PENGUIN
GUJARAT: THE MAKI

Siddharth Varadarajan is deputy chief of the national bureau of the *Times of India*. He has reported on several important political events, from Kashmir and the royal palace massacre in Nepal, to Pakistan, the weapons-inspection crisis in Iraq, the NATO bombing of Yugoslavia and the Taliban regime in Afghanistan. Before his current assignment, he was an editorial writer for the same newspaper.

Among his academic writings are the articles 'The Ink Link: Media, Communalism and the Evasion of Politics,' in K.N. Panikkar, *The Concerned Indian's Guide to Communalism* (Viking 1999), and 'The International Dynamics of a Nuclear India,' in D.R. SarDesai and Raju G.C. Thomas, *Nuclear India in the Twenty-First Century* (Palgrave, 2002). Siddharth studied at the London School of Economics and Columbia University and taught economics at New York University before turning to journalism in 1995.

GUJARAT
The Making of a Tragedy

Edited by
Siddharth Varadarajan

PENGUIN BOOKS

Penguin Books India (P) Ltd., 11 Community Centre, Panchsheel Park, New Delhi 110 017,
India
Penguin Books Ltd., 80 Strand, London WC2R 0RL, UK
Penguin Putnam Inc., 375 Hudson Street, New York, NY 10014, USA
Penguin Books Australia Ltd., 250 Camberwell Road, Camberwell, Victoria 3124, Australia
Penguin Books Canada Ltd., 10 Alcorn Avenue, Suite 300, Toronto, Ontario M4V 3B2, Canada
Penguin Books (NZ) Ltd., Cnr Rosedale & Airborne Roads, Albany, Auckland, New Zealand

First published by Penguin Books India 2002

Typeset in Sabon by Mantra Virtual Services, New Delhi
Printed and bound by Thomson Press (India) Ltd.

For the victims of the train massacre at Godhra and the targetted killings in the rest of Gujarat which followed

For the journalists and concerned citizens who brought us the truth

For all the brave women and men of Gujarat who stood their ground in the face of terrible violence

Contents

The Aftermath

Essays and Analyses

Acknowledgements

This book is intended to be a permanent public archive of the tragedy that is Gujarat. It attempts to bear witness to the unspeakable events which took place there, to write history before it is rewritten, to apportion blame, to ask for justice, to raise questions that all Indians should raise.

A collective endeavour such as this would not have been possible had it not been preceded by the hard work of hundreds of journalists and concerned citizens who gave a voice to stories that might otherwise never have been heard. No less crucial has been the contribution of the relief camp organisers and volunteers, who did all they could during those terrible days and after to provide help and succour to the victims.

In trying to synthesise a coherent narrative from the mass of media accounts and fact-finding reports, my contributors and I have borrowed freely from published material. Where possible, we have acknowledged our debt. But wherever the debt has gone unacknowledged, the omission is purely accidental.

In particular, I would like to express my debt of gratitude to those whose reports have been extracted or extensively referred to: the People's Union for Civil Liberties, Vadodara and Vadodara Shanti Abhiyan, the People's Union for Democratic Rights, Delhi, *Communalism Combat*, the Women's Panel (Farah Naqvi, Malini Ghose, Syeda Hameed, Ruth Manorama, Sheba George, Mari Thekaekara), Sahrwaru, Awaaz-e-Niswaan and the Forum Against Oppression of Women, Shama Dalvai and Sandhya Mhatre, Kavita Panjabi, Krishna Bandhopadhyay and Bolan Gangopadhyay, Medico Friends Circle, Human Rights Watch, Sahmat, AIDWA, the Independent Commission (Kamal Mitra Chenoy, S.P. Shukla, Achin Vanaik, P.S. Subramaniam), Citizens' Initiative, the Editors Guild, the National Human Rights Commission and the Election

Commission of India.

I would also like to thank *Aajkal, Amar Ujala, Economic and Political Weekly, Hindu, Hindustan Times, Jan Morcha, Jansatta, Kathadesh, Nirikshak, Outlook, Seminar, Telegraph* and *Times of India* for permission to reprint material. If this book succeeds in capturing the horror, pathos and immediacy of the situation, this is due in no small measure to the contributions by journalists from these publications. I am grateful to them, and to all the other journalists, named and unnamed, whose work has been referred to in footnotes throughout the book. Though the *Indian Express* produced excellent reportage on Gujarat, I have not been able to reproduce any of its stories since the newspaper, regrettably, declined to grant the necessary permission.

I am grateful to Kamini Mahadevan and David Davidar at Penguin Books India, who first approached me with the idea of a book on Gujarat and who bore patiently with me as the enterprise slowly took shape. Nandini Sundar helped me select and edit a lot of the material and was as keen as me to see this book out. Chinu Srinivasan, Shastri Ramachandaran, Tunku Varadarajan, Om Thanvi, Mrinal Pande and Sarvar Sherry Chand provided help, and had Tejbir Singh and Harsh Sethi not commissioned such fine pieces for their splendid issue of *Seminar* on Gujarat, this volume would have been so much the poorer.

It is perhaps inevitable that a book of this scale and design, produced at great speed, will contain a few errors, especially since the events described within have been the subject of official indifference, concealment and denial. I have tried my best to check, cross-check and verify every fact from as many different sources as possible; any errors that remain are purely inadvertent.

This book has been edited by me in my individual capacity and though I have received the generosity and cooperation of my publishers and colleagues, the views expressed herein should not be taken as the views of the *Times of India*.

List of Contributors

Ranjana Argade teaches Hindi at Gujarat University, Ahmedabad.

Anil Chamaria is a senior Hindi language journalist.

Darshan Desai works for *Outlook* from Ahmedabad.

Mahasweta Devi, one of Bengal's leading writers, is a Jnanpith award winner.

G.N. Devy is Director, Tribal Academy, Tejgarh, Gujarat.

Barkha Dutt is a senior journalist with NDTV.

Vrinda Grover is a legal scholar based in New Delhi.

Ramachandra Guha, sociologist and historian, is author of *Environmentalism: A Global History.*

Shail Mayaram is Visiting Senior Fellow, Centre for the Study of Developing Societies, Delhi.

Mohandas Namishray is a Dalit intellectual and an editor with the Dr B.R. Ambedkar Foundation, New Delhi.

Farah Naqvi is an independent journalist based in Delhi, **Malini Ghose** works for Nirantar in Delhi,

Sheba George is with Sahrwaru in Ahmedabad,

Syeda Hameed is with the Muslim Women's Forum,

Ruth Manorama is with the National Alliance of Women,

Mari Thekaekara is with Accord, Tamil Nadu.

A.G. Noorani, lawyer and political commentator, is author of *The RSS and the BJP: A Division of Labour.*

People's Union for Civil Liberties-Vadodara and **Shanti Abhiyan** are two major forums active in Vadodara for more than a decade.

People's Union for Democratic Rights, is a Delhi-based civil liberties and democratic rights organisations.

Jyoti Punwani, senior journalist and columnist for *MID-DAY,* has reported extensively on communal issues.

Vibhuti Narain Rai is currently IG (Railways), Allahabad. He is the author of the novel *Shehar mein Curfew.*

Rajdeep Sardesai is political editor, NDTV.

Teesta Setalvad is a senior journalist, co-editor of *Communalism Combat,* director of the KHOJ education for a plural India programme and a human rights activist.

Ghanshyam Shah is Professor in Social Sciences at the Centre of Social Medicine and Community Health, Jawaharlal Nehru University, New Delhi.

Prakash N. Shah is vice-president of the Gujarati Sahitya Parishad and editor of *Nirikshak,* Ahmedabad.

Gurpal Singh works in the film and television industry. He appears on the comedy programme *Chhupa Rustam.*

Nandini Sundar is an anthropologist and Associate Professor at the Centre for the Study of Law and Governance, Jawaharlal Nehru University.

Achyut Yagnik, is Coordinator, Centre for Social Knowledge and Action (SETU), Ahmedabad

Overview

Chronicle of a Tragedy Foretold

Siddharth Varadarajan

On 27 February, at approximately ten minutes to eight in the morning, the Sabarmati Express fitfully pulled out of Godhra railway station on the last leg of what was to be one of the most catastrophic rail journeys of post-Partition India. As it left, the train was stoned by an irate mob and some twenty minutes later, a coach had been burned to cinder along with fifty-eight helpless passengers. Who the attackers were and what prompted them to such cruelty are unknown but the rulers of Gujarat promptly decided all Muslims had to be taught a lesson. 'Retaliation' was swift and merciless, some would even say clinical. Over the next few days, several hundred Muslims were killed in a state-wide carnage that is certain to become a part of our 'past that will not pass'.

The mood aboard the train that morning was edgy and tense. Among the passengers were a large number of activists and supporters of the Vishwa Hindu Parishad (VHP) returning home from a political ceremony aimed at forcibly constructing a temple to Lord Rama at the very site where the Babri Masjid once stood. The high command of the Sangh Parivar—the Rashtriya Swayamsevak Sangh (RSS) umbrella tying the Bharatiya Janata Party (BJP) to more violent elements like the VHP and Bajrang Dal—had decreed that regardless of any stand the courts may take, 15 March would be the date when temple construction would begin. The BJP had performed disastrously in the Uttar Pradesh assembly elections earlier in February, coming third after the Samajwadi Party and Bahujan Samaj

Party. Within the RSS there was a growing feeling that the soft-pedalling of the Hindu chauvinist agenda under compulsions of coalition politics was making the BJP lose its distinctive stamp and that it was time to return to the Ayodhya agenda.

In a cynical game of shadow brinkmanship, the extra-parliamentary wing of the Sangh Parivar issued an ultimatum to its members sitting in power in New Delhi demanding that sixty-seven acres of land around the Babri Masjid site be immediately handed over to the Ramjanmabhoomi Nyas for temple construction. Sending in supporters to Ayodhya was seen as an inexpensive, theatrical way of generating a momentum which the Vajpayee government could then conveniently point to as evidence of 'overwhelming public sentiment'—and as a reason to capitulate. BJP MPs used their railway booking privileges to commandeer seats and whole coaches for this political mobilization. In Gujarat, the only state where the party was in power by itself, local ministers regularly flagged off trains full of raucous activists and were often on hand to welcome their flock back.[1]

Flush with the triumphalism of those who know the State is on their side, a section of the VHP passengers had got into arguments and fights with Muslim vendors and passengers while the Sabarmati Express was waiting at Godhra station. At least one Muslim vendor was beaten up by the 'Ram sevaks' after he refused to say 'Jai Shri Ram', and an unsuccessful attempt was made to abduct a young Muslim girl.[2] Some of the Muslim vendors and passengers ran for cover; others tried fighting back. The situation on the platform was deteriorating very fast. Anxious to avoid further incidents, the engine driver blew his whistle frantically and the train pulled away from the station. As it left, stones were thrown at some of the coaches, particularly S-6.

Barely fifteen minutes later, flames engulfed coach S-6. By the time the raging fire was put out and the authorities were able to go in, fifty-eight men, women and children had been asphyxiated and burnt. One passenger succumbed to injuries later. Among the dead identified, more than thirty had been activists or supporters of the VHP. At least one Muslim passenger was amongst the seriously injured.[3] To date, nineteen of the dead remain unidentified, with no relatives coming forward to claim the *ex-gratia* compensation for them.[4] Given the highly organized nature of the VHP mobilization from Gujarat, these nineteen are unlikely to have been 'kar sevaks'.

The Need for a Conspiracy

What happened during those fateful ten minutes will be the subject of controversy and speculation for years to come. Most on-the-spot reports by journalists and fact-finding commissions suggest the attack on the train was a cruel—but probably spontaneous—act of a mob. The mob may have gathered because of what had happened at the station but their callous and cowardly attack on defenceless passengers was completely out of proportion to the 'provocation' they were allegedly responding to. The Godhra district authorities say the mob consisted largely of residents from Signal Falia, a volatile locality situated close to the railway tracks predominantly populated by Ghanchi Muslims. How the mob gathered there and when, why S-6 was singled out, what kind of inflammable material was used and by whom, how it came to be poured inside, as the Forensic Science Laboratory report suggests,[5] are still mysteries. Although the erstwhile collector of Godhra, Jayanti Ravi, suggested that 'anti-social elements' were responsible,[6] both the Gujarat and central governments insisted the attack on the train was a pre-meditated, well-planned act of terrorism by people acting either under the direct orders of Pakistan or under the influence of what Gujarat Chief Minister Narendra Modi has called the 'jihadi mentality'. On 1 March, Home Minister Lal Krishna Advani held a briefing for journalists to plant the idea that the 'needle of suspicion' regarding Godhra pointed towards Pakistan's ISI. Newspapers attributed the remark to 'highly placed sources in the government' and further quoted these sources as pointing out that this view (of ISI involvement) was gaining ground because 'fomenting communal trouble' was 'an important part of the overall ISI strategy'.[7] One report quoted the 'source' as saying that this 'predetermined genocide (i.e. Godhra) was bound to' generate a violent reaction as part of the 'design and objective of the ISI . . . to destabilize India.'[8] Two days later, in Ahmedabad, Advani expanded on the terrorist theme: 'Although facts will be revealed only after the inquiry is over, one feels that only local residents of Godhra were not involved in this horrendous act. The needle of suspicion points to those elements which attacked Parliament' on 13 December 2001.[9] BJP president Jana Krishnamurthy was more forthright. Godhra, he insisted, was the handiwork of Pakistan and the ISI.[10] And Gujarat's home minister, Gordhan Zadaphia, asserted, 'The bogie burning is a terrorist act similar to the attack on the American Centre in Kolkata. The culprits in both cases are the same.'[11]

Though some sixty persons have so far been arrested, the government has not yet provided evidence to back up its claim of a wider conspiracy behind the Godhra carnage.[12] The charge-sheet itself is silent about a conspiracy and by June, presumably because of the lack of evidence, Advani too sought to distance himself from his earlier comments. Speaking to reporters in Ahmedabad, he said that while Godhra appeared to be a 'pre-planned' attack, it was not an act of terrorism. 'No one', he now asserted, 'had ever claimed Godhra was a "terrorist attack".'[13]

But if proof of the wider conspiracy has not surfaced yet, the investigating authorities do not appear to have made headway in other directions either. Even by the shoddy standards of criminal investigation in India, it is evident that the Godhra case is not being probed with the degree of urgency and professionalism that it warrants. The Railways have coach-wise lists of all BJP reserved passengers on board the Sabarmati Express that day but the police have not tried to track them down. At the very least, many passengers of S-5, S-6 and S-7 would be potential eyewitnesses but statements were not recorded before they all dispersed.[14] Similarly, police made no attempt in the crucial hours and days after the attack to limit access to the burnt-out coach, after all, a crime scene. It is almost as if the political authorities—having committed themselves to the theory of a well-organized 'Islamic' terrorist plot—did not want investigative and criminal forensics to come in the way.[15]

While the truth about the degree to which the attack on the Sabarmati Express was pre-planned may never be known, it is worth asking why the BJP sets great store by the theory of a deeper conspiracy. For on the moral or juridical plane, spontaneity cannot in any way be considered a mitigating factor. Whether the mob of lumpen elements lay waiting for the train for hours before or had gathered on the spur of the moment in response to the fracas at Godhra station, nothing can possibly justify or excuse the enormity of the crime which was committed. No legal system in the world would show leniency just because the burning of S-6 was not pre-planned.

However, by immediately stressing the possibility of a wider terrorist plot tied to Pakistan, the BJP has been attempting to tap into and exploit its own propaganda about the Muslims of India being disloyal citizens and willing agents of the ISI and Pakistan. In the coded language that the Sangh Parivar has perfected, words like 'terrorist', 'fanatic' and 'fundamentalist' are subliminal signifiers for Muslims. 'All Muslims are not terrorists but all terrorists are Muslims,' Narendra Modi had famously declared on a television programme soon after the attack on the World Trade Centre.[16] At that point, Modi was only a simple *pracharak* of the RSS but the remark provides a glimpse into his thinking. To blame terrorists for the Godhra attack, then, was his less than subtle way of putting the blame on Muslims as a whole. And the charge of pre-planning a crime, that at one stage was said to have been committed by a mob comprising of 'thousands', was intended to emphasize the collective nature of the conspiracy. Modi, in fact, described Godhra as 'a pre-planned conspiracy of collective terrorism'.[17] Some of Modi's ministers were less squeamish about making the link between Pakistan and Gujarat's Muslims. 'Godhra has a notorious reputation . . . We suspect that many Pakistanis live here illegally' said Gujarat health minister Ashok Bhatt.[18]

In the words of a senior Gujarat-based journalist, Digant Oza, 'Thus the equation was complete. Godhra was a pre-planned Pakistani act carried out by local Muslims. . . This was to become a main weapon in the hands of VHP goons in the coming weeks.'[19]

What Modi and his ministers were doing, in a way, was to identify the target against which 'reaction' would be justified. Having done that, the chief minister issued a chilling warning on state-run television on 28 February of what was in store:

> I want to assure the people that Gujarat shall not tolerate any such incident. The culprits will get full punishment for their sins. *Not only this, we will set an example that nobody, not even in his dreams, thinks of committing a heinous crime like this*.[20] (Emphasis added)

The same day, he made a similar remark on the floor of the Gujarat assembly:

> The State Government, taking seriously this cruel and inhuman offence of the mass violence (on innocent travellers), is firm to take *symbolic strict steps and to punish in such a way* that such an incident may not repeat in the future.[21] (Emphasis added)

Here, it is evident that what Modi had in mind was something other than the law taking its course against the perpetrators of Godhra. Having earlier widened the category of the perpetrator by emphasizing the 'pre-planned', 'collective' nature of the 'terrorist' act, the chief minister was now proposing to widen the ambit of the punishment as well. Apart from giving the culprits 'full punishment for their sins', the state government was threatening to 'set an example'. It didn't matter that these dark warnings came packaged alongside vague appeals to maintain peace and 'self-restraint'. For the message being sent out was crystal clear. Somebody was going to have to pay for what happened at Godhra. Symbolic strict steps had to be taken. 'We will teach a lesson to those who have done this,' said Zadaphia.[22]

The next seventy-two hours were to demonstrate exactly

what the ruling BJP in Gujarat—and at the Centre—had in mind. A pogrom of unimaginable proportions was unleashed with the full sanction of the government. Goons from the RSS, BJP, VHP and Bajrang Dal were given a free hand by the state authorities and police. Voters' lists, arms, gas cylinders and transportation mysteriously became available. Despite Prime Minister Atal Bihari Vajpayee cancelling his trip to Australia for the Commonwealth Heads of Government Meeting in anticipation of a major outbreak of violence, he did nothing to ensure law and order was maintained. The state government delayed asking for the deployment of the Army till the evening of 28 February. Even though troops began arriving in Ahmedabad early on 1 March, lack of logistical cooperation from the local authorities meant they could not be effectively deployed until 3 March, by which time the worst damage had already been done.[23] By then, over 600 Muslims had been killed (the unofficial death toll today is 2,000), more than 200,000 had been displaced because their homes had been looted and burnt, and Muslim property worth several thousand crores of rupees destroyed, all under the watchful eye of the police and state administration.[24] Unlike communal riots in the past, this time, Muslim members of the State apparatus like police officers and judges of the High Court were not spared. In some places, the police assisted the mobs in hunting down Muslims. Elsewhere, they just stood by, or declared they had orders not to protect Muslims. Sporadic incidents of violence continued until July. The Muslims of Gujarat continue to live in great fear and insecurity; and although criminal cases have now reluctantly been registered for some of the worst massacres, there is little prospect of the guilty BJP leaders, policemen and activists of the Sangh Parivar being brought to book.[25]

To understand how and why Gujarat was allowed to burn, one must turn to two separate but inter-related sets of factors. One is specific to the politics and ideology of the RSS and BJP and the nature of its rule in Gujarat, the other to the practice of State power in India since independence, but especially since the 1980s.

In physically targetting Muslims, the Sangh Parivar was being faithful to its old divisive agenda and also carrying forward its programme of communalizing Gujarat to a certain logical point. However, the ease with which it has been able to use the State machinery to sanction, legitimize and orchestrate violence against a section of citizens—something the country first saw in such a raw, naked manner during the Congress-sanctioned massacre of Sikhs in November 1984—points to a more pervasive problem with the nature and structure of the Indian polity and State. As in Delhi in 1984 or Bombay in 1993 (when Muslims were attacked in the wake of the Babri Masjid's demolition) or indeed the violence in Hyderabad in 1990 (when nearly 200 Muslims and Hindus died),[26] the State in Gujarat turned against a section of its citizens and refused to accept responsibility for providing even the most basic physical protection to them. This is a problem that cannot be resolved by simply dismissing a chief minister or voting one political party out of power at the Centre and bringing in another, more 'secular', party.

The BJP in Gujarat

One reason for violence against Muslims being so well-organized was the degree to which the Sangh Parivar has communalized the state administration and society since the BJP returned to power under Keshubhai Patel's leadership in 1998. In June 1999, Patel wrote to the Centre seeking advice on whether the RSS could be deleted from the list of thirty-two political or quasi-political organizations state government employees were prohibited from joining. Within days, the reply came: There was no problem, since the Unlawful Activity (Prevention) Tribunal had cleared the RSS as a lawful organization.[27] Haren Pandya, who was Gujarat's home minister at the time, promptly announced his intention of issuing an official circular to this effect. Keshubhai Patel brushed aside suggestions that allowing government employees to join the RSS would lead to favours being doled out on the basis of organizational loyalty. 'We will not allow anyone to take advantage of their proximity with the RSS,' he declared.[28]   Around the same time, an attempt was made to force all schools in Gujarat to subscribe to an RSS magazine, *Sadhana*. However, the state government was forced by the public outcry throughout India to change course on both counts. In any event, the BJP's failure to change the service rules on RSS membership did not prove to be much of a hindrance. As subsequent events showed, the system of administration in India is so corrupt that when a minister asks senior police officers or bureaucrats to commit an illegality or permit a crime or release a party functionary from jail, more often than not the officers comply.

The massacres orchestrated after Godhra were foreshadowed by a series of attacks launched by the VHP on Muslim property in several Gujarat cities in August 2000.[29] In the wake of the killing of Hindu pilgrims at Pahalgam on 1 August by terrorists, VHP leader Pravin Togadia called for a Gujarat-wide *bandh*. The BJP government in the state supported the bandh. Muslim businesses in Ahmedabad, Surat, Vadodara, Modasa and Lambadia in Sabarkantha district were attacked and burnt. Places of worship, like the dargah of Hazrat Syed Masoom Ali in Ahmedabad were burnt. In Naroda, Muslims from the Municipal Labour Quarters were forcibly evicted and Muslim shops looted. In Surat, Muslim-owned powerlooms were gutted and the loss was estimated to be in the region of Rs 10 crore. In Modasa village, sixty-three business establishments—fifty-one Muslim and twelve Hindu—were burnt down. The estimated loss was Rs 1.5 crore. Apart from killing two rioters in Lambadia, the police in the state by and large did not intervene during the violence. And afterwards, the Muslim victims encountered great difficulty in registering cases. The aim of the violence, to cripple the Muslim community economically, was to resurface with a vengeance during and after the VHP-sponsored bandh of 28 February 2002, when virtually all vulnerable Muslim establishments—big or small—were targetted in much of Gujarat.

Though Muslims now appear to be the main victims of State-sanctioned violence in Gujarat, the Sangh Parivar has also targetted Christians in the state. According to a report prepared by the All India Federation of Organisations for Democratic Rights, there have been over forty attacks on Christian churches, houses, educational institutions and individuals by the VHP and Bajrang Dal during the BJP's rule in Gujarat. The majority of these occurred between December 1998 and January 1999 in Dangs district.[30] These attacks coincided with a stepped up Sangh Parivar campaign against 'Christian missionaries' throughout India. December 1998 was also when the Australian missionary, Graham Staines, was burnt alive with his two young sons in Orissa. The accused, Dara Singh, was once active with Bajrang Dal though the latter insists he was never a member. Instead of forthrightly condemning the anti-Christian violence, Prime Minister Vajpayee, who visited the Dangs during this period, tried to divert the issue by calling for a national debate on religious conversions. 'The root cause of the violence in the Dangs is the conversion issue', he said. Pleased by Vajpayee's equivocation on the anti-Christian violence, Haren Pandya said, 'Initially, we wondered why the Prime Minister was coming here, but now we are happy.'[31]

During this period, the BJP government in Gujarat instructed all police stations in the state to collect detailed information on Christians and Muslims living in the state. For example, one circular sent by the Gujarat director general of police (intelligence) to police commissioners and DSPs in the state asked the following questions for each district:

> What is the total population of Christians? Which all places do they live in?. . . Population of Christians in your district, taluka-wise and village-wise. You are requested to give information about the name, address and telephone numbers of their main leaders. In the last five years, how many cases of class-wars between Hindus and Christians have been registered in your district? What was their result in the court? How many Christians are involved and in which all offences? You are requested to certainly send the name, address and the case registration number of the offender along with their dossiers. In your districts what type of trickery is being used by the

Christian missionaries defilement activities? *(sic)* How are they increasing it? How many and what type of vehicles do they possess? You are requested to inform the number of these vehicles. . . You are requested to send the dossiers of all such Christians who are involved in criminal activities and having criminal attitude. *(sic)*' [32]

The circular was prefaced with the following statement of purpose: 'Presently, the incidents of class-conflicts between Hindus and Christians are increasing very much. It is very necessary to stop these activities.' However, the questions make it quite clear that in the eyes of the police and government, Christians alone are to blame for these conflicts. References to 'Christian Missionaries defilement activities' further highlight the bias and the detailed census-type information solicited seems to serve no logical purpose other than to provide—for any potential anti-Christian group—a detailed list of Christian properties and vehicles. At least one notice was sent around soliciting detailed data on Muslims. In early 1999, P.B. Upadhyaya, director general of police (intelligence) in Ahmedabad wrote to all police commissioners and district police officers:

You are asked to intimate the details of persons (Muslims) involved in communal riots. . . how many Darul Ulams *(sic)* are functioning in your districts and cities. . . the details of existing Muslim organisations in your district with their address and who are the leaders working for their organisations, their names, addresses, total members, telephone numbers, etc. . . Please intimate about the number of Pakistani nationals in your District/cities . . . Please intimate the details of Muslims in your cities who are involved in narcotic and smuggling activities. . . Please open the dossier of Muslim individuals who are involved in the offence of assault with knives or scissors, rioting and murder with their names and the copy of the same to be sent here . . . [33]

This circular is remarkable not just for the way in which Muslim rioters, smugglers, Pakistanis and 'existing Muslim organisations' are conflated into one undifferentiated category of troublemakers but also because of the underlying assumption that 'Muslims' are the source of all criminal activity. To date, no Gujarat police circular demanding similar details about Hindu criminals and rioters has surfaced. But such circulars have another, more sinister dimension. One of the most peculiar features of the anti-Muslim violence in Gujarat following Godhra was the detailed information about Muslim businesses that the Sangh Parivar-led mobs seem to have had. Presumably it was from officially-conducted surveys of some kind that this data was culled.

What has given the BJP's divisive politics in the state a deadlier twist, particularly in urban Gujarat, is the declining fortunes of the organized working class. The onset of what Breman calls 'predatory' capitalism, marked by the casualization of the workforce,[34] has further undermined the socially stabilizing role of labour. Industrial capitalism came to Ahmedabad with the establishment of textile mills at the end of the nineteenth century. An urban working class culture slowly emerged that was both religiously and ethnically inclusive. Trade unions like the Majoor Mahajan Sangh played a 'pivotal role' in the emergence of 'social consciousness produced by factorized employment'.[35] From the 1970s onwards, however, the textile industry in Ahmedabad came under pressure and entered what was to be a two-decade-long process of stagnation and collapse. By the end of the 1990s, according to the Self-Employed Women's Association (SEWA), 80,000 regular mill workers and 50,000 temporary (or 'badli') workers had lost their jobs: 'The ranks of workers in the informal economy swelled significantly. Today, 77 per cent of all workers in Ahmedabad are engaged in the informal economy.'[36]

This informalization of work, Breman argues, has led to labour forfeiting 'its economic value, bargaining power and dignity . . . The trade union movement which used to be the main platform for collective action has withered away'.[37] And it has become easier for the Sangh Parivar to mobilize subaltern groups: 'Whenever communal tensions have flared up and erupted in street riots in the past, these clashes could be defused by appealing to working class solidarity, which transcended the boundaries of primordial loyalties.'[38] During the 1969 riots, members of the Majoor Mahajan Sangh protected each other, Breman notes, but in the Ahmedabad of 2002, 'it is certainly not a coincidence that the orgy of violence that has taken place . . . since the end of February seems to have reached a climax in ex-mill localities populated by social segments from which a major part of this industrial workforce used to be recruited: subaltern Hindus (mainly Dalits, OBCs and intermediate castes, especially Patels) and Muslims.'[39]

The blame for the transformation of Gujarat's political economy—and the decline of organized labour—can hardly be placed at the doors of the BJP alone. However, the party has certainly helped speed the process along, benefiting from it politically. And the state has suffered as a result. As the economist, Meghnad Desai, put it, 'Gujarat is richer in money . . . but of late, especially since the BJP captured the imagination of the Gujarati middle classes, it has become harsh and violent.'[40]

Four years after the BJP took power in the state, Gujarat provides a chilling glimpse into the Hindutva dystopia, a land where hatred and irrationality rule the roost, where minorities are terrorized and killed, where aggressive, economically powerful social groups are able to use the State—and State-sponsored mass violence—to further their own business interests, where disadvantaged social groups like dalits and tribals are politically mobilized against their own interests, and where a major section of civil society is fast losing the moral capacity to distinguish between right and wrong.

An Agenda of Pseudo-Hindu Separatism

In its essence, the ideology of the RSS and BJP is based on the negation of both Indian statecraft—which holds that the State must provide security and prosperity to all—and the idea that in a modern polity, a citizen is defined not by his or her religion, race or ethnicity but by the political and economic rights—and civic duties—he or she shares with other citizens. Heavily influenced by German race-based conceptions of nationalism,[41] the RSS ideologue, M.S. Golwalkar, argued in his 1939 tract, *We, or Our Nationhood Defined*, that only Hindus are true Indians and that Muslims, Christians, Jews and Parsis are all foreigners who should be allowed to stay in India only on terms set by the Hindus.[42] 'Ever since that evil day when Moslems first landed in Hindusthan, right up to the present moment,' says Golwalkar, 'the Hindu Nation has been gallantly fighting on to shake off the despoilers . . .'[43] Lamenting the fact that the Indian freedom struggle—which from the 1857 War of Independence onwards had begun to advance the notion of rights-based citizenship—did not distinguish between Hindus and others, Golwalkar wrote, 'Wrong notions of democracy (have) strengthened the view (that a Nation naturally was composed of all those who happened to reside therein) and we began to class ourselves with our old invaders and foes under the outlandish name—Indian—and tried to win them over to join hands with us in our struggle.'[44]

At a time when the national movement was trying to overcome the communal policies of British colonialism by defining nationhood in a politically inclusive manner and pushing forward the common struggle for rights, the RSS felt that the very term Indian was 'outlandish' and inappropriate. Golwalkar argued that Muslim, Christian and other non-Hindu Indians were not really Indians: 'All those not belonging to the national, i.e. Hindu race, Religion, Culture and Language, naturally fall out of the pale of real "National" life. We repeat: in Hindusthan, the land of the Hindus, lives and should live the Hindu Nation.'[45] And what of the non-Hindus? Golwalkar answers:

> the foreign races in Hindusthan must either adopt the Hindu culture and language, must learn to respect and hold in reverence Hindu religion, must entertain no idea but those of the glorification of the Hindu race and culture, i.e. of the Hindu nation and must lose their separate existence to merge in the Hindu race, or may stay in the country, wholly subordinated to the Hindu Nation, claiming nothing, deserving no privileges, far less any preferential treatment—not even citizen's rights.

There is, at least should be, no other course for them to adopt. We are an old nation; let us deal, as old nations ought to and do deal, with the foreign races who have chosen to live in our country.[46]

Elsewhere in the same tract, Golwalkar provides an example of how an 'old nation' deals with 'foreign races':

To keep up the purity of the Race and its culture, Germany shocked the world by her purging the country of the Semitic Races—the Jews. Race pride at its highest has been manifested here. Germany has also shown how well nigh impossible it is for Races and cultures, having differences going to the root, to be assimilated into one united whole, a good lesson for us in Hindusthan to learn and profit by.[47]

Golwalkar's formulations proved too extreme even for the man he chose to write a foreword for his book, M.S. Aney, of the Hindu Mahasabha. 'I find that the author in dealing with the problem of the Mohmeddans' *(sic)* place has not always borne in mind the distinction between the Hindu nationality and Hindu sovereign State', Aney wrote. 'No modern State has denied the resident minorities of different nationalities rights of citizenship of the State if they are once naturalized either automatically or under the operation of a Statute . . . No modern jurist or political philosopher or student of constitutional law can subscribe to the proposition which the author has laid down in Chapter V.'[48] In subsequent editions of *We*, an unrepentant Golwalkar dropped Aney's inconvenient 'Foreword'.[49]

In *Bunch of Thoughts*, published in 1966, Golwalkar returns to the same theme of Muslims and other non-Hindus being foreigners. Indeed, 'The Muslims' and 'The Christians' figure as chapter titles under the section 'Internal Threats'. Attacking the basic premise of those who took part in the freedom struggle, he wrote: 'They forgot that here was already a full-fledged ancient nation of the Hindus and the various communities which were living in the country were here either as guests, the Jews and Parsis, or as invaders, the Muslims and Christians. They never faced the question of how all such heterogeneous groups could be called as the children of the soil merely because, by an accident, they happened to reside in a common territory under the rule of a common enemy.' (p 142) However, Golwalkar's preoccupation was not so much with questions of history as with contemporary politics. At stake was not some academic point about the indigeneity of the religious beliefs of Indians but the 'unfortunate' notion that all citizens should have equal rights: 'Unfortunately in our country', he wrote, 'our Constitution has equated the children of the soil with the aggressor, and given equal rights to everybody . . .'[50]

Interestingly, the official Gujarat high school textbook on Social Studies for Class IX says in the first paragraph of the chapter 'Problems of the Country and their Solution' that 'apart from the Muslims, even the Christians, Parsees *and other foreigners* are also recognized as the minority communities' (emphasis added).[51] The textbook also makes the curious claim that 'In most of the states the Hindus are in a minority and Muslims, Christians and Shikhs *(sic)* are in a majority in these respective states.'

Though BJP leaders have attempted to distance themselves somewhat from Golwalkar's *We* because of the embarrassing reference to the Nazis—and the RSS no longer openly distributes the 1939 book—the outlook it promotes is deeply ingrained in the ideology and politics of the party. In any case, BJP leaders continue wholeheartedly to identify themselves with Veer Savarkar, another ideologue of Hindutva, who subscribed to the same Germanic racial-religious conception of nationhood as Golwalkar did. Savarkar may have been a leader of the Hindu Mahasabha—an organization distinct from the RSS—but he is equally an iconic figure and ideologue of the Sangh Parivar. In May 2002, even as Gujarat continued to burn, Advani renamed the airport at Port Blair in the Andamans and Nicobar Islands after Savarkar and reaffirmed his personal admiration for the chauvinist leader. In his book, *Hindutva*, Savarkar also describes 'Hindusthan' as the homeland of the Hindus. For Savarkar, Hindus are the only true Indians because the country is 'at once a *Pitrabhu* and a *Punyabhu*—fatherland and a holy land':

That is why in the case of some of our Mohammedan or Christian countrymen who had originally been forcibly converted to a non-Hindu religion and who consequently have inherited along with Hindus, a common Fatherland and a greater part of the wealth of a common culture . . . are not and cannot be recognised as Hindus. For though Hindusthan to them is Fatherland as to any other Hindu yet it is not to them a Holyland too. Their holyland is far off in Arabia or Palestine. Their mythology and Godmen, ideas and heroes are not the children of this soil. Consequently, their names and their outlook smack of a foreign origin.[52]

This ahistorical theory, which ignored the fact that religious ideas not only entered India from abroad but also spread from India to the farthest reaches of Asia, was, in reality, a crude attempt by Savarkar to negate the right to conscience—the right of citizens to believe in whatever religion or creed they like. To endorse this notion today—as Advani implicitly did when he said at Port Blair, 'There is no need to feel shy of Hindutva, propounded at great length by Veer Savarkar'—is tantamount to saying that Hindu citizens of the United States or Britain can never be loyal to those countries because their *'punyabhu'* is India.

Taken to its logical conclusion, the thesis of Golwalkar and Savarkar was that Hindus and Muslims were two separate nations. Indeed, in his presidential address to the Hindu Mahasabha in 1937, Savarkar explicitly referred to the idea of two nations: 'India cannot be assumed today to be a Unitarian and homogeneous nation, but on the contrary there are two nations in the main: the Hindus and the Muslims.' Donald Eugene Smith, who quotes this line in his book *India as a Secular State*, adds wryly: 'M.A. Jinnah could have constructed his two-nation theory, which led to the demand for Pakistan, on the basis of Savarkar's speech!'.[53]

Savarkar's reference to two nations was not accidental, for in its essence, the ideology of Hindutva is nothing other than a credo of pseudo-Hindu separatism. Ashis Nandy is not off the mark when he describes it is an ideology for those whose Hinduism has worn off. Like the Muslim League's separatism, the separatism of the Hindutva advocates was also patronized by the British colonialists as a way of splitting and disorienting the freedom struggle. In turn, 'Hindu' separatists like the RSS and Savarkar (once he was was released from Andamans Jail) kept well away from the struggle for independence. If the separatism of the Muslim League was territorial in nature and emphasized the need for physical distance between a 'Hindu India' and a 'Muslim Pakistan', the separatism of the Sangh Parivar aims to break away from the philosophical, cultural and civilizational mores of the country, including Hinduism itself.

The ideology of Hindutva separatism seeks to distance itself from the idea of India, to reject what Golwalkar called the 'outlandish' notion of an Indian, to secede from everything healthy and enlightened that this country has produced in the struggle for the emancipation of its people. As Nandy *et al.* have argued, the Sangh Parivar's concept of 'Hindu Rashtra' is 'culturally hollow: it is nothing more than the post-seventeenth century European concepts of nationality and nation-state projected back into the Indian past'.[54] The RSS and its leaders and fronts, Nandy *et al.* continue, have 'shown (not) the slightest sensitivity to the traditional Indian concepts of statecraft or village technology or artisan skills . . . There is a complete rejection of not only the pre-British Islamic concept of state in India . . . even the traditional Hindu experience of running large states in India is seen as entirely irrelevant.'[55]

Apart from rejecting India's syncretic culture, the Sangh Parivar tries to negate the achievements of Indian philosophy over the centuries—from the earliest metaphysical and pantheistic speculations of the Rgveda, the development of different schools of Vedanta, the struggle against Brahminism, the democratic, humanist spirit of the Bhaktas and Sufis—and pushes an ahistorical worldview aimed at mystifying rather than clarifying the problems of society. Rejecting the key principle of Indian statecraft as it has evolved from the period of the Mahabharata through to the Mughal era, the 1857 War of Independence and the freedom movement—that the State derives its legitimacy and mandate from its ability to provide security and prosperity to all regardless of religion or class—the RSS operates on a plagiarized European definition of nationalism whose foundation lies in the denial of the very possibility of equality of rights for all citizens.

From Golwalkar to Newton

When one examines the politics of the RSS and BJP today, it is striking to see the manner in which the arguments of Golwalkar and Savarkar about Muslims and Christians as 'foreigners' and 'enemies' resonate in the pronouncements and activities of these organizations. There is a clear line which connects the founding principles of the RSS to the mass killing of Muslims in Gujarat. Golwalkar's obsession with a purely Hindu nation in which non-Hindus would have no rights, the 'Newtonian' rationalizations of genocidal violence provided by Narendra Modi, and Prime Minister Vajpayee's sweeping attack on Muslims in his speech to a BJP meeting in Goa in April are all part of the same chauvinist discourse.

At its Akhil Bharatiya Karykari Mandal meeting in Bangalore in mid-March, 2002, the RSS adopted a controversial resolution titled 'Godhra and After' in which Muslims were cautioned that they would only be safe in India if they won the 'goodwill' of Hindus. By 'Hindus', of course, was meant the RSS. 'Let Muslims realise that their real safety lies in the goodwill of the majority', the resolution stated. It added, 'The reaction of this murderous incident in Gujarat was natural and spontaneous. The entire Hindu society cutting across all divisions of party, caste and social status reacted.'[56] Elaborating on the resolution, RSS joint general secretary Madan Das Devi told the press, 'Hindus live and let live. This does not mean Hindus can tolerate insults. They (Muslims) are safe if they win our goodwill . . . respect us and we will respect you.' Asked to explain the real meaning of what he was trying to say, Devi said, 'Any killing is unjustifiable but at the same time there will be reaction to any action.'[57] In similar vein, BJP president Jana Krishnamurthy told the press during the party conclave in Goa, 'In any communal strife, there is always one who provokes and another (who is) provoked.' Strongly implying that the attacks on Muslims were provoked, he criticized the media and others for 'advising and attacking the provoked. This has given rise to a psychology amidst the provoked that it is the victim in every sense'.[58]

The first use of this morally perverse 'Newtonian' logic of action and reaction to justify the killing of Muslims after Godhra was made by Modi in an interview to Zee Television on 1 March, even as the violence was at its peak. And ironically, it wasn't so much a reference to the burning of the Sabarmati Express as to press reports that former Congress MP Ehsan Jafri—who was lynched by a Sangh Parivar-led mob at his residence in Chamanpura, Ahmedabad on 28 February—had fired at the mob in order to try and disperse them. Modi said that Jafri's 'action' of firing had infuriated the mob and that the massacre which followed was a 'reaction'. Since his remark generated a huge controversy[59] and led the Gujarat information department to deny that he had said any such thing, it is worth reproducing his exact quote: '*Kriya pratikriya ki chain chal rahi hai. Hum chahate hain ki na kriya ho aur na pratikriya.* (What is happening is a chain of action and reaction. What I want is that there should be no action and no reaction).' Asked about the violence which erupted throughout Gujarat on the day of the VHP-sponsored bandh, he said:

> *Godhra mein jo parson hua, jahan par chalees mahilaon aur bacchon ko zinda jala diya, is mein desh mein aur videsh mein sadma pahunchna swabhavik tha. Godhra ke is ilake ke logon ki criminal tendencies rahi hain. In logon ne pahele mahila teachers ka khoon kiya. Aur ab yeh jaghanya apraadh kiya hai jiski pratikria ho rahi hai.* (It is natural that what happened in Godhra day before yesterday, where forty women and children were burnt alive, has shocked the country and the world. The people in that part of Godhra have had criminal tendencies. Earlier, these people had murdered women teachers. And now they have done this terrible crime for which a reaction is going on).[60]

Apart from being a crude attempt to deflect criticism of his failures as chief minister, Modi's 'action-reaction' theory is also morally repugnant. As Vir Sanghvi has argued, 'What Mr Modi and his ilk are really saying is this: Because the riots were a response to a horrific and immoral act at Godhra, they are somehow less morally reprehensible . . . But cause-and-effect cannot be a moral philosophy. You cannot whitewash an event, wipe away somebody's guilt or provide moral justification by pointing to the cause of their behaviour.'[61]

Steeped in the RSS teachings of historical enmity between Hindus and Muslims and unencumbered by the formal trappings of political office, VHP leader Ashok Singhal took Modi's Newtonian logic one step further. For him, the situation in Gujarat was 'a matter of pride.' 'It is a befitting reply to what has been perpetrated on the Hindus in the last 1,000 years . . . Gujarat has shown the way and our journey of victory will begin and end on the same path.'[62] The VHP's Pravin Togadia held out another direct threat. 'Wherever there is Godhra, there will be Gujarat', he said. 'In Gujarat, for the first time there has been a Hindu awakening and Muslims have been turned into refugees. This is a welcome sign and Gujarat has shown the way to the country.'[63] Togadia's inflammatory statement was formalized by the VHP later in a resolution adopted at a conference in Hardwar at the end of June where Muslims throughout India were warned that Gujarat could be repeated and that they could all be driven into refugee camps.[64]

In 1939, Golwalkar had argued that 'only those movements are truly "National" as aim at re-building, revitalising and emancipating from its present stupor, the Hindu Nation. Those only are nationalist patriots, who, with the aspiration to glorify the Hindu race and Nation next to their heart, are prompted into activity and strive to achieve that goal. All others are either traitors and enemies to the national cause, or, to take a charitable view, idiots.'[65] It was left for senior BJP leader and spokesman J.P. Mathur to take this logic forward and describe the killing of Muslims in Gujarat as a 'patriotic reaction' to what happened at Godhra. 'I don't know why the people and the media have been calling the violence in Gujarat riots. These are not riots, but the reaction of nationalist forces to the Godhra carnage ... The so-called secular leaders like I. K. Gujral, Chandrashekhar, Sonia Gandhi, Mulayam Singh Yadav are also in league with the anti-national forces. Whenever nationalist forces come out to challenge the anti-national elements, these people come to the rescue of the Muslims,' Mathur said.[66] There is no ambiguity in Mathur's statement, nothing is left to chance: Muslims are anti-national, those who attack them are nationalists.

When the Mask Slipped

Perhaps the most significant elaboration of the Golwalkar-Savarkar thesis of India as a Hindu nation beset by Muslim trouble-makers in recent times was that provided by Prime Minister Vajpayee in his speech to the BJP national executive meeting in Goa on 12 April 2002.[67] The speech is remarkable for the manner in which it attempts to justify the murder of Muslim citizens in Gujarat by referring to Godhra and contrasting the supposed 'traditional tolerance' of Hindus with the alleged 'intolerance' of Muslims.

Like Golwalkar, who believed only Hindus were true Indians, Vajpayee uses 'us', 'our', 'Hindus' and 'Indians' interchangeably throughout his speech. He begins by making an observation about Hindu kingdoms in ancient Cambodia. 'No king destroyed a temple or damaged the deities' idols at the time of attacking another king. This is our culture. This is our outlook, which treats all faiths equally.' India, he said, was secular before Muslims and Christians set foot on her soil. Once they came, they had freedom of worship. 'No one thought of converting them with force, because this is not practiced in our religion; and in our culture, there is no use for it.' Here, the Prime Minister was trying to contrast the 'tolerance' of Hindus and Hinduism, which he described as 'our religion', with the supposed intolerance of Muslims and Christians. The reference to the destruction of idols and conversion 'with force' is a standard part of the RSS arsenal. At the root of major incidents of violence, he said, was 'growing intolerance'. Since Hindus are, by definition, tolerant, the obvious inference is that this 'growing intolerance' is on the part of the Muslims. Turning immediately to the burning issue of the day, he asked:

> What happened in Gujarat? If a conspiracy had not been hatched to burn alive the innocent passengers of the Sabarmati Express, then the subsequent tragedy in Gujarat could have been averted. But this did not happen. People were torched alive. Who were those culprits? The government is investigating into this. Intelligence agencies are collecting all the information. But we should not forget how the tragedy of Gujarat started. The subsequent developments were no doubt condemnable, but who lit the fire? How did the fire spread?

Here, in as unsophisticated a fashion as Modi had stated it, we find Vajpayee presenting his own version of Newton's Third Law. There is no remorse about the killing of hundreds of innocent people, no apologies for the failure of the government to protect its citizens. He makes no attempt to distinguish between the criminal perpetrators of the Godhra attack and the innocent victims of the 'subsequent tragedy in Gujarat'. For him, Muslims are an amorphous, undifferentiated lot who collectively 'lit the fire'. They were to blame, not his party men who took part in the 'subsequent developments'.

Going from the specific to the general, Vajpayee then launched a frontal attack on Muslims. He asserts that 'For us, the soil of India from Goa to Guwahati is the same, all the people living on this land are the same. We do not believe in religious extremism. Today, the threat to our nation comes from terrorism'. Who is this *we* and where exactly does this 'threat to our nation' come from? The Hindi text provides a clue. Vajpayee deliberately uses the Urdu word *mazhabi* for 'religious' (rather than the Hindi word *dharmik)* when he says 'religious extremism'.[68] We do not believe in religious extremism; it is the Muslims. And terrorism, of course, is synonymous with Islam, or 'militant Islam', as Vajpayee chose to put it. But having first made a distinction between militant Islam and tolerant Islam, he then makes a sweeping generalization about all Muslims:

> Wherever Muslims live, they don't like to live in co-existence
> with others, they don't like to mingle with others; and instead
> of propagating their ideas in a peaceful manner, they want to
> spread their faith by resorting to terror and threats. The world
> has become alert to this danger.

The statement is classic hate speech, but after it generated a huge controversy, Vajpayee claimed his remarks were aimed not at all Muslims but only 'militant Muslims'. The Prime Minister's Office subsequently issued a doctored version of the speech in which the word 'such' was inserted between 'Wherever' and 'Muslims live'. Many newspapers subsequently printed this version. It was not until a privilege motion was raised in Parliament—for Vajpayee had made the mistake of claiming on the floor of the House on May 1 that the doctored version of the speech was the true version—that he was forced to admit the word 'such' had been deliberately interpolated. However, he reiterated that 'no one who reads my entire speech and takes note of the tribute I have paid to the tolerant and compassionate teachings of Islam, can be in any doubt that my reference . . . is only to the followers of militant Islam'.[69]

The allegation of Muslims not living in co-existence with others and not mingling with others is such a standard trope in RSS propaganda that Vajpayee's claim of intending to refer only to militant Muslims does not seem very convincing. Earlier in his speech, he had equated militant Islam with terrorism. 'Not mingling with others' is a peculiar charge to level against terrorists. In any case, it was a bit odd for the prime minister to talk about terrorism and militancy as if they were the preserve of the adherents of Islam—especially at a time when his own Sangh Parivar was heavily involved in acts of terror in Gujarat. But there was a deeper level of dishonesty in the charge against Muslims, for it is precisely the policy of the RSS to ghettoize and isolate the Muslim community. As sociologist Dhirubhai Sheth has argued, it was not accidental that the Muslims who bore the brunt of the Sangh Parivar's violence in Gujarat were those who chose to live in Hindu-majority areas. The communal killings in the state, he says, have exposed the dishonesty of the

'Hindutvavadis' who reproach Muslims for not entering the 'national mainstream' but then beat them back into their ghettos whenever they do emerge.[70]

In another attempt to soften the impact of his Goa remarks, Vajpayee told Parliament that he was as opposed to militant Hinduism as he was to militant Islam. 'I accept the Hindutva of Swami Vivekananda but the type of Hindutva being propagated now is wrong and one should be wary of it.' Having said this, however, he went back to square one by adding that although there were laws to deal with such an eventuality, he was confident no Hindu organization would become a danger to the country's unity.[71] In other words, only Muslim (or Christian or Sikh) organizations have the potential of endangering the country's unity. After maligning Vivekananda—who never spoke of Hindutva but of Hinduism—Vajpayee went straight back to the teachings of Golwalkar and Savarkar.

Apart from reverting to the usual chauvinist line of the Sangh Parivar, Vajpayee was also diverting the debate into a dead end. The issue is not whether he personally opposes militant Islam or Hinduism but whether, as prime minister, he is prepared to defend the constitutional rights of all Indians. Regardless of his own views and beliefs, a prime minister cannot speak for only a section of citizens. Do the Muslims of Gujarat have the right to physical security? Is he prepared to punish those who have committed crimes regardless of their political or ideological affiliation? Rather than dealing with these questions, Vajpayee is trying to cover up his own political failure and culpability.

It is remarkable that Vajpayee's first televised address to the country was only on 2 March—after the seventy-two hours of apparent freedom enjoyed by the Sangh Parivar in Gujarat expired—and even then, all he could do was appeal for calm and tolerance.[72] In fact, his attempt to blame the ordinary people of Gujarat—and their supposed lack of 'harmony'—for the mass killings in their state was a disingenuous manoeuvre aimed at absolving himself, his party colleagues and the state machinery they control, of any responsibility for the crimes. Like Rajiv Gandhi in November 1984 and Narasimha Rao in January

1993, Vajpayee will go down in history as a prime minister who preached the virtues of tolerance even as he turned a blind eye to the massacre of innocent citizens. Instead of using national television to tell the people of Gujarat that the genocidal mobs would be put down with a firm hand—and that policemen failing to protect the life and liberty of all would be punished—Vajpayee delivered a sermon on the need for religious *sadbhavna*.

There was little passion or feeling in what he said, no words of succour for the victims, no anger or opprobrium for the killers. He said the violence was a 'black mark on the nation's forehead' but he couldn't bring himself to say that retaliatory attacks on Muslims for what happened at Godhra would attract the same punishment as the burning of the train. Here was a violent disturbance that had made a mockery of State power as it is supposed to operate yet the prime minister issued no dire warnings to those who were challenging his authority and power as chief executive. In the US, President George W. Bush and his senior aides publicly warned citizens against attacking Muslims, Arabs and other immigrants following the World Trade Centre terrorist strike. In less than a year since 9/11, a man in Texas has been sentenced to death for the 'retaliatory' murder of a Sikh immigrant. To date, however, Vajpayee has yet to even publicly acknowledge that Muslim citizens of India were victimized in Gujarat or to threaten the attackers with the severest consequences.

Indeed, Vajpayee was later to demonstrate that he was so loyal to his party and Parivar that he didn't mind undermining the majesty of the State and his own office. On 17 April, he said that if only Parliament had condemned Godhra, the subsequent massacres would not have happened. The fact is that he is leader of the House and could have ordered a discussion and condemnation of Godhra on the day it happened—instead of the scheduled presentation of the Budget. In early May, he made another curious statement, this time on the floor of the Rajya Sabha: That he had decided to remove Modi in April but didn't act fearing a backlash in Gujarat. 'I had gone to Goa making up my mind on changing the ruler in Gujarat but according to my own assessment, I felt that the change in leadership will only worsen the situation.'[73] At the time, the only people opposed to a change in leadership were the RSS and VHP. Removing Modi may or may not have provided temporary relief for Gujarat's beleaguered Muslims but it was odd for the prime minister to admit being held hostage to the threats of criminals and goons. 'Vajpayee,' wrote B.G. Verghese, 'placed the diktat of the mob above his oath of office . . . the emperor has no clothes, stripped of the last shred of moral authority.'[74]

The State and its Victims

Whatever Vajpayee's compulsions, the Opposition was wrong in making the removal of Modi the main issue. By fixing responsibility on one man at a time when the complicity of the ruling party and state administration, including the police, was so apparent, the Opposition let off the BJP as a whole. Worse, it was also implicitly saying that there was nothing wrong in the way the wider State apparatus had functioned. The Opposition, especially the Congress, probably had its own, narrow compulsions. Demanding the dismissal of the state government would have meant going in for elections—something Congress leaders felt would benefit Modi and the BJP. But there was another, more fundamental, issue at stake. The Congress is unwilling to accept that the mass killing of Muslims in Gujarat is very much part of an established pattern in India where the ruling party is able to use the machinery of the state and lumpen elements or party cadres to orchestrate communal violence. This is exactly what happened in 1984, when thousands of Sikhs were killed, and the Congress was as guilty then as the BJP is today.[75] If Modi invoked Newton, Rajiv Gandhi had said that when a big tree falls, the earth is bound to shake. Of course, what makes Gujarat different is the sheer brazenness of the BJP—both in terms of mobilizing the state machinery and in terms of openly rationalizing the violence.

In the past two decades, most large-scale incidents of communal violence have occurred only because the ruling party has either willed them or allowed them to happen. This is amply borne out by the pattern of police behaviour before, during and after a 'communal riot'. Virtually every 'riot' enquiry commission has established how the police either actively participates in anti-minority violence or takes on the role of a silent bystander. In UP, the Provincial Armed Constabulary—indicted by the state's own CB-CID inquiry report for the 1987 massacre of Muslims in Malliana and Hashimpura near Meerut—has repeatedly been found acting in a communal manner. If one reads the Justice Jagmohan Reddy Commission report on the Ahmedabad riots of 1969, one is struck by a sense of déjà vu. Over 1,000 people were killed, mostly Muslims, and though the role of the police, state administration and ruling party was not so blatant as it was in 2002, the partisanship of the police did not escape notice:

> This commission of inquiry has cited more than half a dozen instances where Muslim religious places adjoining police lines or police stations were attacked or damaged. The argument advanced by the police officers that because they were busy quelling riots at various other places, these police stations were shorn of adequate strength and hence these attacks on religious places could not be punished, did not impress the commission. It has made this observation because not a single case of damage to a Hindu place of worship near a police station was reported to the commission.[76]

Before a riot, the police are politically conditioned to view only Muslim localities as trouble spots and Muslim lumpens as trouble-makers. It is very rare that the police keep an eye on leaders and activists from Hindu chauvinist organizations or organizations affiliated to ruling parties, even though it is from these quarters that trouble usually comes. Once the violence is over, the police tend to refuse to register cases, especially against politically influential leaders. This is what happened in Delhi after November 1984. If forced to register cases, the police will sabotage the prosecution by imprecise or flabby FIRs, destroying evidence or intimidating witnesses. Often, governments will appoint weak public prosecutors as well, to ensure there are no convictions.

Regardless of which party comes to power at the Centre or state level, no serious attempt is ever made to punish the guilty or reform the law enforcement machinery. Accusations about involvement in riots are only used to score political points but not to ensure that justice is actually delivered to the victims and the guilty brought to book. Thus, despite several changes of government in Delhi—in which, at various times, non-Congress parties like the Janata Dal, BJP, and even CPI have held influential portfolios—justice has not been done for the Sikh victims of November 1984. Errant policemen indicted by official commissions of inquiry such as the Kapoor-Mittal Committee have not been acted against; on the contrary, many got promotions.[77] In Uttar Pradesh, the SP of Mulayam Singh Yadav and the BSP of Mayawati have never thought it fit to prosecute those policemen indicted for their role in Malliana and Hashimpura. In Maharashtra, the Congress defeated the Shiv Sena on the slogan of implementing the Srikrishna Commission report on the 1993 Mumbai riots. However, once elected, the new government has shown great reluctance to pursue those cases—either against the Shiv Sena leadership, or against the police. It's almost as if there is a conspiracy on the part of these parties to criticize and attack each other for organizing communal violence while preserving intact the administrative and legal machinery needed for the job.

Since none of the established political parties has shown the least interest in punishing the guilty, it is legitimate to ask whether communal violence is merely an expression of the inability of those who preside over the state to uphold the rule of law, or a tool the authorities use to stay in power. The Congress used communal violence in the past, the BJP is using it today, and the Congress or some other party might use it again tomorrow. Whatever its ideology, the Congress in the past two decades has helped the BJP shift the locus of Indian politics steadily rightward. Although there is a difference between the two—the Congress' communalism tends to be tactical while the BJP's is strategic and long-term—this makes little difference either to the victims who suffer or to the police and lumpens who thrive regardless. In any case, the key to tackling this problem lies in ending the ease with which State institutions can be mobilized for sectarian violence. There is no alternative to strict adherence to the rule of law—and a political process which makes elected representatives and public officials genuinely accountable to ordinary citizens. If the existing system is not able to ensure security for ordinary citizens, it is necessary to start thinking about alternatives. A party that presides over mass violence must be defeated at the polls but the problem will not go away simply by a change of government. Economic questions, too, cannot be side-stepped. A society which fails to generate livelihood and dignity for the majority of its citizens will always be vulnerable to violence. Neo-liberal reforms and the onset of an economic regime in which the State recognizes no obligation towards its citizens are eating away at the civic solidarities which unite people. So long as the direction of the economy is unchanged, the election of a 'secular' government will provide citizens only temporary relief.

At the same time, it is essential that the unique threat the BJP poses to India be properly understood for what it is. As the origins and role of the RSS make clear, anti-minority mobilization is central to the BJP's outlook and strategy. Several official commissions—such as the Madon Commission on Bhiwandi (1970), the Vithayathil Commission on Tellicherry (1971), the N.C. Saxena Commission on Meerut (1982)—have established the role of the RSS in fomenting communal violence. But the critics of the BJP should not confuse the party's stated, rhetorical aims with its real agenda. Its stated aim may be a 'Hindu Rashtra' but its real goal is to use Hindus as a human shield to cover up what is otherwise an unsavoury economic and political agenda for all Indians, including Hindus. Whether on the economic or social front, it is clear that the party has no intention of addressing the concerns of the majority. Economic decisions are taken from the vantage point of enriching those sections of society that are already privileged. The more communal violence there is, the easier it will be to push through unpopular policies. The public space for debate and discussion shrinks. It is not coincidental that large corporate houses like Reliance Industries regularly advertise in the RSS newspapers *Organiser* and *Panchajanya*.

If and when the BJP's 'Hindu Rashtra' ever comes into being, it will be a state founded on the denial of fundamental rights to all citizens, including Hindus, especially poor Hindus. The Sangh Parivar's lack of concern for ordinary Hindus is demonstrated by the manner in which compensation for the victims of the Godhra carnage was halved from two lakh rupees to one lakh. The Modi government, it seems, couldn't bear to give the riot victims, who are mostly Muslims, matching *ex gratia* payments of two lakhs; so when the charge of communal bias in relief was made, the Godhra rate was promptly cut. While the BJP constantly cites the Godhra carnage as a justification for the anti-Muslim pogrom that followed, the victims of both tragedies are united in paying the price for the party's niggardliness in providing relief and compensation.

Another example of how the BJP uses Hindus as a human shield is provided by the plight of Kashmiri Pandits. The RSS likes to counter any discussion about the condition of Muslim riot victims in Gujarat by referring to the plight of Pandit refugees in Jammu. While there is a difference between the two situations—no chief minister or prime minister ever invoked Newton's law to justify the manner in which Pandits in the Valley were targetted by terrorists and forced to flee—it is self-serving and dishonest for the Sangh Parivar to pretend to be concerned about the Pandits. For though the BJP has been in power at the Centre since 1998, it has done nothing to improve the lot of the Kashmiri refugees, to provide them a sense of security or to create the conditions for them to return to their homes. However, it is always ready to exploit their tragedy in order to justify the victimization of others and sharpen communal divisions in Kashmir and elsewhere in India.

Setting up a hierarchy of crimes and victims is a favourite way for governments to indulge their own prejudices, evade their own responsibility, and push their own political agenda. The Muslims who were killed in the Gujarat violence were as much victims as the Hindu passengers who were burned alive at Godhra. Yet, Modi, Advani, Vajpayee and others use the strongest possible words to describe the burning of the train while dismissing what followed as merely 'unfortunate.' An official Gujarat government press release of 4 March 2002 quotes Advani as referring to the train attack as the 'Godhra genocide'.[78] The violence which followed is mentioned only in the context of the 'restoration of peace'. On 5 March, an official press release quotes Modi describing Godhra as 'genocide' three times; the subsequent massacres were simply 'riots' and 'violence'.[79] As the Editors Guild Report notes, 'The phraseology most often used for the Godhra incident (in official press releases) was "inhuman genocide", "inhuman carnage" or "massacre" while the subsequent riots were invariably described as "disturbances", and occasionally as "violent disturbances/ incidents".'[80] But like the Holocaust deniers—those 'Assassins of Memory' who say Hitler did not kill six million Jews but then give all the reasons why he would have been justified in doing so,[81] Sangh Parivar leaders can't keep their genocidal impulses hidden. Prime Minister Vajpayee urged Parliamentarians in early March not to use strong words like 'massacre' to describe the Gujarat killings. BJP spokesman V.K. Malhotra criticized those who used the word 'genocide' for the state-sanctioned attacks on Muslims in the state because the number of victims was too low.[82] But then along comes the VHP with its resolution at Hardwar hailing the Gujarat violence for the immense scale of its impact and threatening to turn all Indian Muslims into refugees. No public condemnation of the VHP was forthcoming, either from Vajpayee or his other colleagues so exercised about the use of 'strong' language.

In a shabby attempt to turn the spotlight away from their crimes in Gujarat, the Sangh Parivar and apologists for the government constantly invoke the 1984 massacres, the killing of Hindus in Kashmir or atrocities on Hindus in Bangladesh. One BJP publicist has even tried to define, in arithmetical terms, when the amount of column space given to Godhra in any discussion about the Gujarat pogrom is inadequate.[83] The truth is that no amount of criticism of Godhra (or of other crimes against Hindus and other non-Muslims) is sufficient so long as one also speaks the truth about what the Sangh Parivar did to the Muslims of Gujarat subsequently.

Like the 'action-reaction' thesis of Modi and Vajpayee, the Sangh Parivar's attempt to establish a hierarchy of suffering is aimed at legitimizing a moral universe in which one set of victims is supposed to feel vicariously recompensed by the suffering of another set of victims. A moral universe in which questions of official accountability and justice can be postponed indefinitely so that the failure of the State to provide security to all is covered up. For the sake of its soul as a nation, India must reject this corrosive notion of morality which sees in the condemnation of the Gujarat pogrom the diminution of the suffering of the victims of the Godhra carnage, or of other victims of other tragedies. For those who have suffered, justice is not a zero-sum game. All victims must be honoured, respected and compensated adequately and equally, regardless of their religious or political beliefs. And all perpetrators must be punished, regardless of the uniform they wear, the political parties they belong to, or the high offices they occupy. A society that cannot guarantee this much for one section of the population today will be unable to prevent a similar tragedy befalling others tomorrow.

Notes

1 *Indian Express*, 28 February 2002.
2 For a detailed account of the Godhra incident, see the chapter by Jyoti Punwani in this volume.
3 A passenger named Ibrahim Bhai was listed amongst those with grievous injuries and was treated in Baroda hospital. The Railways paid him Rs 5,000 ex-gratia compensation. Western Railways note, undated.
4 Sourav Mukherjee, '19 Godhra victims still unidentified,' *Times of India* (Ahmedabad), 2 June 2002.

5   'Godhra bogie burnt from inside, says report,' *Times of India*, 3 July 2002.

6   Cited in People's Union for Civil Liberties, Vadodara and Vadodara Shanti Abhiyan, *Violence in Vadodara: A Report*, Vadodara, May 2002, p 158.

7   'Priority for controlling violence, says Advani,' *Hindu*, 2 March 2002.

8   'Has VHP fallen into ISI trap?,' *Times of India*, 2 March 2002.

9   'Advani clean chit to Modi,' *Telegraph*, 4 March 2002.

10 Smruti Koppikar, 'BJP chief reads riot act to Muslims,' *Indian Express*, 13 April 2002.

11 Quoted in Digant Oza, 'Gaps in the chain of tragedy,' *Hindustan Times*, 17 June 2002.

12 'The case is still being investigated and if there was some deep conspiracy, then we are yet to find it,' Inspector General of Police (Railways) P.P. Agja was quoted as saying at the end of March. Kingshuk Nag, 'Conspiracy theory finds few takers,' *Times of India* (Ahmedabad edition), 28 March 2002.

13 'Godhra not a terrorist act: Advani,' *Hindustan Times*, 17 June 2002.

14 See Oza, *op cit.*, for a discussion of the questions about Godhra that still remain unanswered.

15 The hostile reaction of the BJP to the Forensic Science Laboratory report on how the inflammable material which burnt coach S-6 was poured from inside is a case in point. See Chapter 2, 'The Carnage at Godhra'.

16 The remark was made during a debate on 'The Big Fight: Is Islam the Cutting Edge of Terrorism?,' Star News channel, 14 September 2001. I was a participant in the same programme.

17 'The State Government has taken Stringent Action to Stem Riots and Violence: Narendra Modi,' Press Release of the Gujarat Information Bureau, Government of Gujarat, Ahmedabad, 5 March 2002. Reprinted in Aakar Patel, Dileep Padgaonkar, B.G. Verghese, *Rights and Wrongs: Ordeal by Fire in the Killing Fields of Gujarat.* Editors Guild Fact Finding Mission Report, New Delhi, May 2002 (henceforth, *Editors Guild Report*), p 57.

18 Quoted in Oza, *op cit*.

19 *Ibid*.

20 Broadcast (in Gujarati) on Ahmedabad Doordarshan, 28 February 2002. Reproduced as Annexure 4AA in *Editors Guild Report*.

21 Press Note of Gujarat government's Directorate of Information dated 28 February 2002. Reproduced in *Editors Guild Report*, p 43.

22 Quoted in Oza, *op cit*.

23 Sujan Dutta, 'Where Had All the Soldiers Gone?,' *Telegraph*, 2 March 2002.

24 See Chapter 3 ('A License to Kill') for a detailed description of the targetted violence against Muslims in the state. For figures of displaced, see Chapter 9 ('Little Relief, No Rehabilitations').

25 See Chapter 12, 'The Elusive Quest for Justice' by Vrinda Grover.

26 Asghar Ali Engineer, 'Making of the Hyderabad Riots,' *Economic and Political Weekly*, 9 February 1991, pp 271-274.

27 See Rajesh Joshi, 'Test flights of the Hindutva dream: For the Sangh, Gujarat is id~al turf for its saffron experiments,' *Outlook*, 24 December 1999.

28 *Ibid*.

29 See *Saffron on the Rampage: Gujarat's Muslims pay for Lashkar's Deeds*. Sabrang Communications, Mumbai, 2000. The report was based on a collective investigation into the violence by 10 Mumbai- and Gujarat-based citizens' groups.

30 *Then They Came for the Christians*, Report of an all-India fact-finding team constituted by All India Federation of Organisations for Democratic Rights, Mumbai, April 1999.

31 *Times of India*, 11 January 1999 and 13 January 1999. Quoted in *Then They Came for the Christians*, p 14.

32 Ref No. D.2: Hindu-Christi/83/99 Date 02.02.1999 (1058). Reproduced in full from *Asian Age*, 12 February 1999.

33 D:2/2: Com/Muslim Activity/84/99 dt. 1/2.2.99. Reproduced as Appendix 1 in Kamal Mitra Chenoy, S.P. Shukla, K.S. Subramanian and Achin Vanaik, *Gujarat Carnage 2002: A Report to the Nation*, New Delhi, April 2002, p 34.

34 See Jan Breman, *Footloose Labour: Working in India's Informal*

Economy. Cambridge University Press, 1996.

35 Jan Breman, 'Communal Upheaval as Resurgence of Social Darwinism,' *Economic and Political Weekly*, May 2002.

36 Self-Employed Women's Association (SEWA), *Shantipath: Our Road to Restoring Peace*, Ahmedabad, June 2002, p 3.

37 Jan Breman, 'Communal Upheaval,' *op cit.*

38 *Ibid.*

39 *Ibid.*

40 Meghnad Desai, 'Not a nice Gujarati to know,' *Seminar*, October 1998, p 16.

41 Christophe Jaffrelot, *The Hindu Nationalist Movement in India*, Viking, 1996, p. 53.

42 For an excellent introduction to the ideology and politics of the RSS and BJP, see A.G. Noorani, *The RSS and the BJP: A Division of Labour*, Leftword, 2000.

43 M.S. Golwalkar, *We, or Our Nationhood Defined*. Nagpur: Bharat Publications, 1939, p. 12.

44 *Ibid.*, p 14.

45 *Ibid*, pp 43-44.

46 *Ibid.*, Chapter V, pp 47-48.

47 *Ibid.*, p 35.

48 M.S. Aney, 'Foreword,' in *ibid.*, pp xiii-xiv.

49 Koenrad Elst, 'Was Guru Golwalkar a Nazi?,' Leuven, 14 July 1999. http://pws.the-ecorp.com/~chbrugmans/articles/golwalkar.html

50 M.S. Golwalkar, *Why Hindu Rashtra?* (1960). Quoted in Noorani, *op cit.* p. 23. See also *Bunch of Thoughts*. Bangalore: Vikrama Prakashan, 1966.

51 *Social Studies*, Standard 9. Gujarat State Board of School Textbooks, reproduced in *Editors Guild Report*, p. 245.

52 Vinayak Damodar Savarkar, *Hindutva*. Bharti Sahitya Sadan, 1989 (Sixth Edition), p. 113.

53 Donald Eugene Smith, *India as a Secular State*. Princeton University Press, 1963, pp 459-460.

54 Ashis Nandy, Shikha Trivedy, Shail Mayaram, Achyut Yagnik, *Creating a Nationality: The Ramjanmabhumi Movement and Fear*

of the Self. New Delhi: Oxford University Press, 1995, p 63.

55 *Ibid.*, p 62. See also Ashis Nandy, 'Hinduism versus Hindutva,' *Times of India*, 18 February 1991.

56 The full text of the resolution may be accessed at www.rss.org/reso2002.htm

57 'RSS asks Muslims to shun extremist leaders,' *Hindu*, 18 March 2002; 'Hindu goodwill key to Muslims' safety: RSS,' *Hindustan Times*, 18 March 2002.

58 Smruti Koppikar, 'BJP chief reads riot act to Muslims,' *Indian Express*, 13 April 2002.

59 'Blame it on Newton's Law: Modi,' *Times of India*, 3 March 2002.

60 Interview by Sudhir Choudhury, Zee TV, 1 March, 2002. Reproduced as Annexure 4A in the *Editors Guild Report*, p. 38. The denial issued by the Gujarat Government's Directorate of Information on 3 March 2002 states, 'The Chief Minister has never mentioned such Newton's (*sic*) third law,' and is reproduced in the *Editors Guild report*, pp. 73-4. But though Modi did not himself invoke Newton's name when he spoke of action and reaction, his reference to the law was obvious.

61 Vir Sanghvi, 'Gujarat: Cause and Effect,' *Hindustan Times*, 21 April 2002.

62 'ISI hand in Godhra incident: Singhal,' *Hindustan Times*, 6 May 2002.

63 Amita Verma, 'VHP to test war on jihad in UP,' *Asian Age*, 7 June 2002.

64 *Hindu*, 24 June 2002; *Amar Ujala* (Dehra Doon edition), 24 June 2002.

65 In *We, or Our Nationhood Defined.* p 44.

66 Onkar Singh, 'Gujarat violence is patriots' reaction to Godhra: Mathur,' rediff.com, 3 May 2002. http://www.rediff.com/news/2002/may/03train.htm (Accessed on 20 June 2002)

67 The speech is reproduced unedited in the Appendix.

68 His exact words were '*Hum mazhabi kattarta mein vishwas nahin karte*'. The fact that *mazhabi* is the only Urdu word used in the sentence is not accidental. In Sangh Parivar literature and propaganda, whenever a positive reference to religion is made,

the word used tends to be *dharm*, implying Hinduism; when the reference is negative, the word used tends to be *mazhab*. See M. Zeyaul Haque, 'The Language of Hate,' *Milli Gazette*, 1 June 2001.

69 The ruling by Lok Sabha Speaker Manohar Joshi on a privilege motion moved by Priya Ranjan Dasmunsi on 9 May, 2002, quotes the PM as admitting that the 'video tape of his speech at Goa did not contain the word "such".' 'Privilege motion against PM rejected,' *Hindu*, 17 May 2002.

70 Dhirubhai Sheth, '*Is dangey ko samajhne ke liye...*,' *Rashtriya Sahara*, 9 March 2002.

71 'PM wanted to sack Modi but feared reaction,' *Times of India*, 7 May 2002.

72 'It's a black mark, says PM,' *Hindu*, 3 March 2002.

73 'PM wanted to sack Modi but feared reaction, *Times of India*, 7 May 2002. His remark in Parliament condemning Godhra was made at a public function to felicitate former PM Chandrashekhar. 'A lesson or two for his teacher,' *Hindu*, 18 April 2002.

74 B.G. Verghese, 'Farewell to Rajdharma,' *Times of India*, 23 May 2002.

75 See People's Union for Civil Liberties and People's Union for Democratic Rights, *Who are the Guilty?*. Delhi, November 1984.

76 From the Report of the Justice Jagmohan Reddy Commission on the Ahmedabad riots of 1969, cited in the Srikrishna Commission of Inquiry, http://www.sabrang.com/srikrish/antimin.htm. See also '1969 Communal Riots in Ahmedabad,' *Economic and Political Weekly*, Volume 5, Nos. 3-5, January 1970, and K. Vikram Rao, '1969 and 2002: By what yardstick is the Congress calling the BJP black?,' *The Pioneer*, 25 May 2002.

77 See Vrinda Grover, *Quest for Justice: 1984 Massacre of Sikh Citizens in Delhi*, 2 vols, mimeo.

78 'Godhra genocide had given setback to Four Year BJP Rule in Gujarat: Advani,' Gujarat information department press release, Ahmedabad, March 4, 2002. Reproduced in *Editors Guild Report*, p 50.

79 5 March 2002 press note, *op cit.*, p 57.

80 Editors Guild Report, pp 12-13.
81 The phrase is from Pierre Videl-Naquet, *Assassins of Memory*, Columbia University Press, 1993.
82 'Not "genocide": BJP,' *Hindu*, 27 April 2002.
83 See Balbir Punj, 'Fiddling with Facts,' *Outlook*, 27 May 2002.

The Violence

2

The Carnage at Godhra

Jyoti Punwani

Early in the morning on 27 February, coach S-6 of the Ahmedabad-bound Sabarmati Express was attacked by a mob just outside Godhra railway station. The coach—aboard which were a large number of Vishwa Hindu Parishad activists and supporters returning from Ayodhya—was stoned and set on fire. By the times the flames were extinguished, fifty-eight passengers were dead, many charred beyond recognition. One passenger died later.

Gujarat Chief Minister Narendra Modi called it an act of genocide and Union Home Minister Lal Krishna Advani hinted at a broad conspiracy involving Pakistan, the Inter-Services Intelligence (ISI) and Islamic extremists.

How and why was the Sabarmati Express set on fire? The investigative agencies inquiring into the incident may never disclose the truth, given the political interests involved and the central position the official theory of an 'Islamic conspiracy' now occupies in the BJP's rationalization of the violence which followed. But already, one official investigation has caused a major rethink on the prevalent theory that the mob outside set the train on fire. An experiment conducted in June by the Forensic Science Laboratory (FSL), Ahmedabad, showed that the fire could only have been caused by pouring inflammable liquid from inside the coach and then starting the fire in the bogie.[1] Any satisfactory explanation would also entail meeting all the travellers on that train, and especially those on the adjacent coaches (S-5 and S-7). But after spending a week meeting a few survivors, as many eyewitnesses as possible, railway employees, the authorities as well as residents of Godhra, I have been able to put together the following account.

In order to attract supporters to its 15 March 2002 programme for building a Ram temple in Ayodhya at the site where the now demolished Babri Masjid once stood, the VHP had conceived of a 'Ram Naam Jap' campaign. All this entailed for supporters in a particular locality was to recite 'Shri Ram Jai Ram Jai Jai Ram' non-stop for sixty-five days beginning 26 November 2001. They were then qualified to participate in the *yagna* which was to begin in January in Ayodhya and continue till March.

According to Malaben Rawal, national co-ordinator of the Durga Vahini, the women's wing of the VHP, some 2,000 volunteers had enrolled from Gujarat for this programme. Those who joined the Bajrang Dal were given trishuls, saffron headbands and 'Ram sewak' cards. Those who finally decided to go to Ayodhya left in three batches on 22, 24 and 26 February. They were carrying trishuls, most of them less than six inches long, though some were five feet. Rawal told me in April 2002 that they had made it clear that 'the trishul is not for personal use, but for protection of their *dharm*.'

Police *bandobast* was maintained at all major railway stations when these groups left Gujarat, be it Ahmedabad, Baroda or Godhra. In Godhra specially, because of the large number of Muslim vendors at the station, the police seemed to have ensured, whenever they knew the VHP travellers were passing through, that their stalls remained closed. In fact, a rickshaw-wallah who used to sleep in the station recalled that for five days before 27 February, the police would ensure that no bearded Muslim remained on the platform around 3 a.m., when the Sabarmati normally made its return journey from Faizabad, the railhead for Ayodhya. I could not confirm this. Perhaps the bandobast was for the batches going to Ayodhya. The last batch must have passed Godhra on the night of the 26th, and the police/railway staff may not have expected a return batch to pass through the next morning. But the VHP batch was right on schedule: they left Ahmedabad on the 22nd, reached Ayodhya on the 24th, participated in the *yagna* on the 25th, and left Ayodhya that evening for their return trip.

The rail authorities in Faizabad, including the railway police, didn't seem to have thought it important to inform their counterparts all along the way that the VHP activists were returning. Debashis Bhattacharya, a retired bank employee travelling from Faizabad, told the *Times of India* on 28 February that stone-throwing on the train began at Rudauli station, near Lucknow.[2] Even this did not prompt the railway police to warn their counterparts en route to Ahmedabad to be prepared for trouble. A senior rail official at Godhra told me that the train had been delayed because of the conduct of the VHP passengers at two or three stations early on. But this information did not reach the station authorities before the train did.

Godhra's vendors are not new to hooliganism by mobs. They recalled those travelling for Mahendra Tikait's kisan rally many years earlier—men had simply picked up foodstuff without paying. But no violence had erupted then. Vendors told me that had the railway staff known the Sabarmati was coming back full of VHP passengers, they would have diverted the train to another platform, since platform no. 1 is the only one which has stalls. Senior rail officials confirmed this.

The Train Arrives

The Sabarmati drew into Godhra four hours late, around 7.43 a.m. Platform no. 1 was full of commuters waiting for their regular trains to the nearby stations of Baroda, Dahod and Piplod, all of which normally leave around 8 a.m. Many of these were Muslims who could be identified as such. Forty per cent of Godhra's population is Muslim.

Both Hindu and Muslim eyewitnesses said that trouble started as soon as the VHP passengers alighted from the train. They were carrying sticks, with which they assaulted Siddiq Bakr, a bearded tea-vendor. It is unclear why Siddiq was assaulted. One vendor said it was because he was bearded, not because he asked for money. 'I saw these fellows hitting Siddiq Bakr on the leg and head. He had to be treated and he hasn't come back since, though the police need his statement.'[3] This vendor, himself bearded, described how he coped with the situation: 'As soon as I saw these people with their orange headbands and sticks, shouting slogans, I ran off and hid outside the station. I told my staff to remove their nameplates and if asked, to say that they were Hindus. I told them to say 'Jai Sri Ram' if ordered to do so, and on no account to ask for money. When Tikait's followers had got off here, they had not only grabbed my samosas, but even the tray on which they were kept. However, some of these fellows did pay. They also asked one of my assistants if he was a Hindu, and he said yes though he is not.'[4]

Foodstuff was picked up, a vendor's beard was pulled, another had tea flung on his face, (it is not known whether any of these was Siddiq), a cigarette-vendor's tray overturned, and some Muslims were forced to say 'Jai Shri Ram'. The National Human Rights Commission cites the testimony of a Hindu tea vendor to the effect that the VHP activists had quarrelled with Siddiq Bakr, and that police officers saw some of the kar sevaks trying to force him to raise the slogan 'Jai Shri Ram' and beating him.[5] Anees Piplodwala, a regular commuter on the Dehradun Express, recalled, 'They were saying, "*Ek hi nara bolo Jai Shri Ram to chhorenge*".' He also saw some saffron headband-wearing passengers looting stalls and beating a tea vendor.

National Human Rights Commission on the ruckus at Godhra station

The (NHRC) team went to the railway station and spoke to Shri Jai Singh Katija, station superintendent, and some eyewitnesses of the incident of 27 February. Shri Shafi Ghulam Rasool, a tea-stall owner, said that around 8 a.m. on 27 February, when the Sabarmati Express arrived, he had seen the slogan-shouting passengers who alighted from the train.

He heard about their altercation with tea-vendor, Siddiqui Bokkar, only after the train left. Shri Bhairon Singh, tea-vendor, stated that the kar sevaks had quarrelled with Siddiqui. Constable Karan Singh Yadav of the RPF said that he had seen 2-3 passengers in a scuffle with the tea-vendor. ASI, GRP, Chatter Singh Chauhan, said that the kar sevaks were trying to force the tea-vendor to raise the slogan 'Jai Shri Ram'. He also stated that one of the kar sevaks had pulled the beard of a Muslim tea-vendor and asked him to utter the words 'Jai Shri Ram'. They also beat the vendor. After the train started and before it could leave the platform, the chain was pulled. As the train halted, it was attacked with stones from the left side. The GRP staff rushed to the train, chased away the crowd and the train was made to leave. However, there was a second chain pulling and the train stopped at a distance of about one kilometre from the railway station near 'A' cabin. It was at this spot that coaches S-5 and S-6 were heavily stoned by a mob, which later burnt coach S-6. SI M.J. Jhala, PSO, GRP said that he had learnt about the incident at 8 a.m. and before he reached the spot at 8.15 a.m., the coach had already been burnt. His estimate of the crowd was 500 to 700. He said that on his orders the RPF had fired 4 rounds to disperse the mob.

Extracted from the confidential report on the visit of NHRC team headed by Chairperson, NHRC to Ahmedabad, Vadodra and Godhra from 19-22 March, 2002, pp. 22-23. This report was made public by the NHRC on 31 May 2002.

Some eyewitnesses interviewed by me didn't want to be named. Three were passengers, bound for Piplod and Baroda, and three are railway employees, two of them Hindu. They confirmed that the VHP passengers had sticks in their hands and were chasing bearded Muslims on the platform. One vendor, a Hindu, saw the tray of a cigarette-vendor being upturned. They also saw three lathi-carrying policemen, one in mufti, not intervening while all this was going on. The other Hindu eyewitness deplored the behaviour of the VHP passengers. 'In a democracy, you can't impose your religion on anyone else.'

Piplodwala said he saw some Bohra Muslims complying with the VHP demands to say 'Jai Shri Ram'. But another eyewitness, himself a Bohra standing on the over-bridge, saw a non-Bohra bearded Muslim refuse to repeat the slogan. This Bohra, who asked not to be named, almost became a target himself. He was standing with another Bohra, Umaid Dalal, on the bridge. Both are bearded, one wears a Bohra cap. Suddenly, the VHP passengers looked up and saw them. 'They shouted, "*daadhiwale mullah ko maaro*" and ran in our direction. But the train's whistle blew just then, and they ran back towards the train,' said Dalal. He remembered seeing them freely pick up whatever they wanted from the stalls.

The bearded vendor quoted above said that some of the VHP passengers tried to molest a girl on the platform. 'They also molested a girl who had been sitting on a bench on the platform (*uski beizzati ki*).' The girl referred to is seventeen-year-old Sophiya Shaikh, whom I met at her home in Baroda. She had just sat down on a bench on platform no. 1 with her mother and sister when the Sabarmati drew in. The three women were waiting for the Godhra-Baroda 'MEMU' (local train) to return home to Baroda after a long holiday at Sophiya's aunt's house in Signal Falia, the vast maze-like settlement of Ghanchi Muslims (the majority sect of Godhra's Muslims) adjacent to the station. 'We saw a ruckus on the platform. Passengers with saffron headbands who had got down from the train were shouting loudly and roaming with lathis. We got up to wait outside till the Sabarmati left.'[6] As the three women walked towards the exit, the mother in front, followed by Sophiya's younger sister, and Sophiya bringing up the rear, a well-built man grabbed Sophiya's arm from the back and pulled her towards the train, at the same time cupping a hand over her mouth. But she had already screamed 'Mummy', and the man left her at once. 'He probably thought I was alone,' Sophiya told me.

The threesome immediately ran into one of the rooms in the station and then went home as soon as they could. The women didn't lodge a complaint, nor do they have any intention of doing so. 'We thank God we escaped in one piece', says the mother, still shaken. Told about 'well-wishers' in Mumbai who want her to relate her experience in a press conference there, Sophiya shies away with a 'Never', even as her father shakes his head. This incident has been cited as one of the immediate causes of the burning of the coach. But says Sophiya, 'That can never be. Who committed the crime, and who paid for it!' A Class VIII drop-out, Sophiya said she has Hindu friends and this experience had not changed her relationship with them. 'We don't like living without our Hindu neighbours, we attend each other's weddings and eat together,' added her mother, giving me her contact phone number. It belongs to a Hindu neighbour.

Many of the eyewitnesses I met at Godhra station confirmed seeing this incident; someone yelled at Sophiya's mother: 'Take her away.' Piplodwala saw a burqah-clad lady running up to the waiting commuters and asking them to do something, not just stand there. 'I remember remarking to a friend, it's good it's so early in the morning. Had it been later, everyone in Signal Falia would have been awake.' As he boarded the Dehradun Express, Piplodwala saw the VHP passengers stone it. Other commuters (who didn't want to be identified) also saw the VHP passengers pick up stones from the tracks. One of them heard the passengers on the platform say, 'Don't let them get inside the train,' probably referring to the vendors.

The train halted at Godhra for just three minutes. All this was happening simultaneously on one side of platform no. 1, away from the Government Railway Police (GRP) post which is at the other end. Stones had already begun to be thrown on the train. One vendor said that as soon as Siddiq was beaten, some Muslims began stoning the train. The VHP passengers also retaliated immediately. Mukesh Shah, a Bajrang Dal member, who was on the platform when the stone-throwing began, told me in Ahmedabad, 'We also threw stones back at them, and told the ladies and children to get in and close the windows.' In July, police officers investigating the case told the *Times of India* they were convinced that there was stone-pelting from inside the train at Godhra platform after the quarrel with the tea-vendor but that 'the crime committed by those who burnt the coach is far more serious in proportion to the crime the people inside committed.'[7]

All the survivors I met confirmed that the stone-throwing began within minutes of the train stopping at the station. Said Gayatri Panchal, who lost her parents and two elder sisters in the fire, 'At Godhra, the train had barely stopped for two minutes when Urmilaben, in-charge of our troupe, told us that people were throwing stones and we should close our windows.' Navinbhai Brahmbhatt lost his wife in the fire. He recalled closing the windows when the stoning started at Godhra station. 'The women were told to climb onto the upper berths for safety.'

A lot more was happening. Malaben Rawal of the Durga Vahini said that some 'Muslims' tried to attack other compartments but were repulsed by the Bajrang Dal boys, one of whom hit a Muslim man on the forehead with a five-foot-long trishul. Though Malaben was not on the Sabarmati, such an account from a senior VHP functionary needs to be taken seriously.

The Train Departs

By the time the train was ready to move out, the situation had turned so volatile that Railway Protection Force (RPF) constables were imploring the VHP passengers—'with folded hands' one of them told me—to get back on the train. But none of them intervened to stop the scuffles that had already erupted. Piplodwala remembers stones being thrown from both sides ('*aamne saamne*') when the train stopped the first time, barely a minute after leaving the station. The chain was probably pulled in several different bogies to enable the VHP travellers left behind to get on the train. This was confirmed by the statement of the guard, Satyanarayan Panchuram Verma, to the police.

An affidavit filed before the Justice G.T. Nanavati Commision of Inquiry by civil rights advocate Amrish Patel. 'The guard and the assistant driver stated that the chains were pulled from four coaches (no 83101, 5343, 51263 and 88238), but they were not able to identify the persons responsible for the chain-pulling as the coaches were packed with ". . . kar sevaks returning from Ayodhya".'[8]

Verma, who went down to fix the problem after the chain-pulling incident, gave a statement to the police on 9 March saying, 'I saw people wearing saffron bandanas running towards the train and boarding it. I learnt that they were kar sevaks who were left behind at the station. As they were present in large numbers and since I could not identify anyone responsible for the chain-pulling, I did not take steps against anyone.' The train started moving around 8 a.m., after an 'all-right' sign was given by the guard.[9]

When the train stopped for the second time near Signal Falia, the stone-pelting increased. Rail employees on duty at 'A Cabin' near Signal Falia had to close their doors and windows to avoid the stones. They saw a large mob consisting of Muslims surround the entire train and stone it. One of them heard the mob shouting, '*Hamara aadmi andar hai* (One of our people is inside).' Rail employees and RPF constables told me that the stone-throwing continued even after S-6 caught fire. This was confirmed by Bhattacharya's account to the *Times of India*.[10] A small mob had gathered on the other side of the track too, but the RPF managed to disperse them.

More information about the last few minutes leading up to the start of the fire in S-6 is emerging in the Nanavati Commission. In his statement to the commission, assistant station master Rajendraprasad Meena—who was on duty at Godhra 'A Cabin', close to which the entire tragedy took place—said that there was no mob waiting near the tracks to attack the train or its passengers.[11] Those who gathered near the train and pelted stones had come from behind the train, he categorically stated. Under cross-examination by Dr Mukul Sinha of an NGO, the Jansangharsh Manch, Meena said that the mob which attacked the train had arrived in small groups of ten to fifteen persons, then gathered at the spot. 'They came from a narrow road at the junction between "A Cabin" and Signal Falia near the Godhra railway station, he said, adding that the mob, pelting stones at the train, did not attack him.

Instead, they allowed him to pass through them.'[12] Significantly, he said that he had not seen anyone climbing into or alighting from the train and that he did not think it possible to throw an article inside the train because the windows of the coach were higher than the heads of those standing near the tracks.[13] The report about his testimony continues:

'In his statement, Meena said that the train had stopped near A-Cabin between 7.55 a.m. and 8.00 a.m. On being informed about chain-pulling on the train, he alighted from his A-Cabin office and approached the train. However, heavy stone-pelting forced him to beat a retreat. The assistant station master said that he also saw some persons approaching the train from the engine's direction and pelting stones at the train. This went on till around 8.25 a.m. when he saw black smoke billowing out of S-6 coach that was a little ahead of A-Cabin. Within five minutes, flames engulfed the coach, said Meena. Ten minutes later, the police arrived and opened fire. Following this, the Fire Brigade began extinguishing the fire. In the meantime, the mob dispersed. In his statement, Meena also revealed that while he was standing on the first floor of A-Cabin, he had seen smoke coming out of a motor garage and a truck on the other side of the track where the train passengers had alighted.'[14]

I could not meet anyone who admitted to having seen the train being set on fire, except the survivors from S-6. Not one of them said that anyone inside the compartment had started the fire, as has been demonstrated by the FSL experiment. The experiment, conducted with water and, of course, without the presence of a mob, showed that had the inflammable liquid been poured from outside, the coach would not have caught fire the way it did, as all or most of the liquid would have fallen outside the coach. The report concluded that someone inside the coach must have poured the liquid. The report, filed by FSL assistant director M. S. Dahiya, surmises that three of the four doors of the compartment were open when the fire was raging inside, while all the windows were closed.[15]

However, the survivors I met claimed that the mob broke the windows and poured the inflammable liquid inside. They then threw burning balls of cotton and rags inside the compartment. The smoke was so overpowering, they said, that many of them passed out. Gayatri Panchal remembers the smoke having a strange suffocating smell. 'When smoke began entering our coach, we all got off. The smoke was so much that some people became unconscious,' recalled Mukesh Shah.[16]

Perhaps those who died were asphyxiated by the smoke before the fire reached them. That would explain why no screams for help were heard from the coach, either by the RPF, which first reached the site, or the superintendent of police, who reached around 8.26 a.m. Said Navinbhai, 'The mob broke the windows and threw burning rags and balls of cotton inside. Many became unconscious because of the overpowering smoke. Others lost their voices and must have died where they were, unable to scream for help. The fire was at our feet, the stones were on the windows. Somehow, some of us in the adjacent coach managed to jump out.' Mandakini Bhatia, who survived the attack along with her husband, told me she couldn't speak for days after. The couple, who were part of the VHP troupe, escaped by squeezing themselves through the twisted and broken grills of a window, as did Bhattacharya.

All those outside the train first saw the thick black smoke. Railway employees saw flames coming out from the windows on the track side, not the side facing Signal Falia. Janakidevi Chaurasia, who was an ordinary traveller not with the VHP, told *India Today* that after the windows and doors on the platform side were shut to avoid the stones, her son spotted fire on the other side and bottles landed inside the coach from those windows.[17]

An RPF constable, among the first to reach the burning coach, had another theory about how the coach was set on fire. He surmised that the mob must have set fire to the buffers between the two coaches, since rubber catches fire fast. They must have also poured diesel inside the toilet windows which, unlike the other windows, were not closed, he said. The fire spread to the coach from both ends, trapping the passengers in the centre. By the time the RPF reached the site, the coach was on fire. An elderly constable told us that they had to shout to the passengers to open their doors and windows, which they had locked from inside to protect themselves. However, this is contradicted by the FSL report which suggests three of the four doors were open. Ultimately, the RPF says it broke the windows on the track side, and found some of the passengers unconscious.

When the Fire Brigade reached the site by 8.26 a.m., the fire was raging in earnest. Two Fire Brigade employees told me they had been stopped on the way by a mob led by Haji Bilal, a councillor whom they recognized as he often treated the municipal staff to tea. This forced them to take a detour and reach further away from the train than they normally would have, necessitating a longer water pipe. As they reached the train, they could see a woman, her face all black, coming to the door again and again but unable to jump off. This means that at least one door on the track side was open. 'Had we not been stopped, we might have at least been able to save her,' they said. The SP too saw this woman. However, the Fire Brigade's version has been doubted. Five minutes would be the time normally taken for it to reach the railway station, say police officials. Haji Bilal has since been arrested and is one of the main accused in the train-burning offence.

The Fire Brigade men admitted they could not enter the burning coach as soon as they reached because of the intensity of the fire. The RPF constable, who had worked for twenty-two years in the Fire Brigade, risked going in. He did his best to save as many passengers as he could, holding a blanket borrowed from the other passengers as a shield behind him, till it caught fire. Passengers were bringing blankets, he said, to wrap around those who were being rescued from S-6.

Unanswered Questions

Both the RPF constable and the SP commented on the behaviour of the VHP passengers while the coach was burning. Instead of trying to help save those trapped inside, they were urging the police to tackle the dispersing Muslim mob. However, one of them who died later in hospital of burns, did try his best to save his fellow passengers. The GRP and RPF, both under flak for not saving the lives of the VHP passengers, blamed the latter for the deaths of 'poor, innocent labourers travelling to Ahmedabad to earn a living'. Of the fifty-nine persons who died, the VHP has identified thirty-eight as those who travelled with them, plus three who are missing. The families of two others have been making inquiries of the collector, Godhra, while Jankidevi Chaurasia has been speaking about her missing grandson to many newspapers. Taking into account Pooja Deshpande and one more person who died later in hospital, this leaves seventeen persons unidentified. Could these be UP labourers whose relatives may be too poor and illiterate to travel to Godhra to make inquiries? Another point worth noting is that hardly any of the reserved passengers of S-6 figure in the list of those dead and injured.[18] Could it be that they had all been forced out much earlier by unreserved VHP passengers and hence escaped the fire?

The burning of the train has left some unresolved questions. Was the chain pulled the second time? If so, who pulled it? The RPF claims the vacuum pipe itself had been cut or burnt, thus neutralizing the chain pulling mechanism. In their testimony before the Nanavati Commission, however, the engine drivers stated that the train stopped the second time because of chain-pulling.[19] Raghunathrao Jadhav, the main driver, said the train stopped because the chain had been pulled a second time just after the engine crossed the 'A Cabin' and three minutes after the train started. The train was moving at a speed of nearly 13 km at that time. Assistant driver Mukesh Pachauri, in his statement, said that the coaches from where the chain was pulled were not together.[20] Jadhav stated that there is a gauge in the engine and its vacuum level drops when the chain is pulled. If the chain-pulling takes place from more than one coach, the vacuum level drops further and has to be reset from outside the coach from where it takes place. 'He said that it is not correct to say that if the resetting is not done properly, the vacuum level would drop on its own. He also made it clear that the vacuum level did not drop suddenly, but went down gradually.'[21]

Second, why was there no effective firing to prevent the burning of the coach? The most likely explanation is that by the time the RPF/GRP reached the scene, the coach was already on fire. GRP men told me that though they are always armed, they normally leave their rifles at their outpost at the station because they are too cumbersome to carry all the time. When the GRP finally reached the spot, they did fire, dispersing the mob. A GRP constable heard the shots a little after 8.00 as she was making her way towards the station, and when the SP reached, at 8.26 a.m., the mob had dispersed.

Third, the forensic investigators probing the manner in which S-6 burnt have concluded that no inflammable liquid was thrown on the coach from the outside, nor was there any possibility of it being splashed inside from the doors. How then was the inflammable material—investigators M.S. Dahiya and M.N. Joshi believe some sixty litres of liquid was used—poured in?[22]

Godhra bogie burnt from inside, says report
Times News Network

Ahmedabad: The mystery over the burning of the S-6 bogie of Sabarmati Express at Godhra on 27 February ... has turned deeper with the forensic report on the incident discounting the possibility of the mob throwing inflammable liquid from outside and then setting the bogie on fire.

Investigations made by the Ahmedabad-based Forensic Science Laboratory (FSL) have now shown that almost sixty litres of inflammable material was poured from inside the compartment before it was set on fire. A report by the FSL's Assistant Director Dr M.S. Dahiya, which is part of the charge-sheet filed in the Godhra case about a month back, is based on a study of the pattern of the burns in the compartment and a simulated exercise conducted on 3 May to recreate the incident. The report contradicts the view held so far that the mob which attacked the train threw inflammable liquid at the train using buckets and cans from a distance, even while the passengers had shut all the windows and doors of the compartment.

To recreate how the crime must have been committed, a train

bogie was placed at the same spot. Using a variety of different containers, it was doused with liquid for experimental observation.

The report said the height of the window of the bogie was found to be seven feet. In these circumstances, it was not possible to throw inflammable liquids into the bogie from the outside with the help of a bucket or a jerry-can because by this method most of the liquid fell outside the bogie. At the spot of the incident, at about a distance of fourteen feet, there was a mound of gravel-stones about three feet high. It was spread parallel to the bogie for a long distance. The FSL officials, standing on the mound, threw water on the windows of the bogie, of which only about 10 to 15 per cent entered the bogie. The rest fell on the outside. Since, a major portion of the inflammable liquid fell on the tracks and around it, it would have caused damage on the outside of the bogie and under it.

The report says, 'after inspecting the bogie and the tracks, it was found that there is no effect of fire below the windows. Taking this fact into account and the burning pattern on the outside of the bogie, the conclusion is that no inflammable liquid was thrown into the bogie from the outside'. It further says, 'it also does not look possible that inflammable liquid was thrown in from the doors of the bogie'.

As a next step, using a bucket, about sixty litres of water was thrown into the passage of the compartment from one side and then a large part of the bogie was covered. Water thrown like this went only in one direction; no part of it flowed outside from the open doors or in the direction of the latrine. 'On the basis of this experimental observation, the conclusion is that standing in the passage of the compartment near seat no. 72, using a container with a wide opening, about sixty litres of inflammable liquid has been poured and then immediately a fire has been started in the bogie,' the report says. The FSL report further says that 'it appears that three of the four doors of the compartment were open when it was burning while all the windows were shut. The pattern of burning (alligatoring pattern) shows that the intensity of the heat was four times more towards the eastern side (towards seat no. 72) of the bogie'.

Source: *Times of India* (Ahmedabad), 3 July 2002.

Apart from the mystery of how precisely the fire started, eyewitness accounts do not give a satisfactory explanation for why the train was burnt. The FSL experiment has provoked the Congress to accuse the VHP of having stage-managed the Godhra train carnage to instigate communal violence in Gujarat. Amarsinh Chaudhary, former chief minister of Gujarat and president of the Gujarat Pradesh Congress Committee before his replacement by Shankersinh Vaghela in mid-July, was quoted in the *Hindu* as saying that 'the same elements who indulged in communal carnage were also involved in setting fire to the train'.[23] Chaudhary has only said out loud what many have been saying in private. However, the VHP maintained that the result of the forensic experiment had strengthened its claim that the Godhra incident was well-planned—that 'Muslim' conspirators had travelled in the same train in order to burn it.[24] On his part, L.K. Advani first rejected as 'frivolous' the contention of the FSL report when asked about it in Ahmedabad.[25] However, after the Gujarat police claimed that three of the accused had confessed to entering the coach and pouring the inflammable material,[26] the home minister changed tack. 'I have seen the bogie and anyone can see that the fire is from inside. But that does not mean people burnt themselves. The inquiry commission is seized of the matter.'[27]

Whatever the interpretations being drawn from the FSL report, the fact remains that the accounts of eyewitnesses and survivors do not point towards a well-planned conspiracy—be it by the VHP or by a group of Muslims. If the burning was a spontaneous act, why did it happen? How did the inflammable liquid get inside the train? Were the 'kar sevaks' carrying kerosene to cook food *en route* which then caught fire after the mob attacked? Were the incidents on the platform enough to provoke such an inhuman, barbaric reaction? Did a vendor get on the train to recover his money? Did the mob stone the train to rescue him, or were they trying to save Sophiya, under the impression that she was trapped inside? Did the VHP passengers begin stoning the Muslim settlement at Signal Falia? The women there said they were woken up by the sound of stones falling outside their houses.

Given the volatile situation created as soon as the VHP passengers alighted, the fact that a 1,000-strong mob collected in a few minutes cannot be disbelieved. The garages just outside the station were a handy source of diesel and other inflammable materials. P.P Agja, IGP (Railways) was quoted as saying he was not surprised that a crowd collected so fast.[28]

The report submitted to the investigating agencies by Baroda RPF divisional commissioner S.N. Pandey confirms the conclusion that the burning was a spontaneous act. The RPF document claims: 'A large number of activists of the Bajrang Dal and the Vishwa Hindu Parishad were in the train. They were shouting slogans like 'Bharat Mata Ki Jai' and 'Jai Shri Ram'. There was an altercation between the activists and a few hawkers who were selling eatables on the issue of payment. The vendors were from the local Muslim community.' The RPF has also pieced together a time schedule of events that led to the tragedy:

7:42 a.m.: The Sabarmati Express entered Godhra station.
7:47 a.m.: It was ready to depart. This is when the hawkers began pelting stones.
7:50 a.m.: The chain was pulled to stop the train.
7:55 a.m.: The train resumed its journey, but the stone pelting continued.
8:00 a.m.: The chain was pulled for a second time.
8:07 a.m.: A crowd which had gathered began to burn the bogie, and only dispersed after the RPF had resorted to four rounds of firing.[29]

Despite the use of 'truth serum' (sodium pentothal) on some of the Godhra suspects, the police have not yet been able to establish the wider 'conspiracy' Modi had first spoken of. The *Times of India* reported that, 'The polygraph interrogations conducted on two of the accused are said to have centred around their links with the Students' Islamic Movement of India, terrorist outfits in Pakistan, the militants who attacked Parliament, whether they received funds from the ISI and who masterminded the conspiracy. But there have been no satisfactory results.'[30]

But why did the mob attack the coach? To get everyone out, or to avenge their humiliation at the station? Bhattacharya told the *Times of India* that the mob was roaring: '*Maar dalo sabko* (Kill everyone)' and '*Ek ko bachne nahin denge* (Don't spare anyone).'[31] However, investigators are still reportedly baffled by certain key aspects of the mob, especially its 'composition and character'. The *Times of India* reported from Godhra in July: 'While the whole country may have condemned the mob for being blood-thirsty and perpetrating a heinous act of burning alive fifty-nine persons without adequate provocation, there is a mystery over how almost ninety persons escaped largely unhurt from the burning compartment. There are recorded statements to suggest that there were at least 150 persons in the compartment when the incident took place. "The question here is if this was really a blood-thirsty mob, why did they not kill passengers who were jumping out of the burning train. All the deaths took place inside the compartment and there are only a handful of other passengers with injuries suffered in stone throwing," said a police officer involved with the investigations. The official said that the escaping passengers could have been easily lynched, if that was the intent of the mob.' 'Police officers are saying that the mob psychology of Godhra was obviously different from that of the mobs who attacked Naroda-Patiya, Gulberg Society, Sardarpura or Best Bakery in the Godhra aftermath, where those who tried to escape the flames were hacked and thrown back into the fire.'[32]

The Ghanchi Muslims at Godhra spoke of harassment of Muslims all along the way inside the train as one of the provocations that led to the burning of the coach. I could not meet any victim of such harassment, but Malaben Rawal of the Durga Vahini and a Muslim resident of Rustompura near Godhra both narrated an incident of a Muslim couple being harassed on the train. The couple got off at Godhra. The *Indian Express* dated 10 March 2002, carried an account by one Akbar Shah, a passenger on the Sabarmati, about such harassment all the way from Faizabad. 'Akbar Sirajuddin Shah, Fateh

Mohammed Yedusa and his wife Gulshan Khatum (*sic*) travelled from Faizabad in the coach adjoining the fateful S-6. They escaped while the train burnt and took shelter in Godhra. Shah says, "When we were boarding the train in Faizabad, the canteen-wala told us to remove Gulshan's burqa. When I asked why, he said there were quite a few kar sevaks on the train. So she removed it. We sat on the upper berth. There was a lot of slogan-shouting; three-four of them asked another family to also shout the slogans but they said no. They ordered them again and there was an argument. Finally, that family was forced to get off at a station midway".'[33]

Jan Morcha, a Hindi daily published from Ayodhya and edited by the respected senior journalist, Sheetala Prasad, carried a detailed report on 25 February 2002—two days before the Godhra attack—describing the unprovoked attacks by VHP travellers on Muslims aboard the Sabarmati Express carrying VHP volunteers to Ayodhya, as well as on Muslims waiting at railway platforms en route.[34]

Bajrang Dal activists on Sabarmati Express beat up Muslims, force them to shout, 'Jai Shri Ram!'

Bhalesar (Faizabad), 24 February: *Trishuldhari* Bajrang Dal workers, travelling to Ayodhya on board the Sabarmati Express this morning, let loose a reign of terror upon dozens of helpless Muslim passengers, burqa clad women and innocent children. They also targetted the people waiting at the platform, forcing them to shout the slogan, *'Jai Shri Ram!'* A few even declared themselves to be Hindus in order to escape their wrath.

According to eyewitnesses, close to 2,000 trishul-carrying Bajrang Dal workers, on board the Sabarmati Express coming from the direction of Lucknow, began indulging in these activities from the Dariabad Station. Anyone identified as a Muslim on the train was mercilessly attacked with trishuls and beaten with iron rods. Even women and innocent children were not spared. Burqas were pulled off, women were beaten with iron rods and dragged, people waiting at the platform were also similarly targetted.

This continued between the Dariabad and Rudauli Stations.

According to an eyewitness, a youth who protested against this barbarism was thrown off the train between the Patranga and Rojagaon stations. Several women, badly wounded and covered in blood, jumped off the train as it pulled into Rudauli around 8.00 a.m. The Bajrang Dal activists also got off the train and started attacking those whom they identified as Muslims from among those present on the platform.

Ata Mohammad, from Takia Khairanpur, waiting to catch a train to Allahabad, was badly beaten, some others were forced to shout, '*Jai Shri Ram!*' Some escaped by declaring that they were Hindus. Fifty-year-old Mohammad Absar who lives near the station was grabbed as he stepped out of his house. His long beard was rudely pulled before he was repeatedly stabbed with trishuls. Another man from the Rudauli police station area who happened to be at the station was badly beaten with iron rods. Local residents rang up the police.

By the time the police *chowki*-in-charge, Bhalesar, arrived at the station, the train had left and the injured were being rushed to the hospital. No report was registered at the police station since the officer-in-charge was unavailable. The injured have no idea why they were attacked. Rumours are rife. The people are petrified; respected Hindus and Muslims of the area have condemned the shameful attack, Muslim religious leaders have appealed for peace and requested that there be no retaliation.

Source: Jan Morcha, 25 February 2002. Translated in *Communalism Combat*, March-April 2002.

A team sent by the All India Democratic Women's Association later met one of the victims of these attacks and confirmed the *Jan Morcha* report: 'We personally followed up the story published in the *Jan Morcha* of 25 February describing how kar sevaks travelling on the Sabarmati Express had attacked people visually identifiable as Muslims at railway stations. On 7 March, we met such a victim in the Lucknow Civil Hospital. He was Mohammad Asar, a construction worker. Asar was, as usual, on his way to work in Rudauli, Barabanki district, when he was attacked by kar sevaks at a railway crossing. His stomach was slit open and his shoulder was broken; his crime was that he was a Muslim.'[35]

It could not be confirmed whether the Signal Falia residents had already been informed of these incidents en route. Did the attacks on the platform prove to be the last straw?

Trying to find an answer to this, I met Maulana Hussen Umerji, chief Maulvi of Godhra, who has more than once, at peace meetings called by the collector of Godhra[36], apologized on behalf of his community. He and a few prominent Ghanchi Muslims of Godhra issued a statement in Gujarati condemning the incident, praying for the souls of those who died and offering condolences to their families, but this was not published in any Gujarati paper. At the end of a long interview, the Maulvi said, 'It's worth thinking: so many trains pass through Godhra. For 150 years no Muslim hit or even abused any passenger. Then how could they do this? If the starting point had not been there, if the *badmaashi* had not begun from Faizabad itself, would they have broken this 150-year record?' But was that reason enough to set fire to the train? 'What do you do when the devil takes over? *Shaitaan sawaar ho gaya tha, donon taraf.*'

Why couldn't the GRP/RPF on duty at the station handle these assaults on the platform? Were they afraid of being outnumbered? Or were they, as usual, reluctant to swing their *lathis* against Hindu rioters? Probably it was the same attitude which made the rail authorities in Faizabad and all along the way ignore the belligerence of the VHP passengers. Bhattacharya told the *Times of India* that the latter would get off at every station and shout slogans. And Sajjanlal Mohanlal Raniwal, the ticket collector on the Sabarmati Express, has mentioned how he was stopped from entering the coaches by VHP and Bajrang Dal activists who had forcibly occupied the reserved seats. Raniwal was forced to spend the night in the guard's coach.[37]

In contrast, police authorities in Godhra were used to taking all precautions to avoid any confrontation between the VHP passengers and the Muslim vendors at the station, probably because of Godhra's peculiar history of communal riots, specifically involving the Ghanchi Muslims living around the railway station. Godhra and its Ghanchis are notorious all over

Gujarat. But that did not deter the VHP passengers, most of them Gujaratis, from provoking them there. Till now, no report of any such violent confrontation all through the Sabarmati's journey on that particular day has come to light. I could personally verify that nothing happened at Dahod, before Godhra. Why did the VHP travellers run amok at Godhra? Was the sight of so many bearded Muslims a red rag to them, or did they want to provoke them?

National Human Rights Commission on the failure of intelligence at Godhra

11. The response of the State Government of 12 April 2002 also fails to dispel the observation made by the Commission in its Preliminary Comments that the failure to protect the life, liberty, equality and dignity of the people of Gujarat itself stemmed from a serious failure of intelligence and a failure to take timely and adequate anticipatory steps to prevent the initial tragedy in Godhra and the subsequent violence.

12. The report of the State Government of 12 April 2002 asserts that the State Intelligence Bureau 'had alerted all Superintendents and Commissioners of Police as early as 7.2.2002 about the movement of kar sevaks from the State by train on 22.2.2002 to Ayodhya. Besides the State Intelligence Bureau had also intimated UP State Police authorities on 12th, 21st, 23rd, 25th and 26th February 2002 about the number of kar sevaks who had left the State for Ayodhya by train.' However, 'specific information about the return journey of kar sevaks by the Sabarmati Express starting from Ayodhya was received only on 28.2.2002 at 0122 hrs i.e., after the incident had taken place on 27.2.2002 morning.'

13. It appears incomprehensible to the Commission that a matter which had been the subject of repeated communications between the Gujarat Intelligence Bureau and the UP State Police as to the out-going travel plans of the kar sevaks, should have been so abysmally lacking in intelligence as to their return journeys. This is all the more so given the volatile situation that was developing in Ayodhya at that time and the frequent reports in the press warning of the dangers of inter-communal

violence erupting in Ayodhya and other sensitive locations in the country. In the view of the Commission, it was imperative, in such circumstances, for the Gujarat Intelligence Bureau to have kept in close and continuing touch with their counterparts in Uttar Pradesh and with the Central Intelligence Bureau. The inability to establish a two-way flow of intelligence clearly led to tragic consequences. The Commission must therefore also definitively conclude that there was a major failure of intelligence and that the response of the State Government has been unable to rebut this presumption.

Extracted from the Final Report of the National Human Rights Commission in respect of the situation in Gujarat, 31 May 2002, pp 7-8.

Godhra as a Factor

Stereotyping of communities is not only communal but also often misleading. Keeping this in mind, some attributes for which the Ghanchis of Godhra are known among both Hindus and Muslims in Godhra and outside, may be taken as applicable to a majority of them. They are known as an aggressive, impulsive community, descendants of Afghan soldiers and Bhil women. They were initially harvesters and traders of oil, and later became farmers. Today, they are in the transport business. They are largely illiterate and poor, though the number of educated among them is growing. The Ghanchis have had a long history of violent conflicts with Godhra's Hindus, pre- and post-independence. The Hindu Mahasabha was in the forefront of such conflicts before independence and in 1948, when the government is said to have actually ordered the police to set fire to Ghanchi settlements in order to scatter them. Most of them fled to Pakistan but many returned, impoverished and therefore easily drawn into crime.

After independence, their major riots have been with the Sindhis who settled here after Partition. The two communities have more in common with each other than with others of their faith, and till 1980, used to live as neighbours in mixed settlements. Godhra's Sindhis pride themselves as being the only Hindus who can 'take on' the Ghanchis. The 1980-81 riots between them resulted in the exodus from each other's areas. Responding to a rumour about Ghanchis being attacked by Sindhis, a mob of Ghanchis burnt alive a family of five Sindhis in Signal Falia, an incident that hasn't yet been forgotten by the residents of Godhra.

Most of the sixty-seven Muslims arrested for the Sabarmati incident are Ghanchis. Interestingly, of the first thirty to be arrested, fifteen have been shown as arrested on the spot. But the time of their arrest has been given as 21.30 hours in their remand application. That is not the only anomaly in the two cases involving the burning of the train and the violence that followed. Soon after the Sabarmati was set on fire, the VHP in Godhra attacked a mosque and clashed with a group of Ghanchis outside the station. Though curfew was immediately imposed, Muslim property worth Rs 20 crore was burnt on 27 and 28 February.

Strangely, the main accused in these attacks on Muslim property are the same four Muslims who are the main accused in the train burning offence: President of the Godhra municipality Mohammed Husain Abdul Rahim Kalota, councillors Haji Bilal, Salim Shaikh and Abdul Rahim Dhantia alias Kaankatta. According to the Godhra police, therefore, after burning the train, these four led mobs to burn properties belonging to their own community, including a mosque! These anomalies suggest a political motive behind the arrests of Kalota and company. Kalota had just last year, dislodged the BJP from the Godhra municipality by engineering defections.

But apart from this large-scale destruction of Muslim property, no Muslim was killed in Godhra town, where half the local population must have seen the charred bodies of the passengers. How did Godhra, the flashpoint of the Gujarat violence, escape the 'natural upsurge of Hindu anger'? The main reason was the reluctance of the Sindhis to 'retaliate'. It had taken the community years to rebuild themselves after the 1980-81 riots, and they didn't want to risk another major disruption in their business, which was already adversely affected by the destruction of Bohra *kirana* shops in the villages. It was the Sindhi wholesalers who supplied the Bohras with grain on credit, and they knew they couldn't ask the Bohras to pay up. 'We told others to go ahead if they wanted to `retaliate', but this time, we weren't going to allow them to shoot from our shoulders,' said Kishorilal Bhayani, a former president of the Godhra municipality. There couldn't be a stronger refutation of the theory of 'spontaneous mass anger against Godhra' than Godhra's three months of peace, albeit uneasy, after 27 February.

What the Victims Say

Significantly, the display of 'anger' elsewhere did not have the sanction of those in whose name it was being done. Some of the victims' families, whom I met in Ahmedabad in the presence of VHP activists, had close Muslim friends, and despite the VHP's best efforts to convince them that no Muslim could be trusted, a few remained unconvinced. The VHP's stock question to these families was: 'Shouldn't these people (Muslims) be cut?' Not everyone agreed. That these families stuck to their views in the presence of the VHP members was all the more remarkable because apart from the VHP, BJP and Shiv Sena, no other political party/leader, not even the CM, had bothered to meet them.

Dr Girishchandra Rawal lost his sixty-two-year-old wife Sudha in the fire. Though his son Ashwin, a VHP activist, declared expressionlessly that 'even 5,800 dead bodies will not deter us from our mission', his father was not so stoic. With tears in his eyes, the old man, steeped in Hindu scripture, spoke of the loss of his 'partner in old age—the best period of marriage'. 'Words cannot describe this blow,' he said. 'As a doctor, I know what it is to be burnt alive, the feeling of helplessness . . . such barbarity . . .' But even as the VHP members around him urged him to express his 'instinctive anger', he shook his head. 'I feel such rage that I could set fire to this entire society. But as a

Hindu, I have to control myself. There is no place for revenge in my religion. We are taught to behave well even with our enemies.' A fortnight after we met him, Ashwin was killed in broad daylight by a mob of Muslims. The killers haven't yet been arrested. He leaves behind a wife and little daughter, and, of course, his old father.

Navinbhai Brahmbhatt, too, wept as he recalled how he had managed to escape from the adjacent coach, while his wife, Niruben, burnt to death inside S-6. She was finally identified by her *payals*. For the Brahmbhatts, who were not VHP members, this pilgrimage had a special significance. They were planning to re-open Navinbhai's plastics factory which had been closed for the past few months, after the *darshan* in Ayodhya. Niruben had been a great help in running the factory. Now he was left with his two sons aged eleven and fourteen. Asked whether he felt that the death of his wife had been appropriately avenged, Navninbhai stopped weeping and answered, 'Why don't they show their anger to those in Godhra who burnt the train? Why to our own people? The Miyas do business with us. We have no hatred for them. Those who live here didn't do anything. Why are they being killed? I call up my Muslim friends everyday, but they all seem to have left the city.' Even Rajeshbhai Patel, who lost his only son, twenty-two-year-old Chirag, felt that the violence was wrong.

Thirty-two-year-old Pooja Deshpande had not even been part of the VHP troupe. She had simply boarded the train at Dahod, one station before Godhra, hoping to reach her office in Baroda faster than by the local she travelled in daily. Her husband Deepak, a stationmaster in Godhra, had seen her into the Sabarmati. The next time he saw her was when she was rescued as the fifty-sixth body from coach S-6, still holding their joint tiffin-box in her hand. Deshpande said Pooja used to leave his lunch-box with Siddiq Bakr, adding that he was a 'pleasant mild-mannered fellow.' Siddiq was the same vendor who had been beaten at the station by the VHP passengers. 'Even someone who has never hit anyone would have felt ready to kill, seeing those bodies,' said the soft-spoken Deepak, hurt still writ large on his face, as he showed me photographs of his wife. His six-year-old son had performed the last rites of his mother, who had obviously been the fulcrum of their small family. Did he agree with the violent 'retaliation' being meted out in the victims' name? Pooja's inconsolable mother-in-law answered. 'Will that bring our daughter back? Those who did this should be hanged. But no innocent's family should be ruined the way ours has been.'

The manner of Pooja's death had made the mother-in-law lose faith in God. Asked whether she considered Pooja a martyr for the Ram Mandir, her mother-in-law replied, 'Sacrifice and all that is okay, but our house is ruined.' The Godhra unit of the VHP did not mention Pooja Deshpande's name even once in the hour I spent with them, despite asking them repeatedly whether anyone from Godhra had died. Their list of 'martyrs' was confined to those of their troupe who had died in the train. As for the others, they said the government would look after them.

Govind Makwana, who lost his only son, Umakant, aboard the Sabarmati Express on 27 February, told the *Times of India*, 'I am extremely disturbed over what is happening in our area. I had pleaded with folded hands to all who came to my son's cremation to please restrain themselves and maintain peace.' He was speaking on the day of the *besna* of his twenty-two-year-old son. 'Killing other people is not the solution. Losing a son is shattering, and I want no father or mother to suffer from this feeling,' he pleaded.[38]

Govindbhai's heartfelt entreaties fell on deaf ears.

Notes

1   'Godhra bogie burnt from inside, says report,' *Times of India*, 3 July 2002; Anosh Malekar, 'Mystery of the Bogie S6 Inferno,' *Week*, 7 July 2002.

2   'At Rudauli, near Lucknow, we had our first brush with pelting,' he was quoted as saying. See Raja Bose, 'Godhra survivor recounts horror of burning train,' *Times of India*, 3 March 2002.

3   Siddiq has been made one of the main accused in the Godhra incident and was underground while I was there. The Hindu

railway staffers to whom he used to serve tea described him as a mild and pleasant fellow.

4   Interview with vendor, name withheld, March 2002. Unless stated otherwise, all eyewitness accounts in this chapter were gathered by me in personal interviews with the individuals involved.

5   See box, 'NHRC on the ruckus at Godhra station.'

6   Personal interview with Sophiya Sheikh, Baroda, March 2002.

7   Leena Misra, 'Narco analysis gives some leads in Godhra case,' *Times of India* (Ahmedabad), 9 July 2002.

8   Shyam Parekh, 'Who pulled the chain at Godhra,' *Times of India* (Ahmedabad), 17 July 2002.

9   *Ibid.*

10 See footnote 2 above.

11 'Key witness deposes in Godhra case', *Times of India* (Ahmedabad), 18 July 2002.

12 'No mob was waiting to attack S-6 coach', *Indian Express* (Ahmedabad), 18 July 2002.

13 *Ibid.*, *Times of India*, *op cit.*

14 *Indian Express, op cit.*

15 See footnote 1 above.

16 He claimed that before the train reached Godhra, a Muslim female passenger had told him to leave S-6. It seems doubtful that a Muslim woman would pass on this tip to a Bajrang Dal activist. No other survivor made this claim to me.

17 'As the train pulled out of Godhra station, Janakidevi, travelling with her husband, son and grandson Rishab, heard stones hitting it. Seated on the upper berth, she was scared but safe. The train moved and stopped again. Her husband Lallan told her to stay put because a huge mob had attacked them. By then the doors and windows on the platform side of the train were shut. Suddenly Gyan Prakash, her son, spotted fire on the other side. Just then bottles landed inside the coach. "There was black smoke all around. Somebody pulled me down and pushed me from the train. Then I passed out".' Sheela Raval, 'Tracking the plan,' *India Today*, 18 March 2002.

18 Compare Reservation Chart for Sleeper Class Coach S-6, Train 9166 Sabarmati Express, leaving Lucknow for Ahmedabad on 25

February 2002, posted on the Godhra collectorate's website (http://www.mahitishakti.net/englishversion/what_new/train/reservation_list.htm) with the Western Railway list of ex-gratia compensation to dead and injured (mimeo) and 'List of injured in attack on Sabarmati Express', PTI, Ahmedabad, 27 February, as carried in *Hindustan Times* (http://www.hindustantimes.com/nonfram/280202/dLNAT15.asp).

19 'Sabarmati Express drivers appear before panel,' *Times of India* (Ahmedabad), 19 July 2002.

20 *Ibid.*

21 *Ibid.*

22 Anosh Malekar, *op cit.*

23 Manas Dasgupta, 'Inflammable material was poured from inside the compartment,' *Hindu*, 4 July 2002.

24 *Ibid.*

25 'Advani disputes forensic report on Godhra,' *Times of India* (Ahmedabad), 8 July 2002. The newspaper reports: 'The contention of the Ahmedabad-based Forensic Science Laboratory that the fire, which engulfed two coaches of the Sabarmati Express at Godhra railway station, was ignited from within them was untenable, Advani told reporters here on Sunday. "How could women, children and other travellers keep inflammable material or explosives to take their own lives?" Advani asked during a day's visit here, while rejecting the laboratory's report. "The idea is frivolous".'

26 'Three Godhra accused confess to being part of mob,' *Times of India* (Ahmedabad), 15 July 2002. Reports quoting unnamed police sources appeared around the same time in *Asian Age* and *Indian Express* claiming the three men had also confessed to climbing on board S-6. See Rohit Bhan, 'Godhra: Loopholes Persist,' *Indian Express* (Ahmedabad), 21 July 2002.

27 'Let EC decide dates: Advani,' *Times of India*, 25 July 2002.

28 Kingshuk Nag, 'Godhra attack not planned,' *Times of India.* 12 April 2002.

29 Rajesh Ramachandran, 'RPF saved the day in Godhra: Report', *Times of India,* 12 April 2002; Rajdeep Sardesai, NDTV.

30 Leena Misra, *op cit.*

31 See footnote 2 above.

32 'Godhra mob's psychology still unclear,' *Times of India* (Ahmedabad), 7 July 2002.

33 Darshan Desai, 'For clues to Godhra, stop at Signal Falia,' *Indian Express*, 10 March 2002.

34 *'Bajrang Dal karyakartaon ne Sabarmati train mein Muslimon ko peeta, Jai Shri Ram ke naare lagvaye* (Bajrag Dal activists on Sabarmati train beat up Muslims, force them to say Jai Shri Ram),' *Jan Morcha* (Faizabad), 25 February, 2002.

35 Brinda Karat and Subhasini Ali, 'Investigation as Collusion-II,' *Hindu*, June 1, 2002.

36 The collector, Jayanti Ravi, and the DSP of Panchmahals, Raju Bhargava, were both transferred, reportedly on the insistence of VHP members, in the first week of July. See 'Transfer of Godhra officials could derail peace process,' *Times of India* (Mumbai), 6 July 2002. Both had worked hard to bring the two communities together in Godhra and other parts of Panchmahals. Bhargava had arrested many BJP and VHP activists for rioting, while Jayanti Ravi had herself led the first peace rally held in Godhra on 3 April 2002.

37 Anosh Malekar, *op cit.*

38 *Times of India*, 3 March 2002. Quoted in *Communalism Combat*, March-April 2002.

3

A License to Kill
Patterns of Violence in Gujarat

Nandini Sundar

An eye for an eye blinds Gandhinagar

Ahmedabad, February 28: Gujarat was virtually handed over today to frenzied mobs of the VHP and Bajrang Dal who left a trail of murder, loot and arson in a series of 'Godhra revenge attacks'. The carnage climaxed in the burning of former Congress MP Ehsan Jafri . . . late in the afternoon. Well past midnight, the fires kept on burning and reports of more deaths kept pouring in, along with news of the recovery of 23 bodies in a slum cluster in the city.

(*Indian Express* lead story, 1 March 2002)

Curfew in 26 towns as mob goes berserk

Ahmedabad, February 28: In towns across Gujarat, Muslim shops, offices and mosques were attacked by Vishwa Hindu Parishad and other like-minded people. Cars burned in the streets, Muslim shops were looted and set on fire . . . 70 people have died so far . . . Indefinite curfew has been imposed in 26 towns across the state . . . Police sources said they were not prepared to raid the offices of the VHP just yet. They were more concerned with controlling the volatile situation . . . Meanwhile, Acharya Giriraj Kishore on Thursday asked the minority community to condemn the train attack and warned that the Hindu patience had its limitations.

(*Hindustan Times*, 1 March 2002)

This chapter attempts to provide an overview of the large-scale violence against Muslims which took place in Gujarat following the Godhra incident. The degree of organization behind the attacks—in the mobilization of large crowds, the deployment of what seems like a core trained militia, the distribution of weapons and gas cylinders, the hate meetings held weeks before the attacks, the directions to the police not to intervene—suggests not just a clear pattern of official complicity but also long-term planning by the Sangh Parivar to decimate Muslims. Godhra may have been the immediate impetus, but there is a high possibility that in the run-up to the planned *shilanyas* at Ayodhya on 15 March, some outrage would have occurred or been manufactured and used to justify a massive 'retaliatory' attack.

Although the victims of the Gujarat violence are predominantly Muslim—the attacks aimed not only to eliminate them physically but to destroy them economically—what has also suffered in the process is the space of everyday interaction between communities. Where it has not directly communalized, the Sangh Parivar has terrorized and intimidated the Gujarati populace into silence. Hindus, dalits and adivasis who helped Muslims, citizens engaged in peace initiatives, journalists who reported on the direct complicity of the police or the role of BJP leaders—have all been 'punished' for the sin of being ordinary human beings who believe in peace, or even simply doing the job they are paid for.

The Promise of Impunity

Even as coach S-6 of the Sabarmati Express was burning at Godhra, the VHP activists aboard the train began their 'retaliation'. Some of them attacked a mosque at Signal Falia, and dispersed only when the police fired teargas and a round of live bullets at them.[1] By 12.40 pm, the train, short of two bogies, was on its way to Ahmedabad. The VHP activists attacked Muslims at every station en route, except for Kheda where the SP had ordered all Muslim vendors and porters off the platform.[2]

At Vadodara, they took over the platform with sticks, broken bottles, tridents and daggers, shouting slogans and swearing revenge. Three persons were stabbed, one of whom later died. One Muslim was stabbed to death at Anand railway station when the Sabarmati Express arrived at the station.[3] In Ahmedabad seven buses were burnt that night.[4]

The first call that Gujarat home minister Gordhanbhai Zadaphia received was at 8.10 a.m., from a VHP worker travelling on the Sabarmati, who told him that the train was being attacked. By 9.00 a.m., the control room in the chief minister's bungalow was busy monitoring developments in Godhra. That evening, Zadaphia, Modi, VHP joint general secretary Jaideep Patel and local MLAs Prabhat Singh Chauhan and Bhupendrabhai Lakhanwala visited the site. Jaideep Patel was continuously on his mobile, making arrangements for photos of the burnt bodies to be sent to every newspaper.[5]

By the 27th afternoon, the VHP had taken the decision to call a Gujarat bandh for the next day and an India-wide bandh on 1 March.[6] By evening, the BJP extended its formal support, despite knowing that a similar bandh called two years ago after the Lashkar-e-Taiba had killed pilgrims at Amarnath had led to large-scale devastation of Muslim property.[7] The VHP was informally told that they had till the evening of 28 February to take *turant jawabi karwai* (immediate punitive action), after which the government would be forced to deploy the army. 'Across Gujarat', says Sujan Dutta, 'VHP/Bajrang Dal cadre interpreted the bandh call as a call to action.'[8]

The VHP and Bajrang Dal had been preparing for attacks for months—holding *trishul diksha* (*trishul* distribution) ceremonies in rural areas, where *trishuls* and swords were handed out, and venomous speeches made against Muslims. *Communalism Combat,* a Mumbai-based publication which has been monitoring the situation in Gujarat for several years now, received reports that a 'secret' meeting was held at Lunawada (Panchmahals) on the evening of the 27 February which was attended by all the top brass of the VHP/Bajrang Dal/BJP and RSS, which made detailed plans on the use of kerosene and other methods of killing.[9] Muslim shops were burnt in Lunawada that night itself.[10] Similar but smaller meetings were held across the state on the 27th and 28th in village Leach (Mehsana), village Motera (Gandhinagar), village Prantij (Sabarkantha) and village Sanjeli (Dahod).[11] To give just one example—on 1 March, Subhashbhai Mafatbhai Chota, a local Bajrang Dal leader in Vadodara, is said to have called a meeting at a well between Patarveni and Salaad villages. Some Hindus from Raghovpura village (near Tarsali, Vadodara), also went and later came back and told their Muslim friends that plans were being made to burn their houses. Sure enough, the mobs arrived that night with swords and cans of kerosene.[12] In urban centres too, as the mode of attacks was to show, meticulous planning seems to have taken place.

At least one media report speaks of a meeting called by the Chief Minister on the 27th night to ensure that the police would stay off while the Sangh Parivar mobs enacted a 'Hindu backlash'.[13] This alone can explain what happened at Gulberg society, Chamanpura—when police who were put on alert at 7.00 a.m. allowed mobs of several thousand strong to build up, and joint police commissioner M.K. Tandon who personally reassured Ehsan Jafri that he would be given full protection, then disappeared.[14] This also accounts for policemen at Naroda Patiya explicitly telling Muslims begging for protection that they had orders not to save them and to let the violence run for twenty-four hours.[15]

A plot from the devil's lair

A late-evening meeting convened by Modi on 27 February ensured mobs a free hand the next day
Manu Joseph

What exactly happened on the night of 27 February in Chief Minister Narendra Modi's bungalow in Gandhinagar? All along there have been rumours of a late-evening meeting called by Modi on the day of the Godhra carnage in which he instructed senior police officials to allow 'people to vent their frustration' over the torching of the Sabarmati Express during the VHP *bandh* the following day. These rumours have now been confirmed.

Information with *Outlook* shows that a senior minister from his own cabinet has blown the whistle. Last week, the minister deposed before the Concerned Citizens Tribunal headed by former Supreme Court judge Justice Krishna Iyer. The nine-member tribunal . . . was in Gujarat to record evidence on who or what may have caused the Gujarat carnage. Former Bombay High Court judge Justice Hosbet Suresh, who is on the Concerned Citizens panel and who also heard the deposition, confirms that the minister did depose before him. He told *Outlook*: 'Yes, a senior minister appeared before us for 35 to 40 minutes and talked to us about a few things that led to the Gujarat carnage. Among other things, the minister spoke about the meeting Modi called on the night of 27 February. The minister spoke to the tribunal on the condition that it would not name him in its final report . . .'

The minister told *Outlook* that in his deposition, he revealed that on the night of February 27, Modi summoned DGP K. Chakravarthy, commissioner of police, Ahmedabad, P.C. Pande, home secretary Ashok Narayan, secretary to the home department K. Nityanand (a serving police officer of IG rank on deputation) and DGP (IB) G.S. Raigar. Also present were officers from the CM's office: P.K. Mishra, Anil Mukhim and A.K. Sharma. The minister also told *Outlook* that the meeting was held at the CM's bungalow.

The minister told the tribunal that in the two-hour meeting, Modi made it clear there would be justice for Godhra the next day, during the VHP-called bandh. He ordered that the police should not come in the way of 'the Hindu backlash'. At one point in this briefing, according to the minister's statement to the tribunal, DGP Chakravarthy vehemently protested. But he was harshly told by Modi to shut up and obey. Commissioner Pande, says the minister, would later show remorse in private but at that meeting didn't have the guts to object. According to the deposition, it was a typical Modi meeting: more orders than discussion. By the end of it, the CM ensured that his top officials—especially the police—would stay out of the way of the Sangh Parivar men. The word was passed on to the mobs. (According to a top IB official, on the morning of February 28, VHP and Bajrang Dal activists first visited some parts of Ahmedabad and created minor trouble just to check if the police did in fact look the other way. Once Modi's word was confirmed, the carnage began.) . . .

The minister went on to tell the tribunal that Modi was convinced that since he started the riots, he would be able to control the violence within a day or two . . . The more shocking aspect of the minister's testimony, says a tribunal member, was: 'Scores could have been settled in Godhra itself. Perhaps 100 people may have died there on the whole and that may have been the end of it. But Modi brought the riots to Ahmedabad. He took the riots to rest of the state.'

The riots . . . had a simple political background . . . According to the minister, Modi told the BJP high command (after he became CM) that . . . in the next elections he would bring the BJP back to power. The minister added that when five and a half months into the job Modi realised his charm wasn't working, he decided religious polarization was the only way to survive. As triggers go, Godhra was a strong one. But anything could have served as a trigger. There was talk of making an issue of a cow slaughter video the party had got but that plan was shelved . . . *(Excerpts)*

Source: *Outlook*, 3 June 2002.

———————————

On the evening of 27 February, the VHP and Bajrang Dal asked their activists to organize condolence meetings—*besnas* and *bhajans*—and to ring bells all over Ahmedabad in unison as a mark of grief and protest at the Godhra carnage.[16] Details of when the bodies would arrive from Godhra were relayed on radio and television channels, and when they finally came early in the morning of the 28th, a crowd of some 500 people—relatives and VHP/BJP leaders—was waiting to receive them at the Sola civil hospital. The bodies, which came to the city despite police chief P.C. Pande's objections,[17] were accorded a martyrs' welcome—with shouts of '*Kar Sevak Amar Rahe, Hindu Ekta Zindabad*' and vows of vengeance by some VHP men.[18] At 7 a.m., thirteen bodies were taken in a procession to Jantanagar in Ahmedabad's Amraiwadi locality and from there again to the crematorium in Hadkeshwar. The procession included some policemen, posted to provide protection, who conveniently turned a blind eye to the VHP youth who periodically left the procession, set fire to Muslim shops and rejoined it.[19] The Gujarat assembly adjourned after paying homage to the Godhra victims.

That morning, large-scale violence erupted in Ahmedabad. Large mobs attacked Naroda Patiya, Naroda Gam, Naroda fruit market, Chamanpura, Odhav, Gomtipur, Amraiwadi, Paldi and Vatva. The homes of Muslim judges were attacked. In Gandhinagar, the Wakf Board and the Gujarat State Minorities Finance and Development Corporation—located in the state capital's 'high security zone'—were attacked as the police stood by.[20] Simultaneously, mob attacks took place in the countryside around Ahmedabad, in Vadodara and its environs, in Sabarkantha, Panchmahals and other districts.

Sections of the Gujarati media, particularly the pro-BJP *Sandesh* and *Gujarat Samachar*, did their best to inflame passions and incite violence by carrying front page photographs of the Godhra victims, and even worse, completely concocted stories about the abduction and rape of Hindu women by Muslims at Godhra. One such fictitious front page story in the *Sandesh* on 28 February about the bodies of two women recovered at a pond in Kalol pruriently concluded: 'As part of a cruel inhuman act that would make even a devil weep, the breasts of both the dead bodies had been cut. Seeing the dead bodies one knows that the girls had been raped again and again, perhaps many times. There is a speculation that during this act itself the girls might have died . . . . Is there no limit to the lust?.'[21] VHP leaders circulated copies of the fictitious *Sandesh* article across Gujarat. Eyewitnesses from Naroda Patiya in Ahmedabad reported that the mobs were 'brandishing not only swords and stones but also copies of *Sandesh*, demanding blood for blood'.[22] In the rural areas of Panchmahals district, said Moinuddin of village Mora, men were going around all day on motorcycles selling xerox copies of the *Sandesh* for Rs 2 and mobilizing people.[23] In adivasi areas, the stories of women raped and killed metamorphosed into rumours about attacks on adivasi women.[24] Local TV channels (such as J-TV, Deep and VNM in

Vadodara) also helped to incite mobs by airing inflammatory speeches by BJP/VHP leaders like Ajay Dave, Nalin Bhatt, Deepak Kharchikar, Neeraj Jain, Bhartiben Vyas (mayor of Vadodara), Jitendra Sukhadia, and others.[25]

In most places, the major violence occurred between 28 February and 2 March—within the '72 hours' that Modi claims it took him to restore order to Gujarat.[26] One could equally well interpret this as the time-period for which the Sangh Parivar mobs were promised impunity for any act of violence. However, in several districts, violence broke out much later, towards the end of March or early April. Violent incidents continued well into July. The Union government officially admits that between April and June 'sporadic incidents of communal violence' caused 216 civilian deaths, 790 civilian injuries and property loss of about Rs 417.07 crore.[27]

According to PUCL, Vadodara, there were three distinct phases of violence in Vadodara: the first wave of systematic organized attacks against Muslims and their property that lasted from 28 February to 5 March; the second wave which began on 15 March, the day of the *shiladan* in Ayodhya, when Hindutva processions and *ramdhuns* turned violent and those who had yet not participated in crimes were egged on to do so; and the third wave which spanned the period from 26 April–5 May and was fuelled by rumours of retaliatory attacks by Muslims.[28] It is also in the later phases that vested interests like the 'builders' mafia' and land speculators appear to have got into the act.[29]

Predictably, the Gujarat government looks at the violence differently and openly blames 'Muslims'. In an interview to *Hindustan Times*, state home minister Zadaphia said: 'What happened up to 2 March was a reaction to Godhra. Thereafter, the riots were provoked, and even planned by Muslims.' Zadaphia said the riots happened in three phases. In the first phase there was a huge outpouring from the Hindus, the 'sufferers'. 'Doctors, engineers and advocates from the majority community were out on the roads during the first three days of the riots. This definitely shows it was a spontaneous reaction,'

Zadaphia said. Thereafter, he said, Muslims were responsible for keeping the violence alive. In the third phase, politics took precedence over communal violence. For this, he blamed the Congress. Contradicting his own theory of 'reaction' in the first phase, he said, 'Hindus cannot be violent. If they were, then the 1,700 karsevaks on the train in Godhra would have retaliated'.[30] Echoing the official line, *India Today* concluded, on the basis of very slim and even slanted evidence, that the violence after 2 March was due to Muslims: 'This phase, really, was one of Muslim mobs attacking Hindus.'[31]

While there have been some attacks on Hindus by mobs of Muslims, the vast majority of those killed or displaced are Muslims—victims of Sangh Parivar-led attacks and police operations both at the time and after. Most of the Hindus who died were shot dead by the police, while many Hindus were also killed by the Hindutva mobs who either mistook them for Muslims or punished them for working for, or being friends with, Muslims.[32] Consider this report of the first week's violence in *Frontline*:

> In Ahmedabad, 249 bodies had been recovered until the midnight of March 5. Of these, six could not be identified, while 30 were of Hindus. Of the Hindus killed, 13 were shot by the police, while several others died in attacks on Muslim-owned establishments. Six bodies of Hindu workers were, for example, recovered from Hans Inn and Tasty Hotel. Although there were almost no attacks by Muslim mobs on Hindu-dominated areas, 24 Muslims were killed in police firing.[33]

In any event, so organized was the violence and so total the complicity of the State that what happened in Gujarat cannot be described as a 'riot'. A riot conjures up images of members of two religious communities fighting each other. In Gujarat, Muslims were targetted by leaders and activists of a political organization, the Sangh Parivar, which claims to represent Hindus. Ordinary Hindus may have been bystanders and some may have joined in the violence but the pogrom of Muslims unleashed on 28 February was without doubt a political phenomenon.

Method in the Madness

> 'February 28, 2002 was going to be the day when Hindus would show what they are capable of.' *Haresbhai Bhatt, chief of Gujarat Bajrang Dal.*[34]

The attacks started practically simultaneously in locations across Gujarat, both urban and rural. From around 9–10 a.m. on the 28th morning, large mobs led by prominent local leaders of the VHP, Bajrang Dal and BJP built up wherever there were Muslim houses within Hindu majority areas. Areas where Muslims were in a majority like Juhapura in Ahmedabad or Tandalja in Vadodara were comparatively safe. While in many places the attacks were aimed at killing as many Muslims as possible, those directing the violence seemed equally concerned with destroying all Muslim businesses so as to undermine the economic foundations of the community.

Nature and leadership of mobs

Sharief Khan, who was out on the streets of Ahmedabad from 28 February onwards with his ambulance, told *Communalism Combat* that the mobs were nothing like those he had seen in Ahmedabad riots before: 'It was a full-fledged deployment of a highly organised mob. The numbers were large and the actions were coordinated.'[35] The mobs varied in size from a few hundred to several thousand strong, with some eyewitneses (e.g. in Chamanpura in Ahmedabad or Sanjeli in Dahod) reporting mobs of 15-20,000. Conceivably the mobs could have seemed much larger to the terrified victims than they actually were. Exaggerating the numbers also suits the police and the BJP— the former because they can justify their own inaction by claiming to be outnumbered, and the latter because they can then claim widespread public support and participation in the attacks. That this may, in fact, be a well-perfected strategy is suggested by a Hindutva manual issued two years ago, aimed at teaching Sangh activists how to make an attack on minorities look like a 'spontaneous reaction' by the public. It noted ingenuously, 'Now that we have our own government, we should take proper advantage of it and get our work done by it.'[36]

Newspaper photos[37] and television footage of the first few days of the mayhem in Ahmedabad showed young men in saffron headbands, sword in hand, out on the streets in motorcycles, running in large gangs, against the backdrop of huge clouds of smoke, overturned vehicles and devastated buildings. Nasir Khan Rahim Khan Pathan described the mob which attacked Naroda Patiya on 28 February as 'dressed in khaki half-pants or *chaddis*, saffron *banians* and black hair bands.'[38] Mohan Bundela, a member of Jansangharsh Morcha, a housing rights organization in Gomtipur, Ahmedabad, wrote in his FIR that the crowd which burnt the Muslim huts in Salatnagar 'had tied headbands of saffron colour and worn saffron belts with trishuls on them and many of them had swords also.'[39] In Machchipeeth, Vadodara, in addition to the saffron headbands, several rallyists had saffron flags tied to their sticks and rods.[40]

The mobs were shouting one constant refrain which all survivors, whether in rural or urban areas, recall as *Maaro, Kapo, Looto*, or *Maaro, Miya ne maaro*. (Kill, Hack, Loot, or Kill Muslims).[41] In Ahmedabad, even after the victims had fled, loudspeakers aimed at the camps, especially during the night, relayed these slogans.[42] *Jai Bajrang Bali*, *Har Har Mahadev* and. of course, *Jai Shri Ram* were used as battle cries.[43] The VHP-Bajrang Dal gangs forced their terrified victims to say this as well.[44] Two not-yet-teenage boys in Delol (Panchmahals district) were made to go around a pyre of their relatives, chanting *Jai Shri Ram* before being shoved into the fire themselves.[45] Some Muslims refused to chant Jai Shri Ram. Among them were the former Congress Member of Parliament, Ehsan Jafri, in Chamanpura, Ahmedabad, and Ismailbhai in Delol, both of whom were paraded around and hacked into pieces before being burnt.[46] Even sections of the police began demanding these professions of faith in the superiority of Hinduism. In Navayard Cabin D Area of Roshannagar, Vadodara, two men, Abdul Nabi Bholey Khan and Mohammad

Umar Abdul Latif, who refused to say '*Sabse Bada Hanuman*' (Hanuman is the greatest) were made to sit cross-legged while the police jumped up and down on their thighs.[47]

The killings were marked by a ritualistic frenzy, almost carnivalesque in its abandon. Five-month pregnant B, who was raped by men from Randhikpur, her natal village, recalled them shouting 'Jai Shri Ram' as they fell upon her.[48] Banusabil Qureshi of Randhikpur, who took shelter in an adivasi house, claims she saw some Hindu women dancing the *garba* after burning down Muslim houses.[49] Abuses against Muslims were common. In Machchipith (Vadodara), the mob were shouting '*Bandiao* (circumcised), go to Pakistan, *Babur ki aulado Hindustan chhod do*' as they waved their swords and trishuls. 'Some even took off their pants and danced around in the lanes.'[50]

Several BJP elected representatives at various levels are said by survivors to have taken direct part in the carnage. One Muslim man from Naroda Patiya, whose ten-year-old son was badly burnt and in hospital, alleged that BJP MLA Maya Kodnani gave the signal which let the mob loose on their locality: 'If she is brought before me today I will tell her, we elected you to the assembly and you brought this disaster on us.'[51] Although many eyewitnesses identified Maya Kodnani and VHP joint general secretary Jaideep Patel, as playing key roles in the violence in Ahmedabad, and an FIR was filed against them on 17 March, their names have been kept out of all chargesheets so far.[52] A resident of Jamalpur (Ahmedabad) alleged Haren Pandya, Gujarat Revenue Minister helped set fire to Apna Bazaar medical store on 28 February night, even as the police in the Ellis Bridge Police Station nearby slumbered on.[53] In Visnagar (Mehsana), the lead was said by eyewitnesses to have been taken by BJP MLA Prahladbhai Mohanbhai Gosa Patel and Nayabhai Tribhuvandas Patel, deputy chief of the municipal corporation.[54] In Kalol (Panchmahals), many eyewitnesses allege they saw the local BJP MLA, Prabhasingh Chauhan, and his son leading the attacks.[55] In Vadodara, the PUCL list of people accused by eyewitnesses as being directly involved includes several BJP councillors, corporators or *taluka* panchayat members. BJP corporators also made sure that no help reached the Muslims—in Kadi town (Mehsana), a municipal council member is said to have prevented the fire brigade from responding to calls, while BJP corporators Bhartiben and Anitaben are said to have told doctors at VS hospital in Ahmedabad not to treat Muslim patients.[56]

Although many of the real accused have been let off, the chargesheets filed in several prominent cases corroborate that the leadership was provided by the BJP/VHP and Bajrang Dal. Among the 48 charged in Naroda Patiya, are Babu Bajrangi, Bajrang Dal activist, VHP member P.J. Rajput and BJP leader Kishan Korani.[57]

In rural areas, the saffron headbands seem to have been less *de rigeur*, but here too, many of the attackers were easily identifiable as local VHP, Bajrang Dal, RSS or BJP men.[58] A report on rural Dahod by two women's groups notes that the mob could be divided into three distinct groups. The first lot consisted of local Sangh Parivar leaders who coordinated the attacks on their mobile phones.[59] For instance, Mohamedibhai, who ran a cement business in Ghumali village (Dahod), said he was hiding in an adivasi neighbour's house when a mob of around fifty led by local VHP leader Bacchhubhai Khaber of Chari village came to attack on 2 March. From a small window, he watched Bacchhubhai Khaber burn his house down, with a liquor bottle in one hand and a mobile phone in the other, on which he loudly provided an update to other VHP leaders.[60]

A second group provided the armed backup—with trishuls, swords, petrol, diesel, kerosene. They came in vehicles—cars, tempos, jeeps. In more than one village, the Muslim survivors noted that the men had identical backpacks from which they took out pouches of chemicals. It was these men who burnt and raped, and who carried out the most brutal attacks. Survivors also noted that not all the people in the mob spoke Gujarati—many spoke Marathi and Hindi.[61] This account, which suggests a trained militia operating at the core, is corroborated by the PUDR fact-finding team. For instance, the adivasi *sarpanch* of Anjanwa in Panchmahals, where eleven people were killed, said that one of the attackers was wearing a helmet, and many of them were dressed like city people with boots and socks. One was even carrying a camera bag.[62]

Adivasis were the third group—they provided mass to the mob but their activities were mostly confined to looting and burning. They did not generally engage in rape and murder.[63] For the past ten years, the VHP and Bajrang Dal have been attempting to mobilize adivasi youth in areas like Panchmahals, Dahod, Sabarkantha and Chhota Udepur.[64] Among the fears they routinely play on is that of adivasi women being 'abducted' by Muslim men, and the exploitation of adivasis by Muslim moneylenders, conveniently ignoring the exploitation by Hindu moneylenders.[65] In many places, however, the adivasis who joined the VHP-led mobs were little more than mercenaries. VHP activists went around on 27 and 28 February giving adivasis money to burn and loot.[66] On one estimate, Rs 1,000-1,200 was paid to adivasis in Kawant (Vadodara) to burn Muslim houses. An adivasi schoolteacher in Joj (Panchmahals) claimed that adivasis had been coerced into participating in the attacks. In fact, many adivasi women had wept while watching the destruction.[67] According to Dalwai and Mhatre's sources in Panchmahals:

> Bharat Dangi, a Bhil from Suliyat village was promised suitable reward for his men who participated in the looting and burning of houses indicated by the VHP leaders. After the looting and burning was over, Bharat Dangi demanded his reward. When refused, Bharat Dangi threatened that the VHP leaders would meet the same fate as that of the Muslims if he and his men were not paid their promised reward. The VHP reported the threats to Mora Police Station and Bharat Dangi was incarcerated. Although Bharat Dangi gave the name of the VHP leaders who were with him, none of them was arrested. The police refuse to give any information as to in which jail Bharat Dangi has been incarcerated.[68]

It was not just adivasis but other poor people too who were paid to attack. In Sokhada village near Vadodara, headquarters of one of the Swaminarayan sects (specially popular with Gujarati NRIs), villagers were given alcohol to lubricate the looting. One villager overheard an NRI saying that he was prepared to spend a crore on this (attacking Muslims). He is also reported to have told the mobs to go ahead and make a good job of it.[69]

In both rural and urban areas, the attackers came prepared for a full day's 'work': eyewitnesses from Ahmedabad told Human Rights Watch that many of the attackers were equipped with cell phones and water bottles.[70]

In the urban areas, newspapers and human rights activists both reported a new phenomenon—middle class families coming out in cars to loot shops, phoning friends and relatives to tell them where the best stocks were available, and, when not satisfied with what they'd got, coming back for more.[71] Big stores like Bata and Pantaloons and jewellery shops on posh C.G. Road in Ahmedabad were completely wiped out. Sharif Khan, with the Noble Ambulance Trust, told *Communalism Combat*: 'I even saw women members of the Durga Vahini at CG Road and Ashram Road. Out of the mob of 4-5000 here, 60 per cent were women and they were looting and burning shops.'[72]

High-society looters roam scot-free
Sourav Mukherjee and Amit Mukherjee

Ahmedabad: Apart from the wanton killings that took place during the communal riots in the city on 28 February, the most lasting image that lingers nearly 200 days later is that of the 'high-society looters'—those who had come in cars, plundered plush shops and walked away with suitcases full of goodies. Police had even claimed that they were closing in on such people, who had been captured on hidden cameras installed in some of these shops. But chances are that all these looters are still walking around in Pantaloon trousers and Metro and Bata shoes.

For not a single person from the elite neighbourhoods of Ahmedabad, who participated in the free-for-all at Ashram

Road and C G Road showrooms on that day, has been booked by the police. Instead, the 39 arrested by the Navrangpura police for looting shops are slum dwellers of Gulbai Tekra, Navrangpura gaam and Mithakhali.

The involvement of those who stay in apartments and bungalows is being surreptitiously swept under the carpet.

Shop-owners aren't unduly worried that the looters, who walked away with mannequins, barcode machines, billing machines, fax machines, tyres, spoons and even mismatched shoes have gone scot-free as long as they get their insurance claims.

A senior police official said: 'A local college student had toured Navrangpura and video-taped these social bigwigs shoplifting. But after promising to supply us with the evidence he developed cold feet.'

Initially recoveries were made from a large number of slums in the posh neighbourhood. Goods were also recovered from a few middle-class homes in Navrangpura and Naranpura. These recoveries notwithstanding, big names are missing from the FIRs lodged with the police. Even the victims of this indiscriminate loot do not wish to speak, let alone pursue the matter. Mehul Vaghela, Pantaloons store in-charge, says 'Let's not talk about the issue. Let bygones be bygones . . . I can tell you how I am preparing for Diwali but let's leave this subject aside.' Police records show Pantaloons suffered a loss of Rs 3 crore.

Compared to the losses amounting to more than Rs 9 crore, recoveries of articles worth less than Rs 1 lakh have been made. This reflects just how complacent the police are towards the issue.

The manager at Metro Shoes on C G Road says: 'I don't want to talk on this subject.' He even refused to divulge his name. Says Mohammad Altaf of Cona Shoes at Municipal Market on C G Road, 'I had lost Rs 70 lakh when my shoe store was looted and burnt on 28 February. I spent almost an equal amount to make good the damage.'

Source: *Times of India*, Ahmedabad, 16 September 2002.

Means of attack

Whatever their actual numbers, the mobs were well armed. They had swords, *guptis,* trishuls, guns, stones, acid bulbs, petrol bombs and gas cylinders. Many of the survivors, both rural and urban, reported that people were hacked to death with swords before being burnt.

In the twenty-first century, swords are hardly the kind of thing ordinary people keep at home and bring out in spontaneous anger, as Narendra Modi and the BJP would have us believe. Evidence is rapidly emerging that these were distributed by the Bajrang Dal on a mass scale, much before 27 February at various meetings and training camps held across the state from August–December 2001, and certainly on the evening of 27 February and morning of 28 February, when the attacks were being planned. Jaideep Patel, VHP joint general secretary told the *Indian Express*: 'We've been distributing these weapons since 1985; *trishul diksha samarohs* and *Bharatiya abhyans* are a constant process. Nobody has objected, not even the police.'[73] Patel and Bajrang Dal leaders like Haresh Bhatt claimed that these were meant for self-defence, with Bhatt describing them as 'divine instruments used by our gods.'[74]

The fact remains that the police *should* have objected. One police officer is quoted as saying: 'Look, most of them (swords) are more than four feet long. They slice through flesh on touch. Just touch the edge to a man's throat and he will die.'[75] Sword distribution continued at least through April and May. In mid-April, the Rajasthan police seized a fresh consignment of 1,500 swords and knives en route to Gujarat.[76] A month later, the Rajkot police discovered a large consignment of 99 swords, 200 guptis and other lethal weapons camouflaged in hockey sticks, intended for the Bajrang Dal.[77]

Gas cylinders were another common weapon, used on an industrial scale, especially, but not only in urban centres like Ahmedabad and Baroda. In a country where ordinary citizens still have to bribe to get a gas cylinder, people don't keep extra cylinders handy just in case they need to burn a neighbour or two.[78] When Teesta Setalvad visited Naroda Patiya in Ahmedabad, a tanker used to carry inflammable fuel and gas cylinders was still parked there. Survivors alleged that the gas cylinders were provided by Bipin Panchal, a local VHP worker who also owns Uday Gas Agency.[79] In Gulberg Society, Chamanpura, the police FIR notes that ten to twelve gas cylinders were exploded in the attacks.[80] During the attack on Prof J.S. Bandukwala, a PUCL member in Vadodara, two LPG cylinders which had been stored in a Hanuman temple nearby, were brought by autorickshaw.[81] Even in rural areas, where wood is still the main source of cooking fuel, gas cylinders were used, e.g. in Por (Gandhinagar).[82] More commonly, however, mobs in rural areas relied on kerosene, petrol and diesel. In Jhalod town (Dahod), there was tremendous sale of petrol and acid on 28 February.[83]

The systematic use of gas cylinders to blow up Muslim houses, shops and factories has prompted some police officers to speculate that a core group of rioters might have been given advanced training in the use of cylinders as a weapon. 'How did mobs in Ahmedabad, Vadodara, Himmatnagar, Halol and Mehsana think almost simultaneously along similar lines?,' the *Times of India* reported investigators as asking. 'The question has been dogging many independent police officials who are trying to establish a pattern behind the riots . . . Besides, say investigators, using an LPG cylinder for destruction is something that does not come so easily to everybody. This means that there is a possibility that some persons have been trained in the job beforehand. Not only were these cylinders used to set on fire several premises, they were also used to break open huge gates and doors to enable the mobs to make an entry into shops and godowns.'[84]

The VHP/Bajrang Dal also used chemicals and acid with great effect. In Pandarwada village, some 150 people were locked up in a house by a BJP supporter, Mahendra Vakil, on the pretext of shielding them from the mobs. He is then said to have opened the roof tiles and poured glass and acid in from the top. There were at least ten acid burn victims from Pandarwada in Godhra civil hospital.[85] Ansari Abdul Kader of Millatnagar (Ahmedabad) said that the mob 'had some white powder with them. It was so strong, it would make cracks in the walls and catch fire immediately once it was thrown in the air.'[86] In

Vadodara, the mob drilled holes into shop walls, poured in inflammable chemicals and then set them on fire.[87] In both rural and urban areas, it is common to see Hindu houses, shops and even handcarts standing safe right next to, or, in between, Muslim establishments which have been completely gutted.

There are also many reports of the attackers possessing guns and Muslims dying or being injured in private firing—e.g. in Sanjeli, Jhalod, Piplod, all in Dahod district; in Radhanpur (Patan), in Kadi town (Mehsana).[88] On 15 March, a VHP/ Bajrang Dal crowd which had collected on the terrace of RK Roadlines in Mama-ni-Pole fired twenty rounds at the mosque and general direction of Machchipeeth in Vadodara. When the PUCL team visited, they could still see bullet marks on the mosque.[89]

In Sukhsar (Dahod), eyewitnesses to the attacks told a women's team from Bombay: 'The mob seemed to have a very clear division of labour. There were around 40 people who were continuously firing. When a gun would run out of ammunition, it would be passed to someone in a waiting truck whose job was only to reload used weapons and hand newly loaded weapons to people who were firing. People had both machine manufactured revolvers and "katta" (country) rifles. Another group in the mob was mainly involved in looting and setting structures on fire. They had pouches of chemicals which they would throw to start the fires. One jeep contained all the material for setting fires. Evidence of these chemicals could be seen in burnt buildings more than a month later, as white powdery residue in pools of black oily liquid on the cement and stone floors. People were seen in the mobs carrying mobile telephones and co-ordinating their activities.'[90]

The Sangh Parivar-led mobs did their homework well. In Himmatnagar (Sabarkantha), they managed to burn the fireproof showroom of Harsoliya Motors which was owned by Bohras who had been in the town for nine generations.[91] In Saifee Society, Ahmedabad, 65 solidly built bungalows were destroyed using acid and explosive chemicals. A black timer device was attached to the mains and some solvent poured into it, enabling a short circuit in seconds.[92]

Burning was the primary motif in the attacks. Perhaps this was seen as an 'appropriate' reaction to the burning of the passengers in the Sabarmati. Yet the fact remains that it is also the best way of destroying evidence. In many cases, people left without even the bodies of their relatives are unable to claim compensation. The government, for instance, refuses to recognize that more than eight people were burnt at Limbadiya Chowkdi, since the remaining fifty-nine were charred to ashes in a fire that raged over two hours.[93]

Anyone who was out on the highway was particularly vulnerable. A group of British Muslims, on their way back to Ahmedabad from a tourist trip to Jaipur, were accosted by a mob of 40-100 people at Prantij. The mob demanded to know if they were Hindu or Muslim, pulled them out and chased them. Two men are dead and two are missing.[94] Many Ghanchis are in the trucking business and were easily targetted. Five truck drivers were burnt alive and twenty trucks set alight by a mob at Madhopur Kampa in Sabarkantha district. All that remained of each man fitted into a small cardboard carton. These were later handed over to the Truck Drivers' Co-operative at Modasa.[95]

Horror on the highway: a truck driver's account
Farukh Umarbhai, of Kalol, occupation driver. Case Nn. 3875 at Kalol civil hospital for burns, 28 February 2002.

Farukh has eight children and earns Rs 1,500 p.m. He spoke to us at Godhra relief camp and showed us his right hand which was fully burnt and loosely swathed in a bandage. He was sweating and trembling as he recounted the whole episode: 'I left Indore for Godhra on the 27th. At 7.00-8.00 p.m. I was stopped by a group of 50 on the highway, but I went on. They had put boulders on the roads. At Limkheda I was stoned by a crowd, who repeatedly asked me: Are you Muslim? The mob got me down from the truck and poured petrol over me. I somehow managed to climb back on the truck and reversed. The man who was holding my hair had to let me go, but he threw a lit match at me. The conductor had run away. I somehow managed to drive the tempo 10 km and stopped at

Piplod. I went to the police for help but they refused. I asked them at least to accompany me to Baria civil hospital but they said it wasn't their work. I went to a Muslim family I knew in Piplod and then my brother, who is a conductor, came from Kalol to get me and took me to Kalol civil hospital.

Interviewed on 5 April 2002 by PUDR.

Identifying victims: pre-drawn lists

One of the characteristics of a modern state is its vastly increased reach in terms of surveillance, enumeration and categorization of the population. In the Gujarat case, this modern technology of governance was put to painfully medieval uses. The mobs had detailed computerized lists of Muslim houses and shops which they used to precise, devastating effect. Except for a few instances, even neighbouring Hindu establishments were not damaged. Muslim shops with Hindu names (including, for example, many vegetarian hotels) were targetted, as were businesses which had Muslim sleeping partners.

The police, in fact, strongly suspect that voters' lists were used and that the violence was planned well in advance:

'The manner in which targets were selected indicates that the mobs had perfect information about who was living where and owned what,' said officials of an investigating agency in Ahmedabad. A preliminary report with investigating agencies states that those who lead the mobs were armed with voters lists too. 'This has happened. The people who were at the forefront of the mobs were grassroot level workers of parties. They knew the wards and areas well and who lived where. There is no doubt about the fact that they sat with the lists on the night of February 27 and prepared for what to do the next morning,' an official said.

A senior city police officer said, 'Even they did a survey of Duffnala area in the posh Shahibaug area where most of the senior government officers stay in their official bungalows. It seems now that Godhra was only an issue, this master plan was prepared months back and they were just waiting for a chance . . . It seems, as we go deeper into investigation, everything was pre-planned.'[96]

It is clearly impossible for such lists to be generated overnight, contrary to the claims made by VHP Gujarat chairman K.K. Shastri.[97] Government sources told *Outlook* that months before the massacre, VHP volunteers had made concerted attempts to get lists of Muslim business establishments from the Ahmedabad Municipal Corporation, as well as of Muslim students from professional institutions and universities.[98] Both AIPRF and PUCL were separately told—in Anand, Kheda, Godhra and Vadodara—of household surveys done by a group of women about a month and a half prior to the Godhra incident. In some cases, they were identified as VHP women, whereas others said the women claimed to be from Gandhinagar.[99] Recently revised voters' lists and TV cable operators subscription lists also provided handy lists of Muslim houses and businesses.[100]

The targetting was so precise as to be even mindless. In Himmatnagar, the mob insisted on following their list, despite the pleas of local shopowners that it was outdated. Raj Auto Traders on Dahod road, owned by a Hindu from Godhra, was set on fire since their list mentioned a Muslim owner. A soft drink factory that had recently been sold by a Muslim to a Hindu Kachi Patel was also burnt.[101]

In rural areas, the planning seems to have been as meticulous. Eyewitnesses in Panchmahals and Dahod told Dalwai and Mhatre that the attackers had maps of the village with plot numbers and lists of Muslim families.[102] Of course, local VHP/ BJP supporters also helped to identify Muslim houses—in Anjanwa village, despite the sarpanch's claim that all the attackers were outsiders, there is no way they could have identified the Muslim houses without local guides. The houses are all spread out, each upon its own farmstead.[103]

In many places, from 27 February onwards and sometimes even before, Hindu houses began to put up photos of Ram and Hanuman, or saffron flags to protect themselves from the mobs. In Jhalod town (Dahod) all the Hindu houses were marked with saffron flags as early as 22 February, a day before Eid. The Muslims were surprised as there was no special occasion or tension. This was followed by a rally in the evening and meetings in several places.[104] According to Salma of Vadsar Road (Vadodara), two days before the Godhra incident, Bajrang Dal members had stuck photos of Hanuman on all the Hindu houses. Ever since 21 February, when a large Bajrang Dal meeting had been held in the locality, there had been strong rumours that 'something was going to happen.'[105]

Even before Godhra, a warning . . .

According to the refugees, they were aware that the Bajrang Dal had been regularly holding meetings in Sokhada, but they did not view these as communal at the time. They also reported that they had heard that sadhus from the Swaminarayan Mandir had been giving slogans to awaken Hindus . . . we have to build the Ram temple, how long can we tolerate these Muslims etc. Fifteen days before the incident on 28 February and 1 March (when 100-odd houses belonging to Muslims were looted and burned and the village mosque attacked), one Hashubhai Patel, alias Tikka, had said that the Hindus would break the mosque.

Source: PUCL Vadodara and Vadodara Shanti Abhiyan, *Violence in Vadodara: A Report*, Vadodara, May 2002, pp 104-5.

The surveillance and surveying of Muslims continued even after the first wave of attacks, but this time primarily as a scare tactic. The *Hindustan Times* reported in early April that well-known schools in Ahmedabad were being surveyed to identify Muslim children, in order to scare them off from coming to school. According to one police officer: 'School staff, bus drivers and autorickshaw drivers who ferry the children to school have been asked to assist in leaking information about Muslim students . . . By conducting the survey, these religious maniacs are trying to force Muslim families to get their wards to leave these schools for good. A kind of cleansing of the education system, without spilling any blood.' Hindutva activists were also collecting information on what remained of Muslim businesses.[106]

Hate mobilization

It is important not to forget that the massacre took place against the background of large-scale mobilization for the *shila pujan* at Ayodhya on 15 March. Some Muslims in Panchmahals reported that the atmosphere in their villages had been vitiated since 1991 with L.K. Advani's Rath Yatra. The number of VHP and Bajrang Dal meetings had increased in the past two years, and then again intensified in the six months prior to the shila pujan at Ayodhya.[107] In Pandarwada, for example, a meeting was held at 'Ayodhya' chowk (a common area taken over exclusively and renamed by local Sangh Parivar activists after the demolition of the Babri Masjid in December 1992) barely a fortnight before the massacres, in which VHP leaders talked of the need to fight Muslims. Trishuls were distributed at that meeting.[108] In Tarsali (Vadodara), relations between Hindus and Muslims which had hitherto been cordial, started deteriorating about three months earlier, when the Bajrang Dal started holding meetings. VHP leader Pravin Togadia had addressed a meeting at the end of January 2002 in which he asked Hindus to boycott Muslims both economically and socially. The local cable operator also broadcast this.[109] Bajrang Dal training of cadres in the use of arms had also proceeded apace over the past decade. Succesfully trained cadres got certificates with *patta,* trishul and *danda,* in return for which they paid a sum of Rs 51.[110]

As the carnage continued, nasty communal leaflets—as usual unsigned and unattributed—appeared, SMS messages on cell phones were sent warning Hindus against impending retaliatory attacks by Muslims. One such pamphlet which appeared shortly before Holi called upon the army and police to remember their Hindu roots and threatened to reduce Muslim majority Jamalpur and Dariapur to ashes on Holi.[111] Others called for an economic boycott of Muslims.[112] Whatever the success of these leaflets, the VHP-propagated economic embargo of Muslims is well in place. Salma Aapa of Syedwadi, who had taken refuge in Vatwa Relief camp told *Communalism Combat*: 'Today when we went to the other side of the "border" to buy vegetables, vendors were threatened: "Do not sell vegetables to Muslim women, nor milk for Muslim children."'[113]

Those who did not take part in the violence were punished or humiliated. In areas where violence had not happened, VHP and BJP activists sent around boxes of bangles to the local leaders—sarpanchs, corporators—signifying 'womanly cowardice'.[114] In some places like Dabhoi Road and Fatehgunj in Vadodara, these people 'succumbed,' leading to violence in the second round after 15 March.[115] In Aswamegh society, Tandalja, however, where peace committees had been at work, Hindu residents who received bangles said that they wanted peace and their understanding of Hinduism was different.[116]

Police collusion

It is axiomatic that the mass violence the Sangh Parivar unleased on the Muslims of Gujarat could not have happened without the indulgence and even active active support of the police. And though the communalized sentiments of the ordinary policeman may have been a factor, it is equally true that policemen would not have dared to facilitate the violence through their acts of omission and commission without the knowledge that their senior officers and political masters wanted them to do so.

Even to those inured to the ways of the Indian police the role of the men in khaki is perhaps one of the most shocking aspects of the Gujarat carnage. Having placed the Muslims under curfew, they gave free run of the roads to VHP and Bajrang Dal mobs.[117] In rural areas like Fatehpura, Sanjeli and other places in Dahod/Panchmahals, mob attacks were preceded by police patrols which told Muslims to stay indoors.[118] There are several instances when the police, far from protecting the Muslims under attack, actually fired at them, providing cover to the mobs. In Naroda Patiya, several survivors related how they were caught between the police, who threatened to open fire on them, and a murderous mob. In Behrampur, Dani Limda and Gomtipur, witnesses told Sahrwaru and Human Rights Watch that the police fired upon them. Describing a consistent pattern, Mohammad Salim from Bara Sache ki Chali, near Chartoda Kabaristan, said: 'The Hindus called us outside to fight. When we came out, the police fired on us, twelve or thirteen people died . . . The police were with them and picked out the Muslim homes and set them on fire . . . None of the deaths from our area were from the Bajrang Dal, it was all from police firing.'[119] In Vadodara, PUCL has documented innumerable instances of police brutality against Muslims, especially during combing operations, which seem to have been little more than an excuse to terrorize Muslims. At Ajwa road and Wadi-Taiwada (both in Vadodara) in April, the police fired at Muslims without any provocation, killing three men.[120] While 'combing' Muslim areas, a seventy-year old man on a drip was forcibly removed from it, beaten up, and taken into custody, pregnant women, very small children and handicapped people were all badly beaten and abused with the worst kind of sexual and other insults.[121]

The evidence that the police had been ordered not to act, and that they willingly forsook their constitutional responsibility surfaces repeatedly in survivors' testimonies. Fifteen-year old Asif Daud Karbhari of Naroda Patiya recalled the police telling them: 'We have been ordered not to do anything for 24 hours.'[122] In Sukhsar (Dahod), the police told Muslim residents asking for protection: 'We were given commands by the Gujarat government not to give any kind of protection to Muslims.'[123] In Tejgadh (Vadodara district), PSI Pandya controlled the mobs by firing at a crowd in Limdi market on the evening of 4 March in which 4-5 people were injured. By 5 March, however, he said that he had instructions not to fire.[124] In what senior police officers elsewhere in the country said was a shocking and unprecedented step, two state Ministers, Ashok Bhatt and I.K. Jadeja, sat in the police control room in Ahmedabad and Gandhinagar respectively for several hours directing operations on 28 February.[125] In some instances, the police directly took their orders from VHP/BJP leaders on the ground.[126]

Of course, large sections of the police needed no prompting

from the VHP/BJP to act communally. In several instances they are reported to have told the Muslims that they must pay for Godhra or go to Pakistan, or threatened to kill them.[127] In Fatehpura (Dahod), the police kept victims, including women who had been stripped (some of the women had also been raped), standing in the station for thirty-six hours without food and water.[128] Yet it is important to note that this same communalized force managed to maintain order in districts where the police chiefs and administration held firm. However, those officials who defied government orders and followed their own conscience, soon found themselves shunted out. (See Chapter 5, Teesta Setalvad, 'When Guardians Betray'.) Even after the violence was over, the police stonewalled investigations—refusing to register FIRs till the names of VHP and Bajrang Dal leaders were withdrawn, pre-empting the victims by registering their own bland FIRs, filing omnibus FIRs etc. According to the NHRC, 'almost 90 per cent of those arrested even in heinous offences like murder, arson etc., have managed to get bailed out almost as soon as they were arrested.'[129] There has been no attempt to recover looted goods or collect circumstantial evidence like the traces of chemical powder. The possibility of the victims ever getting justice is remote.

The army was eventually deployed only on 1 March—in what the *Times of India* described as a 'method behind the Centre's laxity'[130]—and even then, the state government did not give it the necessary logistical support.[131] An Army officer posted in Panchmahals told the PUDR fact-finding team that even after they reached the area, it was extremely difficult to get to the affected villages. What should have been a forty-five minute drive from Lunawada to Santrampur took the Army some six hours because of the tree trunks and other road blocks along the way. As soon as the Army managed to clear one road block and move on, someone would come and lay down the trees again.[132]

The Fire Brigade, especially in urban areas, was similarly prevented from reaching the sites to which it had been called. Fireman Jignesh Makwana of the Ahmedabad Fire Brigade said that on 28 February, despite receiving over 150 calls, his colleagues were able to attend to only a few: 'They (the mob) slept in front of the vehicles or formed a human chain to prevent us. After much delay and convincing, we were allowed to go ahead but after we chanted "Jai Shri Ram"'.[133] There are reports, however, of the Fire Brigade too acting in a partisan manner.[134]

The Victims

In the first few days of the violence, there was mass murder. While the official death toll by the end of June was about 1,000, in reality the toll was at least two times higher.[135] As families got separated, it took time to count the living and the dead. Some families had only one or two young survivors left, some none at all. Many of the bodies were reduced to ashes, with nothing left beyond a few brittle bones. Places like Naroda Patiya and Chamanpura in Ahmedabad, or Best Bakery (Vadodara) became household names overnight for the degree of violence and depravity of the Sangh Parivar-led mobs. Only much later, did people begin to hear about places like Limbadiya Chowkri, where sixty-seven people from Kidiyad village (Sabarkantha) were burnt alive in a tempo, Pandarwada (Panchmahals) where thirty-eight people were hacked to death while taking refuge in fields, Sardarpura (Mehsana) where twenty-nine people were burnt and Odh (Anand) in which twenty-nine people were burnt alive in one room.[136] And these were only a few of the many places where violence took place. Contrary to Narendra Modi's claim that out of 18,000 villages in Gujarat, hardly sixty to seventy villages had been affected,[137] a partial listing by just one fact-finding team, covering only six districts turned up seventy-two small towns and villages which had witnessed murder, burning and looting.[138] In all, some nineteen districts were affected by the violence, and curfew was imposed in twenty-six towns.[139]

Class, age and status no bar

The VHP/BJP-led mobs killed quite indiscriminately—the only

criterion was that you had to be Muslim. Old men and women who could not flee, small infants, handicapped youth were all equally fair game. Judges, sitting and retired, had to flee their homes. Ehsan Jafri, a respected former Member of Parliament, was brutally murdered along with dozens of other Muslims at the Gulberg housing society in Ahmedabad. The hundreds of desperate phone calls he made to the police and senior politicians were all to no avail.

Parents were made to watch their children being dismembered and children were left with memories of their mothers rolling in pain engulfed by fire. In some terribly warped re-enactment of a medieval battle scene, an old man in Tarsali (Vadodara) was shown his beheaded son's head on a tray before being killed himself.[140] Mariambi of Naroda Patiya, whose eighteen-year-old handicapped son, Moinuddin, was tied to his bed, made to drink kerosene and torched, wondered: 'What could they gain by killing a boy like that?'[141] Another physically challenged youth, Maqsud Mohammad Hanif Sheikh, was attacked and burnt alive when he could not run away in Diwada Colony near Santrampur (Panchmahals).[142] In Anjanwa (Panchmahals), eight women and children were hacked with swords and thrown into a well, and two old men, one over seventy-five and the other too sick to run, were caught and burnt alive in the fields. Even an otherwise hardened Army officer who arrived soon after the massacres said he had never seen anything so horrible as the bodies of these little children.[143]

Meet Prasad, the Muslim in Gujarat
Vinay Menon

Ahmedabad: What's in a name? The promise of life—and the foreboding of death. Lying swathed in bandages at Ahmedabad civil hospital, Prasad of Bhagalpur believes, in a grotesquely convoluted way, that he can now live by name alone.

Prasad is not his real name. He won't tell anyone what it is. But his younger brother is called Mohammed Akram. It was the name that ignited the flames that engulfed their family on 28 February. The skin on Prasad's face has turned flaky, at several places it is peeling off. It looks like black, chipped paint. The mob had bathed him in petrol before putting a match to him. He had been badly burnt by the time a passerby had taken him to a private hospital.

'*Bataa saale kya hai,* Hindu *ya mian,*' the thugs had demanded of Prasad's family on Ring Road. Hindu, Prasad had lied. They had wanted to make sure—'*utaaro sabke pant*'. But it hadn't come to that; one among the mob had got his hands on an identity card bearing Prasad's brother's name. '*Arrey mian hai, mian,*' he had exulted in murderous triumph. '*Jalaa dalo ek-ek ko.*' It had begun to rain iron rods, sticks and stones. Prasad had been dumped inside a Maruti, driven to the National Highway, and set on fire.

'He gave a Hindu name when he was shifted here,' said a doctor at the civil hospital. 'When we found out, he begged us to save his life.'

A middle-aged man has been visiting Prasad at the hospital. 'He too gives a Hindu name,' the doctor said. 'We have told him he can safely reveal his identity to us. But he insists he is Hindu. They both seem petrified.'

'Save me saheb, save me please. I am scared. Very scared,' pleads Prasad. 'They will kill me if they find out I survived. Don't tell anyone I am a Muslim, I beg of you.'

Prasad wants to remain a Hindu. He wants to go back home to his wife and children.

'Saheb, if you write about me, call me Prasad. That is my name. I want to live. That name will help me live.'

Source: Hindustan Times, 4 March 2002

In Naroda Patiya, where some of the worst massacres took place, burning was accompanied by mass rapes. No longer a topic of silence and shame, this time the violence against women was so widespread that many people, both men and women, spoke of it.[144] A woman who prepared female bodies for burial at a mass gravesite near Dariakhan Ghummat camp told Human Rights Watch: 'I washed the ladies' bodies before burial. Some bodies had heads missing, some had hands missing, some were like coal, you would touch them and they would crumble. Some women's bodies had been split down the middle. I washed seventeen bodies on 2 March, only one was completely intact. All had been burned, many had been split down the middle. On 3 March, fifteen more bodies came. Then I just threw water over them, I couldn't stand to. be around them anymore.' Another gravedigger at the same site said the dead included at least three pregnant women, one of them with foetus partially hanging out.[145] (See Chapter 6, 'Nothing New?': Women as Victims')

Quite apart from the deaths, several victims have been left with debilitating injuries. Naeem Sheikh of Naroda Patiya told Dalwai and Mhatre that as his wife began to run, 'they struck her with a sword and it almost severed her arm—only a little was left—her arm was dangling and had to be operated.'[146] There are many acid and burns victims still in hospitals months after being attacked. Mohammad Javed, a cleaner in Kadi village (Mehsana), whose hand was blown off by a bomb, Rafiqkhan, a factory worker from Shivshakti Nagar (Vadodara) whose skull was broken and had to have two major operations, Hamida Banu Sheikh, a kite maker in Wadi-Taiwada (Vadodara), whose hand was fractured in four places by police beating—are all economic as well as physical casualities of the violence. Many of them are the sole bread earners in their families and it will be a long time before they can work again, if ever.[147] Given that the vast majority of those affected are very poor people—daily wage workers, agricultural labourers, rickshaw pullers, handcart owners—the violence, curfew, loss of their tools (agricultural implements, handcarts) and economic boycott encouraged by the VHP has ensured that even those who survived physical attacks and displacement have now fallen through the economic cracks. Both Muslim and Hindu employees of Muslim establishments have suffered. Even food is hard to come by for many.[148] The paltry sums of money offered for death, injury or relief and rehabilitation do not even begin to skim the surface of economic loss.

Almost everyone has been left with deep mental traumas.[149] Even children as small as one and a half years old, have been affected. One such infant, who survived the massacres in

Randhikpur, refuses to let go of her grandmother. She frequently gets fever, screams loudly and is unable to function normally.[150] Children's schooling has been badly affected—both because of the displacement and trauma, and because many of the exam centres were in Hindu areas and parents were scared to send their children there.[151] On 15 April, mobs attacked Muslim students in two separate exam centres at Delhi Darwaza in Ahmedabad. Terrified students later relayed the story:

> I was giving my class VIII terminal examination on the ground floor but in another class at the far end of the corridor at the Jyot Kanya Vidyalaya. Suddenly we heard ominous shouts. I turned to the Sir who was the supervisor. 'What is the noise, Sir?' 'Looks like a fight. You better not go anywhere,' he said. (The girl was stammering with fright as she recounted the incident.) Suddenly the shouts grew louder. We just ran out of our class and the school. Six to seven of us ran towards the Kanichad mohalla where residents had blocked the entrance for fear of attacks from Hindus. We were banging on the blockade frantically. They would not open. We were screaming, in tears, 'We are Muslims, we are Muslims, please save . . . We are so frightened.'[151]

In Panchmahals and Dahod, there is scarcely a village left with any Muslim houses. The secretary of the Bajrang Dal in Ahmedabad boasted to Dalwai and Mhatre: 'Eight hundred villages from Panchmahals are cleared of Muslims.'[153] In other districts like Kheda or Anand, the situation is little better. Yasinbhai Mohammadbhai Vora, ex-president of the Kheda Municipal Corporation listed the villages which had been thoroughly 'cleansed' of any Muslim presence: Mogar, Sarsa, Chikodra, Bedwa, Samarkha, Odh in Anand district. Jinger, Timba and Khalsar in Kheda district; Chaklasi, Peej, Piplak and Dumral in Nadiad district.[154]

A women's team which visited Dahod noted the complete devastation of Muslim houses, shops and places of worship in villages: 'In every structure, be it a house or a shop: every door, window, window frame, grills, electric wiring, water pipes, taps, switch boards, electric meters, every movable property, even the roof is missing. Every place has been burnt completely. In places, even walls have been broken down. The places look as though they have been bombed. Even bore-wells have been damaged/blocked. Every single big tree, including all fruit bearing trees have been cut down.'[155] In Vadodara, even the goats owned by Muslims in Gotri had acid thrown on them.[156]

People's homes were looted before being destroyed, often by their neighbours and in some cases with the police looking on.[157] Muslims from Sukhsar (Dahod), where the total loss to property is estimated at around Rs 65 million, said that when they saw their stolen goods lying with the neighbours and complained to the police, the police scolded them instead.[158]

In some places, like Piplod (Dahod) and Malvan (Panchmahals), Hindu shopkeepers have usurped the space that Muslim businesses formerly occupied, and the latter are fighting hard to get them vacated.[159] Elsewhere, in Ahmedabad, the administration used the general destruction caused by the mobs to bulldoze 'encroachments' and take over the land. The residents of these areas, who had fled there from earlier riots— have now lost everything they had, including marks of identity like ration cards, and have no proof that they ever existed as citizens of Ahmedabad.[160] While the poor are always the first to suffer in communal violence, this was also the first time in recent history, when the State could not or did not even protect its own. A sitting High Court judge, police officers, war veterans[161]—were all equally targeted because they happened to be Muslim. Military intelligence told Justice M.H. Kadri he should not rely on the local police for his security.[162]

Even judges had to run for cover
Shyam Parekh

Ahmedabad: That the common Muslim in Ahmedabad was fully at the mercy of the rioting mobs is well known. But the dance of death did not spare even two top judges as the events described below reveal.

Justice M.H. Kadri is a sitting judge of the Gujarat High Court.

He lives in his official quarters near Law Garden in the heart of city, with his family which includes his 85-year-old bedridden mother. As riots broke out, he was tipped off that he could be attacked. The two security guards at his gate would be unable to stop the mob. So, calls for more armed guards were made to the director general of police as well as additional chief secretary (home) Ashok Narayan. What transpired is not known, but Justice Kadri was forced to move out.

Chief Justice of Gujarat, D. Dharmadhikari, offered that Justice Kadri move in with him but the latter preferred to move in with some relatives. After witnessing rioting first-hand around his relatives' home. Justice Kadri moved in with a brother judge for a day. All with his bedridden mother. Fortunately, his family was unharmed. Justice Kadri confirmed he had to leave his house but declined to talk further. Narayan told Times News Network: 'Justice Kadri is safe, I don't know why he had to shift.'

Another respected judge of the city, Justice Akbar N. Divecha, also had a torrid experience. Justice Divecha, who served the Gujarat High Court, retired in New Delhi as chairman of the MRTP Commission. After retirement, Justice Divecha made Ahmedabad his home. But last Thursday he became homeless. His house in the Kazima flats in Paldi was attacked and burnt down. He managed to escape just in time and avoided personal injury. On Monday he went back to survey his burnt down house, of course, with military escort. There is little left of what was his home. The incidents have shocked the judicial fraternity. Retired chief justice of Rajasthan High Court A.P. Ravani told Times News Network: 'It is an insult to the secular Constitution that a HC judge of a minority community was compelled to shift his official residence.'

Source: *Times of India*, 5 March 2002

Economicide

Apart from the loss of life, the Gujarat violence was unique for the manner in which Muslim homes and businesses—from the plushest showroom or film studio to the lowliest *laari*, or hand-cart—were systematically targetted. Prof Pankaj Chandra and colleagues at the Indian Institute of Management, Ahmedabad, have evolved a framework for assessing the economic damage to the Muslim community and the state as a whole involving direct loss, indirect loss and opportunity loss.[163] Research is still underway but a rough-and-ready estimate made at the end of March by Batuk Vora, freelance journalist and ex-MLA, puts the figure at several thousand crores of rupees:

- Rs 3,000 crore due to closed down shops, industries and commerce
- Rs 1,000 crore in Surat city alone due to heavy damage to two textile mills, many handloom weaving factories and other industries, according to Kashiram Rana, Union textile minister from Surat
- More than Rs 10 crore due to burning down of 60 Opel Astras parked inside the GM Motors unit at Halol
- More than Rs 2 crore at the Lucky Film Studio nearby
- Rs 4 crore due to burnt down Honda City and Accord fleet of cars at Landmark Honda showroom at Thaltej on Sarkhej-Gandhinagar highway.
- Rs 600 crore loss to the hotel industry at Ahmedabad city due to closure, according to Ratan Prakash Gupta, president of the city's Hotel-Restaurant Association. At least 20,000 workers said to survive on these hotels and restaurants have been rendered jobless; many are missing.
- Rs 500 crore due to burnt down restaurants and hotels at various towns and cities, according to a leading hotelier. That includes two A/C hotels at Bhavnagar and 120 restaurants at Ahmedabad, plus innumerable small cabins and restaurants on highways and small towns.
- According to a leading Gujarati daily, at least 20,000 two-wheelers and 4,000 cars were burnt down at various spots in the city; thousands more were burnt at Rajkot, Vadodara, Bhavnagar; scores of trucks were destroyed on Kalol-Godhra, Ahmedabad-Bhavnagar or Rajkot, Mehsana-Ahmedabad and Surat-Vadodara highways.
- Besides the five industrial units burnt down at Halol, three big industries were heavily damaged at Shapar-Veraval area

in Saurashtra, six plastic and other industrial units at Rajkot, several at Vadodara, Surat, Godhra and Bhavnagar inside GIDC estates.[164]

Vora's figures do not include losses due to arson and torching of thousands of houses and buildings. Other estimates of economic loss made in April put the figure at Rs 2,000 crore.[165] The Self-Employed Women's Association (SEWA) reported that 52,400 of its members had been affected by the violence. SEWA, in conjunction with Dr Jeemol Unni of the Gujarat Institute of Development Research, estimated that workers in the informal sector in Ahmedabad suffered a loss of income of Rs 179 crore during the 40-day period from 28 February to 8 April 2002.[166]

Desecration and destruction of masjids, dargahs, tombs

In both rural and urban areas, the first target of the mobs was invariably the local masjid or dargah, which, like everything else, was burnt, smashed and looted. Many of them have been desecrated, with 'Jai Shri Ram' written across the walls, saffron flags planted on top, and idols of Hanuman installed within. When Teesta Setalvad visited the Babanshah Mosque, Swami Narayan Chawl behind Naroda Fruit Market on 6 March she saw 'not just torn pages of the *Quran* strewn all over the floor; the vandals had even had time to defecate on it. The framed photograph of a Hindu idol was planted at the very spot where the imam stands to lead the namaz. There were tell-tale signs of a puja having been performed at the place.[167]

In Ahmedabad and Vadodara, several old, important and protected mosques were destroyed using cranes and bulldozers, sometimes within hours, like the fifteenth-sixteenth century stone mosque of Malik Asin at Ahmedabad. The historic sixteenth century mosque near the Jethabhai stepwell in Isanpur area in Ahmedabad was demolished using bulldozers and heavy cranes, officials from the Archaeological Survey of India were quoted as saying.[168] The Vadodara tomb of Faiyaz Khan, one of the most famous Hindustani classical vocal singers of all time, was attacked and wreathed in burning tyres.[169] *Communalism Combat* collected a list of some 230 mosques, dargahs and mazars across Gujarat which had been damaged in the first seventy-two hours. The destruction had clear state sanction—for instance, eyewitnesses reported that the demolition of the 400-year old mosque at Anjali Cinema took place in the presence of Gujarat state ministers Haren Pandya and Amit Shah.[170] Almost overnight, the spaces where these shrines once stood—such as the 300-year old grave of the first modern Urdu poet, Vali Gujarati and the 450-year old Pir Geban Shashid Baba Dargah in Vadodara were tarred over with newly-laid roads. Vali Gujarati's tomb was first replaced with a makeshift 'Godharia Hanuman temple' before being completely levelled and tarred over with the help of the authorities.[171] In June, when some NGOs sought to rebuild the tombs, the police prevented them from doing so.[172]

Not all Hindus feel comfortable with this violent redrawing of their cityscape. Shankar, a rickshaw driver told members of the women's panel, as they passed what used to be Vali Gujarati's tomb: 'I always swerve a bit to the side driving over the spot where the mazaar stood. It wouldn't feel right to go over it. I know other drivers do the same.'[173] In Vadodara, Hindu worshippers warded off mobs at the Khanka-e-Riyafat dargah in Dandia Bazaar on 15 March. The next day, however, the dargah was gone.[174]

No less tragic was the vandalism visited upon Muslim scholars, who saw their entire life's work of research go up in flames. Reference has already been made to the burning of Prof J.S. Bandukwala's residence. The house of Nasirmiyan Ganam, a seventy-year old epigraphist in Vadodara who discovered the site of an ancient temple and numerous idols from the ruins of Kayavarohan in central Gujarat, was also attacked and burnt. The mobs had come looking for him and his family but they had taken the precaution of moving to a safer location. His collection of coins was looted and hundreds of precious volumes were consigned to the flames.[175] Sanskrit scholar Mohammad Ilyas Usman Sibhai was also targetted, proving that even Muslims who study the Vedas are not safe from the Sangh Parivar. A lifetime's collection of Sanskrit texts was burnt.[176]

Treasure of Sanskrit scholar goes up in flames
Raja Bose

Ahmedabad: When the flames of violence engulfed Khanpur, 25 km from here, they also burnt down a scholar's hopes to spread his passion for Sanskrit among children in Lunawada in Panchmahals district. His only fault—he was a Muslim daring to read the Vedas, Puranas, Upanishads and the Bhagvad Gita.

For 56-year-old Mohammad Ilyas Usman Sibhai, hounded out of his house in Khanpur on 1 March along with his family, the heartbreaking news came when he heard of his life's collection of Sanskrit texts, many of them rare manuscripts, being burnt down in his house by a mob . . . 'My house being razed did not hurt me,' says Sibhai, a graduate in mathematics and a Sanskrit Acharya from the Vrihat Gujarat Sanskrit Parishad of Ahmedabad. 'But burning my life's collection has come as a big blow to me,' he adds. Sibhai, who now stays in a house in Lunawada town, teaches both mathematics and Sanskrit at the Seth M.L. Vidya Mandir in Khanpur. And, he was happy that his passion was bearing fruit—more and more students from both the communities were learning Sanskrit.

'But that was before all this mayhem happened. I was happy to see the interest among the children about Sanskrit literature,' he says, pointing out the irony. 'I have been working on my Ph.D on the philosophy of *Ekishwarvaad* or the theory that God-is-one,' he adds.

'I heard that my neighbours, most of whom are Hindus, tried their best to save my house. They say that the mob came from outside the village. But it broke my heart to see my life's collection reduced to ashes. I remember having bought the Vedas at Rs 1,000 a book way back in 1969. I had a collection of all major Indian poets, including Kalidas, and even had books on Vanaspati,' says Sibhai, who has been living in Khanpur for the last thirty-eight years. Sibhai read all the four Vedas and other texts like Manu Smriti, the Upanishad, the Puranas, Bhagvad Gita, the epics like Ramayana and Mahabharata and works of many other Sanskrit poets.

Source: *Times of India*, 11 May 2002

Postscript: Moved by Sibhai's plight, K.G. Vanzara, a government official, offered to donate a month's salary to help rebuild his library. Vanzara said: 'I am a lover of books and I have thousands of rare books in Sanskrit, Persian and Arabic in my personal library . . . I can feel the sorrow, helplessness and anguish of Mohammed Sibhai.' In such a situation as an ardent student of Sanskrit literature, Hindu scripture, Koran Majid and Islamic scripture, Vanzara said: 'I extend my heartfelt sympathy, love and solidarity with Mohammed Sibhai and offer my one month's income to Sibhai to rebuild his personal library . . .' ('TOI story moves Gujarat government official to act,' *Times of India*, 12 May 2002.)

Betrayal of trust

Perhaps one of the most painful aspects of the violence in Gujarat has been the way in which some Hindus betrayed their Muslim neighbours. Naeem Sheikh, who survived the massacre at Naroda Patiya, used to sell bread and biscuits from his bakery to people in Gangotri and Gopinath housing societies opposite. Someone from Gangotri told him and his family to hide in a dilapidated hosiery workshop:

> At about 4.30 or 5.30 p.m. the shutter was opened and we were asked to leave. There was a Maharashtrian policeman who told us to get out. So I took my family and walked out and found that we were surrounded from all sides. Three sides were blocked and there was only one opening near Gopinath, we rushed there. Then they threw petrol, kerosene and set the whole place on fire, they threw burning tyres from the top (terraces or upper floor). They struck me with a sword. They blocked the passage to prevent people from going out. They stood there firmly till people died. There was a blazing fire and everybody was thrown in it. At least 250-300 people were killed. I lost my mother, sister, brother-in-law, sister-in-law, two nephews (6 and 8 years old) . . . I have a daughter. She is with her mother.
>
> The attack on us was carried out by people from Gangotri and Gopinath, people known to us. They displayed pictures of the Godhra incident and told us they were now avenging those deaths. I could not believe that all those people who ate my bread and biscuits would be so brutal. They didn't even spare the owner of the two provision stores where they ran a regular account.[177]

The same feeling of shock and disbelief was echoed by Muslims in rural areas where, despite generations of face to face interactions, their attackers showed no humanity. In Por (Gandhinagar), 200 Muslims were packed into two tempos and six of them died of suffocation as they tried to flee from a mob of bloodthirsty Patels. These were the same Patels who had feasted in their houses on Eid, barely a week before. In Abbasana (Ahmedabad), there were only three Muslim houses, whose occupants had lived with their Hindu neighbours for years, attending each others' weddings, festivals, life cycle rituals. A Muslim woman from one of these families had even been elected to the panchayat. Yet on 2 April attackers from their own village killed five of them. More than anything else, it is this betrayal that the families find hard to accept.[178] Saira, a social worker with the Centre for Social Justice in Ahmedabad, who talked to the Women's Panel in Vadali camp said bitterly about her attackers:

> Of course I can recognize them. I saw them everyday. I grew up with them. Now with my work I know everybody here. What could I tell them—don't kill me, you've seen me everyday of my life?[179]

Defending each other

Yet even in this communalized atmosphere, where to be an ordinary person with an ordinary conscience is to invite trouble, there are many cases of people who helped the Sangh Parivar's Muslim victims escape, or provided temporary shelter. Many of the Hindus who protected Muslims were viciously targetted by the Hindutva gangs.

In rural areas, the old Kham alliance (Kshatriyas, Harijans, Adivasis and Muslims) forged by the Congress in the 1980s seems to have had some basis in or lasting effects on social relations. In Harniyav village (Ahmedabad rural), the five Muslim families were protected by their Thakore neighbours when the mob attacked on 2 March.[180] In Katwara (Dahod), Chamar families sheltered Muslims for a day and a half before they were rescued by the camp organizer from Dahod;[181] in Santej (Mehsana), the lone Muslim migrant family was brought to the camp by Rabaris;[182] in Hadmatiya (Sabarkantha), Darbars and dalits helped the Muslims hiding in the forest.[183] In Anjanwa (Panchmahals) and Sukhsar (Dahod) adivasi sarpanches of Congress persuasion tried to get the police to help, through the offices of the local Congress MLA or MP.[184] In several places (Baria-ki-Hatod, Jhamri, Khudra, Chunadi, Ghumali, Mandav, Joj, Bhikapura, Kundala—all in Panchmahals and Dahod), adivasis gave fleeing Muslims from other villages or their own village shelter.[185] Twelve-year old Ayub of village Limkheda (Dahod) recalled that when his family was attacked,

> a Kaka (Baria man) pointed us in the direction of the maize field that my brother and sister had run into. When night fell, Sikandar and Shiraz started crying from hunger and thirst. We saw a torchlight. Kaka and his wife had come to get us. They kept us and fed us for seven days. Kaka also went and spoke to local sarpanches and leaders. He located my mother who had escaped to Halol. That's how we came here.[186]

In some places, Hindus rescued Muslims directly from the mobs. Rabari villagers from Kohkra Kesarpur (Sabarkantha) rescued some fifty Muslims from Talod town who were surrounded by a mob, just as they lit a fire and started stripping the women.[187] In Tulsi Park Society in Ahmedabad, dalit families protected their Muslim neighbours from the VHP-led mobs for two days.[188] In Naroda Patiya, some Muslims escaped because Hindu friends came to rescue them.[189]

Among exemplary individuals, special mention must be made of Ramdas Pillai of Kisanwadi (Vadodara) who along with his wife Lakshmiben, brother Krishnamurty Swaminathan and friend Kanubhai, an autorickshaw driver, sheltered 500 Muslims in their houses and later took them to a camp. Ramdas even managed to keep off a mob from attacking the masjid on 28 February and saved one man just as he was about to be knifed. Ramdas has since been receiving death threats.[190] (See account of Kisanwadi in chapter 4).

James Michael Lyngdoh, the 'Italian'

If ordinary citizens in Gujarat who stood up to the violence were physically attacked or abused by the Sangh Parivar as 'cowards' and 'eunuchs', constitutional authorities who stood by their oaths of office also had to bear the brunt of crude taunts. Chief Election Commissioner J.M. Lyngdoh was one such victim.

When Narendra Modi dissolved the Gujarat assembly in July, he expected early elections. The BJP was confident of returning to power riding on a crest of blood. But the Election Commission of India (EC) under Lyngoh stood in the way. After receiving a negative report about the situation in Gujarat from a special ECI team, Lyngdoh and his fellow Election Commissioners, B.B. Tandon and T.S. Krishnamurty, toured the state on 9 and 10 August. After meeting officials, some of whom tried to obfuscate and conceal facts, and terrified Muslims who were unable to return to their homes to vote, the EC decided to postpone the elections to November-December. *(See pp 329-330 in this volume for extracts from the EC's report on Gujarat)*

The Vajpayee government mounted a legal challenge to the EC's powers in the Supreme Court but Modi vented his anger on the streets. At a rally at Bodeli near Vadodara on 22 August, he launched a personal attack on Lyngdoh. Referring to the CEC by his full name—James Michael Lyngdoh—no less than six times in order to emphasise his Christian religion, Modi said, 'Someone asked me, has Lyngdoh come from Italy? I said we would need to ask Rajiv Gandhi. Some asked, 'Is he a relation of Sonia Gandhi?', I said, perhaps they meet in church.' Modi claimed the CEC was biased against Gujarat. 'People are hired to kill and burn houses and a certain Mr James Michael Lyngdoh comes along and decides that the situation in the state is not good to hold elections.' (*Times of India, Indian Express*, 23 August 2002).

Lyngdoh is a Khasi from Meghalaya and the Khasis must have been surprised by Modi's peculiar geography which pushed them from India into Italy. But then for the RSS, the large majority outside the pale of 'Hindi, Hindu, Hindutva' have never been 'proper' Indians. (*n.s.*)

Source: *Indian Express*, 13 May 2002.

Some of those who gave Muslims shelter—like a Hindu family in Moti Bandibar (Dahod)—also had their houses burnt down.[191] Others live in fear to this day of being attacked by Hindutva gangs.[192] In Surat, Hindus who 'deceived' the mobs into believing there were no Muslims to attack in their locality subsequently needed police protection themselves as mob leaders vowed revenge for this 'deception'.[193] Perhaps many more would have helped Muslims had they not been so afraid of the mobs. In Anupam Nagar (Vadodara), Hindus who tried to help their Muslim neighbours were taunted by the mobs, 'Who are these people to you?', while the Hindu family which sheltered Prof Bandukwala's daughter and PUCL friends, were later 'interrogated' for being helpful to Muslims.[194]

While some people were willing to loot, they drew the line at gruesome killing. Hindu villagers from Sadgal who had come to loot trucks being burnt on the highway at Madhopur Kampa in Sabarkantha, helped two Muslims (a helper and a passenger on one of the trucks) escape from being burnt and dropped them to the camp at Modasa. They even helped the victims identify the attackers.[195]

There are also many instances of Muslims protecting Hindus in areas where they were in a majority. In Kasamala Kabrastan (Karelibaug, Vadodara), Muslim households fed a household of Hindu daily wagers who were unable to go out to work because of curfew and assured them they would be safe. They also gave food and shelter to a Hindu boy whose house had been burnt down.[196] In several places in Vadodara—Tandalja, Kasamala, Fatehganj, Suleimani Chaal—Hindus and Muslims jointly decided to keep the peace. While some of these efforts petered out as in Fatehganj, Muslim-dominated Tandalja, was successful throughout the long months of violence in keeping peace. This, despite severe provocation by papers like *Gujarat Mitra* and *Sandesh*, which persisted in falsely reporting disturbances in Tandalja and claiming that Muslims were gathering in this 'mini-Pakistan' to take revenge.[197]

A candle in the darkness
Manas Dasgupta

Ahmedabad: Those who wanted to 'teach a lesson' to Gujarat's Muslims in the aftermath of the Godhra carnage, will never understand people like Om Prakash Sharma or Radhaben. They and their families live in the relief camps with victims from the minority community. Among the 800-odd inmates of camp number forty-five in Ahmedabad's Saraspur locality are some 120 members of twenty-four Hindu families. They live under the same tattered piece of cloth passed off as a tent, eat the same food and share the same anxiety of an unknown future as the Muslim inmates.

The twenty-four Hindu families, twenty-one of them belonging to the 'Salat' Adivasi community, lived with their Muslim neighbours in the Ambica Mill-ni-Chali. When they were attacked on 1 March, they fought with the Muslims against the attackers throwing stones and a few even used bows and arrows. Radha's husband, Kallu Valia, a small trader, and several other Hindu residents were among the hundreds of Muslims arrested for rioting and later released on bail.

They were able to repulse the first attack but as the numbers grew on the other side, they were forced to flee to the camp where they have been for the last three and a half months. Some Muslim organizations that are repairing damaged houses in the Chali have not left out those of Hindus.

Source: *Hindu*, 23 June 2002.

Attacks on Hindus

While the systematic, genocidal attacks have been clearly directed against Muslims, many Hindus, especially in poor urban communities, have also suffered in the process. Some have been the victims of retaliatory attacks by Muslims, while others have had their homes burnt down by Hindutva mobs who failed to prevent the fire spreading. The numbers of Hindus displaced are much lower, approximately 10,000 compared to perhaps as many as 2 lakh Muslims—and almost all of them are in Ahmedabad.[198] In rural areas, a few Hindus have been killed in retaliatory attacks or self-defence by Muslims (e.g. in Godasar), but life goes on as normal for Hindus—if one can call it that after all one's Muslim neighbours have been forcibly evicted.

Many Hindus saved themselves by putting saffron flags, posters of Hindu gods and goddesses, swastiks, mango leaves, coconuts etc. outside their house.[199] A few like Miraben, a domestic worker who lived among Muslims in Naroda Patiya, who had taken her gods down to clean, had her one room, asbestos-roofed shack burnt down by the VHP-Bajrang Dal mob. But unlike her Muslim neighbours, she was able to return to the site a few days afterwards to see what remained.[200]

There were also a few retaliatory attacks by Muslims using acid, petrol and crude bombs on Hindu settlements like Mahajan-no-Vando within Muslim-dominated Jamalpur. Twenty-five people were injured in the attacks and five homes completely destroyed. These people too were poor wage labourers. In their case, however, Narendra Modi visited the colony on 6 March and police protection was posted outside.[201] TV footage taken in the first few days of violence also showed some incidents of mutual stone pelting between Hindu and Muslim residents of neighbouring colonies. On 21 March, Revadi Bazaar, a wholesale cloth market in Ahmedabad was set on fire by a crowd of Muslims in which some fifty shops were damaged.[202]

Though the number of Hindus killed in mob violence was way below the number of Muslims, the sense of personal tragedy and loss was no less for the families concerned. The father of Dharmesh and Trupa Solanki was dragged away by a mob in April; his mutilated body was found just as they were about to sit for their exams.[203] Vinod Solanki was hit by a police bullet in his left calf on 28 February as he was running from a mob which had attacked the Pooja-ni-chawli in Behrampura, Ahmedabad, where his family lived. Two months later, he was still in hospital and without a home to return to. 'My mother went there a couple of times. The entire *kholi* has been burnt down. All our belongings, including our *laari* (vending van) has been looted,' he told the *Indian Express*.[204]

Many Hindus are scared that Muslims will take 'revenge', a fear which is fuelled by VHP leaflets and rumours, false or twisted stories in papers like the *Sandesh*, and even announcements by police vans 'warning' people of impending attacks by Muslims (as in Abhilasha Char Rasta, Vadodara). As a result, many Hindu colonies have started night patrols and formed defense squads armed with hockey sticks, rods etc.[205] The process of ghettoization is proceeding fast.

Attacks on media and peace initiatives

For the first time in post-colonial India, ordinary citizens have been prevented from helping victims of communal violence or going on peace marches, thanks to continuing violence and an atmosphere of intimidation. In Ahmedabad, the few NGOs and activists who have been working in relief camps have been threatened, and Xavier's, which has been the hub of relief activity, has been repeatedly attacked. Meera Mehta, a social worker at the Shah Alam Relief camp said she routinely got abusive phone calls.[206]

In Mehmedabad, Vipin Shroff's attempt to hold a peace rally had to be abandoned after Sangh Parivar activists turned up at his doorstop, threatened to cut him to pieces and stoned his house for a good fifteen minutes, saying 'We don't want Hindu Muslim unity.'[207] A group of IIMA students who demonstrated peacefully outside the gates of their institution in early March and collected signatures from passers-by were attacked and forced to take their placards inside by VHP goons. A peace meeting at the Sabarmati ashram was disrupted on 7 April by BJP (and Congress) youth activists—and the police officer who saved Medha Patkar of the Narmada Bachao Andolan was immediately transferred. Several journalists were injured by the police in that incident. On 3 April, *Asian Age* reporter Sonal Kellog was beaten up by the police for recording the statements of Muslim women on police attrocities.[208] Elsewhere in the country too, as in Faizabad (UP) where a BJP-BSP alliance is in power, a 100-strong group of students and activists who wanted

to commemorate the unifying, patriotic ethos of the 1857 War
of Independence and protest against the Gujarat carnage was
arrested.[209]

Attacks on relief camps

'The camps make the Hindus feel insecure . . . it is necessary to
remove these camps as some of the outsiders living in these
camps have indulged in rioting.' — *Bharat Barot, Civil Supplies
Minister in a letter to Gordhan Zadaphia, Home Minister,
Gujarat*[210]

The Muslims who were attacked in Gujarat following the
Godhra carnage fled wherever they could—in rural areas taking
shelter in hills and forests, walking long distances, barefoot,
bleeding, sometimes over days before they reached safe havens
in Muslim-dominated villages or towns. In some places, Muslim
community leaders brought them to camps. Sharif Bhai, a
member of the management committee at the Shah Alam Relief
Camp in Ahmedabad, who rescued some of the survivors from
Naroda Patiya recalled: 'I cannot describe the condition of the
victims when we brought them. They were terrorized and
traumatized—many women did not have any clothes on their
body. We made ten rounds in these four buses, from 12 midnight
to 3.00 a.m., to shift 3,000 persons from Naroda to the Shah
Alam Dargah.'[211]

Collecting and burying dead bodies was left to camp
organizers and religious trusts. On 5 March when there was a
mass burial of ninety-six bodies from Gulberg society and
Naroda at Dudheshwar graveyeard, Narendra Modi was visiting
Madhavpura less than a kilometre away. No official or political
leader came to the funerals.[212] Nor did they think it necessary
to go visit the living in refugee camps, till several days after.

As for the injured, where the killers had failed, the authorities
almost succeeded in finishing them off too. In Vatwa relief camp,
people were lying on the ground, with just a sheet covering
their burnt bodies.[213] Attempts to get them to hospital were
foiled along the way. Hafiz Khan Bhatti, a transport contractor
who also runs an educational trust and ambulance, worked non-

stop to bring people to the hospital during the attacks. 'As a reward,' he is quoted as saying, 'the police took my ambulance into custody and seized it for three days. When I went to collect it, I was shocked to find that there were five to ten punctures in each tyre.'[214] In Shah Alam Dargah, at least four people who could not get to hospital in the first few days of the carnage, died for want of medical attention.[215]

Many of the camps had no roofs, no covering for the floor and no sanitation facilities. Chartoda Kabaristan in Gomtipur (Ahmedabad) is a graveyard, with refugees sleeping between the graves. The Sangh Parivar threat, 'Pakistan ya Kabristan' (to send Muslims to Pakistan or the graveyard) has quite literally come true.

Having refused to create the camps, the government has been doing its best to dismantle them, even at a time when Muslims feel insecure about returning to their earlier locations. In villages, people are being forced to go back home in administration brokered 'peace deals' whereby they withdraw the names of their attackers and are 'allowed' to return. The conditions for coming back include everything from converting to Hinduism to not taking part in Hindu festivals and not allowing Muslim children to watch Hindu wedding processions.[216] In many places, there can be no return. To cite just one example: a group of thirty people who went back to retrieve their belongings from Avdhut Society, Vadodara, under police protection, were accosted by an armed mob, who had been fed rumours that the Muslims were returning on a retaliatory mission. Four people died in the lynching. The police simply ran away.[217]

Barot's argument that the Muslim camps made his Hindu constituents feel insecure is even more ironic in the light of the attacks on camps by Sangh activists. In Ahmedabad, residents of Dariakhan Gummat camp in Barot's constituency were gripped with fear in late April when mobs tried to attack them, and the police teargas shells fell into the camp. Seventy-five-year old Fatimabibi Rehmjibhai, was midway through her lunch, died of shock when a teargas shell burst near her.[218] Sukhsar camp in Dahod was threatened every night for ten days in April, even though there was a police post just outside. Some goons would come and fire in the air. On 16 April, they actually fired into the camp, while the police did nothing.[219] As late as 2 May when the Sanjeli (Dahod) victims had shifted back to their village and were huddled in some burnt-out houses, a truck-load of people came and stood outside the house with the truck engine running. Two men in front played the dholak. Forum activists who witnessed this wrote: 'It was clear that there was no reason for this but to add to the fear of these already traumatized people.'[220]

Months after the Godhra incident, the VHP continues to call for a 'final settlement' to the 'communal problem', to circulate pamphlets, videos and colour photographs of the Godhra incident, to keep the press going with anti-Muslim rumours and threaten to turn all of India into Gujarat.[221]

Conclusion

The pattern which clearly emerges from a review of all that has happened in Gujarat following Godhra is one of State-sponsored genocidal violence against Muslim citizens. Simply put, Muslims were attacked and killed in Gujarat because the ruling BJP willed it. The promises of impunity which were made to the cadre of the VHP and Bajrang Dal, the instructions to the police to facilitate the attacks on Muslims, the careful, systematic targetting of Muslims who lived or had businesses outside Muslim-majority areas, the collection of weapons, fuel and transport, the use of voters' lists and other official data, the incendiary communal propaganda fuelled in part by the statements of senior politicians, the dire warnings to Hindus not to protect their Muslim friends and neighbours—all suggest the highest degree of official complicity in the violence. Further proof of the official attitude is provided by the abject conditions in which the Muslim victims of the violence still find themselves, the impunity with which the Sangh Parivar continues to press for an economic and social boycott of Muslims, and the State's refusal to provide adequate security, relief or rehabilitation assistance.

Communal violence has occurred many times before in independent India and the involvement of the State and ruling party is also not something new. But never before has the role of the State administration been so extensive—and open—and never before have its leaders been so brazen and remorseless in pursuing their victims. What has happened in Gujarat should not be taken lightly or dismissed as mere happenstance. Apart from confirming the Sangh Parivar's implacable, murderous, hostility towards India's minorities, the violence marks a new trend in the arrogance and abuse of political power. Unless concerned citizens act to put an end to this trend by ensuring the guilty are punished, there is no telling when and where— and against whom—the *danse macabre* of Gujarat will once again be re-enacted.

Notes

1   Communalism Combat, *Genocide Gujarat 2002*, March-April 2002, (henceforth *GG*), p 13.

2   SP Kheda to Peoples Union for Democratic Rights (PUDR) fact-finding team, PUDR pers.com.

3   'Violence erupts across Gujarat,' *Indian Express*, 28 February 2002.

4   Sujan Dutta, 'When Guardians of Gujarat gave 24-hour license for punitive action,' *Telegraph*, 10 March 2002, Peoples Union for Civil Liberties, Vadodara and Vadodara Shanti Abhiyan, *Violence in Vadodara: A Report*, Vadodara, June 2002, (henceforth *PUCL*), p 5.

5   Sujan Dutta, *op cit*.

6   *Ibid*.

7   See *Saffron on the Rampage: Gujarat's Muslims pay for Lashkar's Deeds*, Sabrang Communications, Mumbai, 2000.

8   Sujan Dutta, *op cit*.

9   *GG*, p 115.

10 Milind Ghatwai, 'First Gujarat verdict is not guilty, courtesy the

cops: Burning Muslim shops, all acquitted in just two sessions,' *Indian Express*, 14 July 2002.

11 PUDR, *Maaro! Kaapo! Baalo!: State, Society and Communalism in Gujarat,* New Delhi, May 2002 (henceforth *PUDR*), p 28.

12 *PUCL*, p 64.

13 Manu Joseph, 'A plot from the devil's lair,' *Outlook*, 3 June 2002.

14 Kingshuk Nag, 'Jafri may not have fired at all,' *Times of India* (Ahmedabad), 9 June 2002.

15 SAHRWARU (Women's Action and Resource Unit, Ahmedabad), *A Holocaust in Gujarat with Epicenter Ahmedabad*: *Crushing a Religious Minority*, Ahmedabad, May 2002 (henceforth *Sahrwaru*), p 6.

16 Shama Dalwai and Sandhya Mhatre, *Godhra and After: Report of Violence in Gujarat,* Mumbai, May 2002 (henceforth *D&M*), p 19.

17 Rashme Sehgal, 'Ahmedabad Cop-out'. Interview with P.C. Pande, *Times of India*, 15 March 2002.

18 *GG*, p. 13.

19 Sujan Dutta, *op cit*.

20 'Curfew in 26 towns as mobs go berserk,' *Hindustan Times*, 1 March 2002; 'An eye for an eye blinds Gandhinagar,' *Indian Express*, 1 March 2002.

21 Reproduced in *GG*, p 127. See also extract from the PUCL report on the role of the media in this volume.

22 *The Survivors Speak: How has the Gujarat massacre affected minority women?*, Fact-finding by a Women's Panel, New Delhi April 2002, (henceforth *Survivors Speak*), p 11.

23 *GG*, p 49.

24 *Survivors Speak*, p 11.

25 *PUCL*, p 146. Neeraj Jain was shot in the neck in mid-July. Since he was named in the PUCL report, he attributed this to the 'hit list' of PUCL. (PUCL Pers. com)

26 Narendra Modi, quoted in the *Indian Express*, Ahmedabad, 6 March 2002.

27 Reply to starred question no. 27 by Minister of State in the Ministry of Home Affairs, I.D. Swami, Lok Sabha, 16 July 2002.

28 *PUCL*, pp 5-7.

29   Pratyush Kanth, 'Builders, lumpens fuelling riots: IB,' *Times of India*, 11 May 2002.

30   'Minister accuses Muslims of keeping riots alive,' *Hindustan Times*, 6 May 2002.

31   Uday Mahurkar, 'End of Hope,' *India Today*, 15 April 2002: 37. The *India Today* article, for example, says that a young man who went to a Muslim-dominated area in Himmatnagar was found with his eyes gouged out. As the PUDR report (p. 19) on the same incident shows, the boy disappeared from the market after parking his scooter outside a Bohra shop. Several prominent Muslims have, in fact, called for a thorough enquiry into the incident. This has not happened, giving the VHP a chance to continue fuelling rumours about this.

32   See, for example, Syed Khalique Ahmed, 'A tale of two Bihar fathers, their missings sons in Gujarat,' *Indian Express*, 4 July 2002. Suhan Das was killed because he worked for a Muslim samosa-maker.

33   Praveen Swami, 'Saffron Terror,' *Frontline*, 16-29 March 2002.

34   Interview with Sujan Dutta, *Telegraph*, 10 March 2002.

35   Sharief Khan, interviewed by *GG* on 5 March, *GG*, p 42.

36   Rathin Das, 'Gujarat rioters did it by the book,' *Hindustan Times*, 26 March 2002.

37   See, for example, the main photograph in the *Hindu*, 1 March 2002.

38   *GG*, p 20.

39   See petition of Mohanbhai Bundela before Gujarat High Court, 6 May 2002.

40   *PUCL*, p 48.

41   See *PUDR* title, *Sahrwaru*, p 4.

42   Human Rights Watch, *'We Have No Orders to Save You': State Participation and Complicity in Communal Violence in Gujarat*, New York, April 2002 (Henceforth *HRW*), p 59; *GG*, p 35.

43   *PUCL*, p 74, 104.

44   Clearly, the mobs were carrying out Guru Golwalkar's teachings on the need for non-Hindus in India to glorify Hinduism or lose their citizenship rights.

45   *PUDR*, p 11.

46 *GG*, p 27; *PUDR*, p 11.

47 *PUCL*, p 88.

48 *D&M*, p 13.

49 *Ibid.*, p 12.

50 *PUCL*, p 48.

51 *D&M*, p 8.

52 Leena Misra, 'Police fighting shy of netting big fish,' *Times of India* (Ahmedabad), 15 May 2002.

53 *GG*, pp 33-34.

54 *PUDR*, p 33.

55 *Ibid.*

56 *Ibid.*; *GG*, p 34.

57 'Are VHP, BJP workers the culprits?' The *Times of India*, 4 March 2002; 'Bajrang Dal hand in Naroda killings: Cops,' *Indian Express*, 5 March 2002; 'Once again police blame victims,' *Indian Express*, 4 June 2002; see also the names of the accused in the accounts of Naroda Patiya and Gulberg society in chapter 4.

58 See, for example, list of accused in *PUCL*, pp 117-119, *PUDR*, pp 55-59.

59 Forum Against Oppression of Women and Aawaz e-Niswan, Mumbai, *Genocide in Rural Gujarat: The Experience of Dahod district*, Mumbai, May 2002, (henceforth *Forum*), p 6.

60 *D&M*, p 13.

61 *Forum*, p 6; see also *D&M*, p 20, for a similar categorization of mobs into three groups.

62 *PUDR*, p 9.

63 *Forum*, p 6, *PUCL*, p 111.

64 Vanraj Damor, Computer Engineer and Dahod District Convenor of Adivasi Youth Congress of Gujarat, to *D&M*, p 16.

65 *PUDR*, pp 32-33; see also *PUCL*, p 109.

66 Chandrakant Naidu, 'Tribals made cannon fodder in Gujarat's communal war,' *Hindustan Times*, 7 May 2002; *PUDR*, p 28; Jay Raina, 'With liquor and cash,' *Hindustan Times*, 4 May 2002.

67 *PUCL*, p 111.

68 *D&M*, p 13. The *PUDR* report also corroborates the story that the adivasis of Suliyath were paid to participate, *PUDR*, p 10.

69 *PUCL*, p 105.

70   *HRW*, p 23.

71   Sourav Mukherjee and Amit Mukherjee, 'The New Middle Class Mobster', *Times of India*, 3 March 2002.

72   *GG*, p 42.

73   Joydeep Ray, 'VHP 'hand' in Gujarat's murder weapons,' *Indian Express*, 10 April 2002.

74   *Ibid.*

75   *Ibid.*

76   'Over a thousand swords, knives seized on their way to Gujarat,' *Indian Express*, 17 April 2002.

77   'Bajrang Dal leader held with swords,' *Times of India*, 17 May 2002; 'Cops corner vehicle, 99 swords, Bajrang man tumble out,' *Indian Express*, 16 May 2002. The leaders were bailed out soon after.

78   See also Kamal Mitra Chenoy, S.P.Shukla, K.S. Subramanian and Achin Vanaik, *Gujarat Carnage 2002: A Report to the Nation*, New Delhi, March 2002, p 19.

79   *GG*, p 20, 24.

80   *GG*, p 27.

81   *PUCL*, p 98; there is also evidence of cylinders used to destroy the masjid in Kisanwadi, *PUCL*, p 81.

82   *PUDR*, p 20.

83   *Forum*, p 20.

84   'LPG blasts baffle riot investigators,' *Times of India* (Ahmedabad), 18 July 2002.

85   *PUDR*, p 20; see also *GG*, p 46.

86   *Sahrwaru*, p 12.

87   *PUCL*, p 6.

88   *Forum*, p 21, 27, 36; *GG*, p 60; *PUDR*, p 21; see also *PUDR*, p 18, 21 for firing which forced fleeing tempos from Kidiyad to stop. 67 people were killed.

89   *PUCL*, p 48.

90   *Forum*, p 36.

91   *PUDR*, p 18.

92   *GG*, p 36.

93   *PUDR*, p 19, 30.

94   *GG*, p 65.

95 *PUDR*, p 30.

96 'Mobs used voters' lists to target victims,' *Indian Express*, 8 March, 2002.

97 'Riots in Ahmedabad . . . it had to be done,' www.rediff.com, 13 March, 2002.

98 Ranjit Bhushan. 'Thy Hand, Great Anarch,' *Outlook,* 18 March 2002.

99 All India Fact Finding Report on Genocide in Gujarat, Preliminary Report (henceforth *AIPRF*), p 4; *PUCL*, p 50.

100 *AIPRF*, p 4.

101 *PUDR*, pp 18-19.

102 *D&M*, p 18.

103 PUDR pers.com.

104 *Forum*, p 20.

105 *PUCL*, p 50.

106 Vinay Menon, 'Muslim schoolkids targeted in Gujarat', *Hindustan Times*, 6 April 2002.

107 *PUCL*, p 104, *PUDR*, p 8.

108 *PUDR*, p 27.

109 *PUCL*, p 62.

110 *D&M*: 19

111 Rathin Das, 'Leaflet threatens Holi bloodbath', *Hindustan Times*, 28 March, 2002.

112 Rajeev Khanna, 'Hate tracts being distributed in Gujarat towns', *Asian Age*, 26 April 2002. See also *GG*, pp 132-138 for a collection of these leaflets.

113 *GG*, p 35.

114 *PUCL*, p 7, 100; *PUDR*, p 15; Vinay Menon, 'Hindu activists taunted for 'less' violence', *Hindustan Times*, 8 April 2002.

115 *PUCL*, p 7.

116 *PUCL*, p 68.

117 Vinay Menon, 'Curfew ties victims, frees killers,' *Hindustan Times*, 2 March 2002.

118 *Forum*, pp 7-8.

119 *HRW*, p 26.

120 *PUCL*, p 35, 84.

121 *PUCL*, p 38, 41, 45, 51, 84, 86, 134. See also *Survivors Speak*, p 21.

122 *Sahrwaru*, p 5.

123 *Forum*, p 35.

124 FIR filed by Khatri Abdulkader Nishar Ahamd and others of Tejgadh, reproduced in *GG*, p 65.

125 Darshan Desai and Joydeep Ray, 'Dial M for Modi, Murder?,' *Indian Express*, 24 March 2002.

126 See *PUCL*, p 48, on Ajay Dave and Milind Ambegaonkar directing the police to fire on Machchipeeth.

127 *Forum*, p 27, *Sahrwaru*, p 6, *PUCL*, p 38, 41, 45, 51, 84, 86, 134

128 *Forum*, p 7.

129 NHRC Final Report on Gujarat, 31 May 2002, p 11.

130 Manoj Joshi and Siddharth Varadarajan, 'Method behind Centre's laxity?,' *Times of India*, 2 March 2002.

131 Rajat Pandit, 'Centre delayed deployment of paramilitary forces,' *Times of India*, 3 March 2002; Rahul Bedi, 'Soldiers "held back to allow Hindu revenge",' *The Telegraph*, 4 April 2002.

132 PUDR interview, 8 March 2002, pers. com.

133 Meghdoot Sharon, 'Firemen battle mobs to fight flames in city,' *Indian Express*, 1 March 2002.

134 *PUCL*, p 64.

135 See for example, *PUDR*, annexure 3 (pp 59-61) which highlights the discrepancies in the official record and the actual numbers killed. 280 people were killed in just 16 incidents in 6 districts. This does not even include any of the major Ahmedabad incidents.

136 *PUDR*, pp 7-9, 16-17, 23-24, *PUCL*, pp 114-115.

137 Interview with Narendra Modi by Anosh Malekar, *The Week*, 12 May, 2002.

138 *PUDR*, 7-27, 50-55. The PUCL report lists some 62 sites of violence in Vadodara district alone.

139 *PUDR*, p 1, 'Curfew in 26 towns as mobs go berserk,' *Hindustan Times*, 1 March 2002.

140 *PUCL*, p 9.

141 *GG*, p 22.

142 *PUDR*, p 53, *Forum*, p 42.

143 PUDR, p 10; PUDR interview, Panchmahals, 8 April 2002. PUDR pers. com.

144 See the excerpts from *Survivors Speak* in this volume, Chapter 6.

145 *HRW*, p 28.

146 *D&M*, p 3.

147 *PUDR*, p 44, *PUCL* p 34, 55.

148 See for example, *PUCL*, p 32, 78, *PUDR*, pp 45-46; see also Hitarth Pandya, 'Muslims forced to give up jobs in Gujarat,' *Asian Age*, 25 April 2002.

149 *Carnage in Gujarat: A Public Health Crisis*, Report of the investigation by Medico Friends Circle, New Delhi, May 2002, pp 18-21.

150 *D&M*, p 12.

151 PUDR interview, Godhra relief camp, PUDR pers. com.

152 *GG*, p 92.

153 *D&M*, p 18.

154 Yasinbhai Mohammadbhai Vora interviewed by *GG* on 9 March in Kheda Town, *GG*, p 59.

155 *Forum*, pp 5-7.

156 *PUCL*, p 6.

157 *HRW*, p 33. Sahmat, *Ethnic Cleaning in Ahmedabad*, New Delhi March 2002, pp 7-8; also *PUCL*, p 51, 72.

158 *Forum*, p 38.

159 *Ibid.*, p 28, 43.

160 Anjali Mody, 'Genocide in the land of Gandhi,' *Hindu*, 10 March 2002.

161 For example, the Vadodara home of Lt Col (Retd.) H.U. Shaikh was stoned, and he and his family were forced to flee. See Robin David, 'I risked my life for this country,' *Times of India*, 8 March 2002.

162 Shyam Parekh, 'Even Judges had to run for cover,' *Times of India*, 5 March 2002. See also the submission of Justice A.P. Ravani to the National Human Rights Commission, 20 March 2002. http://www.sabrang.com/gujarat/nhrc/nh3.htm

163 Pankaj Chandra *et al*, A framework for assessing economic damage due to communal problem in Gujarat,' pers. com.

164 Batuk Vora, 'Collateral damage: crores,' *Times of India*, 31 March 2002.

165 Raju Bist, 'Body blow to Gujarat business,' *Asia Times*, 23 April 2002.

166 Self-employed Women's Association, *Shantipath: Our Road to Restoring Peace*, Ahmedabad, May 2002, pp 13, 26.

167 *GG*, p 33.

168 'Mob used bulldozer to raze heritage mosque,' *Indian Express*, 13 March 2002.

169 Sukumar Muralidharan, 'Cultural Vandalism,' *Frontline*, 11-24 May, 2002.

170 *GG*, p 94.

171 Sourav Mukherjee, 'Nobody knows who built roads over dargahs,' *Times of India*, 11 March 2002; *PUCL*, p 5.

172 'Vali's tomb repair plan scuttled,' *Times of India* (Ahmedabad), 23 June 2002.

173 *Survivors Speak*, p iv

174 *PUCL: 5*

175 Syed Khalique Ahmed, 'He devoted life to ruins, mob turned his house to one,' *Indian Express*, 14 March 2002.

176 Raja Bose, 'Treasure of Sanskrit scholar goes up in flames,' *Times of India*, 11 May 2002.

177 Interviewed at Shah Alam Relief Camp, *D&M*, p 4.

178 *PUDR*, p 30.

179 *Survivors Speak*, p 26.

180 *PUDR*, p 50.

181 *Ibid.*, p 51.

182 *Ibid.*, p 53.

183 *Ibid.*, p 54.

184 *Ibid.*, p 9, *Forum*, p 36.

185 *PUDR*, p 14, *D &M*, pp 12-14.

186 *Survivors Speak*, pp 36-37.

187 *PUDR*, p 20.

188 Stavan Desai, 'For 48 hours, they shielded Muslim friends,' *Indian Express*, 8 March 2002.

189 Radha Sharma, 'A Hindu brother rescues Muslim sister,' *Times of India* (Ahmedabad), 9 May 2002; Tushar Prabhune, 'Brave

lawyer fears for life,' *Asian Age*, 20 April 2002.

190 *PUCL*, pp 80-82.

191 *Forum*, p 26.

192 Veersinh Rathod saved 25 Muslim families in the Naroda area of Ahmedabad. Apart from 'Hindutva fanatics', he said the police are also now harassing him. See Tushar Prabhune, 'Brave lawyer fears for life,' *Asian Age*, 20 April 2002.

193 Shashank Mhasawade, 'Sanity triumphs over madness,' *Hindustan Times*, 5 March 2002.

194 *PUCL*, p 59, 98.

195 *PUDR*, p 19.

196 *PUCL*, p 77.

197 *PUCL*, pp 65-70, 77, 85, 91.

198 Sanjay Pandey, 'Riots hit all classes, people of all faith,' *Times of India*, 18 March 2002.

199 Amit Mukherjee, 'Shops in Gujarat wear religion on their sleeve,' *Times of India*, 18 March 2002.

200 Chandrima Bhattacharya, 'Lonely search for way back to life,' *Telegraph*, 6 March 2002.

201 *HRW*, pp 36-38.

202 HRW, pp 36-37.

203 Shefali Nautiyal, 'Father killed, they appear for exams to live his dream,' *Indian Express* (Ahmedabad), 21 April 2002.

204 Shefali Nautiyal, 'He lost home to hate, neglect almost claimed his leg,' *Indian Express*, 14 May 2002.

205 *PUCL*, pp 148-149.

206 Namita Bhandare, 'Hate mobs deny peace a chance in Gujarat,' *Hindustan Times*, 7 April 2002.

207 *Ibid*.

208 *HRW*, p 34.

209 Uma Chakravarti and Anand Chakravarti, 'Crackdown in Faizabad: Are we governed by the constitution?,' *Economic and Political Weekly*, No. 23, June 2002, pp 2202-2203.

210 Basant Rawat, 'Minister finishes mob mission,' *Telegraph*, 21 March 2002. See also Meghdoot Sharon, 'The latest: 'Riot victims are security risk,' *Indian Express*, 22 March 2002.

211 *GG*, p 24.

212 Joydeep Ray, 'Mass burials sans relatives for Naroda, Gulberg victims,' *Indian Express*, 6 March 2002.

213 Anjali Mody, 'Riot victims deprived of relief, medicare,' *Hindu*, 4 March 2002.

214 *GG*, p 35.

215 Vinay Menon, 'How safe are the safe houses?,' *Hindustan Times*, 3 March 2002.

216 *Forum*, pp 10-11; Vipul Mudgal, 'Forgive and Forget Deal in Gujarat,' *Hindustan Times*, 15 April 2002; Rajiv Shah, 'Refugees: We were asked to withdraw FIRs and go home,' *Times of India*, 29 April 2002; Milind Ghatwai, 'A stamp paper of hate: Muslims asked to sign on the twisted line,' *Indian Express*, 11 May 2002.

217 *PUCL*, p 57; 'Trip back home to retrieve belongings costs riot hit dear,' *Indian Express*, 18 March 2002. See also Maria Abraham, 'Gujarat Muslims not homeward bound,' *Hindustan Times*, 14 May 2002; Sachin Sharma and Robin David, 'Villagers resisting return of minorities,' *Times of India*, 23 April 2002.

218 Stavan Desai, 'Fear grips relief camps as police told to weed out 'criminals' from refugees,' *Indian Express*, 26 April 2002.

219 *Forum*, pp 38-39.

220 *Ibid.*, p 11.

221 Jay Raina, 'Sangh Parivar talks of final settlement,' *Hindustan Times*, 21 April 2002.

4

Narratives from the Killing Fields

Editor's Note: This chapter draws primarily on published reports produced by various citizens'groups that visited Gujarat in the wake of the violence which erupted throughout the state following Godhra. These accounts are meant to illustrate the nature of the violence—nineteen districts were affected in all— but are by no means exhaustive or even representative of the worst. Instead, by focusing on a handful of incidents—in which some six hundred people were killed—the intention is to make the horror of what happened real to readers. Even though survivors' testimonies have been recorded methodically for many of the incidents, it is nearly impossible to reconstruct a definitive account of what happened in each locality in the absence of proper criminal and forensic investigation by the police. In any event, no description of the violence can adequately capture the individual tragedy of the victims, or their sense of desperation and betrayal as the State looked the other way.

AHMEDABAD CITY

Naroda Patiya and Naroda Gaon

28 February—1 March 2002
Between 91 and 200 people killed; many women raped
The VHP's Gujarat bandh on 28 February 28 began with large-scale violence against Muslims in Naroda Patiya and Naroda Gaon, two localities on the outskirts of Ahmedabad city along

a deserted highway. Even though the quarters of the State Reserve Police (SRP) were just across the road, Naroda Patiya burned for the better part of a day and its Muslim residents were subjected to unspeakable brutality and destruction. Officially 91—but probably as many as two hundred or more people—were killed and burnt in Naroda Patiya that day.

The total population of the area is about 12-15,000. There are about a thousand Muslims, who are mostly poor daily wage earners, migrants from Karnataka and Maharashtra. A government-owned state transport (ST) warehouse is situated just opposite the settlement and served as an easy source of diesel and petrol with which to attack the Muslims.

A large mob came to Naroda Patiya on the morning of 28 February at around 9.00 a.m. Many of them were dressed in khaki shorts, saffron vests and black and saffron headbands— regulation RSS and Bajrang Dal gear—and armed with guns, spears, swords, acid and petrol bombs. The mob came from Krishnanagar, and from Gangotri and Gopinath housing societies nearby. The leaders of the mob came in three white Maruti cars (GJ 61418, GJ 1B1593 and GJ 1-3631) while the gas cylinders and inflammable fuel were brought in a tanker (GJ1T 7384). The mob got petrol and diesel from the ST warehouse, helped by a watchman on duty at the gate. (Four Muslim workers at the ST warehouse were, however, rescued by the management and sent back to their homes in Kheda.)

Several eyewitnesses have reported seeing Dr Jaideep Patel (second to Pravin Togadia in the VHP hierarchy) leading the mob. Patel had accompanied the corpses of the Sabarmati Express victims from Godhra to Ahmedabad the previous night. One of the victims of the Godhra arson was a resident of Naroda Patiya. According to survivors, other instigators included BJP corporators Ashok Saheb, Vallabh Patel, Padyuman Mistry, Ballabhbhai Patel of the Bajrang Dal, Harish Lakshmanbhai Koshti and Manoj Lakshmanbhai Koshti, Bharatbhai Rabati, Vijay Dada, all four Shiv Sena leaders, and Bipin Panchal, who owns Uday Gas Agency which supplied many of the gas cylinders. The police aided the mob by firing on the Muslims or standing aside.

They first attacked the Noorani Masjid, breaking its minarets and setting the prayer carpets and Qurans on fire. They then threw in a gas cylinder which exploded after a while, burning down the masjid completely. Dawood Bhai Ghadiyali, a volunteer at Dariakhan Ghummat Relief camp was personally involved in burying at least 192 bodies over sixteen days but says he saw many more come in. Interviewed on 20 March, he said: 'I still cannot sleep because of the condition of the bodies I saw. In many cases, the skull was just not there . . . The volunteers who did this work had to steel their hearts, wear gloves, sprinkle dettol, use *attar*.'

Nasir Khan Rahim Khan Pathan, principal of Sunflower School which catered to both Hindu and Muslim children, saw the attackers pour petrol into the mouth of six-year-old Imran. 'A lit matchstick was then thrown into his mouth and he just blasted apart.' He also saw the crowd burn some eighty others and throw them into a well, including seventy-year-old Tarkash bibi. Eleven-year-old Raja Bundubhai, who saw his mother and sister stabbed and then burnt alive, fell down in shock. When he got up, a man hit him on the chest and stomach. There was a brief argument between the attackers—some of them wanted to kill him, but one old man told him to run away. He managed to crawl into a small shed and watched more people being killed.[1]

Many survivors, who escaped by hiding in toilets, in small sheds, or on a terrace, described young girls and women being raped in front of them. Nasir Khan described how Khairunnisa was gang-raped by eleven men, who then proceeded to burn her and each member of her family alive in turns. Her mother's head was cut off. 'The police was with them', a thirteen-year-old boy told Human Rights Watch. 'At 10 a.m., (the mob) went after our mosque. Thirty to forty tear gas shells were released by the police as we, about fifty boys, were trying to save the mosque . . . They killed one seventeen-year-old and eight to ten other boys were injured . . . We kept calling the police but no one came . . . The police would pick up the phone and hang up when they heard it was from Naroda Patiya.'[2]

'I feel like my mind has been destroyed'

Javed Hussain, 14, the son of a rickshaw-puller father and a tailor mother, lost his family in the Naroda Patiya massacre. He stitched handkerchiefs for a living.

'We had just finished having tea around 9.30 a.m. when we heard a mob outside. They were throwing stones, brandishing swords, dharias and khanjars and chanting 'Jai Shri Ram'. They said they would destroy all Muslims. We tried to run but they had surrounded us. They set fire to houses and started throwing people into the flames. I was standing with my pregnant cousin Kausarbibi, who was to deliver in another two days. They dragged her away, ripped open her stomach with a knife and threw the foetus into the fire. Then they threw my family into the fire, one by one: my father, mother and my seventeen-year-old sister Sophiya. My aunt's family was also burnt alive.

'Someone hit me with a pipe and I fainted. When I came to, it was night. There were corpses all around me. My pants had been burnt off. I walked to my house and put on some clothes. Then, I walked 10 km in the night to the house of my employer. All along the way, I feared someone would leap out and kill me. He took me to the hospital and then they brought me to (Shah Alam) camp.

'I feel like my mind has been destroyed. I can't talk for more than a few minutes. I can't sleep at night. Those scenes keep coming back to me. I think about my mother a lot. She used to say that I was her joy, her support. I want to ask the people who did this: What had my family ever done to you? I don't think all Hindus are bad. I had four or five Hindu friends in my colony and I can't believe that they were involved. It was outsiders who did this.'

Source: Priyanka Kakodkar, 'Sleep and the innocent: revenge, yes, but most children want to forget the trauma they relive every night,' *Outlook*, May, 2002.

Amina Aapa, who was making tea at home when the mob came, ran outside when she heard the shouting, and saw what seemed like an endless line of VHP and Bajrang Dal men stretching all the way from Kalupur station to Naroda Patiya. She managed to hide on the roof of her house from where she saw her friend, Kausar Bano, who was nine months pregnant, killed. Her stomach was slashed, the foetus was removed and both mother and foetus burnt. Reshma, another eyewitness to Kausar's death, gave the names of several other women—her friends and neighbours—who had been raped and killed: Ayesha bibi, Shaheen bano, Noorjahan, Najma Begum, Zainab Bano, Noorjahan Alori, Sufia Bano. Mansoor Yusuf noted that four women were burnt to death just outside the police station with the sub-inspector present.

The State Reserve Police quarters are right next door to Naroda Patiya, but apart from some individuals who allowed a few people to take shelter, the SRP did nothing to help the Muslims. When some residents ran towards the police for protection, Inspector K.K. Mysorewala of Naroda Patiya police station ordered his men to fire teargas at them. Several survivors also told Sahrwaru, a women's rights organization, that those who ran towards the police for help were told to turn back or they would be shot. On the other side of the road was the mob waiting to kill them.[3] The terrified residents repeatedly phoned the police—the commissioner, IGP and the local police station— for help. The commissioner told Sharif Bhai: 'What can I do? The police is not in a position to restore law and order.'

The survivors were finally rescued after midnight on 1 March by Muslims who had set up the relief camp at Shah-e-Alam. Describing the post-carnage scene, Radha Sharma and Sanjay Pandey report: 'On Friday (the day after), communal tension was palpable in the area. Hundreds of youths roamed the streets, brandishing swords, daggers, axes and iron-rods. "The cowards have gone into hiding . . . they will not dare venture this side again", they screamed, breaking into a thundering "Jai Shri Ram". Naroda Road, Memco crossroads, Nutan Mills, Bapunagar, Saraspur and the Saijpur Bogha areas bore the brunt of the rioters, who burnt everything that came their way. Burnt skeletons of trucks, rickshaws, petrol tankers, shops and residences were aplenty in Naroda road. Smoke was wafting from the smouldering debris till late in the night. In Noorani Masjid area, a platoon of SRP men waited, the entire stretch around them littered with burnt trucks, tyres and two-wheelers and shacks.'[4]

Aftermath: *The police filed a chargesheet in the Naroda Patiya case in early June. The* Times of India *reported that five people among the leaders of the mob of 6,000, including Babu Bajrangi, Kishan Korani, P.J. Rajput, Harish Rohera, Raju Chaubal, were arrested.*[5] *Bajrangi is a Bajrang Dal leader and Korani a BJP politician and, ironically, a member of the Gujarat State Minorities Finance Corporation. Although the names of Naroda MLA Maya Kodnani, VHP general secretary Jaideep Patel and other top leaders figure in the earliest FIR of the Naroda Patiya carnage, they were not mentioned in the formal chargesheet and have not been arrested till date. On the contrary, crime branch officials say that 'their names are not mentioned at all.' Although earlier news reports quoted the police as explicitly identifying those accused as Bajrang Dal workers,*[6] *the police were later coy on this aspect. On 13 May, Ratilal Rathod alias Bhavani Singh was arrested for the murder of Kausar Bano.*[7]

Primary source: Communalism Combat, *Genocide Gujarat 2002* (Henceforth *GG*)

CHAMANPURA (GULBERG SOCIETY)

28 February
Some 40-65 people, including ex-MP Ehsan Jafri killed
In Chamanpura, Meghani Nagar, in the heart of Ahmadabad city, the attacks started even earlier on the 28th. Chamanpura has several shops and housing societies. One of these societies—Gulberg society—is almost entirely Muslim and consists of nineteen blocks and eight buildings. Former Congress MP, Ehsan Jafri, aged seventy-six, lived in Gulberg society with his family.

According to an FIR (no. 4/5/200)[8] filed by senior inspector

K.G. Erda of Meghani Nagar police station, they were put on alert early in the morning of the 28th. Meghani Nagar had 130 police personnel on duty that day. 'The police contingent was as needed and armed with teargas shells. There was enough bandobast at Meghani Nagar.' Yet none of this was invoked against the attacking mob.

According to the FIR, from about 7.00-7.30 a.m. onwards, a mob came to Chamanpura, and started attacking Muslim-owned establishments—a mattress shop, a bakery and a cycle shop. The police dispersed them at this stage but they reassembled around 1-1.30 p.m armed with swords, sticks, pipes and kerosene, shouting Jai Shri Ram. Erda's FIR claims the police lathi-charged and let off tear gas but the mob refused to listen, and turned more violent, burning and looting shops, including bakeries, electric shops etc. The mob then entered Gulberg society from the back and started stoning and burning property and people. 'At this stage,' the FIR notes, 'there was private firing by Muslims.'

The story put out by the police to all the newspapers highlighted this alleged 'private firing' by Jafri. Thus after reporting that Ehsan Jafri was on the phone for six hours to get help and none came, the *Indian Express* wrote that he fired a couple of rounds in self defence. 'That', said the *Express* report, 'was enough for the mob: they doused the four bungalows in the colony with petrol and kerosene and set them on fire'.[9] Narendra Modi went on record as saying that 'the firing by the Congressman played a pivotal role in inciting the mob.' When asked what could have led to the ex-MP opening fire, he said, 'It was probably in his nature to do so."[10] Following the lead of their chief, the police chargesheet blames Jafri for firing and infuriating the mobs, completely ignoring sections 96-103 of the Indian Penal Code which provide for the right to self-defence.[11] It now turns out that the whole story of private firing may have been a police concoction.

Jafri may not have fired at all
Kingshuk Nag

Ahmedabad: Did Ehsan Jafri fire on the mob that had collected outside his house? Did this enrage the 10,000-strong mob which then lynched Jafri and killed thirty-eight others at Gulberg Society on 28 February?

Highly reliable police sources now admit that the former Congress MP did not fire any shots at all. 'He wasn't in any position to do so,' said a top source.

But obviously the crime branch of the Ahmedabad city police is not privy to this information. The chargesheet with regard to the Gulberg Society incident, filed last week, says the gruesome incident was precipitated by the firing on the mob by Ehsan Jafri. The chargesheet thus vindicates the 'action-reaction' theory and provides an implicit defence for the accused.

From the sequence of events as found out by the *Times of India*, a crowd had begun to collect outside Gulberg Society from the morning of February 28, a day after Godhra. Since the crowd had not yet become a mob, Jafri was able to come out of his house. Sources indicate that he actually travelled to the office of the then police commissioner, P.C. Pande, and met him around 10.30 a.m. Pande assured him help and Jafri returned home.

However, the crowds continued to swell, alarming Jafri. In the meanwhile, Muslims from nearby slums, fearing attack, also got into Gulberg Society. At the same time, some toughies who used to live in Gulberg Society, made good their escape. 'Jafri could have escaped too, but he preferred to stay back,' says a top source.

At 1.30 p.m. the then joint police commissioner, M.K. Tandon arrived. He spoke to Jafri, who came down to the gate of the housing society. Jafri talked about the imminent danger to the residents and Tandon, in turn, promised to rush police reinforcements. But he himself did not wait at the scene. He left for Naroda-Patiya.

Jafri had always thought himself a man who had respect in society. So, around 3.00 p.m., he came down once again to the gate of the housing society to appeal to the mob to disperse. In what was a gamble that failed, he suggested that the mob take him but leave the others in the society alone. The mob readily complied: it got hold of Jafri and killed him in a gory fashion. By 3.30 p.m. everything was over.

'In all respects, Jafri was a brave man. He could have slunk away, but he did not,' says a top source, adding, 'Tandon made a blunder. If he had stuck on at the society, the very presence of the joint commissioner would have deterred the mob.'

Source: Times of India (Ahmedabad), 9 June 2002

According to eyewitnesses,[12] Ehsan Jafri was pulled out of his house around 3.30 p.m., stripped, paraded naked and asked to say *Jai Shri Ram* and *Vande Matram*. He refused. His fingers were then chopped off and he was paraded around the locality badly injured. His hands and feet were then cut off, and he was dragged down the road with a fork like instrument at his throat before being throwing into a fire. Along with Jafri, three brothers and two nephews were killed. Before that, the mob caught hold of two men, Yusuf and Anwar, cut them up and torched them to death.

The official death toll is 39 but eyewitness say that 55-65 people were murdered that day—at least 45 from the society itself and 10 or 12 who had come from outside to take shelter. At least two women had their jewellery taken from them, and were then gang-raped, cut and burnt. The police rescued some 150 survivors in the evening. The *Asian Age* quotes K.G. Erda as saying that the Fire Brigade did not turn up till the next evening. When the reporter reached, everything was burnt and all that was left of bodies were heaps of ashes and unrecognizable body parts.[13]

Eyewitnesses also provided the names and addresses of at least 25 people who led and instigated the mob but despite this, the police has not arrested them all.[14] Some of the instigators as indicated by witnesses included: Jagrupsinh Rajput (formerly with BJP, now with Congress, ex-deputy mayor of Ahmedabad), Chunilal Prajapati (ex-municipal corporator, formerly BJP, now independent), Mehsingh Chaudhary (Congress ex-corporator, who was denied a ticket by Jafri this time), Girish Prabhdas

Sharma and Dinesh Parbhudas Sharma both of whom supplied
five-litre kerosene drums for arson, Kapil of the Bajrang Dal
who works in a petrol pump and supplied trishuls and petrol,
Bharat Rajput, Lala Mohanji Darbar who is involved in illegal
liquor business and was seen raping women and several others.
In all 28 people have been arrested for the Chamanpura killings.

ANAND DISTRICT

Odh village, Umred taluka

28 February—2 March
At least 29 people burnt alive in one incident
Odh is called an NRI village. There are many rich businessmen
running tobacco businesses. The 200 Muslim households—were
mostly those of workers in these tobacco fields. They are now
refugees in the Sureli and Bhalej camps, and this account is
based on their testimonies.

Over the past five years, attempts were made to pick fights
with Muslims at any excuse and escalate tension between the
two communities. The situation worsened about two months
back, when the RSS/VHP held a meeting at the house of
Harishbhai Valabhbhai Patel. Since then, posters of the VHP
and RSS became visible everywhere, Muslim boys were accused
of teasing and troubling Hindu women, and secret meetings
began taking place in the fields. When Muslims asked, they
were told that the meetings were about the fields.

On 28 February following the Godhra incident, there was a
lot of tension in the air. On 1 March people did not even go to
the mosque for *namaaz*. After the *namaaz* time, some people—
Harishbhai Valabhbhai, Vasantbhai Poonambhai Patel and
Natubhai Sanabhai Patel—went to meet Yusufbhai Yakubbhai,
who lived in a Muslim *mohalla*, and told him not to worry.
They said they would only take out a rally and nothing more.
However, there was no rally. On the same day, at 2.00 p.m., a
large mob armed with stones and petrol bombs came screaming,
'*Maro* (kill), *Kapo* (cut)'. They abused the Muslims, calling them
'*bandiya*', and urged people to kill them and burn their houses.

After a few hours, the mob told the people not to leave their houses. Those who listened to them and stayed behind were locked inside their homes, which were set on fire with petrol and kerosene. There were thirty people trapped inside. Two men managed to run away with serious burns. Of the remaining twenty-eight, seven were young girls and two were older women. The bodies were set alight repeatedly so that no evidence would remain. For six people, only parts were found, it was not possible to tell whether they were male or female. Twenty-two bodies had been burned to ashes.

Rehana Yusufbhai Vohra, who later filed an FIR at Khambolaj police station, was an eyewitness to the burning. Her family had keys to the house of a Hindu friend, and nine of them ran and hid there for three days without food or water. Escaping from there, they walked to Sureli camp, which was quite far to seek shelter.

By the night of 2 March the four Muslim mohallas, 200 houses, shops, the two mosques and five dargahs in the village were all burnt, using LPG cylinders and bombs. A bulldozer was used to level the land so that the area where all these were located now looks like an open ground.

The remaining survivors were rescued by Farid, a Congress worker from Sureli village. One little boy and his grandfather were left behind. The grandfather says Ghulam Hussain was burnt alive.

The police arrested twenty-three Hindus in the case. Despite the gravity of the crime, initially the first class magistrate rejected police remand, and gave eighteen accused interim bail on the grounds that they needed to celebrate Shivratri.[15] Sixteen people were then released on regular bail, and now only seven people are in jail. A BJP ex-minister, Dilipbhai Mani, and his personal secretary are helping the accused with their cases.

Source: PUCL Vadodara and Shanti-Abhiyan, *Violence in Vadodara: A Report*, Vadodara, May 2002 (henceforth *PUCL*), pp 114-115.

DAHOD DISTRICT

Randhikpur village, Limkheda taluka
28 February—5 March
20 known dead, several women raped and killed

Randhikpur is a small village with sixty to seventy Muslim families who are poor agricultural labourers. Some have a few bighas of land, some keep cattle, and some have petty shops, e.g. a recycling store. The village witnessed communal tensions in 1998 following inter-religious marriages, when the VHP had alleged that Muslim boys abducted Hindu girls. Some Muslim houses were burnt, and goods and animals looted. The Muslims migrated to Baria for three months, but were called back by the Hindus who said that they would repay the damages. When they returned to the village, however, they discovered that all they were wanted for was their votes in the local panchayat elections. There is an RSS shakha in the village. The present sarpanch is PA to the local BJP MLA who is an adivasi. The Muslims have largely voted for the Congress in elections.

This time, the devastation was of a different order altogether. On the morning of 28 February, a large mob of adivasis came from outside villages and started setting fire to the Muslim houses. Even as the local villagers assured the Muslims that nothing would happen to them, some among them led the attack. All the Muslim houses, in three separate *mohallas* of the village, were burnt and razed to the ground by the mob. The village is surrounded by hills on all sides. The attackers had blocked all the roads. The Muslim men, women, some pregnant, and children ran in different directions to save their lives. About 100 to 150 women and children ran and took shelter at the adivasi sarpanch's house in neighbouring Jhamri village for three days. During the day, they would run to the hills and hide themselves. In Randhikpur, one Chamra Magan sheltered some five women and children, before the police finally rescued them. A group of seventeen ran from village to village (Chundagi to Khudra to Chaparwad). One of them, Shamim, delivered a baby girl at a mosque where they were taking shelter for the night.

The next morning, she again set out with the baby in her arms. Her clothes were soiled, and she was hardly able to walk. At Khudra, they stayed with adivasis who protected them and gave Shamim clothes to change, but they had to leave again. As they were going from Chaparwad to Panivel, village men from Randhikpur and Chaparwad came in two cars, gang-raped the women and then killed them. Shamim and her newborn child were also killed. B, a five-month pregnant young woman, was gang-raped by three men from her village. Her three-year-old daughter was snatched away from her and killed in front of her. The only survivor of this group of seventeen, she spent a day and a night alone in the hills and then was brought to the Godhra camp by the Limkheda police on 5 March where the rest of the Randhikpur victims are staying. No traces of the remains of the dead bodies, not even the ashes of the people burnt alive, are left behind for the relatives to recover. The victims allege that the police was present in the village but they did nothing. The *Indian Express* reports that the village leaders will only allow Muslims back if they drop rape charges.[16]

Source: Peoples Union for Democratic Rights, '*Maaro! Kaapo! Baalo!*': *State, Society and Communalism in Gujarat*, New Delhi, May 2002, (henceforth *PUDR*), pp. 14-15.

SANJELI VILLAGE, JHALOD TALUKA

28 February—2 March
16 known dead, entire Muslim settlement burnt
Sanjeli is a large village with about 700-800 houses. About 50 per cent of the population is Muslim, making it the largest Muslim settlement in the area. This includes about sixty-five Bohra families who are mainly shopkeepers and traders. It has a police outpost with five policemen. As in Randhikpur, there had been tension in 1998 over Muslim-adivasi marriages and Muslims had to leave the village. Some three months before the current attacks, the VHP and Bajrang Dal had held meetings in which they had announced that 'Sanjeli would burn'.

On 28 February, a group of adivasi youth on their way home from a wedding party stoned some Muslim houses in Nani Sanjeli. There was some retaliatory firing in which eight adivasi boys were injured, two requiring minor surgery. They were taken to hospital in Limkheda and a complaint and FIR lodged by Dalsukh Maharaj, a local VHP adivasi activist. He used this incident, however, to go around villages telling people that seventy to eighty boys had been injured in Muslim firing and that the bodies of eight girls had been found in the Sanjeli masjid. He distributed boxes of bangles to the sarpanchs of villages to incite them to send their people.

Owing to this and other VHP mobilization, a massive crowd came to the village on 1 March at around 3.00 p.m. and started burning the outlying houses. About 100 to 150 houses were burnt that day, and their residents fled to the masjid. The mob stayed outside the village all night, throwing stones, shouting and shooting arrows.

The next morning, a peace committee rally was called at the village centre by the VHP/Bajrang Dal leaders to which some Muslim elders also went. After the meeting, the VHP leaders went around neighbouring villages ostensibly to spread the peace message, but actually, it turns out in hindsight, to mobilize crowds. Soon after, a mob descended from neighbouring villages up to a distance of 10 kms away, armed not only with bows and arrows and catapults, but also with private guns, shouting *Bolo Jai Shri Ram*. Some in the mob had come in jeeps and Tata Sumos.

According to the ex-ruler of Sanjeli estate, Kalika Kumar, who witnessed the entire attack, the crowd stood outside the village for a while waiting for a signal. The first charge came from the Limkheda side, including from the SRP jawans who had been assigned to Jivabhai Damor, BJP MLA for his personal security. They had automatic rifles. Most of those who had arms came from Methan and Vandeli village as there are many ex-servicemen in that area. Ilyas bhai Tura, a young driver in the PWD, was shot in the chest at close range. Seventy-year-old Zubeida bibi and sixty-five-year-old Morawala Salam

Mohammad were also shot dead. Some others were injured by gunshots in the chest and legs.

The crowd started burning houses again. The majority of the Muslim houses were torched on 2 and 3 March, after being looted. However, some looting went on for 5-6 days. In total, 600 shops and houses were burnt. A church in Sanjeli was also burnt and the local pastor badly beaten up when he tried to stop the mobs from attacking Muslims. The local police did nothing. Both on 1 and 2 March, when Muslim villagers appealed to the police, they said they had orders only to shoot Muslims who violated curfew, not Hindus, and chased them away.

Many Muslims sought shelter in their respective mosques (Sunni and Bohra), or with some dalit families. DSP Jadeja arrived at Sanjeli at about 5-5.30 pm on 2 March with a posse of policemen and did some effective firing. On seeing him, the mob moved away slightly. The DSP did not have enough vehicles to transport everyone to Dahod, but there were some eight large Muslim vehicles still intact and Kalika Kumar also helped by arranging two trucks from Hindus. Thanks to the roadblocks consisting of electric poles and nails, and the large mobs all along the way, the convoy had to take a longer and more circuitous route than normal. The trucks were continuously stoned—Kadar Mohammad Bhatiyara, a tailor, had his jaw dislocated by a heavy stone. At least six children ranging from the ages of two to six, and one middle-aged woman, were stoned to death en route from Sanjeli to Dahod.

One Tempo containing some 80-100 people had a puncture 1 km out of Sanjeli, caused by the large nails on the roads, and then another puncture 8 km away near village Rainiya. At Rainiya, they were attacked by a Tata Sumo containing nine men equipped with swords, stones and iron pipes. Four people who had got down, all Bohras, were killed and burnt. Two women—Zainab ben Burhanbhai Mulla Meetha and Fatima Murtaza Gadbadawala—were also raped before being killed. Survivors who hid in bushes and managed to walk to Sukhsar police station alleged the attackers included leaders of the VHP and Bajrang Dal like Mukesh Kumar Nand Kishore Purohit, a VHP activist, Jagdish Premchand Jain, a Bajrang Dal leader in the transport and hardware business, and Dimple Kumar Ochavlal Desai, an RSS leader and garment shop owner.

The remaining ten vehicles reached Dahod safely. The majority of Sanjeli refuges were at Dahod but by 24 April were made to go back and camp in their burnt houses.

Source: PUDR, *pp* 15-16.

FATEHPURA, FATEHPURA TALUKA

28 February—4 March
Women raped and forced to walk naked to the police station; refugees kept standing at the station for two days without food or water

Fatehpura and its twin settlement, Karodia, have a total population of about 6,000. The 200-250 Sunni houses and 200 Bohra houses are scattered all over. In all, four lives were lost.

Tension started on the evening of 28 February around 8.30 p.m., when a Hindutva mob came to the main bazaar area and to the village mosque, shouting slogans and throwing stones. On 1 March one house and a few vehicles were burnt on Ukhreli Road on the outskirts of Fatehpura. Women were verbally and physically harassed. In Fatehpura proper, the mob made threatening noises and put Hanuman posters on Hindu houses to ensure their future safety.

Curfew was clamped in the town on 2 March at 9.00 a.m. Apparently, a police patrol came with two policemen in it and asked people to get into their houses. The mob was at this point at some distance. Once the mob entered the village, the police was nowhere to be seen. The mob was large and the attackers were both from the town and outside.

The mob surrounded the whole settlement and started their looting and destruction from one end. Since the houses were scattered, people started congregating in the bigger concrete houses. One or two families were also sheltered for a day by an adivasi family near the town and then sent to the police station at night as their hosts were also threatened. One house, where 100 people were hiding was set on fire. People managed to escape from the roof, and somehow managed to reach the police station in the evening. As the women came out, many of them were stripped and harassed, and at least one woman was raped.

Another concrete house, where people from some fifteen households (including thirty women, ten children and many men) were sheltering, was attacked at noon. First, the mob surrounded the house and then went in. After taking their money and jewellery from them, they took all the young women and children out. The children were pulled away from their mothers and the women were then stripped and raped. Two men who tried to intervene were killed. This went on till six in the evening. The house was also set on fire; when the doors burnt and fell down, the Muslims inside came out. Many people suffered burns.

The police station is almost a kilometre away from this place. These women, who had been raped and doused with petrol had to walk naked and brutalized all this distance and no one—not even one of the Hindu women who were part of the watching crowd—gave them anything to cover themselves. Trying to cover themselves with some leaves on the road, they managed to flee to the police station.

The police station was packed with almost 2,000 people and there wasn't even enough space to sit. So most of them just stood there from Saturday evening to early Monday morning. All through this period, no one got any water or food, except for the children, who were once given a little water. The police did not let them out and did not try to help them in any way at all. In fact, the police said that if they went out they would not be able to stop the mob from killing them.

When the arson and violence in the town ended late night on 4 March not a single Muslim house or shop was left standing. On Monday morning, the police took the Muslims to Rajasthan, where they were handed over to the Rajasthan police. The vehicles were overcrowded and one three-year-old child, who lost his mother's grip, fell down and died. The Rajasthan police was good to them. They stayed in Rajasthan for ten days until 13 March when the Dahod collector came to take them back.

Source: Forum Against Oppression of Women and Aawaz-e-Niswaan, Bombay, Genocide in Rural Gujarat: The Experience of Dahod District, *Mumbai, May 2002 (henceforth* Forum), *pp. 15-19.*

MEHSANA DISTRICT

Visnagar, Visnagar taluka
28 February
At least 32 killed
Visnagar town has about two to three thousand Patel families, 1,200 Thakur families, 600-700 families of Rabaris, 1,000 Dalit families, and about a hundred Muslim families. The Muslims here suffered substantial devastation and casualties. A violent mob attacked the various Muslim clusters on the afternoon of 28 February. The attackers were armed with swords, *dharias*, sticks, acid, petrol, lighters and country made bombs. About 1,200 victims of the town have been staying in a relief camp in village Sawala since the incident. They recognize some of the attackers who were all Patels. According to them, even Patel women participated in the attack by throwing stones on the Muslims from the rooftops.

In one of the Hindu localities, Deepda Darwaza, there were ten shacks/huts belonging to really poor Muslims. Some of these Muslims were labourers, others ran a paan shop, a cycle repair shop or pulled a hand cart. The attackers surrounded their houses, put petrol and burnt them. Eleven people belonging to the families of two brothers were hacked and burnt to death, leaving just three survivors—Yusufbhai, his thirteen-year-old nephew Pathan Arif Khan Yakub Khan, and his eleven-year-old niece Noorjahan Yakub Khan. Those killed included five women, one man and five children. One of the children was just six months old. The two surviving children saw their family members being hacked and burnt with their own eyes. With a deep sense of hurt and pain Yusufbhai tells everyone that even till the last minute he believed that since the attackers were all neighbours, they would not kill his family.

The attackers took the bodies, cut and packed them in sacks and dumped the sacks in a pond on Kada Road. The police later recovered the bodies. While the attack started at around 2.30 p.m., and the police were called repeatedly, they finally came only at 5.00 p.m. The trapped Muslim residents were rescued only after that. The survivors have named sixty people in their complaint to police. However, according to Yusufbhai they were arrested in connection with earlier smaller offences.

In another area in the town called Kaziwada, one Ashrafbhai was attacked by the mob and struck with a sword. His sister, Zainabbibi, and his neighbours, Hanifbhai and Yunusbhai Mansuri, took him in a hand cart to the Civil Hospital, Visnagar. The attackers caught them in the Civil Hospital. Yunusbhai escaped and has not been seen since. Zainabibi, Hanif and Ashrafbhai were taken to the third floor of the hospital and thrown down from there. While Ashraf and Hanif died, Zainabibi did not die the first time round so she was dragged up the stairs and thrown again. Then acid was thrown on the bodies, and they were also slashed with swords. In another locality, Khada Darwaza, about fifteen to twenty Muslim men and children were injured in an attack. As the mob approached this locality, about 100 women hid in a house, while the men tried to resist the attack by throwing back stones. The confrontation continued for about two to three hours.

The survivors allege that the local MLA was the main instigator. He organized meetings in the town and had been heard guaranteeing that there would be no case or imprisonment against the attackers.

Muslims from Visnagar who have fled to Sawala are too scared to go back. Eighty-four auto rickshaws stand forlornly as it is dangerous for the drivers to ply them. School students who attempted to go to school continued to be threatened by groups of ten to fifteen people, and numerous isolated incidents of attacks on Muslims continued to take place, at least till April.

Source: PUDR, pp 22-23

Aftermath: Following the granting of bail to forty-three accused, Yusuf Pathan got the High Court to issue a show-cause notice to the state government. Though thirty-two Muslims are said to have been killed, the police accepted only eleven deaths.[17]

Sardarpura village, Vijapur taluka

28 February—1 March
At least 33 dead, 29 in 1 house
Muslims constituted about 10 per cent of the total population of the village, which included about twenty-five families of Pathans, twenty of Sheikhs (Ghanchis) and about twenty families of Mansuri Muslims.

On 28 February, at about 9.00 p.m. several kiosks owned by Muslims, dalits and Rawals were burnt by a mob from Sardarpura and neighbouring Sunderpura. Though the police were called, the attack continued despite their presence. Fearing further attacks the following day, the Muslims again called the police. Two jeeps with policemen arrived led by two sub-inspectors. A peace committee meeting was fixed for 4.00 p.m. Apart from the sarpanch and an ex-sarpanch (both Patels), representatives from dalits, Rawals, Prajapati and Muslims reached the venue but the Patels did not come. The sarpanch left the venue shortly thereafter, making the excuse that he would try to get the Patels. He did not return.

Strangely, the streetlights of the village, which were not working for about a month prior to the incident, were suddenly repaired that evening. A halogen light was installed near the colony of the Sheikhs and a long wire and a metal conductor were connected to it. The sarpanch took away the key to the bore well from a Muslim bore operator. By 9.30 p.m., a large mob led by a Bajrang Dal activist and consisting of people from eight to ten villages started collecting in Sardarpura. All the three localities of the Muslims (of Pathans, Sheikhs and Memons) were simultaneously attacked. The two sub-inspectors were still in the village when the attack started. They made some excuse about leaving to rescue the Memon shops, and told the DSP that every thing was all right in the village.

In the Sheikh locality, a two-year-old girl was thrown and killed by the mob. Some of the Muslims ran to Rawal houses for shelter and together with the Rawals then ran away through the fields. One person saved himself by hiding in a grave.

Thirty-one people, mostly women and children, had taken shelter in a house in the Sheikh locality. The mob surrounded the house and threw acid at them through openings in the room in which they were locked. The metal conductor, an iron rod attached by a wire to the newly installed halogen light, was also used to try and electrocute people. An eight-year-old girl, Salma, received electric shock on her thigh and waist. Later petrol was poured in and ignited.[18] In all, 29 persons were killed, mostly burnt to death. Two children who fell beneath the pile of bodies of the dead survived the attack.

Finally, after desperate phone calls by other Muslims, DSP Ashok Gehlot reached the village with two vehicles at about 2.30 a.m. The survivors were rescued and taken to Sawala village. Even this was difficult as all the roads out of Sardarpura were blocked at frequent intervals till Ladol, 9 km away, to prevent the Muslims from escaping. An FIR was lodged and twenty-eight persons named by survivors. One of the chief accused, Bajrang Dal activist Chandra Kant, had not been arrested till April.

Source: PUDR, p 23.

PANCHMAHALS DISTRICT

Pandarwada village, Khanpur taluka

28 February—1 March
At least 38 people killed
Pandarwada village has 500 to 600 Hindu families and about

70 to 80 Muslim families. The Hindus are Brahmins, Patels and Vanias, who are prosperous wholesale traders and own cloth and grocery shops in the village. The Muslims are largely agricultural labourers and small peasants, some of whom own land on both sides of the canal that flows by the village. This land is fertile and, according to the victims, some of the village Hindus want to acquire control over it. Some of the Muslims are also daily wage labourers with Hindu shop owners. Several of village notables (sarpanch, lawyer, doctor) have been active in organizing VHP meetings for over a decade. The main *chowk* of the village, where Hindu and Muslim festivals were held together earlier, was named 'Ayodhya chowk' after the Babri Masjid demolition on 6 December 1992 and Muslims stopped using it since then. In the past six months, several VHP meetings were held where Bajrang Dal activists were also called. These activists wrote anti-Muslim slogans on the public walls, asking Muslims to go to Pakistan. A meeting was held about fifteen days before the ghastly massacres took place. Faiz Mohammad Ahmadbhai recalled,

> Nearly 300 to 400 people from nearby villages, men and women, had collected at the meeting. There were VHP leaders, sadhus and others. The entire meeting was broadcast on the loudspeakers, provided by Anil Modi. One leader said, 'there ·were 2-3 households of Muslims earlier. Now they have 100-125 houses. The Muslim population is increasing. We must do something now. We have no arms. In Muslim houses arms are ready for use. We must prepare to fight them.' The principal of Shri K.M. Doshi High School, Kantibhai Ambalal Pandya, who chaired the meeting said, 'We must give serious thought to what the speakers have said today; and we must prepare ourselves so that we can confront them. The Muslims don't believe in family planning so their population increases. Let our population also increase' . . .

The killings in Pandarwada were organized in amazing detail. The local Hindu leaders had mobilized a large mob of Bhils from nearby villages who came on 28 February and again on 1 March when they went on a rampage for nearly the whole day. The mob looted the goods and took away Muslim livestock, destroyed and set fire to their houses and killed several of them as they ran to save their lives. It is said that they were offered Rs. 50,000 for every Muslim killed. The survivors said one of the leaders of the mob was the franchisee of the ration shop, BJP leader Jaswant Patel, who is also the taluka up-pramukh. He had not given any kerosene to the Muslim villagers since Eid, and this very kerosene was then given to the attackers.

In two major incidents during the attack on 1 March in Pandarwada, local village leaders who were BJP supporters deliberately deceived the Muslims by offering to shelter them. Mahendra Vakil told one group of some 150 Muslims, to hide in his old house, while Jaswant Patel told another large group, to take shelter in his wheat fields. According to the survivors they trusted these men because they were their neighbours. Mahendra Vakil told the Muslims to take in the wood lying outside his house so that the mob would not use it to set the house on fire. Then he led the mob attack and burnt the house down. Jaswant Patel similarly led the mob in attacking, hacking and burning those who took shelter in his fields. At least thirty-eight Muslims, including several children, were killed in these several attacks. Some of them were guests from outside who were part of a wedding party. During the attack, eyewitnesses state that a Bajrang Dal leader drove through the village on his motorcycle to see that Muslims did not run away and were executed according to their plans. Similarly, a Tata Sumo with men wearing saffron dupattas, went through the village to supervise the killings. Even the mamlatdar (Taluka Development Officer, TDO) and the police were present, silently watching the massacre. Women saw their husbands hacked and burnt before their eyes. Mumtaz found her three-year-old son sitting next to the body of her husband, Fakir Mohammad, whose face had been so badly dismembered that only his Adam's apple was left.

According to the survivors, a large number of people from the village are still missing, and the number of people killed is much higher than the officially recognized number. Many of those who managed to escape were badly beaten up and stabbed with swords incurring severe injuries. Some had their heads pierced through with sharp iron rods (*gupti*). Some of them are still in critical condition in hospitals in Godhra and Lunawada. All the survivors of the attack including women and small children, fled from the village and hid wherever they could, in the hills and jungle, some for three to four days, without food or water, young children chewing the leaves of the trees to survive.

Today, with their houses completely destroyed, their property looted and animals taken away, their mosque and dargah burnt, there are no Muslims in Pandarwada. They are staying in camps at Godhra and Lunawada. Some of the widows are several months pregnant and have no families who can take care of them and their children. None of the Muslims in the two camps have the courage ever to return to their village. Here too, village leaders want various conditions fulfilled before they will allow the Muslims to return.[19]

Source: PUDR, pp 7-9

Anjanwa village, Santrampur taluka

2–5 March
11 known dead, women and children thrown into a well
Anjanwa is a village with 39 Muslim and about 500 other families. All except three Muslim families have about two to three acres of land in the village. The Hindus (all backward caste, mostly Baria) and the adivasis also have land. Muslims have lived in this village since Santrampur was a princely state. The settlement is scattered with each family having a house on their own agricultural land. The Muslim houses are, in fact, two kilometres away from the main road. There are no newspapers, television or telephones in the village. Vehicles can go only up to a point on the undulating kuchha road in the village. The houses are accessible only on foot. The sprawling village is surrounded by hills on all sides.

With no communication facilities Anjanwa did not immediately receive news of the Godhra incident. On 2 March two Muslim shops belonging to Idris Abdul Sheikh and Burhan Abdul Sheikh were burnt. The owners used to commute from Lunawada so were not there at the time. On 3 March, a mob of 500 men came in the morning from the east, armed with weapons and beating drums. They burnt the mosque and then the Muslim houses. Then they went off at 3.00 p.m. and came back again at 6.00 p.m. again with the frightening beating of drums and shouting '*Maaro! Kaapo! Baalo!*' (Kill! Cut! Burn!) and stayed till the early hours of the next morning.

The Muslims who had been hiding in the hills during the attack, returned after the mob left, in the early hours of 4 March. They asked the sarpanch to call for police protection. According to the sarpanch, he called the Congress MLA (an adivasi) of the area that morning, who in turn told the police. The police said they would send a force. The police van finally did arrive at around 7.30–8.00 p.m. on 4 March. However, some villagers told them that nothing was wrong, and unable to see signs of the attack from the main road, the police returned to Santrampur. The next morning, the sarpanch once again made frantic phone calls to the Santrampur police station, and was told that a van would come to collect the villagers. He asked the Muslims to collect in the village high school so that they could leave immediately when the police came.

In the evening, two sets of mobs came from opposite directions and attacked the waiting Muslims. As the Muslims ran to save themselves in different directions, sections of the mob followed them. Forty-two-year-old Rukaiya Gafur and her two daughters were not able to run fast enough. They were surrounded by the mob at one end of the village. Rukaiya was brutally hacked to death with swords. Her body was thrown into a dry well (known as Wazir Amdu's well). Her two daughters, thirteen- and one-and-a-half years old respectively, were also attacked, but managed to survive. Two men, one over Seventy-five-years-old and moving slowly with difficulty, and another too sick to run were also caught by the mob. They were burnt alive in the fields.

Some women and small children who were unable to escape

were gheraoed by a section of the mob near the sarpanch's well. They were attacked with swords and *dharias*, and eleven of them were thrown into the well. Three women managed to survive in the crevices of the well and were pulled out later by the army, which arrived on the 5th evening. Eight others who had been hacked and thrown died, including four children. All the dead bodies were recovered on 6 March. The army rescued some people on the 5th and the rest who had hidden in the hills on the 6th.

The survivors have identified twenty-seven men of their own village and of the surrounding villages who led the mob. Like those in Pandarwada, they are unwilling to return with many of the killers at large.

Source: PUDR, pp 9-10.

Delol village, Kalol taluka

28 February—1 March
At least 24 dead, 13-year-old girl raped
Delol village is located at a distance of about five km from Kalol taluka town. It had about sixty Muslim households and about 500-600 Hindu households. On 28 February, the day of the Gujarat bandh, a large crowd of mostly outsiders came at about 10.00 a.m. and attacked, looted, burnt and destroyed the mosque, shops and establishments of the Muslims, leaving at 4.00 p.m. Later at night, Ismailbhai was dragged out of his house by a crowd which included people from his own village, made to go through the village twice with a garland of shoes and asked to say 'Jai Shri Ram'. When he refused to say this, he was doused with kerosene and burnt to death in the early hours of the morning.

At 10.00 a.m. on 1 March, a much larger mob came to the village shouting, 'Today is Bharat Bandh—drive the Muslims out, hack them, kill them.' Survivors allege that a local BJP MLA, Prabhasingh Chouhan, was involved in the attack. In the late afternoon, a group of about fifty to sixty Muslims who had taken shelter with the Hindus in the village were chased by a large group of attackers to the main road and from there to the fields. The fleeing Muslims knew many of the members of the mob, but disregarding all their pleas, eight of them were killed. In another incident on the 1st morning, a family of eleven members who had hidden in a Hindu house on the night before was attacked. They first ran towards the Delol bus stand, chased by attackers who hit them with *dharias* and sticks. Here too, the victims recognized many of the attackers. They then ran towards the dry bed of the river Goma, and managed to hide under a tree all day. At night a crowd of 500 to 700 people surrounded them, comprising people from Delol as well as surrounding villages. First they told the petrified Muslims that they would not kill them and gave them water to drink. Then they asked them to leave. Just as they started to leave, they attacked them from behind and hacked and burnt 10 people. According to one account, thirteen-year-old Yasmeen, the daughter of Mohd. Ibrahim, was gang-raped before she was killed. In a symbolic act of conversion, the dead were put in a pile and set on fire. Ten- and twelve-year-old Hameed and Aijaz, sons of Kulsum Ayyub (who was also killed) were made to go around the pyre and shout 'Jai Shri Ram'. They were then shoved into the fire. Only one survivor, Javed, managed to reach the main road, where someone he knew helped him to reach Kalol.

Source: *PUDR*, p 11; see also account of S, village Delol in chapter 6.

SABARKANTHA DISTRICT
Kidiyad village, Modasa taluka
2 March
8 'officially' dead, 67 'unofficially' dead, burnt alive in a tempo
Kidiyad village has about forty-five households of Muslims and 200 of Dalits, Bharwads and Thakars. On 28 February and 1 March, reports about houses being burnt in neighbouring

villages like Haloder started pouring in. When they asked for police protection, PSI Mukesh Patel of Malpur PS sent only one policeman supposedly to provide effective police protection. On 2 March, the mobile police armed with .303 rifles came to the village at about 3.00 p.m. and told the Muslims to run to save their lives as they would not be able to provide protection. The sarpanch requested the police to escort them till Malpur but the police refused.

The scared Muslims then started trying to cross the rivers Eru and Vatrak across the dryer parts of the riverbed. After trying for almost an hour, they returned to the village by 3.45 p.m. or so where they were confronted by a mob of about 400-500 people from their own village and outside, shouting 'Kill them! Hack them! Don't let them go!' The mob was carrying *dharias*, swords and trishuls. There were 224 Muslims in the village at the time, as well as 20 guests from outside. Desperate to flee, 118 of these boarded two tempos and set off. Those who could not do so, hid in the fields around the village.

About thirty-four people had boarded the first tempo (GJ 17 T 9283), which left at about 4 p.m. to try to make its way towards Modasa. Zakirbhai Shamsuddin Sindhi was driving this tempo. The sarpanch of Kidiyad, Saleembhai Jamubhai Sindhi, was also there on this tempo. They reached the Godhra-Modasa highway and found the road blocked at Malpur with stones and about a 1,000 people all around who stoned the tempo, breaking windows and injuring the people inside. However, the tempo managed to turn towards Lunawada, and crossed Limbadiya Chowkri in Panchmahals district. On the way, from Naroda village near Limbadiya, a jeep and a motorcycle (with three riders) started following them. One of the pillion riders had a sword in his hand and the other had a *dharia*. The road was blocked at various places by large trees and the tempo had to take various twists and turns. As they passed through villages, the tempo was stoned sporadically. Finally between Sanparia and Badesara villages, the motorcycle overtook the tempo and forced it to stop. As those in the tempo tried to jump off and escape, they were attacked by the men on the motorcycle. The driver, Zakirbhai Shamsuddin Sindhi, was hit and his four-month-old son, Mohsin, fell from his hands and died. He picked up his dead child and ran.

The Muslims ran towards Kaaranta village across the Bhadrod river nearby, hoping to take shelter in the dargah there. The Patels of Sanparia, however, came out in support of the attackers and killed six people. One woman, Sarabibi, who is an eyewitness to the murders, was able to hide beneath a tarpaulin sheet in a shed behind a Patel house. In fact, the Patel's wife gave her shelter till the police arrived to take her to the Modasa relief camp two days later. Other survivors somehow managed to reach the security of the Karanta dargah. The driver, Zakir Mian, finally buried his dead child there. The survivors filed a police complaint when they reached the Modasa relief camp 10.00 days later.

The second tempo (no. GJ 9T 6439) left Kidiyad at about 4.15 p.m. in order to try to reach Modasa. Eighty-four people, including a large number of women and thirty-two children, were packed tightly into the cramped tempo. Heavy stone pelting started from village Punjarani Muvadi. When the tempo reached Choriwad Crossing, a crowd of about one thousand was standing there. All other roads were blocked. In desperation, Ayub Mian, the driver turned the tempo towards Lunawada, Panchmahals district. From Babaliya, four motorcycles, a jeep, a truck and a tempo (no. GJ7Y 2131) started chasing the tempo. On one of the four motorcycles was Naresh Bhai, a resident of Gogawada. As soon as the tempo reached Limbadiya Chowkri, about 15 km from Lunawada, the motorcyclists overtook the tempo and fired at the front tyre, which burst, bringing the tempo to a standstill.

A large armed crowd which had been alerted by the passing of the first tempo a little while earlier surrounded the tempo along with the pursuers. About sixteen people, including the driver of the tempo managed to run away. These were mostly men with the exception of one woman and two small children. They hid in the fields and saw what followed. After hacking at those who remained on the tempo with swords, the attackers threw tyres on them, poured petrol and set the tempo on fire. Eight people who tried to jump off were fired at and hacked to death. One woman, Arzoo Bibi Ayub Mian Sindhi, sitting in the driver's cabin was also attacked when she jumped off but she survived albeit with severe injuries by pretending to be dead. Those inside the tempo were completely burnt to ashes, as the fire raged for over two hours.

According to the SP (Panchmahals), only eight deaths have been registered in the case as only the bodies of those killed while trying to jump off have been found in a half burnt condition. In fact, Arzoo Bibi was told to identify these bodies and could only identify one of the eight bodies as that of Pirzada Gulabuddin Imam Mian, a resident of Karanta (eighty years old) who had come to Kidiyad on 27 February to offer Friday prayers. The other seven bodies were charred beyond recognition. Yet there are eyewitnesses who state categorically that 59 other people were charred to death, bringing the total to 67. The dead included 37 females and 30 males, of whom 15 were boys below 12 years. Four infants less than a year old perished in the attack. The eyewitnesses have also identified the accused.

Complaints have been given to all authorities by survivors and also to the Khanpur PS investigating the case. The driver of the tempo, Ayubbhai Subha Mian Sindhi, is the main complainant. In the absence of any concerted effort to collect evidence and locate bone fragments if any, the huge disparity between eyewitness accounts and the official story remains.

Source: *PUDR*, pp 16-18.

VADODARA CITY

Best Bakery, Dabhoi Road

1 March
At least 13 dead, including Hindu employees
Best Bakery is in Hanuman Tekri, on Dabhoi Road on the outskirts of Vadodara. It is a lower-middle-class and poor

neighbourhood. Most of the residents are Hindus; there were very few Muslim families. The *basti* consists of small one-storeyed, tin roof houses and very narrow lanes. The Best Bakery was one of the few structures that had more than one storey.

Habibulla Abdul Rauf, the owner, died of natural causes tendays before the incident. He had started his bakery a few years ago, but the family shifted to this area only six months before the attack. All other Muslims staying in the area had already left their houses before the incident. Only this family stayed on because Jayantibhai Chaiwala, a tea-shop owner, sanitation contractor and an influential person of the area, had come to the house on 1st morning and assured them safety saying 'don't worry, we are there.' Eighteen-year-old Zahira Sheikh, daughter of Habibulla Abdul Rauf, told PUCL-Shanti Abhiyan:

'Nothing untoward happened during the day, but my uncle, fearing something, had told us all not to go out of the house.

'Around 8.30 at night, the mob came from Ganeshnagar side. They were shouting loudly and had swords bottles, stones, tins of petrol and kerosene, and were beating metal plates (*thalis*). There were about 200-300 men and boys. Two well-built persons were leading the mob. They were looking very fierce. I don't know their names but can recognize them if I see them. The mob was talking to us in Hindi, not Gujarati.

'When we saw all this, my uncle ran inside and locked the doors. We ran upstairs. Soon, Lal Mohammed's timber shop in front was burnt down. We had heard rumours earlier in the day that it was going to be burnt. So when it was actually burnt, we started getting really scared.

'At 8.30 p.m. itself, when Lal Mohammed's godown was burning, we rang up Panigate police station. They said they would send someone. We rang up three to four times, and each time they said someone would come. After about an hour, the police van came to the area, but the mob ran behind Lal Mohammed's godown and hid there. The police vehicle didn't come into the lane, but turned off from the main road itself. The phone wire was cut off some time at night.

'At first, they looted the bakery. The mob began pulling out all the things. Then they set fire to the room on the ground floor. We had just got fresh stocks of wood, and the room began to burn easily. We were all on the terrace, but my uncle (whose leg was hurt) went down to the first floor. My sister went with him to help him. But the mob came up, sprinkled petrol and set fire to the room. My uncle and sister got burnt in it. Firoze Pathan (a 'chacha') and his wife and children, who used to live next door, were also in their house; all of them were burnt.

'The whole night we were on the terrace, and the mob kept pelting stones at us, abusing us and trying to make us come down. Some of the people in the mob whom I could recognize were Jayanti Chaiwala and his two sons; Mahesh (Jayanti's relative); Munna, another relative; Sanjay Thakkar; Santosh Thakkar; Jagadish Rattiwala; Dinesh Bakeriwala; Shanabhai; a person known as Painter.

'In the morning, we kept pleading and asking for forgiveness (*'hum ne maafi maanga'*), but the mob, who had been joined by more people in the morning, just laughed. Jayantibhai told us to come down after throwing down our weapons. We told him we had no weapons, and swore on Allah's name. After a while, they put a ladder at the back and helped us come down. They snatched Rs 2,000 from my brother, as well as his watch. They kept beating us and pushing us, and brought us to an empty house. The mob kept yelling, *'Maaro saalon ko'*. They beat the boys more, and when the Hindu workers were trying to escape, they killed them with swords right there. They kept saying 'rape these women', and were trying to drag us (the women) into the jungle. By that time, around 11 a.m. on 2 March, the police arrived, and fire engines also arrived to put out the fire. Then the Fire Brigade brought my grandmother down from the terrace where she was still hiding.'

There were twenty-four people in Best Bakery at the time. Of these at least eleven were killed and burnt, including two small children who were hacked and burnt to death, and three Hindu workers. Many others were seriously injured.

The total property loss (buildings and bakery raw materials) is estimated as Rs 9,35,000. Damage due to vehicle loss and household goods would be another two lakhs. All that the family has got is Rs 1,250 as 'compensation' for the house and Rs 80,000 for the death of two family members, Kausar Ali and Shabira.

Source: PUCL Vadodara and Vadodara Shanti Abhiyan, Violence in Vadodara: A Report, *Vadodara, May 2002 (henceforth* PUCL*), pp 59-62.*

Kisanwadi

28 February
Mosque demolished, Muslim homes destroyed, Hindu social worker saves lives
Kisanwadi is in the eastern part of Vadodara. There are ninety-four slum pockets with approximately 10,000 families, mostly from dalit, adivasi, Muslim and other socially and educationally backward sections. The majority of the people in this area live in poor working and living conditions. The slum pockets in this area have mixed population but middle-class-housing societies in the area are clearly demarcated on communal lines.

Approximately 125 Muslim families live in Kisanwadi. All, except five or six families, living next to Hindu families, were affected by the violence and fled the area. They have been described as very decent, poor working class people.

Since 27 February, there was unease in the neighbourhood. There were rumours going around the area. On 28 February, Ramdas Pillai, a local social worker, and his wife Lakshmiben, decided that in the evening they would walk around the *basti* and assess the situation. At 5.30 p.m., one person from the neighbourhood, Nizambhai, came to Pillai's house and asked him to urgently come to his place. Ramdas Pillai went to Nizambhai's place at around 6 p.m. A lot of people had gathered around. They all decided to walk to the masjid together at 6.30 p.m. From there, they proceeded to the wedding of another Muslim family. They were all having dinner when at around 7.00 p.m., there were shouts of '*Aayaa, aayaa, aayaa*!' ('They've come!') A big mob of around 250 to 300 persons came towards the Jhanda Chowk and started climbing on the masjid. Ramdas stood in front and tried to reason with the mob. He kept telling them that whatever happened at Godhra was done by other Muslims; do not punish these people for something wrong done by others. He managed to prevent people from damaging the masjid at that time.

The mob then dispersed and started moving into the *galis* of the *basti*s. The mobs kept increasing. They had *dharias* and *talwaars*. About 500 Muslims were sheltered at Pillai's home and the home of his brother Swaminathan. Kanubhai, an auto-rickshaw driver and a friend of Pillai's, also sheltered his Muslim neighbours in his house. Among the affected persons was a woman who out of fear and panic had rushed out of her house leaving her three-month old daughter inside. Kanubhai went to the house and brought the baby safely to her mother. Suleman, one of the residents, was about to be killed by a person from the mob who was wielding a knife. Ramdas picked up the person and threw him away. An old woman was left behind when her family fled to safety. The next evening Ramdas found her alone at home and rescued her.

The mobs went repeatedly to the Muslim houses and destroyed everything. One wealthy Muslim, Siddiqbhai of Jhanda Chowk incurred a loss of around Rs 2 lakh. Another Muslim who had returned from Dubai had 15-20 *tolas* gold and cash taken away. One provision shop was looted and six tempos and eight rickshaws were burnt. On 14 March, when a PUCL team visited the area, Kisanwadi looked like a haunted neighbourhood, with broken down homes and shops, and burnt *laaris* and auto-rickshaws. At Hussaini Chowk, Jhanda Chowk and Indiranagar, all that was left of their homes were smashed TVs, glass and crockery, sewing machines, cycles and fans twisted out of shape.

The masjid/madrassa was completely razed to the ground. The people living around told the PUCL team that the mob spent two to three days to break down the masjid. The previous day they had set fire to it, but Ramdas was successful in extinguishing it. The mobs went back and attacked it a second time. The team saw remnants of gas cylinders that had been used as bombs to break down the masjid.

By 2.30 p.m. on 1 March, Ramdas was able to arrange for two tractors from his friends, Harishbhai and Mohanbhai Savalia, and a Tata Sumo from another friend. With police escort, he was able to safely reach the people to Qureshi Mohalla Jamaat Khana at Mughalwada. There was no other help from the police.

All reports spoke highly of Ramdas Pillai. Well known in the area, he is a young man of around thirty-five years, well-built and muscular. He is originally from Kochi, now three generations in Vadodara. His wife Lakshmiben is a Gujarati. Ramdas Pillai and his family have been hearing rumours of threats from various quarters. His daughter's tuition teacher told her to convey to her family that he heard a group of 10-12 men at the *paan*-shop saying 'Ramdas *ko pita do- Miyan ko bachaya.*' (Kill Ramdas—he has saved Muslims). Similarly in the vegetable market people heard some such rumours.

Aftermath: According to Ramdas Pillai, in his testimony before the Citizens' Tribunal on 8 May, more than two months after the Muslim residents of Kisanwadi were forced to flee their homes, the situation continues to be grim. Local lumpen elements are stealing whatever little is left of the Muslim homes, the doors, the iron roofs and so on, and are threatening to beat up people if they come back. The police claim they don't have enough staff to post in the area permanently.

The few arrests made were tokenistic. The accused have been seen hobnobbing as '*netas*' with the police in recent peace meetings and have been pressurizing the Muslims to withdraw their complaints.

On 4 April, P.I. Kanani took away his brother, Krishnamurthy Swaminathan on a false pretext and subsequently arrested him on charges of attempt to murder (Section 307). Police Officer J.D. Rana was heard pressurizing Muslim complainants to identify Swaminathan as a perpetrator.

The Muslim complainants kept insisting that Swaminathan, in fact, was one of those who saved them!

Wadi Taiwada, Wadi-Panigate

15 March—30 April 2002
Police brutality during combing operations and cold-blooded murder

This is a very old and prominent area of the walled city, which has a majority of Muslim households, but also quite a few Hindu families. It has always been prone to communal violence. After 28 February, women from the area formed peace committees to convince residents not to get provoked by the events taking place. The area was affected in the second and third phases of violence, starting 15 March.

On 15 March people were expecting trouble. The *arti* at the temple had been particularly aggressive and Hindu boys were roaming freely, while the police warned Muslims to stay indoors. Early evening, the streetlights suddenly went out, and acid was thrown at Kalubhai's house, right next to the police chowki. That night, around 7.30 p.m., Saiyyad Photo Studio was completely burned down. The owner, Saiyyad Masood had invested all his resources in the studio, which he set up seven years ago. As Saiyyad Masood described it: 'The police point was right next to the studio, and so was a temple. If they had wanted to, they could have prevented it . . . We rang up the police several times, even giving Hindu names because they just were not responding to any Muslims on the phone that night. They said on the phone that they were taking orders from only one side that night. Local Bajrang Dal people were certainly involved, with help from the police and outsiders. We saw elders from their houses cheering and urging the younger people to carry on with the violence and not to fear anyone.' The family named several individuals associated with the RSS.

That night, the police began combing operations. One reason for this seems to have been a rumour that the Swaminarayan Mandir in the area was going to be attacked by Muslims.

Shamsuddin Navsariwala said that he heard a senior police officer instruct his men to round up Muslims. At 10.30 p.m., fifteen to twenty policemen, all in plainclothes and wearing helmets, arrived in the Taiwada area. They were led by PI Kanani of the DCB. While the police version is that they came on a tip-off about stone-throwing in the area, residents claimed that there was stoning in a neighbouring area but not in Taiwada. They said that the combing took place in Taiwada when the police should have been deployed in nearby Rangmahal, where a masjid and Muslim homes were burnt.

Combing operations were arbitrary and brutal, and women were targetted for highly abusive treatment. The team met a number of women who had suffered in the police action. Hamida Banu Ibrahim Sheikh (40) had her right hand in plaster. The police broke four fingers. On 15th night Hamida Banu stepped out to go to the toilet, which is right behind her house. There were around fifteen policemen along with PI Kanani. 'They asked me where I was going. I told them. They would not believe me and started abusing me. I simply asked them "why are you doing that" and I got beaten badly. Had I said anything provocative, I would not have minded being beaten, but I only asked them why they were abusing me and they hit me so badly.' She had four fractures on her right hand, for which she underwent four operations at SSG Hospital. Because of the injury to her hand, Hamida Banu did not know whether she would be able to make kites again and who would fend for her family.

Nineteen-year-old Zarina had delivered hardly a month earlier. The police smashed open the house door and it fell on her back. They smashed her foot with the butt of a gun. Zarina has three small children. She pleaded with the police not to take away her husband. They hit her on the back. They took away her husband after beating him up.

Fourteen women were hit that night, including old women, all requiring medical attention. The police broke down doors of homes. They took away twenty-five to thirty men in the combing operations, after beating them up on the road for two hours. No weapons were found. The men were arrested under

Sections 307 and 436. They were also beaten heavily in the lock-up and jail and were released after seven days.

According to residents of Taiwada, from 26 April onwards, attempts were made to engineer retaliation by Muslims through provocative stone-throwing from some neighbouring Hindu localities and was coordinated by the VHP/RSS office in Pratap Rudra Hanuman Mandir. A resident, Mehndi Hussain, was injured in an acid attack.

On the night of 30 April, around 1.30 a.m., two men—Abid Ibrahimbhai Delawala (26), who worked in a cupboard factory, and Noorbhai Yaroobhai Karvania (40), a self-employed car mechanic—were killed in police firing. The police version of the incident is that the two men were shot when police fired to disperse a mob which had attacked a temple, tried to burn a State Reserve Police tent, and was indulging in throwing stones, bottles, acid bulbs, etc. Two Gujarati newspapers, *Sandesh* and *Gujarat Samachar* carried this story in their morning issue. While other mediapersons who came in response to the phone call from the locality immediately after the incident were not allowed to enter, the local VNM and DEEP networks covered it under police protection and gave out the police version.

Residents of the area, however, claim that Delawala and Karvania were shot by the police in cold blood. According to eyewitnesses Mohammad Sharif and Suleman Walibhai Tai, six persons were sitting on night vigil on the veranda of a house near the mosque. Five policemen, in uniform, including PI Parmar, quietly entered the area from the street in front of Dabhoiwala Chaal. They shouted to the men to run or be shot. Then, without any teargas firing or *lathi*-charge, they opened fire from close range, killing the two men as they tried to run away. Both were shot in the head, indicating that the police were shooting to kill.

The policemen approached the bodies of the two men to see if they were dead. They were overheard saying that their work was done, though they had to 'finish 10 of them'. About half an hour later, thirty to forty policemen arrived. When local people tried to talk to the police, they were threatening and abusive.

When the police commisioner was contacted, he asked the callers not to bother him with such small details and to get in touch with the local police. The local media was contacted, and an ambulance was called. However the police stopped them from entering the locality saying that the situation was volatile. They later tried to construct evidence of 'rioting' in the area by bringing an old autorickshaw, stones and glass bottles to the site.

Source: PUCL, pp 32-37.

TWO PERSONAL TRAGEDIES

Raja Rasul Masani, Vadodara

22 March
Muslim teacher, killed for being married to Hindu woman

The brutal murder of thirty-two-year-old Raja Rasul Masani, owner of Venus Academy, located on the first floor of Apsara Building occurred in the fresh outbreak of violence in Vadodara after 15 March. Masani was married to a Hindu Brahmin woman, and lived at Kunj Plaza, a Hindu-dominated building. The following is based on newspaper coverage of the incident.

On 28 February, a mob had attempted to set fire to Venus Academy, an English coaching class. Raja Masani was apprehensive about further attacks. On 22 March, he called his friend and former student, Bhupesh Joshi, to discuss what steps he should take. Joshi arrived within fifteen minutes. He advised him to shut down the classes and shift elsewhere for the time being. Around noon, some ten masked and armed intruders barged into the office and started abusing Masani. Joshi tried to reason with the mob, telling them that Masani was not a fundamentalist, that he was in fact married to a Hindu and should be spared. 'But they just did not listen and began attacking him,' recalled Joshi.

While one of the men attacked Joshi, accusing him of being

a saviour of Muslims, one of the assailants attacked Masani with a sword. Bleeding profusely, Masani jumped from the first floor but could not escape as he fractured his leg. The mob then rushed downstairs and kept stabbing him. Masani was declared brought dead to SSG Hospital. Joshi also jumped from the window to save his life and sustained severe injuries.

As soon as the news of Masani's death reached family members, his wife, Purvi Trivedi, along with her parents, rushed to the hospital. Shocked and inconsolable, Purvi wondered why her husband had been killed. 'He never harmed anyone. Why did they kill him?' she wailed.

People who lived across the road from the academy saw Masani jumping from the first floor. They claim that they had closed their doors immediately and therefore did not see the assailants. According to a news item (*Times of India*, Ahmedabad, 26 March 2002), the Raopura police arrested eight persons accused in the murder.

The report of the incident in *Sandesh* the next day was crude and sensational. Splashed on the first page were colour photographs of Raja Masani's bloodied face, and a photograph of his friend, Joshi, bloody and injured, sitting on the pavement below. A last page report carried the headline: 'Hindi Film Thriller Scene on Apsara Apartments' First Floor'.

Source: PUCL, pp 52-53.

Geetaben, Ahmedabad

24 March
Hindu woman killed for trying to save Muslim friend
Geetaben, a twenty-eight-year-old woman, was dragged out of her house, stripped naked and stabbed to death by a mob in the Guptanagar area of Vejalpur for trying to save her Muslim friend, Munnabhai Salim Sheikh. (Some accounts say Munna and Geetaben were husband and wife). According to news reports, the two were riding on a scooter at about 8.30 a.m. when they were attacked by a mob near her flat. The exact

sequence of events is not clear but there was a fierce exchange of words between her and the mob before Munna was set upon with swords and other sharp-edged weapons. With deep gashes on his head and body, he managed to escape to the Vejalpur police station. The police then took him to V.S. hospital.

Geetaben, in the meantime, managed to run to her flat but the mob followed. They pulled her out and when she ran, they chased her to the nearby bus stand before her cornering her. She was then stripped and repeatedly stabbed in full public view and left for dead in the middle of the street. By the time the police arrived, she was lying face down in a pool of blood.

Later, in hospital, Munna, who did not know Geetaben had been killed, told reporters, 'She was married to a South Indian. We fell in love, she divorced her husband. I don't even know where she is now.' Munna, who owns an autorickshaw, says he met her when he was a cycle-rickshaw driver and she used to sell idlis at Teen Darwaza. He said he would go out in search of her as soon as he was released. The doctors said Munna was in a state of delirium.[19] Two BJP leades have been arrested in the Geetaben case.[20]

Notes

1   Shefali Nautiyal, 'Old man in the mob said *Bhag Ja* and I ran,' *Indian Express*, 23 March 2002.

2   Human Rights Watch, *'We Have No Orders to Save You': State Complicity and Participation in Communal Violence in Gujarat*, New York, April 2002 (henceforth *HRW*), p 15.

3   Asif Daud Karbhari, Mariumbibi Hassanbhai, Fatimappa and many others to Sahrwaru, pp. 5-6; Shefali Nautiyal, *op cit*.

4   Radha Sharma and Sanjay Pandey, 'Mob almost wipes out locality, returns for more,' *Times of India*, 2 March 2002.

5   *Times of India*, 28 May 2002, 'Once again, police blame victims,' *Indian Express*, 4 June 2002.

6   Joydeep Ray, 'Bajrang Dal hand in Naroda killings: Cops,' *Indian Express*, 5 March 2002; 'Are VHP/BJP workers the culprits,' *Times of India*, 4 March 2002.

7 'Kausar Bano case sees some action,' *Times of India*, (Ahmedabad) 16 May 2002.

8 FIR reproduced in *GG*, pp. 27-28.

9 'An ex-MP's murder tells the tale,' *Indian Express*, 1 March 2002.

10 'No let up in Gujarat carnage,' *Hindustan Times*, 2 March 2002; *Times of India*, 2 March 2002.

11 'Jafri blamed for his murder,' *Indian Express*, 4 June 2002.

12 Eyewitnesses quoted in *GG*, pp 29-31; Human Rights Watch, pp 18-20.

13 Shramana Ganguly, 'Ex-MP's building looks like a crematorium after attack,' *Asian Age*, 3 March 2002.

14 Eyewitnesses quoted in *GG*, pp. 29-31.

15 Peoples Union for Democratic Rights, *'Maaro! Kaapo! Baalo!'*: *State, Society and Communalism in Gujarat*, New Delhi, May 2002, (henceforth *PUDR*), p 38.

16 Milind Ghatwai and Rohit Bhan, 'You can come back to your homes *only* if you . . .,' *Indian Express*, 6 May 2002.

17 'Bail to Visnagar carnage accused challenged,' *Times of India* (Ahmedabad), 22 July 2002.

18 Darshan Desai, 'Majority Rules: Sardarpura,' *Indian Express* (Ahmedabad), 7 April 2002.

19 Milind Ghatwai and Rohit Bhan, *op.cit.*

20 'Two BJP leaders held for Geetaben's murder,' *Indian Express* (Ahmedabad), 27 March 2002; 'Woman stripped, stabbed to death for having Muslim friend,' *Indian Express*, 27 March 2002; 'Worst not over for victim: he waits for wife long dead,' *Indian Express*, 29 March 2002.

5

When Guardians Betray
The Role of the Police in Gujarat

Teesta Setalvad

One of the most disturbing aspects of the large-scale anti-Muslim violence that convulsed Gujarat after 27 February is the manner in which the police force willfully abandoned the state and its citizens to the depredations of homicidal mobs.

When VHP and Bajrang Dal activists taunted Muslims with the cry '*Yeh andar ki baat hai, Police hamare saath hai* (It's an open secret/the police is on our side)', this was no empty boast. For the cancer of communalization—which has been spreading within the police forces throughout India for the past two and a half decades—has, in Gujarat, become full blown and malignant. Indeed, the ease and speed with which some 2,000 Muslims were killed and the thoroughness with which Muslim businesses were destroyed with the police force barely lifting a finger suggests the state is in the terminal stage of this disease.

In Gujarat, the utter failure of the law and order machinery to protect lives and property when these were under obvious and direct threat is, first and foremost, an extreme example of the complete politicization of a police force that functions as per the dictates of the ideology of the government in power and not on constitutional principles of equality and non-discrimination. Second, it is not simply the influence of politicians on policemen or policewomen that is the problem here but the kind of hate politics that the party in power believes in.

Gujarat 2002 provides horrific proof, if any were still needed, of the systematic infusion of hate politics in the minds of some police officials from the top echelons who are now wedded to principles that are hostile to the rule of law. Paralysis and inaction at best, and active connivance and brutality at worst— including the shooting of young men and even minors, often at point blank range[1]—were on full display in Gujarat right from 28 February until the middle of May.[2] Since then, some measures, cosmetic and otherwise, have been undertaken to 'bring things under control' but the underlying problem of politicization and bias remains.

Ever since the BJP rode to power with a two-thirds majority in Gujarat in 1998, the Sangh Parivar has undertaken careful and methodical attempts to infiltrate a police force that functions within a colonial-era structure that is susceptible to political interference and influence. Infiltration has taken place at several levels. The first is by placing at the helm officers who are either too weak or are politically malleable. Equally important has been the use of hardline RSS, VHP and Bajrang Dal cadres— backed by elected BJP representatives—directly to subvert and influence the functioning of the police.[3] Where communalization, infiltration and subversion from within have not worked, the BJP government has simply used its administrative powers to ensure compliance. During the killings of 2002, police officers who remained true to their constitutional duty and defended Muslim citizens under attack were invariably shunted out or punished.[4] 'According to the grapevine in Indian Police Service circles', the *Times of India* reported, '27 transfers announced by the government had targetted officers who had not only controlled the riots but also booked cases against influential persons close to the current political establishment.'[5]

Acts of Omission and Commission

When violence of such an unprecedented scale and brutality swept Gujarat and affected as many as nineteen of the state's twenty-four districts for nearly three months, the first question this raises is the quality of police intelligence. But the failure of the police to anticipate the carnage was also a function of its inability to look at the VHP and Bajrang Dal as organizations inimical to law and order. In the weeks and months that preceded Godhra and the violence which followed, the police simply ignored the incendiary implications of the poisonous pamphlets being circulated by the Sangh Parivar, the hate speeches its leaders were delivering around the state and the distribution of trishuls and other weapons to the Hindutva organization's rank and file.

Indian law—be it the Arms Act, the Unlawful Practices Act or the Police Act—is clear on the issue of organizations that strike terror among people and those that are armed. Carrying of swords 'capable of being used for carrying out physical violence' is prohibited under section 37 of the Bombay Police Act.[6] Yet the police has allowed this arming and fatal use of swords unchecked. The VHP and Bajrang Dal, through *trishul dikhsa samarohs,* have been distributing small sharp knives that can be used to kill disguised as trishuls. They proudly announce to the press that they conduct arms training for young children and women.[7] In Gujarat this arms distribution has assumed astronomical proportions. Distribution of trishuls, swords and other arms openly continued until at least the end of March, 2002. Police officers made seizures in Bejalpur, Shahpur, Maninagar, Vatwa and Kalupur only by mid-April whereas state intelligence ought to have been of informed them and acted on this earlier. VHP joint secretary Jaideep Patel has publicly admitted that swords and trishuls are regularly distributed. 'We have been distributing these weapons since 1985—*trishul diksha samarohs* and Bharatiya Abhiyans have been held. Nobody has objected, not even the police.'

By noon of 27 February when the full extent of the Godhra tragedy had become evident, the Gujarat police should have started taking precautions to prevent the eruption of revenge attacks by the VHP and Bajrang Dal. Especially since Ahmedabad police commissioner P.C. Pande had advised against the bodies of the Godhra victims being brought to Ahmedabad and then taken out in a procession, presumably because he knew that would allow the VHP to inflame the situation.[8] That evening, the VHP made its intentions apparent with its belligerent call for a 'Gujarat Bandh' on the 28th. Since a similar state-wide bandh by the VHP had led to the widespread destruction of Muslim property in August 2000,[9] the police should have anticipated trouble. Throughout India, it is a standard practice for the authorities to make preventive arrests of habitual trouble-makers ('Bad Characters' in police parlance) before any major event when violence is anticipated. In Gujarat, however, by the evening of 27 February only two men—Mohammed Ismail Jalaluddin and Fateh Mohammed who were picked up at Astodia in the night for shouting slogans—were taken into preventive custody in the sensitive areas of Ahmedabad.

Preventive arrests on 27 February after the Godhra incident in Ahmedabad

Police Station	Arrests
Naroda	0
Gomtipur	0
Shaherkotda	0
Vejalpur	0
Kalupur	0
Gaekwad Haveli	0
Eliss Bridge	0
Navrangpura	0
Naranpura	0
Ghatlodia	0
Astodia	2

Source: Official police figures obtained by the author. First published in Genocide Gujarat 2002, *Communalism Combat, March-April 2002, p 126.*

Given the situation on the ground, it was disingenuous for director-general of police (DGP), Gujarat, K. Chakravarty to claim—as he did on Doordarshan news that evening—that 'the entire state police machinery has been put on red alert . . . The state reserve battalions have been positioned in all the communally-sensitive areas and instructions have been given to all the SPs and the commissioners to take strict action against all anti–social elements and such action is already is in progress.'[10] Finally, on the night of 27 February some companies of the State Reserve Police (SRP) were hustled into action. One was sent to Godhra from SRP Group-III Naroda, and another to Ahmedabad rural. Some more companies from Ghodasar were moved into parts of Ahmedabad by early morning. But they were split into groups of four or five jawans each, which rendered them largely ineffective against the rampaging mobs which took to the streets on the morning of 28 February.

The supposed inadequacy of forces is often touted as an excuse by serving police officers who fail in their primary duty. 'The police tried their best, but they couldn't stop the mobs. They were grossly outnumbered when the mobs grew,' claimed P.C. Pande.[11] However, in more than one place and on more than one occasion, where good officers held out against the pressure, the same small deployment was enough to act decisively and control the situation.[12] In the vast majority of cases, unfortunately, the police either did not act or acted on the side of the mob.

On the morning of 28 February at around 10.00 a.m., the bodies of those burned alive in coach S-6 of the Sabarmati Express were brought to the Sola Civil Hospital in Ahmedabad, kept there for several hours as religious-political incantations and speeches were made suggesting revenge and retribution. Influential and aggressive leaders of the VHP and BJP were present. The police only watched these developments. The same morning, violence broke out throughout the city.

Despite the fact that the minority community was being attacked by huge and well-armed mobs, Muslims seem to have been the main target of police firing. Of the forty people killed in police firing at Morarji Chowk and Charodia Chowk in Ahmedabad on 28 February all were Muslims.[13]

Who died in police firing?

On 2 May, law minister Arun Jaitley told Parliament it was not true Muslims had been targetted by the Gujarat government. At the same time, he refused to provide a religion-wise breakdown of those killed in police firing.

He had good reasons not to do so.

For on the same day, the police in Ahmedabad was admitting it had killed more Muslims than Hindus in its ostensible attempts to stop what was clearly mob violence directed against Muslims. 'Of the 184 people who died in police firing since the violence began, 104 are Muslims, says a report drafted by Gujarat Police', Vinay Menon of the *Hindustan Times* reported ('Cops admit killing more Muslims', 3 May 2002). 'The statistic substantiates the allegation . . . that not only did the local police not do anything to stop the Hindu mobs; they actually turned their guns on the helpless Muslim victims'.

For example, on 28 February, 40 men shot dead near the Bapunagar police station in Ahmedabad were all Muslims, most shot in the head and chest. They had been defending themselves from a 3000-strong mob. (Janyala Sreenivas, 'Who shot them point blank?', *Indian Express*, 9 April 2002).

Though the number of Muslims and Hindus killed in police firing has been collated by the Gujarat government, noted Menon, this has so far not been released. 'Coming out with the truth would only inflame the situation, it is feared'. The government argues that in the first 72 hours of violence, more Hindus were killed in police firing. State home minister Gordhan Zadaphia told Menon: 'I have data that shows more Hindus were killed in police firing till March 3, but it cannot be disclosed.'

By the third week of May, 75 of the 105 people killed by police firing in Ahmedabad were Muslims. 'But the real numbers,' said Raveen Thukral, 'are probably likely to be far larger: major manipulations are alleged to have been done at the stage of carrying out autopsies.' ('The missing are dead, Gujarat toll may go up,' *Hindustan Times*, 24 May 2002).

Elsewhere in the city, the pattern was similar. Abdul Aziz, a resident of Panna Lal ki Chali, told Human Rights Watch:

On the 28th afternoon at 3 p.m., my younger brother was returning from work. The police said that a curfew was in place. A crowd gathered to attack. The police was leading the crowd. They were looting and the people followed, looting and burning behind them. The crowd was shouting, 'Go to Pakistan. If you want to stay here become Hindu'. The police very clearly aimed at my brother and fired at him. He was twenty-three years old . . .'[14]

In rural areas, the pattern does not appear to have been very different. The *Times of India* reported that an 'eleven-year-old girl in Dudhia village was hit on the head by a bullet in police firing and was now recuperating at the SSG hospital, Vadodara. A fourteen-year-old was killed in police firing at Kisanwadi. The bullet went through his chest. In Halol, a bullet ricocheted from a wall on a veranda of a one-storied-house, injuring a two-and-a-half-year old.'[15] The People's Union for Civil Liberties, Vadodara/Shanti Abhiyan report on the violence in Vadodara notes that the 'overwhelming majority of those injured in police firing were Muslims.'[16]

However, in areas like Chamanpura and Naroda, where police firing could have dispersed the attacking mobs and saved hundreds of Muslim lives, officers and constables were passive bystanders. At least one officer, inspector K.K. Mysorewala, is said by survivors to have fired teargas shells at those trying to flee the mobs.[17] In other localities too, policemen literally handed Muslims over to the mobs. 'Fatima Bi was one of hundreds who tried to hide in the State Transport staff colony,' Praveen Swami reported from Ahmedabad. 'The police pushed us out of there,' she says, 'saying it was our night to die.' The people who lived in the colony were giving the mob tyres and petrol to burn people with. While Fatima Bi found a place to hide, others were less lucky. She watched as her pregnant friend, Saliya Behn, had her belly slit, and was then set on fire along with her children, three-year-old Muskan and six-month-old Subhan. Her badly injured son Khwaja Husain now sits in the Shah Alam refugee camp, unable to talk.[18]

Prompt and effective action by the police goes a long way in controlling a situation that could otherwise go completely out of hand. 'No riot can continue for more than 24 hours unless the State wants it to continue,' Vibhuti Narain Rai, a senior serving IPS officer of the Uttar Pradesh cadre has pointed out.[19] Even where individual policemen or officers have their individual biases, it is only when the top political and police leadership tolerate and encourage these prejudices that the police force as a whole colludes in the violation of law. Ahmedabad's police commissioner conveniently turned this fact upside down. In an interview on 28 February on *Star News*, he said: 'These people also, they somehow get carried away by the overall general sentiment. That's the whole trouble. The police is equally influenced by the overall general sentiments.'[20] What Pande was doing, in effect, was giving sanction to his policemen to act according to 'sentiment' rather than to stringently enforce the law. Harsh Mander, the Indian Administrative Service (IAS) officer who resigned in disgust at the complicity of the State in the violence, has dismissed excuses like Pande's as 'a thin and disgraceful alibi . . . The same forces have been known to act with impartiality and courage when led by officers of professionalism and integrity. The failure is clearly of the leadership of the police and civil services, not of the subordinate men and women in khaki who are trained to obey their orders.'[21]

Where had all the soldiers gone?
Sujan Dutta

March 1: Gujarat today is the Indian soldier's nightmare come true: while he is eyeball-to-eyeball at the border, there is no one to watch his back. Caught in the classic security conundrum—a war on two fronts—the army is taking the flak for delayed action. After 36 hours of bloodletting, the first of the troops flown into Ahmedabad, Rajkot and Vadodara began moving into riot-torn localities at 11 this morning. They had to be flown from reserves' stations in south India because the bulk of the forces is on the border. On the face of it, the delayed reaction is a monumental failure of the Army in Gujarat . . .

Fact is: by 28 February afternoon, the southern command in Pune, liasing with the 11 Division headquarters in Gandhinagar, had contingency plans ready, well before a formal request was made by the Gujarat government. Even so, the first request made by the Gujarat government in the evening—after a full day during which frenzied VHP-led mobs ran amok—was for the army to be put on 'stand-by'. It was later at night, nearly an hour after the Cabinet Committee on Security had met, that the decision was taken to deploy the army.

But it still took about 12 hours for the army to move into Ahmedabad ... At the defence headquarters in New Delhi, the top brass is blaming the Gujarat government ... 'Our forces are as familiar with the state as can be but there is little we can do blindfolded,' said an officer ...

From midnight last night, after the defence ministry issued orders to bring reserves into Gujarat, the air force has flown several sorties on 16 aircraft—four Ilyushin 76s and 12 Antonov-32s from Andhra Pradesh, Karnataka, Maharashtra and Tamil Nadu ... Defence minister George Fernandes said that two brigades of the army—roughly 4,000 troops—have moved into Ahmedabad, Rajkot and Vadodara. The last of the sorties were still being flown early this evening.

The immediate decision taken at army HQ was not to bring troops from the front. Since most of the formations in Gujarat have sent their men to the borders, the troops brought in from south India could not move with their own vehicles ...

By 2.30 a.m., the first planeloads of troops were in Ahmedabad. At army HQ, it was taken for granted that the troops will fan out by dawn. But that was not to be. The troops flown in were unfamiliar with territory, did not have maps, guides and vehicles, and asked the civil administration for 65 vehicles. By law, the troops also had to be accompanied by magistrates. If they had to open fire, it would be only with the permission of the magistrates. There weren't enough magistrates available.

Asked why the army needed such elaborate preparations in cities where rioters were running amok, official sources said the army was going 'by the book'. Meaning the army was going step by step: (a) Mapping the trouble-torn area, (b) sending out reconnaissance patrols, (c) conducting flag marches, (d) Getting magistrates to accompany them, and (e) combing/taking action as the situation demands. For nearly nine hours since the first troops landed and till 11.30 a.m. this morning when 12 columns—between 70 and 90 troopers make up a

186 *Gujarat: The Making of a Tragedy*

column—finally began the flag marches, the army was in Gujarat, ready, to move in, but did not have the wherewithal. Those nine hours will have made the difference to over hundred lives.

Source: Telegraph, 2 March 2002.

Several judicial commission reports on communal riots have indicted the police for partisan conduct[22] and also laid down fairly stringent guidelines for police functioning in a communally sensitive situation. Justice D.P. Madon first enlisted these in his eight-volume report on the Bombay-Bhiwandi-Jalgaon riots.[23] Countrywide, these observations and recommendations by senior judicial officers to *pre-empt* future conflagrations have been observed in their breach.

As per guidelines laid down in the Police Manual of the Bombay Police Act, the police did not contact religious and community leaders to make appeals for peace following Godhra. M.M. Mehta, Ahmedabad's former commissioner of police, who won the National Citizen's Award for his handling of riots in Vadodara many years ago, told *Frontline*, 'The city [Ahmedabad], like other communally-sensitive areas, has a well-established preventive drill to contain potential riots. The director-general of police, the additional director-general in charge of intelligence, the commissioner of police, the home secretary, the chief secretary and the home minister or the chief minister meet to discuss what must be done to deal with the situation'. Each police station carries out preventive arrests, curfew is imposed and the deputy commissioners of police meet their commissioner regularly to review developments, he added.[24]

In Gujarat 2002, not only were such standard guidelines ignored but a new low was set by the presence of senior cabinet ministers in police control rooms who, presumably, directed the police not to act even as mass killings were engineered in thirty different locations all over the state. Gujarat state health minister Ashok Bhatt—who, incidentally, faces a criminal charge of murdering a police head-constable on 22 April 1985 at Khadia in Ahmedabad—was in the police control room (PCR) at the Ahmedabad police commissionerate in Shahibaug for more than three hours on 28 February. And in the state police control room at Gandhinagar, the Gujarat urban development minister, I.K. Jadeja, considered Modi's right-hand man, parked himself for four hours beginning 11.00 a.m.[25] One of the critical messages received by the Ahmedabad control room while minister Ashok Bhatt sat there was that his son, Bhushan Bhatt, a local BJP councillor, had been mobbed by a group at Bhandari-ni-Pol in Gaekwad Haveli area because he was seen leading and guiding a mob. The minister is reported to have instructed the staff to send forces there immediately to rescue his son.[26]

In a situation of crisis, the control room is a critical area of operation since this is one place where all the detailed information sent to and fro from various locations is received and responded to. The officer-in-charge of the control room is always kept informed on wireless about what is happening. It is critical at this time that the police are left uninterrupted and undisturbed to do their job. Professionally. Given the track record of the BJP, especially at a time when an attempt is being made to engineer communal polarization, 'instructions' or 'orders' from politicians who directly or indirectly are playing a part in the violence could only be detrimental to the cause of law enforcement. A senior police officer was quoted by *Outlook* as saying: 'During the initial days of the riot, SPs at the district level were contacted by ministers and told not to fire at Hindus.' 'As the riots unfolded', he added, 'it was not unusual for ministers to visit the districts and demand the release of arrested party workers.'[27]

Is the presence of senior ministers in police control rooms the 'smoking gun' which explains why desperate calls for help made by the Muslim victims on 28 February and 1 March went unheeded? The whole country now knows of the hundreds of futile telephone calls Ehsan Jafri made from his Chamanpura residence[28] but victims from many of the worst-affected areas uniformly testified to being completely unable to contact senior policemen.[29] In Rajkot, police chief Upendra Singh switched off his mobile and was nowhere to be found. 'With their chief out of sight', the *Times of India* reported, 'the local police let matters slide.'[30] The specific message given by the top political leadership to senior policemen was that 'minimum action should be taken against mobs and offenders', that there should be a 'minimum response and action on panic calls from citizens' and most of all, that the armed mobs be left to do their business and complaints should not be registered or should be doctored. During the first two days of violence, there were a number of cases of the police faithfully following these instructions:

• A few hundred calls from Naroda Gaon and Naroda Patiya were made to P.C. Pande and even DGP, Gandhinagar, on 28 February but no help was forthcoming. K.K. Mysorewala, police inspector, Naroda police station, who is indicted by several eyewitness accounts, told the *Aaj Tak* television channel on 2 March: '*Subah ko 11 baje se le kar shaam ke 7-8 baje tak poora danga raha. 15-20,000 tak ki tadat mein yeh aadmi log yahan par aaye the . . . police was here, police bhi yahan thi. Firing bhi kiya hua hai, tear gas bhi chode hain. Mob aisa tha ki woh control kisi se na ho paya. Aisa bada mob tha.*' ('The rioting continued from 11 in the morning to 7-8 in the evening. There were about 15-20,000 people here . . . police was here, the police was also here. Firing was done and teargas shells were also exploded—the mob was such that it could not be controlled by anyone. It was such a big mob.') However, Amina Aapa of Hussain Nagar, Naroda Patiya, a survivor of the massacre, told *Communalism Combat*, 'The PI, K.K. Mysorewala is responsible for the massacre. He burst teargas shells at us when we were running towards him for protection. When approached for help, he replied, "*Jao, mera to upar se order hai* (Go away, I have orders from above)".'[31]

• This was also the time the Naroda Patiya massacre began in which, by the end of the day, over ninety-one Muslims had been torched. There are at least fifteen reported cases of gang-rape of girls and women. Over two dozen survivors from Naroda Gaon and Naroda Patiya confirmed that they had made over a hundred distress calls to Pande. They say his mobile was permanently switched off. There was a similar callous response from most of the DCPs and additional CPs, except Tandon, who finally helped the rest of the Naroda survivors to safety in the dead of the night. Had he not done so, the massacre would have continued and the numbers lost would have been much higher.

- There were several calls from the Gulberg Society, Chamanpura, where former Congress MP Ehsan Jafri was pleading for help in the face of a mob that, in the words of Inspector Erda, was '20-22,000 strong'.[32] He kept calling the control room until he was charred to death along with sixty-five of his relatives, neighbours and persons from neighbouring tenements who had come to his home for shelter. Police officials, speaking anonymously, confirmed that Jafri had made frantic telephone calls to the director-general of police, the police commissioner, the chief secretary, the additional chief secretary (home) and others. Three mobile vans of the city police were on hand around Jafri's house but did not intervene. Sources within the police confirmed that the MP fired *in* the air in a desperate last-ditch attempt at self-defence when he had utterly failed to get police assistance. At that point, the marauders broke into his house, and among other inhuman deeds, quartered him and burned him alive. At least eight girls and women were stripped and raped during the massacre at Gulberg society. It was only the Rapid Action Force (RAF) of the central government that intervened when it was far too late, around 5.00 p.m.

- The police could not or did not respond to pleas to protect a retired and a sitting judge of the Ahmedabad high court (Justice Akbar Divecha and Justice M.H. Kadri) compelling them to seek army protection for their safety. None less than the chief justice of the Gujarat High Court told the judges not to rely on the police.[33]

- The state police allowed huge mobs on the Ahmedabad-

Modasa highway (where sixty-five persons fleeing their village in two tempos were burnt alive; there is a lone survivor[34]), and the Baroda-Godhra route (where over twenty-five large factories and farm lands were burnt in broad daylight). Havoc was wreaked by organized mobs and their motorcycle pilots armed with mobile phones for coordination. These motorcycles (especially on the Godhra-Modasa route through Panchmahals district) would track fleeing families and villagers after which a mob would descend upon them, rape, brutalize, hack and kill. There was no patrolling of the highways, which displays the utter indifference of the state police to the activities of the BJP, RSS, VHP and Bajrang Dal.

- In the Baroda BEST Bakery Case, policemen simply drove past the road on which the Muslim-owned bakery is located, totally unmindful of the huge mob that had encircled the building on the night of 1 March at 9.30 p.m. The attack from the mob had begun at 8 p.m. 'At 8.00 p.m. itself, when Lal Mohammed's godown (nearby) was burning, we rang up Panigate police station. They said they would send someone,' a survivor later told the PUCL, Vadodara and Shanti Abhiyan fact-finding team 'We rang up 3-4 times and each time they said someone would come. After about an hour, the police van came to the area, but the mob ran behind Lal Mohammed's godown and hid there. The police vehicle didn't come into the lane, but turned off from the main road itself. The phone wire was cut off some time at night.' [35] In all, fourteen persons including women and children and three Hindu workers were burned alive there. The police, by failing to intervene even as they drove past, are guilty of complicity in the massacre.

- The Panchmahals police[36] were party and privy to the burning alive and hacking of villagers. The police post at Pandharvada village did nothing to stop the killings. The Dalol and the Mehsana police were also guilty of the same misconduct when they failed to prevent massacres like the one at Sardarpura; similarly in Anand district and Kheda district (where massacres have taken place) the police presence was no help.[37]

Police role in Vadodara

Of the more than 1,300 incidents of violence or attempted violence in the city for which PUCL-Vadodara and Shanti Abhiyan have information till mid-May, the following is the profile of police involvement:

Police absent at time of attack:	814
Police informed but inactive:	397
No response from police:	60
Police present and actively involved:	25
Police prevented incident:	27

Source: People's Union for Civil Liberties, Vadodara, and Vadodara Shanti Abhiyan, *Violence in Vadodara: A Report*, Vadodara, May 2002, pp 132-135.

From major incidents like killings to 'minor' incidents like looting and the destruction of Muslim shrines, the complicity of the police throughout the state was all-pervasive. Manas Dasgupta, Ahmedabad correspondent of the *Hindu*, wrote: 'In many places, shops were looted and set afire right under the nose of the policemen and they even collected a part of the booty. Even as the hooligans were breaking a small mausoleum in the middle of a road barely a few metres away from the police commissioner's office, the police vehicles passing by, not only did not bother to intervene, the police actually gestured to the hooligans to go ahead. There had been at least fifteen incidents of damaging and destroying minority places of worship which were overnight converted into "temples" with the police remaining a mute spectator.'[38] In the Khokhra-Mahemdavad area of Ahmedabd, sub-inspector N.A. Modi was seen by an NGO activist allowing a mob to take diesel out of his police jeep on 1 March. The mob then used his diesel to set fire to some huts.[39]

The partisan, communal role of the Gujarat police continued long after the first spate of brutal massacres. In Vadodara, brutal treatment of Muslim women by the city police continued until early May 2002.[40]

Women not spared by police
Jahnavi Contractor

Vadodara: Noorbibi Rasul, fifty-five, staying at Kagdachal in Bawamanpura, was attacked on 19 April at 10.30 p.m. by lathi-wielding cops—all of them drunk, spewing abusive language and hitting women on the chest, buttocks, thighs, hands and legs. Twelve women from the area filed complaints against the policemen even as they had to undergo medical treatment. Among those injured was an eight-month pregnant woman. 'The cops abused her and said "let's kill them, so there's less trouble later",' alleged one of the victims in her complaint.

When Sahiyar, a women's organization, complained to the Delhi-based delegation of the National Commission for Women, the city police commissioner promised an inquiry. Sources say that joint commissioner P.C Thakur was entrusted the job of conducting an inquiry and give a report on the allegations. 'The inquiry is done, yet no action has been taken against the accused. Instead, they are continuing to abuse women and hitting them with lathis—all this despite the fact that it is completely illegal to do so,' says Jahan Ara of Sahiyar, which is documenting the police excesses.

'Legally, no policeman can lathi-charge women, nor can they enter the homes of women at night and abuse them. They are supposed to use women police to do so. But they have not done so in any of their "late night combing" operations,' says Trupti Shah of Sahiyar, a fact corroborated by the victims. 'These "late night combing operations" are nothing but ways to abuse women and threaten them so that the men in the house come out and later they can be arrested and lathi-charged,' says Bilkis, one of the victims.

At Husaini Chawl, the police personnel did not spare eighteen-year-old Hamidabanu who was crying as her father and uncles were being beaten and taken away. 'They ransacked the house and damaged property and kept shouting abuses,' she said, while showing her injuries to this correspondent.

Source: Times of India (Ahmedabad), 3 May 2002

According to PUCL, Vadodara and Shanti Abhiyan, police 'combing operations' in Vadodara were almost exclusively aimed at Muslim areas. 'The police often acted with great brutality, beating people (resulting in serious injuries, including multiple fractures), destroying property, issuing threats and making arbitrary arrests under a range of charges including Section 307 (attempt to murder). Since the men were often hiding away from their homes—out of fear of vindictive police action— when combing took place, women bore the brunt of police repression. They were subjected to verbal abuse of a highly sexualized nature and often mercilessly beaten. Even pregnant women were brutally beaten; indeed, they seem to have attracted special attention from the police, and in many cases, the beating was accompanied by statements such as "Let it die before it is born" . . . People have lost all faith in the police after their traumatic experiences in so-called combing operations and the cynical and persistent denial of justice.' [41]

Police conduct throughout the state, simply failed to inspire confidence among the affected even after the first round of brutalities. In the third week of March, Muslim women who had gathered for majlis were the victims of unprovoked firing by the police. 'All the women had gathered for majlis—a ceremony before Muharram which is attended by women only' Mumtaz told the *Indian Express*. "We were returning home when we saw smoke around Navapura area . . . the women came outside to check what was happening when suddenly, police personnel barged inside our homes and started firing directly at the women," she alleged. The eighteen-year-old Mumtaz Bano Darbar, a physically challenged girl, escaped death, though a police bullet hurt her. "They didn't even throw teargas shells or lathi-charge first," claims Sherbano Abbas Bukhari, an eighteen-year-old girl who was shot in the chest. "The policewala was only five metres away when he fired directly at me", sobs Sherbano, who is in a very critical condition.' [42]

On the eve of Prime Minister Vajpayee's visit to Ahmedabad, on 3 April the police were at the forefront of the assault against minority sections of the population in the curfew-ridden parts of Ahmedabad. The police, led by inspector S.D. Sharma, in the presence of Mr Parmar of the Ahmedabad collectorate, led a violent attack on the 750 refugees of the Suleiman Roza Relief Camp (behind Nutan Mills), Saraspur and actually shot two persons, Pirujbhai Mohammad Sheikh (30) and Khatoonbi Sharfuddin Saiyed (45).[43] As a result, the 750-strong camp was violently wound up. Advocate Nizam was shot dead by the police inside his home on 3 April and Dr Ishaq Sheikh, vice-president of the Al-Ameen Garib Niwas Hospital, was assaulted violently by the police. On 14 April two more persons were shot dead by the police at Dariapur as they were being attacked by a violent mob. All in all, former Mumbai police commissioner Julio Ribeiro was not off the mark when he said that the police, and indeed the Indian State, 'abdicated their responsibility to defend every citizen irrespective of his or her caste and creed.' The carnage in Gujarat, he told a meeting of Parliament's Standing Committee on Home Affairs in April, has again exposed the police force and its tendency to follow the line of least resistance to please the politicians. After every riot the same facts emerge: the police, apart from a few exceptions, toe the line of their political masters, forgetting everything they learnt in the academy. 'The root cause of the police abdicating their responsibility lies in the politicization of the police force across the country, caused by misuse of the power of appointment and transfers by the politicians,' he said.[44]

Punishing the Good Cops

Not satisfied with ensuring that the police abandoned Gujarat's Muslim citizens during the worst of the violence, the Narendra Modi government took its complicity in the genocide one step further by punishing those police officers who had refused to obey the 'hands off' diktat and had arrested VHP leaders or had dared to name them in FIRs. On 24 March 2002, a total of twenty-seven senior police officers were transferred and shifted in what BJP leaders said was 'part of a larger process of routine transfers which governments frequently undertake'.[45]

One day before the transfers were announced, Gujarat CM Narendra Modi convened a meeting between senior police officers, ministers and BJP MLAs from Ahmedabad to discuss the law and order situation. 'I was ashamed to attend the meeting,' a senior officer told the *Asian Age* later. 'The BJP ministers and MLAs were talking as if they were addressing a Hindutva *sammelan*. They kept on referring to Hindus as "us" and Muslims as "them". And our top bosses, instead of being stern, were looking for political guidance. In this situation, to expect Gujarat to return to normalcy is a dream,' he was quoted as saying.[46] At the meeting, the then police commissioner, P.C. Pande, is said to have pleaded with Modi to be 'allowed' to take action against VHP and Bajrang Dal activists, a plea some other officers found 'shocking'. 'Under the provisions of the Criminal Procedur Code, the police is empowered to act autonomously and they do not need the state government's guidance and permission to act. It is demoralizing to see our boss pleading for permission in this manner when hundreds of Hindus and Muslims have been dying in the state in a politically-motivated communal frenzy,' an officer said.[47]

Among the twenty-seven were five senior officers who were among the very few police chiefs in the state who actually ensured the VHP-led mobs were dispersed and unable to carry out any violence. These were Kutch SP Vivek Srivastava, Ahmedabad DCP Praveen Gondia, Bhavnagar SP Rahul Sharma, Banaskantha SP Himanshu Bhatt and Bharuch SP M.D. Antani. Apprehending that the transfer of four officers who had fulfilled their obligation to the Constitution would demoralize the police force, Gujarat's director-general of police, A.K. Chakravarty—who until then had remained a mute spectator to the complicity of his force in the violence—finally broke ranks and dashed off a protest note to additional chief secretary, Ashok Narayan.[48] But his protest was to no avail.

Vivek Srivastava, the SP of Kutch, had offended the BJP government because he had arrested local VHP leaders for their role in an attempted attack on Muslims in the area. Now, he has been shunted out to the Prohibition commissionerate of the

Gujarat police in Ahmedabad. One week after he was transferred, violence broke out in the Anjar town, the first incident there since Godhra.[49]

When the rest of Gujarat went up in flames, Srivastava ensured Kutch remained peaceful. Not one death was reported, nor was there any major case of arson or damage to property. On 1 March he ordered the arrests of Nakhtarana taluka VHP president Vasant Patel and home guard commandant Akshay Thakkar, also an active VHP member. Thakkar had helped a mob lock up six persons inside a *dargah* in Nakhtarana. 'They were about to be attacked with swords and set on fire, but they managed to break open the door and flee. We had information on who was behind the attack, and we picked up the commandant and a Shiv Sena leader,' police sources told the *Indian Express*. After a shop was burnt down and a dargah damaged, Srivastava identified the culprits and made them pay for the reconstruction. The police also foiled the attempts of a mob which tried to stir up things in Angia village. The police stepped in again when VHP activists attacked a dargah in Bhimsar village a few days later.

Srivastava held his ground despite being badgered by phone calls from the minister of state for home, Gordhanbhai Zadaphia, and other ministers. The chief minister's office also made two calls. When contacted by the *Indian Express*, Zadaphia admitted that he had called up Srivastava twice. 'I thought the leaders who were arrested were innocent and had been picked up by mistake,' said the minister. 'I did my job. As a police officer, I did whatever was required of me to keep law and order . . . The mobs tried everything at hand—petrol bombs, swords . . . But we foiled them. This must have upset some people,' Srivastava was quoted as saying.[50]

In the case of Praveen Gondia, DCP Zone IV, Ahmedabad city, his 'crime' was to register FIRs against prominent Sangh Parivar leaders like BJP MLA Mayaben Kodnani and VHP general secretary Jaideep Patel for their role in the Naroda Patiya massacres.[51] He was transferred to Civil Defence. Banaskantha SP Himanshu Bhatt had suspended a sub-inspector who let a mob plunder Muslim homes in a village in the district. The sub-inspector is close to several BJP and VHP leaders and soon the chief minister's office began putting pressure on Bhatt, who was eventually shunted out to a desk job in the state intelligence bureau.[52] Bharuch SP Manoj Antani, who came down fast and hard on rioters all across the communally-sensitive district, was transferred as SP, Narmada, a less important, smaller district.

Rahul Sharma, the SP of Bhavnagar, had been in-charge for only a month when the riots erupted. He fired on a mob that was trying to set a *madrassa* on fire and put all its leaders behind bars. He also gave an order to the men under his command that any policeman with a gun not opening fire to save human lives from a violent mob would be prosecuted for abetting murder.[53] By his firm act, 400 young lives were saved. A local BJP leader wanted them released. Sharma refused. On 1 March the young 1992-batch officer broke up a rally and ordered the arrest of Shiv Sena leader Kishore Bhatt and twenty-one VHP activists after they raised inflammatory slogans. This brought the situation under immediate control. For twenty-five days, he held his ground, resisting pressure from BJP MLAs, Gordhanbhai Zadaphia and others. Finally, he was transferred to the police control room in Ahmedabad.

In the face of these vindictive transfers, the IPS officers' association decided to meet for discussions, and the state's DGP lodged a protest. To pre-empt any challenge to the abrupt transfer orders, the Gujarat government was quick to file an application with the Central Administrative Tribunal, pleading that it should, before taking action on appeals against transfers, allow the state government to have its say. 'This is the first time that the police in any part of the country have been taught inaction,' said a senior officer. 'The fallout of this would be disastrous. The next time we have a riot and a constable sees a senior officer being assaulted by a mob, he'll probably just stand back and watch.'[54]

Jobs for the Boys

While those police officers who performed creditably were

sidelined, the Modi government also ensured that 'reliable' officers were placed in certain key posts. Soon after Praveen Gondia made the 'mistake' of filing an FIR naming BJP and VHP leaders for their role in the Naroda-Patiya killings, the government decided to hand over the actual investigation of the case to another assistant commissioner of police, P.N. Barot. As soon as he assumed charge, Barot began questioning the wisdom of the local police naming senior Sangh Parivar leaders in their FIRs. At the end of April 2002, the case was transferred to another officer, ACP (Crime) A.K. Surolia. Twelve days before the ninety-day deadline for filing the official chargesheet for the crime, Surolia was transferred out.[55] When the chargesheet was filed finally, there was no mention of the senior BJP and VHP leaders and the sequence of events was described in such as way as to suggest the Muslim victims of the massacre had provoked the mob into killing them. 'Nobody, least of all the courts, would believe what these preliminary chargesheets have to say,' Gujarat security adviser K.P.S. Gill told the press.[56]

It is precisely in order to sabotage any eventual prosecutions that the Modi government has tried to hand-pick investigators. R.J. Savani, a police officer who is a personal friend of VHP leader Pravin Togadia, was put in-charge of the entire crime branch of the Ahmedabad police.[57] The crime branch will be supervising all riot-related investigations in Ahmedabad. Another example of a motivated transfer appears to be that of A.K. Sharma. DSP of Mehsana until January, Modi shifted him to Rajkot when he decided to contest the by-election from there in February. During the communal killings in March, Mehsana was one of the worst-affected districts: in Sardarpura village alone over twenty-nine Muslims were burnt to death in a single house. 'There are over sixty-eight complaints against various BJP and VHP activists that are pending investigation in Mehsana,' the *Asian Age* noted.[58] Perhaps in order to help clear their names, Mehsana police chief Anupam Singh Gehlot, who cracked down on the rioters, was shunted out to Bhavnagar[59] while Sharma was brought back to the district on 24 March. Similarly, Sanjay Gadhvi, 'a classmate of Togadia whose promotion had been denied because he had been chargesheeted in a corruption case and been suspended, has been cleared of all charges and been given a good posting in Ahmedabad.'[60]

Though police appointments throughout India have become politicized, in Gujarat they seem to be especially so. Under the BJP, even MLAs have been given a say in the appointment of police inspectors in their constituencies. 'As a result, they owe more allegiance to politicians than to the chain of command in the police. There is a tremendous erosion of authority,' a senior police officer noted.[61] Apart from the police, the Sangh Parivar has also managed to wield enormous influence over the home guards by filling its ranks with its own members and supporters. 'A case in point,' say Kakodkar and Bhushan, 'is the home guards commandant of Surendranagar, Lalit Thakkar, who was found to be representing the VHP in peace committee meetings. Officials say they are also under pressure to recruit personnel from the Sangh Parivar for the gram sevak dal, an ad hoc force to be used to maintain law and order in the villages.'[62]

There is a policy decision under the home guards scheme to create a post called '*suraksha sahay*' (or security help). Under this scheme policemen are hired at Rs 2,500 for four years. Their recruitment procedure is ad hoc. It does not follow the normal rules, the intention obviously is to make them permanent after four years. The present government has already created health, education '*sahays*'; now there is a strong move to follow the same pattern for the police force.

There are presently, 4,000 vacancies for policemen in Gujarat. Recruitment through the normal route, like the Gujarat Public Service Commission, is a procedure not easily prone to manipulation as there are arduous tests and other procedures to be followed. However, now this novel idea is being pushed to introduce the police *sahayak* at Rs 1,500 to 2,000 per month. After six months of this ad hoc induction, and through which active infiltration has been attempted, BJP leaders have been arguing for regularizing the employment of these inductees into the permanent category. Through the backdoor, then, cadres are being recruited. After four years of ad hoc service, they are inducted directly into the force. The recruitment procedure for the police *sahayaks* is deliberately lax. Nearly 4,000 cadres of the VHP, Bajrang Dal and RSS have already been inducted as police *sahayaks*. These are the persons that are creating havoc with the police system and have been used successfully in the recent genocide.[63]

Over the past five years, as many as 12,000 VHP workers have been inducted into the state home guards, with many district chiefs being VHP office bearers. Barring one or two, all the twenty-five home guard commandants in the state are primary members of the VHP and Bajrang Dal. The home guard's position is a critical one for the maintenance of law and order in rural areas. Through massive infiltration over the past four years, the BJP and its affiliated organizations have virtually taken control of the home guards' machinery. It's an arrangement that has worked well for the Sangh Parivar in Gujarat in recent weeks.

Plight of Muslim Policemen

If on the one hand, the Sangh Parivar has been successful in infiltrating the police force, it has also managed to marginalize or sideline Muslim police officers. From February 1998, when Keshubhai Patel came to power, began the calculated displacement of Muslims in the force. While some Muslim IPS officers were promoted, they were given only 'peripheral postings . . . The rot is so deep that not a single top officer from the minority community has field postings.'[64] All Muslim officers began to be given administrative posts (they were assigned to Law and Order—Crime Investigation). Eight out of the 141 IPS officers in the state who are Muslims were deliberately keep away from decision-making posts. As a result of this well-known and blatantly unconstitutional policy of the Gujarat government, the younger batch of Muslim IPS officers who entered service in 1992-93 have never exercised their executive abilities; they have never seen executive policing. Gujarat is the only state in the country where IPS officers who are Muslim have never been assigned the post of DSP, which would put them in direct charge of maintaining law and order in half or one-third of a district. Two Muslim officers who are qualified to be given the post of DSP have been deliberately denied the opportunity. Of the sixty-five Muslim officers of inspector rank in Gujarat, only two are handling field jobs. Most Muslim officers below the rank of superintendent have been relegated to the CID/crime department. One Muslim DGP is looking after training, one IGP is in-charge of police housing, two IGPs are doing desk jobs at the DG's office. One of these officers has sought and received a transfer out of the state.[65] During the recent anti-Muslim violence in the state, former Mumbai police commissioner Julio Ribeiro said it was surprising that 'IPS officers from the minorities are given only less important postings in Gujarat.'[66]

For an IPS officer, the charge of SP or DSP is a critical training opportunity to gain experience of execution and supervision of policing duties. Every police *chowki* has a constable with a head constable who could be in-charge of a beat, out-post, or a chowki. Since the BJP has assumed power in Gujarat, it has ensured that were a head constable to be a Muslim, he would not be in-charge of the beats/outposts under the chowki. A minister from the state cabinet, while addressing a meeting of Baroda range officers in 1999, laid the cards on the table. He demanded that the names of all head constables and officers above that grade be read out to him publicly. The signal was that the charge of an outpost should not be given to a Muslim.[67]

In 1999, Mahen Trivedi, the minister of state for home, stated publicly at a police function: 'We have told you that we don't want Muslims in controlling posts. Why is he posted there?'[68] At the DSP and inspector level, there are sixty-five Muslims in the service all over Gujarat. With the exception of one officer who has a close relationship with a minister, all others have been shunted to CID, crime, training, computers, civil defence and railways.

In the three critical government departments concerned with recruitment—the GPSC, the Panchayat Service Selection Board and the Gram Seva Samiti—there is not a single member from any minority community. In the vital departments of government—establishment, recruitment, law and order, finance and loans department, there are no minority persons at all. This is blatantly anti-constitutional as it violates the principles of non-discrimination and equal opportunity.

The intense insecurity felt by Muslims in Gujarat is borne out by the fact that even Muslim policemen are afraid to wear name tags on their uniforms and have sought special permission to be on duty without their name tags. Special IG AI Saiyed, with over twenty-five years of service, was asked to help a group on his way to Karai. He stopped and tried to help but was assaulted when they saw his name.[69] Other IPS officers were fearful of their own security during the worst days of the violence.[70] Most shocking of all, in some places like Danteshwar in Vadodara, Muslim policemen were attacked by their Hindu colleagues.[71]

Hate Speech

The final aspect of the institutional complicity of the police in the mass violence against Muslims in Gujarat in 2002 that needs examining is their incredibly lenient attitude towards hate speech. Since February 1998, when the BJP returned to power in the state, a large number of incendiary pamphlets instigating violence against the state's minorities have been widely circulated. Media reports have frequently drawn attention to these obnoxious publications.[72] The VHP, RSS, Bajrang Dal and BJP had made 'good use' of hate speech and hate writing earlier, too, to create a 'suitable' social climate for their political agenda. Even before the Godhra incident, since early-February, a highly provocative pamphlet exhorting cadres economically to boycott Muslims was in circulation across the state. The Gujarat police is guilty of not initiating or pursuing criminal action against the authors and distributors of these pamphlets. Sections 153(a) and 153(b) of the Indian Penal Code (IPC) are the sections of Indian penal law relating to hate speech and disturbance of public tranquility; unfortunately the police and the judiciary have been reluctant or tardy in their punitive measures against offenders even when, in the case of Bombay 1992-1993, hate speech was actually used during a period of extreme violence to guide mobs and cadres.[73]

In Gujarat, the government and the police have condoned criminal actions over the past few years. The message that is sent home is: the law will not check violators in Gujarat. At a public meeting held at Law Garden in September 2001 (the details of which were obtained from interviews by the author with the police),[74] highly provocative speeches were made in gross violation of section 153. No action was taken. One of the comments made at this public meeting: 'There are thirty-six *ayats* of the *Quran* that should be removed because they perpetrate violence; to make Islam less violent, these thirty-six *ayats* should be removed.'[75]

In a riot situation, it is critical that the police respond to rumours that are spread by provocateurs. In Gujarat, from 27 February onwards, the police failed miserably to act decisively and reassuringly to quash the wild rumours which were used to spread violence. The Gujarati newspaper *Sandesh* was used actively to promote fear and insecurity amongst Hindus while the Muslims were being targetted, and the police did precious little to diffuse the situation. A *Sandesh* report of 28 February 2002, 'From among those abducted from the Sabarmati Express two bodies found near Kalol in a mutilated state,' was found by the police after investigation to be an entirely fictitious report. Yet the police did nothing to alleviate the damage caused by its publication.[76] In any case, the law for prosecuting individuals under section 153 of the IPC requires the government to sanction the registration of a case, something the Modi government would be unlikely to do.

The Need for Police Reform

The utter collapse of public confidence in the police and the dismal deterioration in their collective conduct in the state are issues that need urgent debate. It is clear that the police performance in Gujarat is seminally linked to the wider issue of police autonomy and reform. Senior officers who have dealt with communally-volatile situations have repeatedly stressed the urgent need for accountability and reform within the police. Three reports of the National Police Commission,[78] a professional body that studies, analyses and reflects on the state of police functioning in the country, have also noted with alarm the growing evidence of prejudicial conduct and made harsh and specific recommendations. The content of these have, unfortunately, never become the basis for national debate and concern.[79]

After some officers in the Los Angeles Police Department were found through videographic evidence to be kicking suspected criminals or innocents simply because they were Black, attempts were made to inject institutional safeguards against racial discrimination within the police there. In the aftermath of 9/11, the numerous unrecorded arrests of innocent immigrants have been the focus of a studied campaign by the American Civil Liberties Union. The Stephen Lawrence case in the United Kingdom led to the MacPherson Commission which attempted some reform within the British police, also on the issue of racial bias. The issue, then, is not whether we will have institutions that are entirely bias-free but whether we have the moral and ethical honesty to accept that the malaise exists and, thereafter, to try and find a cure.

For this to happen, the institutions—and all those who represent or man them—need to rid themselves of their state of denial. Since the 1980s, there are just too many concrete examples to show that communal bias not only exists but seriously hampers the professional and neutral functioning of the force and leads to denying citizens equal treatment by— and protection from—the law. Apart from the reports of numerous commissions of inquiry, this author taped police wireless messages during the second round of the Bombay riots in January 1993, the transcribed text of which reveals a deep and abiding anti-Muslim hatred operating and affecting actions among a section of the force.[80]

The radical measures needed include a re-vamping of the structure of the police. As important are prompt and punitive measures against officers and men guilty of crude and gross misdemeanors that include communally-driven criminal acts including murder, loot and arson. In Hashimpura, Meerut, 1987, the Provincial Armed Constabulary of the UP police shot dead, in cold blood, forty Muslim youth. Not a single man in uniform has been punished to date. In Bombay 1992-93, the then joint commissioner of police, R.D. Tyagi, shot dead nine innocent men claiming them to be Kashmiri terrorists.[81] Though charge-sheeted, his trial is yet to begin. In Gujarat, too, in all the scenes of recent massacres, significant sections of the police were party to the crimes committed—either through acts of commission or acts of omission. Even as the struggle for justice against the criminals in uniform is waged through the courts and on the streets, it is imperative that the demand for drastic, radical police reforms be pushed with equal vigour.

Notes

1 See, for example, the report on police firings in Dudhia, Kisanwadi and Halol villages in the *Times of India*, Mumbai, 1 March 2002; Joydeep Ray, 'Ahmedabad flares up again, 6 killed by police point-blank,' the *Indian Express*, 22 April 2002; Janyala Sreenivas, 'Who shot them point blank?,' the *Indian Express*, 9 April 2002.

2 The testimonies from over seventy-five survivors of the genocide in Gujarat, recorded by this author in *Genocide-Gujarat 2002, Communalism Combat*, March-April 2002, provide abundant evidence of dereliction of duty and in many cases even complicity of sections of the police force in the ethnic cleansing of Muslims.

3 'Face to Face with Fascism,' *Communalism Combat*, April 2000.

4 See Priyanka Kakodkar and Ranjit Bhushan, 'Unkindest cut: the police establishment is in the midst of a storm over the transfer of some dutiful IPS officers,' *Outlook*, 8 April 2002.

5 'Police chief takes up cudgels on transfer issue,' the *Times of India*, 26 March 2002.

6 The Act, which dates back to 1857, applies to Gujarat. Conviction

can lead to imprisonment of four months to a year. See *GG*, p 18.

7   'Bajrang Dal activists take up arms,' *Times of India*, 13 June 2001; 'Desi Mossad is getting ready at Bajrang Dal's Ayodhya camp,' *India Abroad News Service*, 29 June 2002; 'VHP, Bajrang Dal set up private army,' *GG*, April 2000; 'Arms and a Hindu rashtra,' *Times of India*, 29 September 2000.

8   Asked why the bodies were brought to Ahmedabad, Pande said, 'Don't ask me. It was not my decision. I gave my view on the situation but it was overruled.' Interview of P.C. Pande by Rashme Sehgal, 'Ahmedabad Cop-Out,' the *Times of India*, 15 March 2002.

9   *Saffron On the Rampage*, Collective Fact-finding Report, Mumbai, November 2000.

10   Statement on Doordarshan channel, 27 February 2002.

11   The *Times of India*, 1 March 2002.

12   Bhavnagar SP Rahul Sharma and Kutch SP Vivek Srivastava, for instance, ensured that the VHP-led mobs were controlled easily. See Janyala Sreenivas, 'Bhavnagar SP: Advani praised, Modi disposed,' *Indian Express*, 28 March 2002.

13   See box, 'Who shot them at point-blank?'.

14   Human Rights Watch, *'We Have No Orders to Save You': State Participation and Complicity in Communal Violence in Gujarat*, New York, April 2002, p 26.

15   *Times of India*, Mumbai, 1 March 2002.

16   People's Union for Civil Liberties, Vadodara, and Shanti Abhiyan, *Violence in Vadodara: A Report*, Vadodara, May 2002 (henceforth *PUCL*), p 132.

17   See 'Survivors Testimonies', *GG*, pp 20-27.

18   Praveen Swami, 'Saffron Terror', March 16—29 *Frontline* , 2002.

19   'No communal riot will last more than 24 hours unless the State wants it to'. Interview of Vibhuti Narain Rai then DIG, BSF, by Teesta Setalvad, *GG*, February 1995. The interview speaks in detail of the erosion in constitutional principles among policemen, a development that has coincided with the aggressive legitimization in the pubic and political sphere of the ideology of Hindutva that, as, one of its fundamentals, consistently demonises sections of the religious minorities.

20 Statement of P.C. Pande on 'Newshour', Star News, 28 February 2002. The statement was rebroadcast on 10 March 2002.

21 Harsh Mander, 'Cry the Beloved Country,' *Outlook*, March 2002.

22 Teesta Setalvad, 'Who Is to Blame?,' *GG*, March 1998.

23 *Damning Verdict*, Mumbai, Sabrang Communications & Publishing Private Limited, p 230.

24 Praveen Swami, *op cit*.

25 See box, 'Dial M for Modi, Murder?'.

26 Confidential interviews with the author for *GG*, p 117.

27 Kakodkar and Bhushan, *op cit*.

28 'An ex-MP's murder tells the tale: before he and family were killed, Jafri was on phone for 6 hrs,' *Indian Express*, 1 March 2002.

29 Interviews with the victims of the Naroda Gaon and Naroda Patiya massacres by the author, *GG*, p 20.

30 Sudhir Vyas, 'Police chief leaves Rajkot to its fate,' the *Times of India*, 2 March 2002.

31 *GG*, p 25.

32 *GG*, p 27.

33 Justice A.P. Ravani, retired judge, Gujarat HC, former chief justice, Rajasthan, in written testimony to the NHRC, reproduced in *GG*, p 37.

34 Testimony of Arjubehn, *GG*, p 55.

35 *PUCL*, p 60; *GG*, pp 87-88.

36 *GG*, pp 45-53.

37 *GG*, pp 20-92

38 Manas Dasgupta, 'Saffronised police show their colour,' *Hindu*, 3 March 2002.

39 'SI charged with aiding mob transferred,' *Times of India*, Ahmedabad, 11 June 2002.

40 Jahnavi Contractor, 'Women not spared by police,' *Times of India*, Ahmedabad, 3 May 2002; Jahnavi Contractor, 'Women protest police atrocities in Vadodara,' *Times of India*, Ahmedabad, 6 May 2002; See also testimonies recorded by the Concerned Citizens Tribunal, May 8, 9 and 10 and People's Union for Civil Liberties, Vadodara and Shanti Abhiyan, *At the Receiving End: Women's Experiences of Violence in Vadodara*, Vadodara, May 2002.

41   *PUCL*, p 132.

42   'We were just watching, why did they fire at us?,' *Indian Express*,
     22 March 2002

43   *GG*, p 92.

44   Seema Guha, 'Ribeiro sees communal virus in police,' *Telegraph*,
     17 April 2002.

45   Interview of Arun Jaitley by Smita Gupta, 'Modi Matters,' *Times
     of India*, 10 July 2002.

46   Deepal Trevedie, 'Gujarat police disgusted with Modi,' *Asian Age*,
     24 March 2002.

47   *Ibid*.

48   Priyanka Kakodkar and Ranjit Bhushan, *op cit*.

49   'Riots spread to new areas, curfew in Anjar,' *Hindustan Times*,
     3 April 2002.

50   Janyala Sreenivas, 'I started with the earthquake, left with riots,'
     Indian Express, 26 March 2002.

51   Deepal Trevedie, 'Modi punished good officers,' Asian Age,
     25 March 2002.

52   Priyanka Kakodkar and Ranjit Bhushan, *op cit*.

53   Harsh Mander, 'Call of Conscience, Cast of Character,' *Outlook*,
     22 April 2002.

54   Senior police official sharing details of application, *GG* 121.

55   'Naroda probe headless, again,' *Indian Express*, 16 May 2002.

56   'Naroda, Gulberg chargesheets blame Muslims, upset Gill,' *Times
     of India*, 12 June 2002.

57   Deepal Trevedie, 'Modi punished good officers,' *op cit*.

58   *Ibid*.

59   Vasant Rawat, 'Minority hole in Gujarat police force,' *Telegraph*,
     27 March 2002.

60   Deepal Trevedie, *op cit*.

61   Priyanka Kakodkar and Ranjit Bhushan, *op cit*.

62   *Ibid*.

63   *GG*, pp 120-121.

64   Robin David, 'Muslim IPS officers isolated: Ribeiro,' *Times of
     India*, 9 April 2002.

65   Basant Rawat, 'Minority hole in Gujarat police force', *Telegraph*,
     27 March 2002.

66 Robin David, *op cit.*

67 Gujarat police source speaking to author on condition of anonymity, *GG*, p. 119.

68 *Ibid.*

69 Sonal Kellog, 'Muslim policemen scared to wear name-tags in Gujarat,' *Asian Age*, 24 March 2002.

70 Sonal Kellog, 'Muslim IPS officers targeted, arrange for their own security,' *Asian Age*, 3 March 2002.

71 Milind Ghatwai, 'Behind police lines too, it's the same story,' *Indian Express*, 6 March 2002.

72 'Welcome To Hindu Rashtra,' *GG* October 1998; 'Pamphlet Poison', *GG*, p 132.

73 Teesta Setalvad, 'Hate Speech and Indian Democracy,' *ILS Pune Centenary Volume* (forthcoming); 'Crime and Punishment', *GG* January 1993.

74 *GG*, pp 117-118.

75 *Ibid.*

76 See Aakar Patel, Dileep Padgaonkar, B.G. Verghese, *Rights and Wrongs: Ordeal by Fire in the Killing Fields of Gujarat*, Editors Guild Fact Finding Mission Report, New Delhi, May 2002, pp 6-10; See also *GG*, p 127, for the complete translation of the fabricated news item.

77 Hindutva document accessed by the author from Gujarat and reproduced in translation in full; 'Face to face with Fascism's; Hindutva document: How to bend and break the law'; p 15.

78 The Sixth Report of the National Police Commission, March 1981 noted 'several instances where police officers and policemen have shown an unmistakable bias against a particular community while dealing with communal situations', adding that the composition of the police is 'heavily weighted in favour of the majority community.'

79 'Who Is to Blame?,' *GG*, March 1998.

80 *Dongri 1 to Police Control:* Two military trucks have come carrying milk and other rations, led by Major General (retired) Syed Rehemtullah. Therefore, a crowd has gathered at IR road near Bhendi Bazar, please send some more men.
    (Voice): Why the f—are you distributing milk to them *laandyas*

(abuse for a circumcised person)? Do you want to f—their mothers? *Miyan* (Muslim), bastards live there.

Dongri 1, (agitated): There are lots of police here. Let them distribute milk.

Voice: Why are you distributing milk to them? Are you doing them a favour or what?

V.P.Road to Control: A mob has gathered outside Maharashtra garage, Ghas galli, Lamington road with the intention of setting it on fire. Send men.

Voice: Must be a laandya's garage. Let it burn. S— don't burn anything that belongs to a Maharashtrian. But burn everything belonging to a *miyan,* the bastards.

(Excerpts from transcripts of police wireless messages taped by Teesta Setalvad between 10 and 18 January 1993)

81 *Damning Verdict,* Report of the Srikrishna Commission, Mumbai, Sabrang Communications, p 114.

An open letter to my fellow-police officers
Vibhuti Narain Rai[*]

Dear Colleagues,

I am writing to you at a very difficult time as an Indian Police Service officer and with a sense of anguish. The recent events related to the communal holocaust in Gujarat are a matter of great concern for the country and should inspire serious introspection among all of us IPS officers. The terrible carnage that occurred at Godhra was an early warning of the fact that big events of communal destruction could occur the next day all over the State and the expectation from a professional police force was that it would oppose all actions of revenge and counter-violence with all the force that it could muster. But this did not happen. Not only was the police unsuccessful in containing the violence of the next few days but, it seemed, that in many places policemen were actively encouraging the rioters. The failure of the police should not be attributed to the lower ranks but must be seen as a failure of leadership, that is, a failure of the IPS.

The events that followed the beastly incident at Godhra did not surprise a person like myself who is not only a police officer but also a keen student of social behaviour. The same old story was repeated everywhere from Ahmedabad, the capital, to the rural areas. Since 1960, in almost all riots that have occurred, the same picture has been painted in the same colours, a picture of a helpless and often actively inactive police force that allowed wailing members of the minority community to be looted and killed in its presence, that remained a mute witness to some of their members being burnt alive.

Whatever may be my concerns as an ordinary citizen, as a police officer my greatest concern is the preservation of the professional character of the police force. An insensitive chief minister can pat his incompetent police force on the back and the senior police leadership can also blame the 'misleading

---

[*] A senior serving Indian Police Service officer currently posted as IG (Railways), Allahabad, Vibhuti Narain Rai circulated this letter to all members of the IPS in mid-March. He has decided to make his letter public in the interests of furthering a debate on issues of conscience within the police force.

212 Gujarat: The Making of a Tragedy

media' and the 'anti-national minorities' for any criticism made
of its handling of the situation. But the truth is that after every
riot, the same criticism is made of the police—that of its not
only having failed to protect the lives and property of the
minorities but of siding with Hindu rioters and encouraging
them. And after this recent rioting also the same criticism is
being levelled against the Gujarat police.

Whatever happened in Gujarat is not something new. It only
once again underlines the fact that the senior leadership of the
police will have to sit down and think as to why after every
riot the same story is repeated: that of incompetence, inactivity
and criminal negligence. Until we accept that all is not in order
in our own house, nothing can be put right.

The first: institutionalised opposition to communal violence
is initiated by the police. This occurs at several levels. Collection
of intelligence before the outbreak of violence, preventive
measures while tension is escalating, use of force to stop violence
and, after peace is restored, initiation of legal proceedings
against the guilty. These are some of the steps taken by the
police to combat communal riots. None of these steps can be
taken effectively if we ourselves are infected with a communal
bias.

For an average policeman, collection of intelligence is limited
to gathering of information about the activities of communal
Muslim organizations. It is not easy to make him realize that
the activities of Hindu communal organizations also come
under the purview of anti-national activities and, therefore, it
is necessary to keep an eye on their activities also. It is a fact
that very little input on the activities of communal Hindu
organizations and their activists is to be found in the police
station records.

Similarly, preventive arrests, even in riot situations in which
Muslims are the worst sufferers, are restricted to members of
the minority community. Further, even where Muslims are
being attacked and the police resorts to firing, their main targets
are Muslims. House-searches and arrests reveal the same bias.

What happened in Gujarat was a repetition of the above but
on an unprecedented scale where the extent of violence and
destruction was unparalleled and one-sided. The other
difference was that for the first time, the inaction, connivance
and bias of the police were all on display on television screens
in every Indian (and many foreign) homes. Now we have lost
even the fig-leaf of alleged misrepresentation by the print media.

It may be relevant to mention here that on many occasions when leadership was provided which was professionally sound and free from any communal bias, the same bunch of policemen have won the confidence of various sections of society and made their organizations proud of them. The old truism is borne out that Generals fail and not the troops. Very often, the officers blame lower ranks of the force for their inability to control communal conflicts effectively. But we have seen even in the recent Gujarat happenings that in the midst of failures, there were success stories in which upright IPS officers led their men from the front and ensured that there was no loss of life and property in their area of responsibility.

It is a sad fact that police officers who have not just failed to control riot situations but who have actually given them their active support have not been punished in even one instance. The anti-Sikh riots of 1984, especially in the Capital of the country, one of the best-policed cities, saw the killing of thousands of Sikhs that could not have taken place without the active connivance of police. Despite indictments, not only by the press but by several inquiry commissions, in some of which distinguished IPS officers like Sri Padma Rosha were also involved, not one police officer was punished and none of their careers was adversely affected. The Madon Commission and Srikrishna Commissions have suffered the same fate.

It is very clear that no outside agency can reform us. This is a job we will have to do ourselves. If we have any sense of pride left in the service to which we belong, which has had an illustrious past and has enjoyed great prestige in the country, the time has come for us to set about this task in right earnest. We must call a general house of the Central IPS Association and demand that the government take action against Gujarat officers who have failed in their primary duty to maintain law and order and prevent violence; and against all officers who have failed in similar situations since 1984. We should not treat the association as a trade union body to fight for better pay and service conditions but as a medium to improve the service itself. If the government does not take any action, the very least that we can do is remove such officers from the membership of the Association.

Hoping to hear from many of you shortly,
Vibhuti Narain Rai, IPS (UP, RR, 3 1975).

6

'Nothing New?'

Women as Victims in Gujarat

'. . . *Yeh jo sara rona roya ja raha hai ek-ek kahani batakar, jaise yeh kahani pehli bar desh mein ho rahi hai ki kahan ma ko markar pet se bachche ko nikala, kahan ma ke samne uski beti ke saath balatkar hua, kisko aag mein jalaya gaya. Kya yeh sab pehli baar ho raha hai? Kya 1984 mein Dilli ki sadkon par aisa nahin hua tha?. . .'*

(All these sob stories being told to us, as if this is the first time this country has heard such stories—where a mother is killed and the foetus taken out of her stomach, where a daughter is raped in front of her mother, of someone being burnt. Is this the first time such things have happened? Didn't such things happen on the streets of Delhi in 1984?)

Defence Minister George Fernandes, defending the Vajpayee government on the floor of Parliament during the debate on Gujarat, 30 April 2002.[1]

Editor's Note: What did George Fernandes mean when he said that the 'sob stories' being told about atrocities on women in Gujarat were nothing new? When a victim of violence cites other examples of violence, it is an act of solidarity and empathy. But when a minister in a government which is on the mat for its complicity in mass murder speaks of 1984 and Gujarat in such an insensitive manner—almost hinting that two wrongs make a right—it is tantamount to belittling the suffering of victims of both tragedies. In any event, Fernandes is doubly wrong because the violence in Gujarat *was* different from earlier incidents of communal violence, both for the scale of the assaults and for the sheer sadism and brutality with which women and girls were victimized.

This chapter begins with an eyewitness account of what happened when a victim of rape in Gujarat tried approaching the police for justice. This is followed by extracts from the landmark report of a women's panel which toured the state at the end of March and highlighted for the first time the systematic and widespread nature of sexual violence. The last section, drawn from the report by PUCL Vadodara and Vadodara Shanti Abhiyan, deals not only with the continuing concerns and fears of the Muslim women victims but also with how political forces in Gujarat are fuelling the fears of Hindu women in order to spread communal hatred.

The Rape of Reason
Barkha Dutt

The police station was true to every imaginable stereotype: a raunchy, pot-bellied inspector, uniformed henchmen and hapless, pleading villagers waiting in vain for that precious document called the FIR. An ugly circus of intimidation unfolded before our helpless eyes. Fathers who came armed with names of the men who had murdered their sons were turned away. The police told them to omit all individual names if they wanted an FIR quickly. Cases were instead being filed against the nameless and faceless. And how do you even begin to investigate a mob of five thousand people? Arguing with the guardians of the law proved fruitless. Reason was a stranger in this part of Gujarat.

An emotionally exhausted aid-worker turned to us and asked, 'Now you try and put yourself in the place of a woman who's suffered physical abuse, who has had a man violate her body again and again. Will she have the courage to walk into a police station and say, "I have been raped?"'

We looked around. Not a single woman constable in sight. But media presence can create the illusion of security. For minutes later, a small group of women—young girls actually—walked in, huddling together nervously.

Among them was S, a waif-like woman of eighteen, who hid her pain behind a thin muslin dupatta. Her eyes had a vacant stare, numbed by the brutality. She could barely speak. But the women around her did. On 2 March, S had clambered onto a tempo along with forty other villagers to escape the mob. They didn't get far. The tempo was set on fire and as it overturned, S fell behind with her son Faizan. Her clothes were torn off and one by one the men raped her. What she remembers most vividly is the sound of her son crying.

It was a bizarre coincidence, but we remembered that day as well. We had reached the spot just thirty minutes after the tempo (it was a milk-van) went up in flames. Our camera had filmed and broadcast images of the tin cans, the silver handlebars gleaming through the flames, the charred bodies lying strewn across the tall grass. But there was also something else we knew would never make it to the TV screens, especially in those first few days of violence. It was the body of a woman, mouth agape, legs wrenched open, her head thrown back against the thorny bushes. One arm was still flailing the air, probably her last attempt to fight the man or men who had raped her, before killing her.

S, as we discovered at the police station, was still alive only because she fell unconscious and her rapists took her for dead. And here she was, two months later, trying to register an FIR for Rape. No policeman thought it appropriate to escort this young woman into a closed room or even a quiet corner. Her story had to be told in front of a gawking crowd of constables. And when it was over, a brazen policeman declared that a separate FIR for 'simply rape' could not be filed.

'Why?', we screamed, anger and exasperation now replacing mere journalistic instincts. 'Madam,' said deputy inspector Parmar with a smile and an evil glint in his eye, 'it's like this. If a shopping centre is burnt down and there are 100 people inside, we can't give individual FIRS to all hundred. For one attack, there can only be one FIR.' The police claimed that several complaints had already been recorded in the 'tempo incident', another FIR for rape, they said, would be 'making a case out of a case'. At the most, S's testimony could be a statement attached to the common FIR.

This is how sexual violence is being made invisible across the state. Tomorrow, if Gujarat's history is written by police records and government files, stories like S's and those of hundreds of other women like her, will remain untold and unread. Clubbing rape with complaints of murder is only one part of the problem, the law's insistence on immediate medical evidence is the other. One woman we met had spent twenty-four days hiding in the forest and had walked over 300 km with her two children before she could reach the safety of a relief camp. Which doctor could she have gone to? Will her story simply fall into a black hole?

Ironically, in camp after camp we found that the traditional shroud of secrecy and shame that normally shadows rape survivors was completely missing. Sexual abuse, this time, had been so public and so widespread, it had taken the form of every woman's narrative. Women wanted to talk to anyone who was prepared to listen.

At Godhra's Iqbalpur camp, we sat by the dim light of a gas lamp and heard B's story. B is one of only three women who have managed to record a complaint of rape across the entire Panchmahals district, and that too only because of the intervention of Jayanti Ravi, the district collector. When the collector found a battered B, she had ordered a medical examination, even though the stipulated three days had long passed.

It's been two months now but B's hand is still in a cast and her back is ridden with bruises. She was three months pregnant when she was raped and her first born, a three-year old, killed. And that is only one part of her horrific nightmare. B tells us how she lay flat in the grass, pretending to be dead, while her

45-year old mother, her two sisters, and her sister-in-law were raped and killed. She knows who did it. They were three men from her own village. She has named them in her FIR. But they walk free till today and have sent threats through their henchmen that B must withdraw her complaint of rape, if she ever wants to come back home. George Fernandes, are you listening?

Source: Outlook, May 2002.

The Survivors Speak[*]
Farah Naqvi, Malini Ghose, Syeda Hameed, Ruth Manorama, Sheba George, Mari Thekaekara

A six-member team of women from Delhi, Bangalore, Tamil Nadu and Ahmedabad undertook a five-day fact-finding mission from 27 March—31 March 2002, to assess the impact of the continuing violence on minority women in Gujarat.

Other fact-finding teams have also visited Gujarat post-Godhra. However, given the particular targetting of women in this carnage, there was an urgent need for a sectoral investigation into how women in particular have been affected. The objective of the fact-finding was to determine the nature and extent of the crimes against women; find evidence of the role played by the police and other state institutions in protecting women; determine 'new elements' in the current spate of violence that distinguish it from previous rounds of communal violence in Gujarat; determine the role of organizations like the VHP and Bajrang Dal in both the build-up to the current carnage as well as in actually unleashing the violence.

The team visited seven relief camps in both rural and urban areas (Ahmedabad, Kheda, Vadodara, Sabarkantha and Panchmahals districts) and spoke to a large number of women

[*]   Exracted from *The Survivors Speak: How has the Gujarat massacre affected minority women?* Fact-finding by a Women's Panel constituted by the authors and sponsored by Citizens' Initiative, Ahmedabad, New Delhi, April 2002.

survivors. Ensuring that women's voices are heard was a matter of priority for the entire team. The team also spoke to intellectuals, activists, members of the media, administration, and leaders from the BJP, including MLA Maya Kodnani, accused in an FIR in the Naroda Patiya massacre. The fact-finding was conducted under conditions of continuing violence and curfew in many parts of the state.

We have been shaken and numbed by the scale and brutality of the violence that is still continuing in Gujarat. Despite reading news reports, we were unprepared for what we saw and heard; for fear in the eyes and anguish in the words of ordinary women whose basic human right to live a life of dignity has been snatched away from them.

Our main findings: The pattern of violence does not indicate 'spontaneous' action. There was pre-planning, organization, and precision in the targeting; there is evidence that the current carnage was preceded by an escalation of tension and build-up by the VHP and the Bajrang Dal.

There is compelling evidence of sexual violence against women. These crimes against women have been grossly underreported and the exact extent of these crimes—in rural and urban areas—demands further investigation. Among the women surviving in relief camps, are many who have suffered the most bestial forms of sexual violence—including rape, gang rape, mass rape, stripping, insertion of objects into their body, stripping, molestations. A majority of rape victims have been burnt alive.

There is evidence of State and police complicity in perpetuating crimes against women. No effort was made to protect women. No Mahila police was deployed. State and police complicity in these crimes is continuing, as women survivors continue to be denied the right to file FIRs. There is no existing institutional mechanism in Gujarat through which women can seek justice.

The impact on women has been physical, economic and psychological. On all three fronts there is no evidence of State efforts to help them. The state of the relief camps, as mothers struggle to keep their children alive in the most appalling physical conditions, is indicative of the continued abdication of the State's responsibilities.

Rural women have been affected by communal violence on this scale for the first time. There is a need for further investigation into the role played by particular castes/ communities in rural Gujarat in unleashing violence. There is an alarming trend towards ghettoization of the Muslim community in rural areas for the first time.

Finally, sections of the Gujarati vernacular press played a dangerous and criminal role in promoting the violence, particularly in provoking sexual violence against women.

Sexual Violence against Women

The fact-finding team found compelling evidence of the most extreme form of sexual violence against women during the first few days of the carnage—in Ahmedabad on 28 February and 1 March and in rural areas up to 3 March 2002. The testimonies point to brutal and depraved forms of violence. The violence against minorities was pre-planned, organized and targeted. In every instance of large-scale mob violence against the community in general, there was a regular pattern of violence against women. Given the fact that the data on crimes against women has not been systematically collected, it is impossible to ascertain the extent of the outrage. We believe, however, that crimes against women have been grossly under-reported. For instance, in Panchmahals district only one rape FIR has been filed, though we heard of many other cases.[2] There has been a complete invisibilization of the issue of sexual violence in the media.

The situation is compounded by the apathy of law-enforcement agencies and the indifference of political representatives. In our interview with Maya Kodnani, BJP MLA from Naroda Patiya, where several brutal gang-rapes and rapes of minor girls have been reported, we found that she was indifferent, complacent and even bemused. When questioned about the reported rapes, she said, '*Accha, kya ye sach hai?*

Suna hai. Ek police wale ne mujhe bataya ki aise hua hai par usne dekha nahin (Is this true? One policeman mentioned this to me but he had not seen anything)'. She had not taken the trouble to investigate further, and clearly indicated no intent to do so.

Given the gravity of the situation, it is incomprehensible that until the writing of this report the National Commission for Women, mandated as the apex body for protection of women's rights guaranteed under the Constitution of India, had not visited the State. This indicates a complete institutional breakdown as far as issues such as violence against women are concerned. As the district collector of Panchmahals clearly told us, 'Maintaining law and order is my primary concern. It is not possible for me to look into cases of sexual violence. If something is brought to my notice I can take action, but nothing more than that. NGOs should take on this job. I would welcome their involvement.'

During our visits to the camps, we were besieged with detailed testimonies from rape victims themselves and from eyewitnesses—both activists and family members who witnessed the crime. For instance, in the short time we spent at Halol camp (Panchmahals district) we were able to get information about four incidents of rape. The fact-finding team also saw video footage where women spoke of witnessing rapes. In the film, we saw slogans like 'Muslims Quit India—or we will f*** your mothers' written on the walls of charred houses.

We reproduce below some of the testimonies that we were able to record.

Testimonies of Sexual Violence

Witnessing mass rape (including of minor girls)
Naroda Patiya, Ahmedabad
28 February 2002
The mob started chasing us with burning tyres after we were forced to leave Gangotri society. It was then that they raped many girls. We saw about eight to ten rapes. We saw them strip

sixteen-year-old Mehrunissa. They were stripping themselves and beckoning to the girls. Then they raped them right there on the road. We saw a girl's vagina being slit open. Then they were burnt. Now there is no evidence.

Source: Kulsum Bibi, Shah-e-Alam camp, 27 March 2002

I saw Farzana being raped by Guddu Chara. Farzana was about thirteen years old. She was a resident of Hussain Nagar. They put a *saria* (rod) in Farzana's stomach. She was later burnt. Twelve-year-old Noorjahan was also raped. The rapists were Guddu, Suresh and Naresh Chara and Haria. I also saw Bhawani Singh, who works in the State Transport Department kill five men and a boy.

Source: Azharuddin, thirteen years. He witnessed the rapes while hiding on the terrace of Gangotri Society. The Chara basti is located just behind Jawan Nagar.

The mob, which came from Chara Nagar and Kuber Nagar, started burning people at around 6.00 in the evening. The mob stripped all the girls of the locality, including my twenty-two-year-old daughter, and raped them. My daughter was engaged to be married. Seven members of my family were burnt including my wife (aged 40), my sons (aged 18, 14 and 7) and my daughters (aged 2, 4 and 22). My eldest daughter, who later died in the civil hospital, told me that those who raped her were wearing shorts. They hit her on the head and then burnt her. She died of 80 per cent burn injuries.

Source: Abdul Usman, Testimony recorded by Citizens' Initiative

S, *a rape survivor, speaks*
Village Delol, Kalol Taluka, Panchmahals District
28 February 2002
On the afternoon of 28 February, to escape the violent mob, about forty of us got on to a tempo, wanting to escape to Kalol.

My husband Feroze was driving the tempo. Just outside Kalol a Maruti car was blocking the road. A mob was lying in wait. Feroze had to swerve. The tempo overturned. As we got out they started attacking us. People started running in all directions. Some of us ran towards the river. I fell behind as I was carrying my son, Faizan. The men caught me from behind and threw me on the ground. Faizan fell from my arms and started crying. My clothes were stripped off by the men and I was left stark naked. One by one the men raped me. All the while I could hear my son crying. I lost count after three. They then cut my foot with a sharp weapon and left me there in that state.

Source: S, Kalol camp, Panchmahals district, 30 March 2002

Additional facts about the case:
- We had heard about S's case from her relatives in Halol camp. The details and sequence of events of both testimonies matched.
- S has not undergone a medical examination. Her leg had been swollen for three weeks as a result of the injury inflicted by a sharp weapon, but it is healing now.
- No FIR has been filed though a written statement has been submitted to the DSP. In her statement she names some men from the mob (Jitu Shah, PDS Shop owner of Delol village; Ashok Patel alias Don Dadhi of Ramnath village).
- When we spoke with her and her sister-in-law they both said they were feeling numb and lost, as they did not know where to go from the camp. She categorically stated that they could not go back to her village. She was terribly worried about the future especially her children's. Sultani has still not been told that her husband had died in the attack. She believes he is missing.
- Eyewitnesses state that Mumtaz, another woman from Delol, who died in the same attack was raped before being killed as she was fleeing from the tempo.[3]

A *mother's account of her daughter's rape*
Village Eral, Kalol Taluka, Panchmahals district
3 March 2002

My father-in-law, a retired schoolteacher, refused to leave the village with the other Muslim families who fled to Kalol on 28 February. He believed no one would harm us. From the 28th, about thirteen members of my family sought refuge in various people's houses and the fields. On Sunday afternoon (3 March) the hut we were hiding in was attacked. We ran in different directions and hid in the field. But the mob found some of us and started attacking. I could hear various members of my family shouting for mercy as they were attacked. I recognized two people from my village—Gano Baria and Sunil—pulling away my daughter, Shabana. She screamed, telling the men to get off her and leave her alone. The screams and cries of Ruqaiya (Madina's sister-in-law), Suhana, Shabana, begging for their *izzat* could clearly be heard. My mind was seething with fear and fury. I could do nothing to help my daughter from being assaulted sexually and tortured to death. My daughter was like a flower, still to experience life. Why did they have to do this to her? What kind of men are these? The monsters tore my beloved daughter to pieces. After a while, the mob was saying 'cut them to pieces, leave no evidence. I saw fires being lit. After some time the mob started leaving. And it became quiet.

Source: Medina Mustafa Ismail Sheikh, Kalol camp, Panchmahals district, 30 March 2002

Additional facts about the case:
- Medina's testimony has been corroborated by the other two living witnesses, Mehboob and Khushboo. Khushboo, in her testimony, also recounted how her grandfather (Medina's father-in-law) and Huriben were killed. She also narrated how Ruqaiya's pyjamas were taken off and then one by one the men started 'poking her in the lower part with their body'.
- We saw a copy of Medina's FIR, where the police has

charged five persons with murder under section 302. Charges of rape have not been included. The FIR uses the colloquial phrase 'bura kaam' rather than the specific term 'rape'. We were also given the case report prepared by the camp leaders. The names of some of the accused are mentioned in the FIR.

- On 9 May, police arrested the BJP's Kalol unit president, Chandrasinh Parmar, on charges of rape and murder.[4]

Gang-rape of 25-year-old Z: a husband's account
Hussain Nagar, Naroda Patiya, Ahmedabad
28 February 2002

It started at 9.00 a.m. on 28 February. That's when the mobs arrived, shouting '*Mian Bhai nikalo* (Bring out the Muslims)'. Many of them were wearing *kesari chaddis* (saffron shorts). The mob included boys from the neighbouring buildings—Gopinath Society and Gangotri Society. I ran out of my house with the entire family—mother, father, sister, sister's daughter, my wife Z, my brother, my sister-in-law, and my niece . . . there were eleven of us. We all ran towards the police chowki. The police said, 'Go towards Gopinath and Gangotri.' In the melee, I was separated from my wife. What happened to her, she told me later. She tried to escape the mobs by leaping over a wall. But found herself in a cul-de-sac. They gang-raped her, and cut one arm. She was found naked. She was kept in the civil hospital for many days. Now she is recovering with her mother near the Khanpur darwaza.

Source: Naimuddin, thirty-year-old husband of Z. Shah-e-Alam camp, 27 March 2002. Naimmudin's testimony was corroborated by Mumtaz, who was among the women who found Z naked in the maidan.

Rape of 13-year-old Yasmeen
Village Delol, Panchmahals district
1 March 2002

The extended families of Mohammad Bhai and Bhuri Behn—

about twenty people—were chased by the mob to the river. Javed and another boy who managed to escape and hide behind a bush saw the mob kill Mohammad Bhai and rape Yasmeen. They were about to kill the mother of the other boy who was hiding with him. So he screamed and ran out from behind the bush and was caught. He was made to walk around the dead bodies that were burnt (as if around a pyre) and he was then pushed into the fire.

Source: Women from Delol at Halol camp, Panchmahals district, 30 March 2002.

Stripping and brutalizing of an entire family, Limkheda village

Dherol Station, Halol Taluka, Panchmahals district,
28 February 2002

Thirty-five-year-old Haseena Bibi Yasin Khan Pathan along with her entire extended family of 17 people ran from Limkheda on the morning of 28 February. At 7.00 a.m., they caught the train from station, disembarked at Dherol station at 10.00 a.m. That's when they encountered the mob. Every one ran helter-skelter and the family got separated. Haseena, her husband, and young daughter managed to run towards Halol. Two children, Farzana (10) and Sikandar (7) escaped into the fields. Four boys—Ayub, (12), Mushtaq, (12), Mohsin, (10), and Shiraz (7) managed to hide behind bushes, and witnessed what happened. There was a large crowd. They were brandishing swords. According to Ayub, the mob caught his sister Afsana and cousins Zebu, Noorjehan, Sitara, Akbar, Rehana, Yusuf, Imran, Khatun (aunt) and Zareef (brother). They were all stripped naked and made to run towards a nearby canal. That's the last Ayub saw of them. The bodies turned up charred near the canal the following day. He doesn't recognize the mob. No FIR has been lodged.

Source: Ayub, Halol camp, Panchmahals district. The first part of the testimony is corroborated by his mother, Haseena Bibi.

Activists' Experiences of Dealing with Rape Survivors

Shah-e-Alam Relief Camp, Ahmedabad

Naseem and Mahmooda, from nearby Millat Nagar, work with Sahrwaru, a voluntary organization. They are presently working at the Shah Alam camp. They testified that many women arrived stark naked at the camp. Men took off their shirts to cover the women's nakedness. Some could barely walk because of torn genitals as a result of gang-rapes. While talking to them we met Zubeida Apa, an elderly woman who has witnessed girls being gang-raped. Her trauma was writ large on her face. We did not dare to rake up her pain by asking her more questions. We were told about N who was brought to the camp unconscious, her body covered with bites and nail marks. She was bleeding profusely. Pieces of wood, which had been shoved up her vagina were extricated by the women who dressed her wounds. N herself was too traumatized to recount her own story. She says she does not remember anything, except being chased by the men from Gangotri Society. Accounts like these require further follow-up.

Source: Naseem and Mehmooda, Millat Nagar

The following testimonies have been taken from documentation supplied to the fact-finding team by Citizens' Initiative, Ahmedabad:

Mass rape and murder
Naroda Patiya
28 February 2002
By now it was 6.30 in the evening. The mob caught my husband and hit him on his head twice with the sword. Then they threw petrol in his eyes and then burned him. My sister-in-law was stripped and raped. She had a three-month-old baby in her lap. They threw petrol on her and the child was taken from her lap and thrown in the fire. My brother-in-law was also struck on the head with the sword and thrown in the fire. We were at the

time hiding on the terrace of a building. My mother-in-law was unable to climb the stairs so she was on the ground floor with her four-year-old grandson. She told them to take away whatever money she had but to spare the children. They took away all the money and jewellery, then burnt the children with petrol. My mother-in-law was raped too. I witnessed all this. Unmarried girls from my street were stripped, raped and burnt. A fourteen-year-old girl was killed by piercing an iron rod into her stomach. The mayhem ended at 2.30 a.m. Then the ambulance came and I sat in it along with bodies of my husband and children. I have injury marks on my both my thighs and left hand, which were caused by the police beating. My husband (48 per cent burns), my daughter (95 per cent burns) both died in the hospital after three days. The police was on the spot but they were helping the mob. We fell at their feet but they said they were ordered from above not to help. Since the telephone wires were snapped we could not inform the Fire Brigade.

Source: Jannat Sheikh, testimony to Citizens' Initiative.

B: *Account of a rape survivor*
Randhikpur Village, District Dahod
3 March 2002

Twenty-one-year old B was five months pregnant. When Muslim houses in her village were attacked on 28 February by a mob comprising upper caste people from her own village and some outsiders, she and several of her family members fled. For two days they ran from village to village. At a mosque near Kuajher, her cousin Shamim, delivered a baby. But there was no respite for them. They had to leave immediately, including Shamim who could barely walk, carrying her newborn baby.

'On 3 March we had started moving towards Panivela village, which was in a remote and hilly area. Suddenly we heard the sound of a vehicle. A truck came with people from our own village and outsiders too. We realized that they had not come to help us. They stopped us and then the madness started. They pulled my baby from my arms and threw her away. The other women and I were taken aside and raped. I was raped by three men. I was screaming all the time. They beat me and then left me for dead. When I regained consciousness I found I was alone. All around me were the dead bodies of my family, my baby girl, the newborn baby, their bodies were covered with the rocks and boulders used to kill them. I lay there the whole night and most of the next day. I do not know when I was conscious and when unconscious. Later, I was found by a police squad from Limkheda police station. I was taken to the hospital and then brought to the Godhra Camp.'

Testimony to AIDWA and Anandi, an NGO

Additional facts about the case:

- Her FIR has been filed and a medical examination done on the insistence of the district collector, Jayanti Ravi, even though six-days had passed. Rape has been confirmed.
- She has named the people who killed her family members and those who raped her: Sailesh Bhatt, Mithesh Bhatt, Vijay Maurya, Pradeep Maurya, Lala Vakil, Lala Doctor, Naresh Maurya, Jaswant Nai and Govind Nai (the last three gang-raped her).
- Initially all her family members were missing. Her father and husband have been traced to another camp at Dahod and her brother, Saeed, is with her in Godhra.

Kausar Bano: A meta-narrative of bestiality

'But what they did to my sister-in-law's sister, Kausar Bano, was horrific and heinous. She was nine months pregnant. They cut open her belly, took out her foetus with a sword and threw it into a blazing fire. Then they burnt her as well.'

Source: Saira Banu, Naroda Patiya (recorded at the Shah-e-Alam Camp on 27 March)

During our fact-finding mission, we were to hear this story

many times. We read about it in other fact-finding reports. Many survivors at the Shah-e-Alam camp told us about it. Sometimes the details would vary—the foetus was dashed to the ground, the foetus was slaughtered with a sword, the foetus was swung on the point of the sword and then thrown into a fire. Each teller of the story owned it. It was as if it was their own story. Were these simply the fevered imaginings of traumatized minds? We think not. Kausar's story has come to embody the numerous experiences of evil that were felt by the Muslims of Naroda Patiya on 28 February 2002. In all instances where extreme violence is experienced collectively, meta-narratives are constructed. Each victim is part of the narrative; their experience subsumed by the collective experience. Kausar is that collective experience—a meta-narrative of bestiality; a meta-narrative of helpless victimhood. There are a thousand Kausars.

Members of the fact-finding team have seen photographic evidence of the burnt bodies of a mother and a foetus lying on the mother's belly, as if torn from the uterus and left on the gash. We do not know if that was Kausar Bano.[5]

Sexual Violence and the Media

In many ways, women have been the central characters in the Gujarat carnage, and their bodies the battleground. The Gujarati vernacular press has been the agent provocateur. The story starts with Godhra, where out of the 58 Hindus burnt, 26 were women and 14 children. But to really arouse the passions of the Hindu mob, death is not enough. Far worse than death is the rape of Hindu women—for it is in and on the bodies of these women that the *izzat* (honour) of the community is vested. So on 28 February, *Sandesh*, a leading Gujarati daily, in addition to reporting the Godhra tragedy in provocative language, also ran a front page story saying the following: '10-15 Hindu women were dragged away by a fanatic mob from the railway compartment.' The same story was repeated on page 16 with the heading 'Mob dragged away 8-10 women into the slums.' The story was entirely false. The police denied the incident, and other newspapers, including the *Times of India* could not find confirmation of this news. A day later, on 1 March, *Sandesh* carried a follow-up to this false story on page 16 with the heading 'Out of kidnapped young ladies from Sabarmati Express, dead bodies of two women recovered—breasts of women were cut off.'

Violation of Hindu honour was now compounded by extreme sexual violence and bestiality. Both the abduction and the cutting of breasts were lies—totally baseless stories, which were denied by the police. The fact-finding team was told that later *Sandesh* did publish a small retraction, buried in some corner of its pages. But the damage had been done. The murder and rape of Hindu women, emblazoned in banner headlines across the vernacular press became the excuse, the emotional rallying point, the justification for brutalizing Muslim women and children in ways not ever seen in earlier communal carnages. '*Unhonne hamari auraton aur bachchon par hamla kiya hai. Badla to lena tha* (They have attacked our women and children we had to take revenge)'—goes the sentiment of the angry Hindu. The newspaper literally became a weapon of war. According to a series of eyewitness accounts from Naroda Patiya, the worst-affected area in Ahmedabad, the mobs who attacked Muslim shops and homes, and brutalized Muslim women and children, were brandishing in their hands not only swords and stones, but copies of the *Sandesh* with the Godhra attack as the banner headline, shouting '*khoon ka badla khoon*' (blood for blood).

This one false story about the rape and brutalizing of Hindu women has spread like wildfire across Gujarat, almost assuming proportions of folklore. It now rests easily in the annals of undisputed common knowledge, and cannot be dislodged. Wherever the fact-finding team went, we heard some version of this story, spreading through word of mouth, through the channels of overworked rumour mills—sometimes it was ten Hindu women raped, sometimes it was six Hindu women—but the essential contours remained the same. In one place we heard details like 'The Muslims took the Hindu women to their madrasa and gang-raped them there.' Because the madrasa is the site of learning, raping women there projects the perpetrators as truly bestial men to whom nothing is sacred. In another village, 'Adivasi women' had replaced 'Hindu women' and this was given as the justification for Adivasi participation in the attacks on Muslims.

When the fact-finding team met Aziz Tankarvi, editor of *Gujarat Today*, known to represent the 'Muslim voice' He said clearly, '*Murder ho jata hai, chot lagti hai, to aadmi chup sahan kar leta hai, lekin agar maa, behen, beti ke saath ziyadti hoti hai to voh jawaab dega, badla lega.*' (When someone is murdered you are hurt. But a man can bear it quietly; it is when your mothers and daughters are violated, then he definitely responds, takes revenge). The fact that rape is perceived in this manner— as violating the honour of men, and not the integrity of women— is problematic in and of itself. What is particularly heinous is the fact that the *Sandesh* newspaper should fabricate stories of sexual violence, and use images of brutalized women's bodies as a weapon of war deliberately designed to provoke real violence against women from the Muslim community. What provocative lies *a la Sandesh* do is to provide justification for the carnage—both in the minds of the mobs who carry out the violence, and in the minds of the general 'Hindu' public which may be far removed from the site of the violence.

Ironically, while false stories about the rape of Hindu women have done the rounds, there has been virtual silence in the media, including in the English-language papers, about the real stories of sexual violence against Muslim women. Barring *Gujarat Today*, none of the Gujarati vernacular papers has carried stories about the brutal, bestial ways in which Muslim women were raped and burnt. Even *Gujarat Today*, despite being sympathetic to the Muslim experience, could only supply us with one clipping where the brutal experience of rape has been written about. The *Times of India*, since the beginning of the carnage, until 1 April 2002, carried only one story about rape—'Women's Day Means Nothing for Rape Riot Victims', on 8 March.[6] When members of the fact-finding team spoke to senior journalists in Ahmedabad, their explanation was that rape stories are provocative, and that in the early days of the violence, they had to play a socially responsible role, and not incite more violence. But in the weeks that followed, the press has continued to practice self-censorship about rape stories.[7]

No justice in sight for B—, S—

For the women who were raped during the Gujarat carnage, the first obstacle they faced in their struggle for justice was the attitude of the police. Simply put, many officers flatly refused to believe they had been raped. Despite all the documentation and personal testimonies, Gujarat police officers are today still a disbelieving lot. 'In my view, it is not scientically and psychologically possible to have a sexual urge when the public is rioting', B.K. Nanavati, a deputy superintendent of police told the Agence-France Press. (Praveena Sharma, 'After being raped in riots, Gujarat women face police inaction', AFP, 20 September 2002).

With attitudes like this, it is hardly surprising that the victims get no help even in those rape cases which the police agreed to register. B— of Randhikpur, who was raped and managed to lodge a complaint at the Limkheda police station is a case in point. The People's Union for Democratic Rights reports that as recently as September, 'Those named in the FIT by B— are known to have directly issued dire threats to her family. The accused told her uncle, Ismail, when he tried to go back to Randhikpur, that unless she withdrew the names of the accused from her complaint, her family would not be allowed to return, and 'it would be worse for her'.' (PUDR, *Act Two of Genocide*, September 2002). S—, of village Delol, who was raped by eight men, is nowhere near securing justice. 'The police have done nothing against the accused; they are still scot-free. But I'm determined to get justice,' she told AFP. She is yet to return home.

We find that, yet again, Muslim women are being victimized twice over. They have suffered the most unimaginable forms of sexual abuse during the Gujarat carnage. And yet, there is no one willing to tell their stories to the world. Women's bodies have been employed as weapons in this war—either through grotesque image-making or as the site through which to dishonour men, and yet women are being asked to bear all this silently. Women do not want more communal violence. But peace cannot be bought at the expense of the truth, or at the expense of the right of women to tell the world what they have suffered in Gujarat.

'People don't need revenge. They need to live again.'

Rizwana is 26 years old. An advocate, she lives in Vatva with her parents. She has experienced animosity many times while attending court. A couple of years ago there was a stabbing incident—one of the girls in court remarked, 'You people do a lot of stabbing, You must have learnt it'. An action by one individual would be attributed to the entire community. The Indo-Pak cricket matches would always become points of tension—No matter what happens, they always raise the issue of Pakistan. Eight per cent of the advocates in the court are Muslim. Once it so happened that at one particular meeting most of the advocates who attended were Muslims. A Senior Advocate walked into the room and remarked, 'This is looking like a Pakistani court.' I used to feel 'We are Indian. Please don't say things like this to us.'

She hasn't been to the city civil court where she practices since 27 February 2002. 'I normally go by scooter. I could go, but if I don't come back then what is the point. They haven't spared women and children this time. Women are not going to be allowed to roam about freely for a long time.'

What was she feeling? Anger, helplessness and desire for *badla* (revenge)? She looked startled by the word *badla*. 'Our people are *laachaar* (broken). They are not being able to do anything.' 'If it was a question of revenge we would have taken it long ago.' 'Now I can only think wistfully of the time when I was free. I would hop on my scooter and go wherever I pleased. Now we are prisoners in our own city. People don't need revenge. They need to live again.'

Women's Experiences: The Aftermath
PUCL *Vadodara and Vadodara Shanti Abhiyan*[*]

Fact-finding teams who visited various affected *bastis* and relief camps run by the *jamaats* in Vadodara have gathered a large number of testimonies and accounts of the violence from women. PUCL fact-finding teams focused, by and large, on discussions and interviews with Muslim women as they had borne the brunt of the violence. However, several discussions have been held with women from across various communities. Apart from interacting with and interviewing a wide cross-section of people affected by the violence, many discussions were also held with the police and the administration. The following account has been put together on the basis of detailed interviews with women as well as from direct observation of the prevailing situation.

The wide range of data collected by fact-finding teams reveal that the violence in Vadodara affected most women in some way or the other. Lives of minority women have of course changed drastically. However, women from all communities were also affected by the fear and terror promoted by the state and the police. Hindu women were caught in a fear psychosis about attacks by the 'other'. This largely stemmed from rumours that were being systematically spread by communal organizations in different areas, through various pamphlets and booklets, as well as rumour-mongering by the local press.

Although the livelihoods of all poor, working-class women have been affected, the situation in Muslim households has been far more serious, with hunger being an acute problem because minority men were unable to go out to work fearing attacks. The deep sense of betrayal that women feel by neighbours and children 'who grew up in front of my eyes (in my *aangan*)' is seen across classes. Thus all women, regardless of caste, class

[*]   Extract from, 'Women's Experiences: 27 February—10 May 2002, Vadodara', in People's Union for Civil Liberties, Vadodara, and Vadodara Shanti Abhiyan, *Violence in Vadodara: A Report*, Vadodara, May 2002, pp 122-130.

and community, have been significantly affected by the ongoing violence that has systematically dislocated their everyday living.

Women as Victimizers

There have been multiple effects on Hindu women. At one level, they have gained a new visibility in and access to the public sphere. This was evident in the *'Ram Dhun'* program of 15 March where they participated enthusiastically in celebrations in the many temples in the city in large numbers. Also noteworthy is the fact that they have taken active part in violence, in small though significant numbers. Area reports from Baranpura, Bajwa and Navayard, among others, reveal that women have been active members of the attacking mobs. Some prominent women leaders have also been named in affected persons' testimonies. On 1 March in Atladara, the sarpanch, Kantaben Sanabhai Vasava, was one of the main persons in the mob. Kanchanben Barot, a BJP councillor in the ESI Hospital area was seen to move around with a sword along with others in the mob. In Bajwa, Jayaben Thakkar was part of the attacking mob. Women have played a role in looting as well, as is evident in arrests made in Vadodara. These arrests were widely reported in newspapers in mid-March.

Importantly, they have taken the lead in mobilizing and organization of various activities. Several women's delegations which included members of the BJP and VHP made representations and complaints to the several investigating teams and commissions including NHRC and NCW. These new roles seem to have been played with increasing ease and social sanction.

At another level, women are undeniably an agency through which the ideology of hatred is being perpetuated. PUCL fact-finding teams report that the level of hate among the Hindu women was alarming. Although they started off sounding sympathetic (*'bahut bura hua'*, etc as seen in the infamous Best Bakery case) very soon they defended the violence saying, 'they had it coming', etc. Women are very much part of a systematic hate-the-Muslims campaign that has been in place for the last few years. They feel threatened by Muslims, economically and socially: 'They have four wives and twenty children, they will overrun us, they don't use contraception, etc. They are taking away all our business, we are becoming poor.' PUCL teams have pointed out the manner in which the line between hating Muslims to condoning their killing and encouraging it has been crossed, at least partly on account of the fear psychosis that centres around the notion of the 'dangerous Other.' The insecurity of Hindu women is, in many ways, a product of Hindutva ideology that sets them up as vulnerable to sexual attack by Muslim men. These perceptions are irrational and have no sound basis; nevertheless their fear is clearly real.

Concerns over safety and security have reshaped their daily lives even as they participate in the creation of such an environment. Affluent Hindu women routinely stayed up all night with the men in middle/upper class housing societies for fear of Muslim attacks, albeit in traditional gender roles, providing tea and snacks at regular intervals to the local vigilante men. Others, who have not gone along with the dominant outlook, have been threatened/abused for helping Muslims or even professing secular ideology.

Dalit women have, more or less, allied with the upper castes during the violence. This has been seen in areas like Baranpura, Navidharti, Navayard and Fatehpura. This has resulted in the Hinduization of dalit women on a scale never before witnessed in Vadodara. Dalit women, frequently working class, have been badly hit by the post-Godhra violence. Continuous curfew as well as the atmosphere of fear has resulted in acute economic distress. Many women who worked as daily wagers or domestic help could not reach their places of work, and many have lost employment. Loss of earnings has resulted in a rising incidence of impoverishment and hunger. PUCL teams observed greater anxieties among dalit women regarding life and property as compared to upper-caste women, at least partly because dalit *bastis* lie almost always alongside Muslim *bastis*. In Kagda Chawl, a Hindu woman who is a head loader in the wholesale vegetable market, and lives amidst Muslim families recounted how, during combing operations, the police barged into her home too. Because she is on good terms with the Muslim youth (and probably helped shelter them) the police call her a traitor.

Further, longstanding alliances forged by dalit and Muslim women on the basis of shared socio-economic concerns, as also neighbourhood spaces, seem to have broken down. The women of Jhanda Chowk of Kisanwadi as well as the women of Baranpura articulated this very clearly. Bhanuben Parmar, a resident of Fatehpura recounted in her testimony before the Citizens' Tribunal how she is still very concerned about her Muslim neighbours and friends, but is forced to keep herself aloof from them. All Hindu women in her *basti* feel that the police will punish them if they maintain their earlier close relationships with their Muslims friends. Nevertheless, some women have shown great personal bravery in order to safeguard life and property of their Muslim neighbours. In Kisanwadi Hussaini Chowk, Maharashtrian women stated that they had been salvaging the belongings of their Muslim neighbours and storing them till the Muslim families could return home. Dalit bastis, have also been more prone to 'combing operations' conducted by the police, and many women have been beaten and injured by the police, though the scale bears no comparison with that of Muslim women.

The position of minority households is not comparable to that of any other group. With their life and property under systematic attack, contending with unresponsive, indeed, biased police and administrative personnel, women of minority households have been facing a grim situation. Hunger is an acute problem as neither women nor men were in a position to go out to work, though as of 1 June 2002, the situation has improved somewhat. Hundreds of families have been displaced and rehabilitation is a distant possibility. The social tensions of living in unsafe times is exacerbated by the deep sense of betrayal experienced by the women especially when they have suffered attacks by neighbours and children who 'grew up in front of our eyes'.

Key Emerging Issues

From the testimonies and personal accounts of the women, several persistent themes emerged. Because the patterns and nature of violence changed during the three phases, the experiences of women and what they articulated as their issues also differed over the three phases. In the first phase of violence between 28 February and 8 March for instance, women recalled their pain and terror as they left their homes and saw them being looted and burnt. Many women were separated from their husbands and expressed their anxieties about their husbands' whereabouts. In the second phase following 15 March what stood out more was their suffering at the hands of the police. In fact after the first phase, most testimonies centered around the police atrocities on women during the combing operations.

Women have consistently complained about police brutality during 'combing operations.'[8] Women were also very angry about police bias during the violence. Many of the women were witnesses to police inability and sometimes unwillingness to protect them. The brutal actions of the police during 'combing operations' affected many women. The testimony of Kaushal Bano Mansuri of Bawamanpura on the 'combing operations' speaks for itself: 'I was putting my child to sleep at 9 p.m. on March 23. Suddenly I found lots of policemen in my house. They did not find our men at home. They started giving us *gaalis*. Put two *dandas* on me, one on my hand, the other on my stomach, and then they saw I was pregnant [9 months] and hit me in the thigh. They were all saying Kanani, Kanani [DCP of the area]. They were his staff. Only today I have started moving around [since I was so badly injured]. I had to go the hospital. I went into the dargah and hid there. I told them I was *pet se* (pregnant). They still said "We have to hit her." My *saas* [mother-in-law] also said that I am pregnant. They said, "We have to kill it before that happens."'

Humiliation and sense of violation
The effect of verbal abuse on women was stark, and members

of the fact-finding teams believe that this arena of violence against women is, perhaps, underrated. Humiliation, as a result of verbal abuse, rankled for long and carried almost as much weight as physical abuse. In almost all testimonies, women remembered abuse and slogan shouting very vividly. But it was not just the verbal abuses that angered the women. Rehana Pathan, a recently widowed woman in Kagda Chawl recalled with horror how the policemen barged into her *purdah* while she was in *iddat*. They showed no respect for her grief or for their religious practice of not seeing a man's face for three months after the husband's demise. Women of Kagda Chawl and Imran Chambers described their sadness at how on the evening of Moharram, the combing of the police rudely upset their feast and other religious celebrations. 'My son could not even eat the food that I had made for him!'

Many women recounted damage done to mosques/dargahs in their area. They were also knowledgeable about damage done to other mosques/dargahs, of which they spoke as much with sadness as with indignation. A woman from Badri Mohalla almost cried as she recounted how the police had torn up her Quran and thrown it into some water during the combing operations. 'How would you feel if they did this to your Gita?' she said.

Fear of the future

Overarching fear has become a part and parcel of life for women. Every woman we met displayed a fear of the future—for herself, her family and her community. Although fear and insecurity has permeated society at large, women contend with additional fears about sexual assault and abuse as well as with fear for safety of family members, particularly children. Insecurity is far more apparent at relief camps and when women have themselves experienced or witnessed violence.

All women reiterated their fears for a future where even a basic guarantee to life and property could not be taken for granted. Even women who had not suffered personal loss felt caught in the violence, merely by virtue of belonging to the minority community. PUCL team reports from Qureshi Jamaat Khana Relief Camp: 'The women were concerned about their future. They could not see beyond the camp. "How long will we stay here?" "How long will they feed us?"' they kept asking.

Hamida of Taiwada whose wrist was broken in three places as a result of police *lathis* on her stated that her work of making kites was at a standstill. Both men and women have been unable to work and earn. Lack of mobility and fear of attack on life and property has made venturing out a risky proposition for the minority community, and many could not access necessities like milk and food grain even when they had the means. Long-term prospects are equally grim — the well-planned attack on the livelihood resources of Muslims, whether large industry/business or the humblest *larri*—has rendered economic rehabilitation a daunting task. This has been aggravated by the VHP-Bajrang Dal call for economic boycott of Muslims. It is in this context that productive economic activity of Muslim women takes on a new urgency. We have reports of Muslim women, hitherto employed in home and small-scale industries, not being taken back to work, post-violence. Sadduben Ashrafbhai who worked as plasterer in Baroda Tiles factory in Manjusar was fired on 28 February with ten other Muslim workers of the company. Noorjehan Ismailbhai Ghanchi of Makarpura stated 'On 28 February, the *bandh* was announced. I was told to come back after fifteen to twnty days when things cool down. When curfew opened, I went and signed and was told by Santoshbhai, the supervisor, to come back later. I was at Tandalja Aashiana Camp for a month. On 24 April, when I went back Santoshbhai told me we have cancelled your card.' Many erstwhile employers of these women feel threatened by the current call for a blanket economic boycott of Muslims given by the Hindu right-wing organizations.

The amounts received as compensation for their losses has become a big issue with many women. Their losses are up to a few lakh of rupees and all that they have received is a few thousands. Justifiably they are indignant. A few women in the Qureshi Jamaat Khana stated that they had refused their cheques of Rs 10,000—their loss of property and personal effects was around Rs 12 lakhs. Other women said that they had accepted their meagre cheques because beggars can't be choosers, but they had registered their protest.

Concern for children's well-being and education

Women consistently showed concern for the effect the violence was having on their children's lives. On one hand, they were worried about the effects of uncertainty and dislocation on children as well as about the psychological fallout on children who witnessed violence and experienced arrest. Raeesa Shaikh of Tulsiwadi said poignantly, 'We have brought up our sons with such care, taught them never to harm anyone, to be peace-loving. Now they have taken away these young ones. If they turn into *aatankwadis* (terrorists, as a result of this experience in the jail) we'll be left with nothing.' On the other hand, they were deeply distressed at the way their children's education was affected. Women at Tandalja Relief Camp, for example, specifically asked for volunteers to teach the 250-odd children in the camp. Nevertheless, in view of the prevailing situation, many parents of girl students taking the tenth and twelfth class examinations were unwilling to let them give their papers. Women feel that the insecurity felt by the Muslim community as a whole would also have ramifications not just on education, but even on the individual liberty of their children, especially daughters in the long run.

Betrayal of trust

Muslim women have been traumatized by multiple betrayals. Corrosion of trust is most apparent in women who have been directly affected by the violence and arson. At one level, women acutely feel betrayed by people in their neighbourhood. Women felt upset that long-standing intimate relations did not count for anything during the violence. As Sajida Bano of Baranpura said, 'We had good relations with our neighbours, we used to visit each other at festivals and on other occasions. We would invite them. *Amara thi moon fervi lidu chhe* [now they have turned their faces away from us]'.

Witness to the fact that neighbours, with whom they have lived all their lives, participated in and sometimes led the attack on their community and the looting of property has undermined their belief in a common humanity. As Mehrunissa of Kasamala Kabristan put it, 'Who is a friend and who is a foe? *Insaan par se vishvas hi uth gaya hai.*' The communalization of neighbourhood spaces has also hit women very hard. They live in constant anxiety that children or livestock will cross the 'border.' They are sometimes unable to access civic amenities such as medical facilities, water etc., which lie on the 'other' side. Tragically, suspicion has entered relationships that have lasted for decades, and it is very doubtful if the common cause that women have forged across communities can be rebuilt.

At another level, women feel deeply let down by state institutions, particularly the police. The partisan attitude of the police, 'police *ektarfi,*' has dismayed them. Apart from suffering excesses at the hands of the police, many women have seen police indifferent and inactive, sometimes even colluding with mobs attacking them, conducting arbitrary combing operations in their localities, even though *their* localities were the ones under attack. They have watched innocent family members, old men, underage boys arrested while perpetrators of violence roamed free despite being named in FIRs. Women have lost faith in the fairness of almost all government institutions, and the ruling party, including the chief minister is held responsible for the current crisis in their lives. At the present moment, women feel secure only in the midst of their own community. There is a fear that this would lead to ghettoization of the community.

Reiteration of loyalty to Gujarat and India

Women interviewed by the PUCL compulsively sought to prove their loyalty to India. They recounted with anguish, the sloganeering which branded them traitors, and which told them to leave India for Pakistan. They kept asking where they could go. A woman from Badri Mohalla in her testimony to the Citizens' Tribunal said, 'We are born here, we will die here.

This is our home. Where will we go?'

Leadership

Many women have taken the lead in protecting themselves and their families. Key decisions regarding safety of the family, including determining places to hide, length of time of concealment, flight, its mode and direction, have often been made by women. The situation has also forced women to collectivize, for example, on 2 March women braved curfew restrictions to try and meet the defence minister, George Fernandes to apprise him of shortage of food, milk and other basic amenities. Women have also got together to protest police atrocities against themselves and the arrests of underage sons, as in Bahar Colony, Ajwa Road. They have led initiatives to meet the commissioner of police and register FIRs.

Despite enormous pressures, women have protected their neighbours, menfolk and others in vulnerable and sensitive areas of the city. In Kasamala Kabristan, Muslim women looked after their Hindu neighbours and provided them food during the curfew days. Women have also been organizing relief for those in camps or sheltering with families. Among others, Sherbanoo, Jahanara Rangrez, Sajida Bano of Baranpura, Najma Sheikh, Raeesa Shaikh of Tulsiwadi, Lakshmiben Pillai of Kisanwadi and Sonia Bhoi of Rain Basera have responded with tremendous courage and against great personal odds to protect their neighbours and their families. Middle- and upper-class Bohra women came out, probably for the first time, in the daily *satyagrah* programme (30 April to 4 May) to protest against combing in Mughalwada.

During curfew, women have had to play dual roles. Since curfew was often lifted for women alone, many women managed important work outside the home in addition to their household chores. Irrespective of the tension between the two communities, some women of both communities took grave risks to save lives. Many women helped each other out in terms of everyday necessities.

Notes

1   For the full transcript of the debate, see http://www.
    parliamentofindia.nic.in/lsdeb/dailydeb/30042002.html

*   This chapter consists of excerpts from the report, *The Survivors
    Speak: How Has the Gujarat Massacre Affected Minority
    Women?*, Fact-finding by a Women's Panel with help from
    Citizens Initiative, New Delhi, 16 April 2002.

2   At the time of writing the report.

3   PUDR, p 12.

4   Milind Ghatwai, 'BJP leader held for "rape" as mother refuses to
    give in,' *Indian Express* (Ahmedabad), 14 May 2002.

5   Kausar Bano's father, Khaliq Sheikh, has since been interviewed
    about the incident. Mukta Chakravarty, 'The face behind gujarati
    foetus headline,' *Indian Express*, 23 May 2002.

6   The *Indian Express* consciously decided not to run a story in
    early March on the Kausar Bano case. The story was written by
    Shefali Nautiyal in Ahmedabad on the basis of interviews with
    Naroda Patiya survivors but the newspapers editors in New Delhi
    felt the report might be provocative. See Jyoti Punwani's report
    of the 8 June seminar on the media and communal violence in
    Gujarat organized by the Network of Women in Media,
    Bangalore, www.thehoot.org

7   Senior journalists in Ahmedabad say they can be accused of
    rumour-mongering if they carry stories about rape, given that a
    bulk of the victims are either dead, or if alive have neither had
    medical examinations nor lodged FIRs. Why has it not been
    possible for these papers to carry stories saying that women on
    the run from rampaging mobs cannot be expected to undergo
    medical examinations within 72 hours? When no Muslim victim
    in Gujarat today can enter a police station confident that he/she
    will get a hearing or leave with a copy of their FIR, how does a
    rape victim manage to get an FIR lodged? Why is not possible for
    the press to carry these perspectives?

8   See the description of the incidents at Wadi-Taiwadi in Vadodara
    in chapter 'Narratives from the Killing Fields' and chapter 'When
    Guardians Betray' of this book.

7

Adivasis and Dalits

Tribal Voice and Violence
Ganesh Devy

When Gujarat was burning between 27 February and 4 March, the tribal belt on the eastern border of Gujarat was quiet. The only exceptions were the two districts of Panchmahals, for which Godhra is the main town. Elsewhere in the tribal areas, tribals, Hindus and Muslims continued to coexist peacefully. The only disturbing sight was the long lines of tribal labourers walking the distance from the curfew-bound cities to their villages, in some cases a walk of 100 kilometres. They walked silently, carrying the burden of all their belongings on their heads, a lot of misery in their hearts and terrified like trapped animals.

Nearby 60,000 tribal labourers migrate to Baroda every year in search of employment between October and March. From the third day of the riots they started returning to their villages. No public transport was available to them. So they decided to walk back like refugees trying to escape a devastated country.

The first Muslim shop set on fire in any tribal village was in Tejgadh. This case of arson took place on the evening of 4 March. During the night, two more shops were torched. The rural branch of Baroda district police had not expected this late reaction to the Godhra incident. On Tuesday, Senior DSP Keshav Kumar, who has prepared the first ever book on the Indian Penal Code (IPC) in a tribal language, asked me to join him in his efforts to restore peace. When we arrived at Tejgadh, we saw a cloth shop being looted and set on fire by a mob. The

DSP instantly fired tear gas shells and dispersed the mob. From there, he proceeded to Chhota Udepur together with the MP (BJP) and the former MP (Congress) to discuss the arrangements. He had expected five trucks of army to arrive in the area for night patrolling.

During that night, no army personnel were present in Tejgadh. More shops and houses were burnt in the village. Tejgadh has a miniscule Muslim population; 75 per cent are tribals, 15 per cent Hindus and 5 per cent Muslims. Those who burnt shops and houses in the initial stage were quite drunk and came from the neighbouring villages. But once the first attack was over, other villages joined in on their own with no further need for instigation and the looting continued.

The incidents in Tejgadh displayed a method as well as a sequential growth in the theme of the disturbance. In the cities, at least for the first three days, the riots had a clear stamp of a well-researched and well-orchestrated strike. The attacks there were marked by an amazing precision. As against this, the villages in Panchmahals, Kheda and Baroda districts displayed a blind anger. The incidents at Tejgadh were different from both. They showed that it was not included in the master plan of violence. Nor were the incidents unfolding in Tejgadh a frenzied reaction to the Godhra outrage.

The Muslim population in Tejgadh continued to stay in the village carrying out its daily work without any apprehension of intimidation. On that day, the local population reportedly threatened Muslims in some other village. It was initially maintained that all Muslims of Tejgadh went over to the other village to defend them. It is said that the residents of Tejgadh felt angered by this aggressive attitude of the Tejgadh Muslims. As a result, one Muslim shop was set ablaze in Tejgadh on the evening of 4 March.

It is said that Sarpanch Krishnakant Shah had tried to prevent the burning but had to give up in the face of pressure and threats. Also, that the arsonists came from outside. After the incident, none in Tejgadh was prepared to name the arsonists. And nobody said why the Muslims had gone to another village and why none returned to Tejgadh to save the shops, houses and vehicles that were burnt in installments with great punctuality. No one was prepared to say how so much kerosene was available, and who led the mobs. And no one would explain why only properties belonging to Muslims were set on fire.

The Tejgadh carnage was leisurely; everyday one or two shops were burnt. In the very first instance, the mob was collected from Timla, Koraj and Achhala segments of the panchayat, all at a distance of one or two kilometres from Limdi Bazaar, the centre of the riots. In the second and third instances the distance increased. Tribals from neighbouring villagers wanted to have their share of the booty. The residents of Tejgadh shut the doors of their houses and in a self-imposed curfew locked themselves in. When the curfew was officially imposed, it was only a technical detail.

The police force provided to watch over the village was meagre, and after dispersing two or three mob attacks, it fell into the same kind of conspiracy of inaction that the villagers had already hatched. Thus, even on the twelfth day of the Tejgadh riots, yet another house was burnt, with neither the villagers nor the police ready to intervene. On the thirteenth and the fourteenth day, one or two more houses were burnt down. The ritual continued. If the violence in the cities was marked by its precision hitting, and in other rural areas by its blind frenzy, the violence in Tejgadh stood out for its ritual quality. It showed cold-bloodedness in slow-time. This ritual quality was a clear indication that at this end of the Gujarat riots, the theme of communalism was taking a back seat, having been taken over by the norms of tribal culture.

Therefore, when trouble began in Panvad two days later, and at a distance of thirty kilometres from Tejgadh, the stage for a tribal takeover of the riots was already set. Those interested in fanning the trouble had already planted rumours that would provoke tribals. Among the rumours that I heard, the following five deserve mention.

One: A tribal dreamt that a majestic Mahuda, the most sacred tree of the Rathwas, was chopped down and used to block the road. Babadev, or the Babo Pithora God, was very angry and demanded revenge on those who had harmed the Mahuda.

Two: The police believe that tribals have a *mantra* with which they can spell-bind the rifles used by the police. Therefore, policemen are scared of using their weapons.

Three: A certain Badwa, a *shaman,* had received divine inspiration to become the biggest Badwa, though only twenty-two years old. Having learnt all aspects of magic and since he cannot be killed, he would lead the tribals.

Four: Muslims have raped tribal women and kidnapped tribal girls to sell in the cities.

Five: Muslims have taken away Kashmir (a place or a girl) by exploiting tribals, and have kept fifty tribal women in custody.

The location of Panvad is unique. Almost twenty small and big villages are accessible from there in a short time by walking cross-country. A number of Hindu sectarian movements have been active in the area for several years. Some Jain monks, probably from Rajasthan or Madhya Pradesh, who live in a nearby village called Kawara, have considerable influence on the people. The Muslim businessmen in Panvad are affluent, and many were engaged in moneylending at interest rates ranging between 60 to 120 per cent.

Whether it was because of hatred for the moneylenders, or because of rumours about the magical impediments against the ability of the police, or whatever, the congregation of tribals at Panvad was alarmingly large. Newspapers report that their numbers were up to 5,000. But considering that every village sent about 50 to 100, the number who actually participated in the looting was a little less than 200 at any given time.

The ritual quality introduced by the Tejgadh events was in evidence on a magnified scale in Panvad. This time, the tribals were carrying their ceremonial bow and arrows. Normally, they do not use arrows as weapons. When they want to kill someone, they use the sharp metallic *paliyu* or *dhariyu*; and when they want to fight a thief or an enemy, they use guns. Many of them do possess a gun licence; others buy them illegally from Madhya

Pradesh, just a few kilometres away. Only children use arrows for hunting birds. As a result few birds are to be seen in that area.

So when the first mob attacked Panvad, it carried bows and arrows as a ritual decoration. But when it realized that mere *mantras* could not stop the policemen from firing, the next wave on the following day seems to have brought guns as well. Senior DSP Keshav Kumar, a courageous and conscientious officer, told me that he had encountered tribals who stood before him with bared chests, daring him to fire. Such is their faith in the power of the rumoured mantra.

From the perspective of the tribals it is necessary to raise some questions about the riots: Did the tribal population of Chhota Udepur region have any plan of rising up in revolt? Was there any explicit or latent movement in the area bordering on a militant opposition to the state? Did the communal BJP make such inroads in tribal life that the spirit of Hindutva overtook the local tribal culture? In other words, how much of the Muslim persecution in the tribal regions of Gujarat during the 2002 March riots was tribal in character and how much of it was a measure of the BJP's success? Answers to these questions are important for understanding the riots, as well as the tribal situation.

A Proxy War

During those days, an educated young Rathwa friend sent me a note. It contained his reflections on the demise of a tree. This was the giant neem, called Limda in Gujarati and which gave the name 'Limdi Bazaar' to the area in which arson was going on. The neem was set on fire by the arsonists. It had been standing there for more than a century; and it was burnt alive. It burnt for ten days, slowly, ritually. The note by Arjun Rathwa said, 'Did the Limda have any religion apart from giving shade to the wayfarers? Was it not like an adivasi, neither Hindu nor Muslim? Why have they destroyed it? Was it anybody's enemy? The adivasis too are being destroyed like the neem. They are neither Hindus nor Muslims. But now they are being uprooted altogether.'

I would like to consider this note as typifying tribal non-involvement in communal politics. What then was the source of the wrath let loose on the Muslim community? The most likely answer to this question is that the tribals were made to fight a proxy war on behalf of the baniyas.

Two incidents from the earliest days of the Gujarat riot will illustrate the tribal unwillingness to participate in the communal frenzy. On the evening of 27 February, a truck carrying Muslim passengers from Panchmahals sped through Tejgadh, causing another vehicle, a jeep carrying passengers, to pull closer to the edge of the road. Such jeeps, the most popular mode of transport in the area, are impossibly over-crowded, with passengers hanging on to the vehicle on all sides.

This one pulled itself so close to the edge of the road that four passengers, three men and a woman, died on the spot, crushed between the vehicle and the trees on the side of the road. The villagers knew that the other vehicle, which had caused the accident, was carrying Muslims, not from any other district but from Panchmahals, not on any other day but the day of the Godhra outrage. The villagers in Tejgadh allowed the vehicle a safe passage without any expression of anger, which under those circumstances would have been justified even on an ordinary day.

The second incident happened on 28 February in Haridaspur, the oldest segment of Tejgadh. Haridaspur, which has 170 households, all having a clan relationship, had gathered during the forenoon to cremate and mourn the death of an inhabitant. In that assembly of approximately 1,200, some elected panchayat members from another locality talked of avenging the Godhra incident. But this did not find favour even after the gathering had been served the ritual drink of wine. Such was the support to the Hindutva appeal the day when all newspapers carried headlines about the Godhra carnage. Those present reported (on condition of anonymity) that free supply of kerosene and liquor was promised to all those who had the 'courage' to attack Muslims.

The trouble-makers approached the sarpanch of Tejgadh on 1 March to participate in burning Muslim families, but he reportedly refused to allow any violence within the limits of his panchayat. It appears that on 2 and 3 March, the communal elements of the village changed their argument by giving up the purely communal angle and introduced the more acceptable business angle. They said that Muslim businessmen had become arrogant and, to use the local idiom, 'they have put on too much fat.' This argument clinched the issue, and on the evening of 4 March, when in Chief Minister Modi's ridiculous phrase, 'the riots had been brought under control within a record seventy-two hours,' the first Muslim shop was set on fire.

This shop, owned by the fifty-five-year-old Yakub Khatri, had goods like biscuits and mints. Yakub Khatri owned five acres of agricultural land and his brother, Ghanibhai, was a respected figure in the affairs of the Tejgadh mosque. However, the sweetmeat shop does not give a clear picture of Yakub's financial status. He owned a large house and two more shops, selling foodgrains, cutlery, bangles and shoes, some distance away. Obviously, by targetting Yakub Khatri it was possible for Hindu communal forces to combine the theme of religious revenge with that of business competition.

When this instance of arson happened, the Muslim community in Tejgadh was still present in the village. It tried to counter the attack, but the mob that had gathered was large, and its resistance inadequate. There were no policemen present on the location of this crime. During the three preceding days, the Muslims in Tejgadh had obviously feared such an attack and were prepared to flee. The riots that began during the late hours of the noon continued during the evening with two more shops gutted by fire. During the night, all Muslims fled. None seemed to know where they had sought asylum. It was rumoured that during the Yakub Khatri incident, Muslims had fired shots at the mob, implying that they were in possession of unlawful weapons and strengthening the stereotype of all mosques being places for hoarding weapons.

The next shop destroyed was owned by Kadarbhai, fifty-five years old, and owner of a flour mill, a cloth and a grocery shop. Dilawarbhai, forty, who owned a cloth shop and an adjacent shop selling cutlery and shoes, was the next in the line of fire. Ahmedbhai, fifty-five, owned a foodgrains business as well as an outlet renting *pandals* and public address systems for functions. Nasirbhai, who too had a cutlery and foodgrains business, was the next target.

At this juncture, communal interests seem to have faded from the minds of the rioters. Those who organized the riots and funded them appear to have started looking at this operation purely as a business strategy of eliminating competition and ensuring total control over the market; and those who participated in the riots appear to have started looking at the incidents as an opportunity to loot in a manner of an unusual public ritual.

It was at this moment that the five rumours previously listed were planted because an internal contradiction had started breaking up the momentum that the communal force had managed to create with great difficulty. The contradiction appears to have come up from the intention of tribals to attack businessmen (who invariably have been moneylenders), and the baniya intention of targetting Muslim businessmen alone. The Hindu baniyas who were behind the riots started fearing that the tribal enthusiasm for looting shops would lead to their own shops becoming targets. Therefore, once again the riot machine at Tejgadh chose to bum down the two shops of Yakub Khatri, which were spared during the first round of arson.

The next to be attacked was an elderly and respectable Muslim, popularly known as Lakhpati (a millionaire), who had been a king-pin in the local moneylending business, though in recent years his fortunes had declined. When the communal passion was ignited, the rioters had no time to think of the financial status of the victims. Therefore, the houses of Bhikha, the tailor, Fakirbhai, the poor peasant with a land holding of less than an acre, the house of Yusufbhai Khatri, a retired prison-clerk, were all reduced to ashes.

But, the business interest in the riots did not wane and a warehouse where Muslim merchants stocked their goods was also set to fire. The houses deserted by its Muslim inhabitants were searched by the mobs and vandalized. The last to be attacked was Basheer Khatri's soft drinks and cloth shop. The police presence in Tejgadh throughout the days of the riots, a long period of two weeks, was more marked by its complicity than by inadequacy. What is perhaps the most explicit comment on the motive and the nature of the riots is that not once after 4 March did the panchayat members or the local Hindu baniyas make an attempt to dissuade the rioters.

Their only act of 'grace' was to spare the house of Shabirbhai, who has been an elected member of the panchayat and represents, at present, the Muslim community in Tejgadh. Thus, the 500-odd Muslim inhabitants of Tejgadh were 'punished' for someone else's attack on the Sabarmati Express at Godhra, and, more importantly, for competing with the Hindu moneylenders in the tribal area. Similarly, throughout the few days of the intense rioting in Panvad, one repeatedly heard that the riots were meant to teach a lesson to the Muslim moneylenders who had 'put on too much fat.'

It would be completely wrong to assume that the rioting in support of Hindutva was something that the tribals wanted at any stage. The facts show that the truth is far from it. There had to be a considerable amount of coaxing before any tribal village joined in the riots. There was free use of intimidation too. Generally, a group of fifteen to twenty persons went to the sarpanch of a village to ask him to give 'forces' for attacking Muslims. One or two of the ring-leaders spoke. They promised protection from the law to all those who joined and threatened those who refused the 'invitation'. Since the instigators belonged to the ruling party, it was intimidating to encounter such promises and threats.

Before and during the main days of the Panvad riots, a young Rathwa—who became the shaman in the widespread rumour—promised Rs 2,00,000 to the family of any possible casualty or alternately threatened those who refused. This person himself neither possessed so much wealth to promise compensation nor political clout to hold out the threat. It must be kept in mind that the Rathwas are a people of few words, do not speak beyond a monosyllable in their normal conversation, and rarely tell lies. If a Rathwa commits a murder, it is often said by the police, he will report to the police station himself and confess to his crime. Therefore, when this person was going round making the offer, he was, in all probability, not using empty words. Surely, other persons with money to offer had backed him, and clearly, he was working at their behest.

All in all, therefore, the tribal riots were organized by the moneylenders, even if the legal evidence to establish this fact will be slow in coming forth. Any combing operation undertaken by the state following the riots will be a superficial exercise and will end by only a large number of poor rioters being booked on the basis of stolen goods such as utensils, foodgrains and cloth found in their dwellings.

Obligated by Debt

There have been excellent studies on the role of the *sahukar* in the Panchmahals during the nineteenth century and on how they 'generated' the tribal resistance movement to protect their own right to trade salt in Sirohi district of Rajasthan. Thanks to these studies, one can say with confidence that the tribals in western India have remained under the yoke of the moneylender for centuries.

The ability of tribals to meet any contingencies requiring large cash payments has considerably gone down, particularly from the time the tribals lost their sovereign rights over the forests and had to identity themselves with a given piece of land that was recorded in the books of the revenue department. The land available for cultivation gets divided every passing generation, though such division is not necessarily reflected in the land records. In rain-fed agriculture, the tribal tiller manages to produce just enough for subsistence, and even a single year of poor rain leads to indebtedness.

As against the documentation requirement of any bank deal, which is beyond a tribal's capacity, the private moneylender asks for no documents. He knows by name every tribal who comes to him as a client. His terms are sufficiently flexible to accommodate modifications in the schedule of payment should it be required due to failure of the monsoon. In exchange for all this kindness the moneylender charges a high rate of interest. It ranges between Rs 5 to 12 per month, that is, 60 to 144 per cent for a year. The interest for the first three months is deducted from the principal at the time of the lending, which means that an amount of Rs 70 is handed over to the borrower out of a notional Rs 100 if the interest is 120.

The loan does not have to be repaid in cash. The moneylender accepts foodgrains, forest produce or timber in lieu of cash at a rate that he will decide according to the going rate in the local market; and if the foodgrains are not enough to repay the loan with the interest, the borrower approaches another moneylender in order to procure cash to repay the first loan in full. Two centuries of this lending practice have made the moneylenders prosperous beyond imagination and the tribals indebted beyond redemption.

The politicians too are greatly dependent on the moneylenders for their political success, for the sahukars control the vote banks. It is almost impossible for the politicians not to be sensitive to the views and interests of the moneylenders. Even when the elected representatives of people belong to tribes in reserved constituencies, they are severely restricted from undertaking developmental activities that will harm the interests of the moneylenders. Therefore, while one finds that an impressive developmental activity of a cosmetic nature takes place in tribal areas, economic empowerment is deliberately given a back seat.

Poor infrastructure, chronic cash-crunch, pervasive unemployment, illiteracy, and technological backwardness, which in other sectors are considered unfavourable for economic growth, are the minimal necessary conditions for growth in the private moneylending sector. The situation may differ in degree from one tribal district to another, but the general pathology of tribal underdevelopment and chronic indebtedness does not.

Playing on Tribal Anxieties

The use of bows, arrows and guns by the tribals against the police during the riots is not sufficiently explained by an analysis of their indebtedness to the moneylenders and being coaxed by them into eliminating Muslim competitors. The mob-militancy of the Rathwa tribals has other roots. In order to explain those we need to look at the sociology of Panvad more closely and also how its confrontation with modernity has produced unique discontents.

Panvad, among the tribal towns of Vadodara district, is closest to Madhya Pradesh. The Bhils, who are no different from the Rathwas in language or customs and who live on the other side of the 'notional' border, were at one time notified during British rule under the Criminal Tribes Act (1871). The reason was that they had earlier worked as seasonal soldiers for the Maratha princes in Indore and Dhar. But their 'denotification' in 1952 has left them no real choice but to take up a life of occasional crime. As a result of the possible menace of the denotified Bhils across the border, the villages surrounding Panvad have launched upon a massive deforestation of the low hills for increasing the range of visibility as a security measure. The timber merchants at Chhota Udepur who controlled the Forest Kamdar Sangh during the 1960s encouraged deforestation of this region.

All the ecological dangers that follow deforestation have been visited upon the Panvad region. Agricultural income in that area is lower in comparison to corresponding agricultural holdings in other tribal areas of the district. As a way out, Panvad tribals have moved to literacy and education, but for want of an institution of higher learning nearby, the young tribals end up with high school education and little or no employment. Many migrate to places like Surat for diamond cutting and Kutch as construction or agricultural labour.

For many years the Gujarat Mineral Development Corporation's project at nearby Kadipani provided them employment. But some years back it ran into rough weather due to legal and administrative hassles. Since then, the young tribals in the area have taken to drug trafficking and selling minor arms. The arms are brought in from Madhya Pradesh and taken to Baroda where customers in the region are located. Those who make this easy money then move on to become small-time moneylenders and start acquiring Hindu names and traits. They are the ones who become hospitable to various sect movements. These new arrivals in the Hindu fold have been the special constituency of the Hindutva movement in the area. For the young, neo-Hindu, semi-educated, unemployed, indiscriminate generation, the Hindu moneylender has become the role model, and drugs and unlicensed guns are the order of the day.

The ultimate source of violence is the mind and not the weapons in one's possession. The tribal mindset is not feudal, but it certainly is medieval. It is not feudal because of the tribal attitude to state formation in which the clan replaces the state. But precisely for reasons of preserving clan autonomy and purity, the attitude to women among the tribals is dictated by a limitless fear of women's pollution by an external agency. There is invariably bloodshed when a tribal woman expresses the desire to marry a person outside the particular tribal clan. This social code, however, is increasingly coming under stress from the rapidly changing economic context.

The tribal district north of the Panvad-Chhota Udepur area, that is the Panchmahals, has witnessed social transition of women's status on an unprecedented scale. Among the tribals, the groom gives dowry to the bride's parents. The bride-price among most tribes is nominal or notional. But, among the heavily indebted Panchmahals tribals, this bride-price has come to be perceived as an alternate source of income. In recent years, it has soared to Rs 60,000, while earlier it used to be one or two thousand rupees. The result is that as soon as the wedding takes place, the groom takes the bride with him to a city like

Ahmedabad or Baroda and the two start work as labourers so that the huge amount borrowed from relatives and moneylenders can be repaid over a period extending to several years.

The condition of migrant women labourers in the cities is pitiable, and they face sexual exploitation from labour contractors and city-dwellers. Now the tribals in Panchmahals have started receiving lucrative offers from caste Hindus for purchase of their daughters. The tribals in Panvad area are familiar with these changes. To the east of Panvad is Madhya Pradesh (MP). The tribal women in MP have faced humiliation worse than those in the Panchmahals. Some of the denotified tribal communities such as the Bedias and Kanjars have reached a situation where forcing young girls into sex work is seen as most natural.

In the Panvad region, a fear of violation of tribal women has gripped the tribal psyche. The police records for the period 1990 to 2000 show that the highest number of murders in the region was related to the perceived fear of a woman being taken away. Therefore, it would have been surprising had the tribals in that region not reacted violently after being fed a generous diet of rumours about fifty of their women being sexually abused by Muslims. Those who planned the pogrom did not use this rumour in Tejgadh, and therefore the scale of violence in Panvad was higher than in Tejgadh.

No Room for Adivasis in Hindutva

Those who want to understand the unexpected rise of violence among the tribals of Gujarat may find it useful to note that during a short period of six weeks preceding the March 2002 riots, in a small segment of Tejgadh, Haridaspur, with a population of 1,200, the following sudden deaths had occurred: (*i*) Mansukhbhai Dalasukhbhai, 55; (*ii*) Chikhabhai Dalasukhbhai, 45; (*iii*) Kanchanbhai Chhaganbhai, 40; (*iv*) Kamriben Tersinghbhai, 40; (*v*) Maniabhai Ruplabhai, 40; (*vi*) Singliben Nathiyabhai, 55; and (*vii*) Sansubhai Soriyabhai, 13. In addition, two children of ten and one respectively, died, whose names are not in my records. Not all of them died of Sickle Cell. The general lifespan for Sickle Cell patients ranges between ten to twenty-five years. Many of these, therefore, have to be described as deaths due to malnutrition and medical neglect. No government would admit to the fact that so many poor people died for want of sufficient diet.

If a large section of population is left to fend for itself, to face poverty, hunger, exploitation, and if their semi-literacy and unemployment lead them to a harsh zone of conflict of social values, if the new role models are based on the idea of making easy money, it is likely that the space for an irrational militant tendency will be created. Panvad could not have been an exception.

Yet, it would be completely off the mark to believe that the tribals in Chhota Udepur and Kawant talukas of Vadodara district had, at any time prior to the riots of March 2002, made any plans or conspiracy of an armed attack on the haats in Tejgadh or Panvad, or that there was any local leadership with an apolitical ideology in which violence is the means for social change.

Did the tribal attack on Muslim properties signify a victory for the ideology of Hindutva? One who is not familiar with the tribal traditions will be inclined to answer the question in the affirmative. It may seem that the tribals have come to be staunch supporters of the BJP. But the fact is that the tribals are neither Hindus nor Muslims. In India, there are two types of communities—those that conform to castes and religions and those that do not. Therefore, one is either a subscriber to a religion and member of a caste, or alternately, one is a tribal. Since it has become necessary to write in all official forms if one is a tribal-Hindu, a tribal-Christian or a tribal-Muslim, most tribals have started believing that they are Hindus, Muslims or Christians.

However, when the tribals claim to be Hindus, would any Hindu say that he is a tribal? Though from the tribal point of view 'tribal' and 'Hindu' are not mutually exclusive social categories, from the Hindu point of view they are so. The political discourse in India during the last fifty years, which has come to talk of the SC and the ST in a single breath, is largely responsible for the shifting sense of tribal self-identification.

If one were to look at the actual religious practices, spiritual spaces and belief systems, one would find that tribals are markedly different from Hindus even when the points of convergence may be several. For instance, tribals do not have notions of *yoga, sanyasa, varnas* and *ashramas*. Many tribes do accept some of the Hindu godheads as icons of worship, but no tribe accepts all of them *in toto*. The tribal myths related to gods and demons are markedly different from the Hindu myths. The tribal Ramayanas and Mahabharatas are strikingly different in plot and purport from the Hindu versions of those epics. The institution of priesthood operates very differently among the tribals than it does among Hindus.

In fact, a tribe is bound by its clan affiliation and cannot develop 'caste' as a social institution, which depends on a social hierarchy bound to the accident of birth in a given family. All tribals in a given tribe belong to the same 'caste' and therefore do not have a social hierarchy similar to that, which stratifies the caste Hindus. That was precisely the reason why, while making a listing of socially disadvantaged communities in India, a Schedule of Castes had to be conceptualized as distinct from a Schedule of Tribes.

There was a brief period of Indian history during the early days of colonial rule when all communities in India were described by the term 'tribe'. Thus, the Portuguese travellers in India used the terms 'tribe' and 'caste' as freely interchangeable. But, by the time of Lord Dalhousie it had become amply clear to the British colonial government that the tribes and the castes responded differently to the state. The castes were prepared to accept the notion of state, the tribes were not. Therefore, two official listings were made by the colonial government, one for the 'Criminal Tribes' in 1871, and the other for the 'Tribes' in 1872. The list of tribes has been accepted in the post-colonial times as a useful sociological apparatus, while the legally discriminated 'Criminal Tribes' have been 'denotified' and distributed between the STs, SCs and OBCs.

Given that the tribes have a distinct past, cultural traditions, attitude to the state and spiritual bearings, the tribal identity as Hindus, Muslims or Christians becomes a far more complicated issue than the identity of a Hindu as a Hindu, which too has its own complications. Hence the assertion that tribals are Hindus, when they are not Christians or Muslims, can at best be stretched to mean that in the vast and amorphous cultural federation of the subcontinent's civilization, tribal communities too are a presence, albeit on the farthest margins of the caste hierarchy, and mostly far outside it.

It is pertinent to ask why any tribal would feel attracted by the concept of Hindutva, unless he has willingly decided to enter the Hindu caste fold, which in his case will invariably be at the lowest rung of the hierarchy. But in order to answer this puzzling question, one must also spell out that Hindutva does not mean, and by its proponents is never expected to mean, being a Hindu. In other words, 'Hindutva' to a Hindu is not the same thing as 'Christianity' is to a Christian.

Hindutva really means, as understood by its advocates, conformity to the idea that India has primarily been a Hindu *rashtra*. It is not a religious philosophy or a social reform movement. It is a political philosophy based on cultural chauvinism, which insists that the non-Hindus of India accept their place as 'minorities', whose safety and security will depend on their ability to earn the 'goodwill of the majority'. At the heart of the Hindutva ideology is the idea that the good of a majority should also be seen as the good for any minority, and that any assertion of minority rights is essentially a threat and a challenge to the political authority of the majority. Such minorities, therefore, are seen by the Hindutva advocates as anti-national and anti-social. Besides, any attempt by a minority to swell their numbers is seen by the Hindutva votaries as aggression. Hence, conversion to Christianity or a Hindu girl's marriage to a Muslim or a Christian are seen as undesirable and provocative acts.

There is a major difference, however, between the Islamic

fundamentalists in Iran or the erstwhile Afghanistan and the proponents of Hindutva. The Islamic fundamentalists are not concerned with nationality and numbers. They want all Muslims to follow the tenets of Islam as 'faithfully' as the fundamentalists insist. The Hindutva ideology is primarily bound to the idea of rashtra and it revolves round the idea of a politically powerful majority. Islamic fundamentalism is theocractic militancy. Hindutva is nationalistic puritanism. The former creates internal repression to stop liberalization of Islam; the latter creates threats to the surrounding communities and faiths so that those communities and faiths do not assert their own identities. But, despite these differences, both these ideologies share a profound distrust of cultural diversity.

The advocates of Hindutva dream that some day India will become a Hindu rashtra. The tribals, who are not Hindus, therefore, need not have much enthusiasm for Hindutva. How is it then that in the riots of March 2002, the tribals fell upon the Muslims with such brutality?

The tribals do not know who Babar was and that he or any of his successors may have destroyed Hindu temples and built mosques on those sites. They do not know anything about Savarkar or Hedgewar. They do not know what the RSS stands for. None of them has volunteered to be a Ram sevak and been to Ayodhya. They have never heard of the Shah Bano case or of the Imam of Jama Masjid. The only face of Islam that the tribals have seen and known is the one presented by the local moneylenders. The only face of the Hindutva movement known by the tribals is the presence of the BJP in the panchayat and assembly elections. Though it is true that the tribals feel somewhat closer to Hindus than to Muslims, what is more true is that their affinities are entirely dictated by local issues and local politics.

The Congress leadership knew well the severe limitations on the tribal awareness of national and international issues. Throughout the years of Congress domination of the tribal areas, the party took great care not to educate and sensitize the tribals. They had to be kept as a vote bank, pure and simple; the only issues that could keep them so were underdevelopment and poverty. Throughout the four decades of Congress control in the tribal areas, it spared no effort to drive home to them that they were underdeveloped. This led the tribals to believe that their underdevelopment was an axiomatic truth. Today, when a tribal says 'we are *pachhat*', backward, there is not even a shade of questioning or skepticism about this condition. The Congress knew that if the tribals were kept poor, they would not become political.

The BJP does not know how to remove the poverty of the tribals. Not that it has much interest in the economic progress of the tribals, because it too wants the tribals as a massive vote bank. For about a decade now, the Sangh Parivar has been active in the tribal areas in every state. Through one of its sister organizations, the Vanavasi Seva Sangh (VSS), it has been spreading the message of Hindutva among the tribals. The VSS insists on calling the tribals *vanavasis* and not *adivasis* which means 'the indigenous people', since the VSS shares the RSS view of history in which the Aryans are the original inhabitants of India. How can adivasis, who in the VSS opinion are non-Aryans, be the original inhabitants? Thus the adivasi-ness of the tribals is a serious threat to Hindutva.

The VSS has been positing the Christian missionaries as the major enemy of the adivasis. The tribals know the missionaries well. They understand the talk about conversion. They know that the missionaries do not allow them to sing their traditional songs and paint their traditional gods like Babo Pithoro or Itelan and worship them. In the Dangs district of Gujarat, and in other states like Orissa and Bihar, the Christian missionaries had to face the wrath of the tribals supporting the Hindutva agenda in recent years.

It is interesting, however, to note that those tribals who participated in the attacks on Christian churches in the Dangs and the Muslim shops and houses in the Panchmahals, Banaskantha and Vadodara districts, still describe themselves as adivasis. They do not feel comfortable in calling themselves vanavasis. In other words, the VSS and the BJP have achieved a measure of success in providing the tribals a political agenda of hatred, but they have not succeeded in changing the tribal sense of identity.

Tribals have acquired a strong sense of hatred for their perceived enemies. The poverty preserved for them by the Congress and the politics of hatred introduced among them by the BJP can become a deadly mixture. Since the logical end of Hindutva will be to demand an unquestioning subservience from all minorities, including the tribals, and their total loyalty to the idea of a Hindu rashtra for which the Aryan indegeneity will be the cornerstone, a violent conflict between the adivasi tribals and the vanavasi Hindus is inevitable.

What the Hindutva ideology has gained by inciting the tribals to attack Muslims may look attractive in a limited perspective of the next assembly elections. However, the long-term implication of the political process unleashed cannot but be disturbing for the state. During the March 2002 riots, the authority of the state has visibly eroded in the tribal areas. To establish it again will be a difficult task.

The outcome of the riots is that the Muslims are languishing in relief camps. They have lost all that they had. They feel so insecure that they will not be prepared to go back to their burnt dwellings and shops amidst hostile neighbours. The earthquake in Gujarat left 20,000 dead. Despite tremendous cooperation and help from all comers of the world, the state government has not been able to rehabilitate all the families affected by the quake. The riots have left nearly 100,000 uprooted and economically ruined others. Those innumerable Muslims who have lost their employment are not even counted in this figure. There is just no possibility that these huge numbers will ever be rehabilitated.

Another outcome of the riots is that the tribals of Gujarat have been fed on a politics of hatred. It can easily turn against the non-Muslims as well. There are eight million tribals in Gujarat, most of whom are extremely poor and starving. The long-term effects of this thoughtless political bravado are frightening. While the villages like Tejgadh and Panvad are limping back to normalcy, they can hardly forget the deafening *kikiyario* they have heard in March 2002. The *kikiyario* during the Gujarat riots had a strange combination of pathos and terror, and no touch of divinity at all. It is a pity that the tribals found their voice during the riots but not for any idealistic purpose, nor for improving their own homes and hearths, but for destroying another community and for carrying out a pogrom encouraged by the state.

Throughout the days of the Gujarat violence, Albert Camus' disturbing novel *The Plague* repeatedly came to my thoughts. It depicts the unusual life in the city of Oran in the times of a great plague. The bureaucrats use the calamity as an opportunity to make money. The religious leaders look at it as proof of how the gods are angry with man. Others merely want to escape to another place that could possibly be normal. Dr. Meursault, the central character, decides not to budge at all. He declares, 'To do what I can in my place is my choice.' The epidemic recedes after a while, not because Dr. Meursault has been fighting to bring it under control. It just vanishes as mysteriously as it had erupted.

In Camus' vision, the eruption and the end of the disease are equally absurd. Camus is keen that one makes a conscious choice and takes moral responsibility for the choice made, since in the existential view life is nothing but a series of choices, and it is difficult to make choices since there is no essence like God, Truth, Justice.

For us today, even making a choice is not possible. We are in a situation where if we do not act every moment, we will have to own up to the responsibility of complicity to violence. Constructive action is our only future. There is none other, for otherwise there will be no future for us.

Seminar, May 2002

The Violence in Gujarat and the Dalits
Mohandas Namishray

At the height of the recent communal violence in Gujarat, newspapers in Delhi and other metros, especially the Hindi newspapers, devoted considerable space to: the participation of the Dalits in the violence there.

Those unfamiliar with the volatile situation in Gujarat should study the roots of the communal disturbances. Even if Hindus in Gujarat are not communal, the majority of them are upset with the visible signs of progress amongst the minorities, especially the Muslims and dalits. Though progress has largely been made by the upper castes, when the Muslims and dalits gained economically as a result of education and political awareness, their well-being became a sore point for these castes. In Gujarat during British rule, the Muslims along with the Hindus became wealthy. At that time, the dalits did not enjoy a high status. But after independence, they gained access to education. They got good jobs and took to trade and other businesses. On the other hand, hatred against the dalits and Muslims spread among the newer generation of the upper castes. They made Scheduled Caste/Scheduled Tribe reservations a target of their attack. Gujarat was in the forefront of the nationwide stir against the Supreme Court's decision on reservation. I would like to mention an incident in this respect. To protest against the disrespect shown to a statue of Babasaheb Ambedkar, dalit organizations held a bandh in Gujarat on 16 July 1997. On that very day, a group of upper castes, allegedly abetted by the police, went on a rampage in Ahmedabad's poor *bastis*. Anti-social elements indulged in arson and seriously wounded several people in the dalit areas. After that, whenever dalit youth came out to assemble in a group, the police swung into action. Dalit women, elderly men and women and children

---

* 'Gujarat ki Hinsa aur Dalit', *Amar Ujala*, 24 May 2002. Translated from the Hindi by Kamini Mahadevan.

bore the brunt of police rage. Even girls were not spared.

It would not be wrong to say that the attitude of the Hindutva organizations towards dalits and Muslims has been the same. The strategy of crushing opponents by turn began here. If dalits were to help in attacking the Muslims, they would be co-opted; in other words, the pests got ground with the grain. Last year, when the Bajrang Dal terrorized the Muslim workers, the dalits wholeheartedly supported the Muslims. This time also, where dalits were strong, they helped the Muslims. But dalits cannot be seen as homogenous. The dalits who were adherents of Ambedkar's ideology continued helping the Muslims. On the other hand, the dalits influenced by Gandhi and his ideas got mobilized into attacking the Muslims. Thus, this violence is the result more of the vitiated thinking among those who organized the violence rather than the dalits.

This situation is true not only in Gujarat but in other parts of the country too. Dalit conversion to Islam and Christianity has inflamed the votaries of Hindutva. The tactic pursued by the Hindutva organizations is to target dalits converting to Islam, or to try and bring them back into the Hindu fold. Likewise, to try and ensure that the dalit followers of Ambedkar are also reclaimed by Hindu tradition. With this in mind, the Sangh Parivar has been active among the dalits and adivasis in the past few years. In various urban areas, they have found a space in the Bajrang Dal and other local bodies.

It has also been seen that the Hindutva forces have taken advantage of the poverty and unemployment among dalits to advance their communal politics. For example, in the past few years, the dalits have been roused to anger by spreading rumours about Muslims being responsible for dalit workers losing their jobs in the cotton mills. Hence, given the grave situation in Gujarat, the dalit intellectuals have to consider whether they will go along with the Sangh Parivar or come forward to protect the Muslims and ensure peace in the country.

The Sangh Parivar declares that to live in India one must become a Hindu or set aside one's own religious identity. This logic is applied not only to Muslims but also to Christians and dalits. In 1977, advocate Sundarlal Sagar from Uttar Pradesh wrote in the introduction of his book, *Untouchable and Untouchabililty*, that 'A nation may be a country, but it is not always that a country is a nation.' Nationalism requires that people of a particular geographical entity be united by kinship, tradition, language and culture and a desire to live together. People of two geographical entities bound by tradition and blood can form a nation if they have the consciousness and desire to live together, as was the case for East and West Pakistan for a while. South Africa is a country but not a nation. Blacks and whites are both citizens of South Africa, but are not parts of a nation, because (in the main) they do not desire to live as one.

Prior to Partition, the Hindu Mahasabha and others like V.D. Sarvarkar did not consider India a nation. They thought of Muslims and Hindus as separate nations. Has their view changed after 1947? I believe it hasn't. Dalits need to be even more cautious given the current communal wave. They should be the shield for all minorities and come forward to counter the Hindutva forces. Likewise, among the Muslims, those treated like dalits, should take the support of the progressive Hindu forces and join hands with the dalits and other minorities.

A Hate Pamphlet circulating in Gujarat in March 2002
Wake up . . . Get up . . . Be united . . .
Reply to bricks with stones

Today the minority community is trying to crush the majority community. The Muslims should be ashamed that even after 50 years of independence they have not become Hindustanis, but they have no idea of the strength of the majority community. Muslims are traitors as compared to Hindus—the Godhra killings and the razing of the Sindhi market have proved this. Till now, Muslims were showing their treachery only in Kashmir, then they extended their activities to Parliament in Delhi and now they have made a great blunder by challenging Gujarat. Now the Muslims cannot be protected from the Hindus by either the police or the army—or the vote-seekers or the political parties who pamper them.

When India got her independence, there were 3 crores (30

million) Muslims in India. Now on the 50th anniversary, there are 35 crores (350 million). Understand . . . be warned . . . in five to ten years they will be as many as us. Nobody is preparing a cricket team here; an army is being prepared by Pakistan.

Police and army you also beware, you are also Hindus. You can also be attacked. You should also support Hindus. We Hindus support the police and the army fully.

My Hindu brethren, unite and form a Free Indian Army just like the one during the struggle for independence. Annihilate the enemy and lighten the burden of sin, which the country is carrying.

From Vatva to Naroda, Bapunagar to Kalupur,
On 29th March there will be a call, take Ram's name and attack,
We will kill Muslims the way we destroyed Babri,
We will burn Jamalpur and empty Dariyapur,
Whether it is an old chawl or *miyas* (Muslims), we will not leave you,
We Hindustanis swear we will seek you out and kill you,
This is the tradition of Raghukul and we never foreswear,
Let Sonia have dogs like Faroukh Shaikh or Haji Bilal,
We will treat them like Ehsan Jafri,
Muslims have darkened the skies with the smoke from burned shops,
We will cut them and their blood will flow like rivers.
Free Indian Army is the union of Hinduism. Thousands of our brethren have joined it.
You also join and give your support to save Hindustan.
Thanks to Narendra Modi. We salute you! After Sardar Vallabhbhai Patel, a hero is born!
Gujarat is proud and the glory of India is in your hands.
Every Hindu is requested not to stone the police or army. They are our brothers.
— An Indian

(*Reproduced in Communalism Combat*, Genocide Gujarat 2002, *p 136.*)

8

The Truth Hurts
Gujarat and the Role of the Media

Siddharth Varadarajan

A day after his televised address to the nation regretting the 'disgraceful' violence in Gujarat, Prime Minister Vajpayee told a group of concerned citizens that the media was presenting an 'exaggerated' account of the situation in the state.[1]

As violence continued in Gujarat, home minister L.K. Advani asked the media to take lessons from the American coverage of 11 September and suggested that 'sometimes, speaking the truth may not be an act of responsibility' . . . Advani reminded the gathering that the 'practice' according to a code of ethics formulated by various media bodies was not to name the community of the victims of clashes or rape. 'But now all that has been flouted.'[2]

More than at any other time in the past, the Indian media's coverage of communal violence in Gujarat in 2002 has come under sharp and critical scrutiny by both State and civil society. While Narendra Modi hailed those Gujarati newspapers like *Sandesh* and *Gujarat Samachar*—which vitiated the atmosphere by spreading false and dangerous rumours—the central and Gujarat governments repeatedly charged 'sections' of the national media with bias. What seems to have irked the BJP is the fact that the national media did not flinch from bearing witness to the complicity of the ruling party and state administration in the violence. This was as true of the English language media as for much of the vernacular, non-Gujarati press.³ The role of the Sangh Parivar and its front organizations like the Vishwa Hindu Parishad and Bajrang Dal also came into open view. As evidence of the orchestrated, targetted nature of the violence mounted, the mythic, politically harmless discourse about 'riots' in which 'two communities' clash made way for a new media narrative in which 'carnage', 'pogrom' and 'genocide' were the watchwords. No one who read or watched most of what was coming out of Gujarat during those days should have been in any doubt about one thing: That the violence did not stem from 'Hindus' attacking the 'minority community' but from the *carte blanche* the State gave members of the ruling political organization to attack Muslims.

The broad conclusion of the Editors' Guild Report was that 'the national media and sections of the Gujarati media, barring some notable offenders, played an exemplary role in their coverage of Gujarat, despite certain lapses, many of them inadvertent or minor.

> There were, however, some notable offenders, especially *Sandesh* and *Gujarat Samachar* and certain local cable channels. Technology has introduced a new learning curve and there are lessons to be learnt, internalized and developed into codes of best practice. But the notion that the media should shy away from telling the country how it really is must be firmly rejected. The freedom of the media derives from the citizen's inherent right to expression and information. This freedom carries with it an equally great responsibility that must be honestly and honourably discharged.
>
> It is not for nothing that the nation's motto is *'Satyamev Jayate'*, Truth Shall Triumph.⁴

Stunned by the Indian media's near unanimous reaction to what was happening in the state, the Gujarat government made an attempt to ban Star News, one of the television channels singled out by the BJP for its realistic and critical reportage.⁵ In Delhi, when their efforts at spin didn't yield results, senior ministers tried other, less subtle tactics to try and manage the media. 'Hitlists' of journalists were apparently drawn up.

'Bulging dossiers of clippings on Gujarat have been put together, one of which is devoted to a particularly critical correspondent . . .' *Outlook* wrote. Political circles are awash with rumours that the Vajpayee cabinet's July decision to allow foreign direct investment in the print media was taken in order to 'punish' large English-language newspapers for their truthful coverage of Gujarat.[6]

At the heart of the government's criticism of media coverage of the Gujarat violence lies the morally corrosive notion that reports about the systematic killing of Muslim citizens should have been 'balanced' by accounts of the Godhra carnage and of other incidents where Hindus have suffered.[7] This criticism is the equivalent of the Newtonian 'action-reaction' theory which Narendra Modi and Prime Minister Vajpayee used to justify the violence, as if redemption could somehow be ensured through the repetitive incantation of 'Original Sin.'

Apart from ignoring the fact that 'balance' can only be between two opposites and that Muslim and Hindu victims are really part of the same side—the side of victimhood—the BJP's criticism is, in any case, not even factually correct. There is no major newspaper or TV channel which did not extensively cover the Godhra incident when it happened, criticize the attack in the strongest possible terms, and interview the survivors and victims' families. Had the BJP not 'retaliated' for Godhra, it is likely that much of the media space devoted to the killings which ensued would have been and exclusively devoted to the Godhra tragedy. In any event, it is significant that Advani and other BJP leaders like Arun Jaitley criticized what they said was graphic TV coverage of the violence only when this coverage started reflecting badly on their party. They did not object when the Godhra victims were identified as 'Ram sevaks', and their burnt corpses were turned into an undignified, inflammatory public spectacle by the Modi government and shown repeatedly on TV channels, including Star News. And the fact is that after that one occasion when dead bodies were shown, no channel, not even Star News, showed viewers footage or photographs of the corpses of those who died in Gujarat subsequently.

I have argued elsewhere how the media 'convention' of not identifying communities while covering communal violence works to increase the sense of suspicion and anxiety amongst ordinary citizens not just in riot-affected areas but also elsewhere in the country.[7] In a communally polarized situation where rumours circulate widely, people tend to assume that the victims are 'their own' while the attackers are 'the other'. The veneer of anonymity might conceivably serve a positive purpose when the violence is truly a result of sustained, widespread clashes between 'two communities' but it has absolutely no utility in situations like Gujarat where one community is targetted in such a well-organized manner by political activists with the complicity of the State. No utility, that is, other than to cover up the role of political parties. In Gujarat, Advani was squeamish about 'naming the community of the victims' precisely because Muslims were targetted and the Sangh Parivar got a bad name.

While accurate, honest reporting is desirable in and of itself, my contention is that its consequences would also be benign. Apart from building public opinion in favour of the rule of law, identifying the victims helps generate empathy amongst ordinary Hindus who might otherwise read in the anonymous phrase 'members of a particular community were attacked' a reference to themselves rather than to Muslims. It is not a coincidence that those Gujarati newspapers which inflamed the situation through rumours have pointedly refused to educate their readers about who the victims of the violence which followed Godhra really were. I am personally convinced that it was the accurate coverage of Gujarat by the Indian print and electronic media which forced the BJP finally to stop the violence. Some 2,000 people died but had the media not cried murder, perhaps many, many more would have fallen victim. It is unfortunate, therefore, that once the worst was over, most national newspapers reverted to the old 'guideline' of not identifying victims. Thus, even though Muslims in Gujarat continued to be targetted by the Sangh Parivar until May, vague newspaper descriptions like 'one man killed, two stabbed' have helped the BJP create the false impression that the continuation of the violence for so long was because 'Muslims' had started 'retaliating' against 'Hindus'.

While journalists will debate the issues raised by Gujarat for years to come, there appears to be a consensus on the fact that the media *should* identify the religion of the victim if the victim has been attacked for his or her religious identity. Muslims in Gujarat were attacked for being Muslims; this information was central to the news event and helped to alert the wider citizenry to the true nature of what was happening. However, care should be used in describing the identity of the attackers in news reports. Loose or lazy phrases like 'Hindu mob' or 'Hindus' should not be used to describe what is usually a politically mobilized crowd consisting, very often, of lumpen and criminal elements.

The discourse of communal riots has no room to acknowledge that some Hindus brought together by political or economic motivation to attack Muslims at large cannot really be referred to as 'the Hindus' or even as ' some Hindus'. It is not necessary to grant the Congressmen who attacked Sikhs in 1984 or the VHP mobs who targetted Muslims in Gujarat the apellation 'Hindu' in order to recognize that their victims all belonged to one particular religion. By what logic can a politically instigated mob that enjoys the tacit backing of the State law enforcement machinery be labelled a 'Hindu mob'? The only purpose such a labelling serves is to mask the *political* nature of the violence which is perpetrated and protect the politicians involved.

The Media Did Not Ransack Shops,*
Take Lives, Mr Modi
Rajdeep Sardesai

The messenger has been shot yet again. Kargil, Kandahar and now Gujarat: the media, and more specifically 24-hour news

* *Indian Express*, 7 March 2002

networks, have become target practice for a government seeking to cover-up its own ineptitude. In Kargil, the media was accused of breaching national security even while the obvious intelligence failure on part of the military apparatus was hidden away in bureaucratic files. In Kandahar, the media was charged with placing undue pressure on the government to negotiate with the hijackers even though not one channel had even remotely suggested that the external affairs minister should take along Masood Azhar as a travel companion on a flight to Afghanistan. And now in Gujarat, the accusation is of 'inflaming communal passions' when the fact is that the flames of communal hatred have been stoked by a mob, a section of which at least has been patronized by the ruling establishment in Gandhinagar.

Was it the media that provoked the horrific violence at Godhra's railway station? Was it the media that called for a 24-hour Gujarat bandh the next day that saw the violence spiral out of control? Did the media ask people to come out on the streets and ransack shops and business establishments belonging to one community? The pogroms that were committed in Ahmedabad, Vadodara and other parts of the state were surely not sanctioned by the media.

The government chargesheet against the news networks is that we kept showing visuals of the carnage, and in the process incited violence. But does anyone seriously believe that the telecasting of burning shops and houses motivates people to immediately rush out and start a fire? After all, it was the mob that was determining the pace of events, and not the channels which were merely reporting what was happening on the ground. Since post-September 11, our government ministers see the American media as the barometer for 'television ethics' and have often castigated the Gujarat coverage by comparing it with 'responsible' networks in the US. In that case, they might well wish to see the network coverage of the Los Angeles racial riots a decade ago when the channels kept showing the Rodney King assault incident that sparked off the violence.

The flip side of the government argument would be that the television channels should have been restrained to the point of virtually blanking out the mob frenzy, and instead stated that the government was firmly in control of events. Unfortunately, nothing could be further from the truth, especially in the first 48 hours of chaos. To indicate, for example, that the police was simply not acting against the law-breakers could hardly be seen as 'demoralizing' the police force, but only emphasizing the fact that the mob on the streets was being allowed to get away with their actions.

Again, if any reporter, whether print or television, sees large-scale violence being committed, is the journalist to ignore the hard reality and merely present the facts as seen through government binoculars? If the chief minister says that the situation is returning to normal even while reports are streaming in of continuing violence in several parts of the state, are not the lies to be exposed? And if the government insists that the army is out on the street when the fact is that the army has been kept on stand-by and is waiting for transport trucks, whose version is to be broadcast?

The government chargesheet also says that television reporters were often using words like 'Hindus' and 'Muslims', and thereby further vitiating the atmosphere. It is apparently a long-established tradition that communities will not be named in riot situations. Instead, we are told, that 'group clashes' or terms like 'minority' and 'majority' community should be used to describe the violence. No one is quite sure who initiated this practice, but once again it does seem a bit like obfuscation, and an attempt to inject a false blandness to the harsh and grim reality of a communal riot. If the shop of a Bohra Muslim has been attacked, should that be disguised by suggesting that a shop belonging to 'a member of a minority within the minority community' was attacked?

The more serious accusation against the media is that we were somehow biased against the state government in particular, and in the process against Hindus in general. It's a charge that has been repeatedly made over the years by the Sangh Parivar, especially against the English-speaking media, both print and television. By attempting to pigeonhole a section of the media as the so-called 'secular Taliban', the aim appears to be to create a divide between the Hindutva 'patriots' versus the 'anti-national pseudo-secularists'. This divide has been at the heart of the Sangh Parivar's propaganda campaign.

The sheer viciousness of the campaign has pushed the media on the defensive, and perhaps made some of us even more conscious of the need to be even-handed at all times. In Gujarat, for example, no one has shied away from emphasizing that local Muslim leaders in Godhra were involved in the train tragedy. At the same time, the fact is that VHP and Bajrang Dal activists were leading mobs in several areas where some of the worst attacks took place. The chief minister may have tried to push the Newtonian law by saying that every action invites a reaction, but for the media such comments only expose the state's rather shameful attempt at rationalizing the violence. The charge of bias should not lie at the door of the media but at the gates of Gandhinagar, where the political leadership has ridden the back of the VHP-Bajrang Dal tiger for much too long to now quickly climb off.

This does not mean that the media does not need to introspect. High drama—war, violence, terror—is staple diet for the 24-hour news channel. Such is the nature of the beast that the powerful images that are captured on film in a riot situation can make for gripping viewing. In such situations, journalism can become a glamourous performance and can blur the essence of a report. This is a serious danger. The 'tabloidisation' of the medium is grave concern; and makes some element of self-censorship essential. But as news networks evolve, so must the government's response to the new media revolution. This is the first government in the country that has had to deal with 24-hour news channels. In Gujarat, the absence of credible information being provided on a regular basis by the government was once again glaring.

In America, for example, the state has perfected the art of using the media's reach and power to try and defuse crisis situations. Here, the attitude on the other hand is to ration information and then to question the credentials of those who try to go beyond administrative platitudes. Ironically, Narendra Modi is supposed to be one of the country's most media-savvy politicians who even did a course in New York on media management. Maybe, he needs to go in for a refresher before he begins issuing diktats banning television coverage.

A Survey of the Print and Electronic Media in Baroda
*PUCL-Vadodara and Shanti Abhiyan**

PUCL-Vadodara and Shanti Abhiyan monitored the local press in Vadodara throughout the period of violence starting 28 February 2002. The following report is based on our submission to the Editors' Guild on 5 April 2002, in which we analysed the role played by the vernacular (and English) press in representing the situation to its readership. Constraints of time, resources and people made it difficult for us to do a more detailed analysis of the role of the electronic media. We have, however, tried to put together some details of local news channel programmes in Vadodara.

The Gujarati Press

Sandesh (Baroda edition)

Our fact-finding into the incidents of violence in Baroda has made it possible for us to compare facts unearthed during our field visits with the news reports. According to our framework, the Gujarati newspaper *Sandesh* crossed all limits of responsible journalism during the violence in the state. The following is a description of some characteristics of news articles, reports and

---

* Extracted from People's Union for Civil Liberties, Vadodara and Vadodara Shanti Abhiyan, *Violence in Vadodara: A Report*. Vadodara, May 2002, pp 140-160. The description of the Machchipeeth incident has been taken from another section of the same report, pp 47-48.

editorials which appeared in *Sandesh*.

Sandesh used headlines to provoke, communalize and terrorize people. On 28 February 2002, the main headline said: '70 Hindus Burnt Alive in Godhra'. Another report on the front page says: 'Avenge Blood with Blood'. This is a quote from a statement issued by a VHP leader. *Sandesh* simply used his words as a headline. The Godhra attackers are consistently referred to as 'Muslim *Junooni*'. On 6 March 2002, the headlines screamed, 'Hindus Beware: Haj Pilgrims Return with a Deadly Conspiracy'. In reality, hundreds of terrified and anxious Haj pilgrims returned accompanied with heavy police escorts to homes that could have been razed to the ground. On 8 March 2002, a news item had the headline 'When Muslim Leaders Shouted Slogans like "Hindustan Zindabad".' The report goes on to say that the Circuit House witnessed 'an unprecedented event' when Muslim leaders of the city got together to shout slogans like the above, and appeal for peace. The implication is clear: that Muslims are inherently anti-national and violent.

Most reports concerning the post-Godhra violence usually began with a preceding sentence e.g. 'In the continuing spiral of communal rioting that broke out as a reaction to the "demonic/ barbaric etc. Godhra incident . . ."' The denunciatory adjectives used liberally to describe the Godhra incident were strikingly absent in reporting the subsequent genocide. This introductory statement reinforced a hierarchy in the two sets of crimes that were being committed, one that was consistently underlined by the VHP (as well as by Chief Minister Narendra Modi, when he justified the genocide in Newtonian terms).

Machchipeeth: A case study of misreporting

There were several instances of misreporting, which were instrumental in fuelling rumours. For example, the incident in Machchipeeth, reported on 16 March, was completely misleading.[8] Machchipeeth, in the old city area, is inhabited by middle- and lower-middle-class people of both Hindu and Muslim communities. Many of them ply businesses and some are in the service sector. About forty Hindu families and 400

Muslim families reside in the area. Machchipeeth has been regarded as a communally-sensitive area, although its past history, going back to the times of Gaekwad rule, hardly bears out this reputation. For example, in 1969 the Bhoi community led by Durga Bhoi stood side by side with the Muslim community in order to prevent outsiders from vitiating the communal harmony prevailing in the area. According to local memory, even in 1985 and 1990-2, no significant instances of 'rioting' occurred here . . . The team met Hindu families staying in the area who vouch for the peace-loving nature of all—Hindus as well as Muslims—in this area. In fact, they have signed the first memorandum submitted to NHRC and are going to submit an affidavit on this matter. On 15 March 2002, violence broke out here. This is how *Sandesh* reported it:

Angry Muslims fire on and attack Ramshobha Yatra: What happened in Machchipeeth that caused the city to burn?

In the afternoon the city was infused with spirit of Ram. Women, children and youth burst into the main roads, Ram had suffused the city. At a time like this, the entire city was plunged into violence because of the attack by the fanatics of Machchipeeth. When a shobha yatra emerged in the Raopura area in the afternoon chanting Ram dhun, people were dancing and chanting Ram. Everybody was immersed in devotional sprit. The police was also present. The shobha yatra reached the Machchipeeth crossing. Dhols and manjiras were played.

At Suryanarayan Baug an acid bulb shot out from a rooftop in Machchipeeth. The Ram bhakts of the shobha yatra looked towards Machchipeeth to see where the acid bombs were coming from. And an armed mob was spotted. They had swords and were shouting. The women in the shobha yatra ran in panic. The youth ran towards the police.

But by then a shower of acid bulbs was raining down from not one but five rooftops in Machchipeeth. There was the armed mob down on the streets and up on the rooftops were acid bulbs raining down. Violence disrupts *bhakti ras* (the spirit of devotion) and mobs face each other. The Machchipeeth mob comes forward taking advantage of the 'coverage fire' of acid bulbs from the rooftops. Stones, bottles rain down from the sky and the police is surprised. The violent Machchipeeth mob comes on to the street. Before the people and police understand what is happening the notorious elements of this area, namely Nooru Mistry, Ayub Clubwala and Yusuf Kadia start private firing. On the one hand was the 'covering' stone throwing from the rooftops and on the other was the mob on the road. The police was outnumbered. There was panic. The violent mob was ready to attack the people on the road. Eight to ten people could have died but the police came right on time and fired.

Analysis: In fact, the entire city was terrorized, not suffused with the spirit of devotion. The Ram dhun programme was part of an aggressive call given by the VHP, it was not a show of intense devotion. Such shobha yatras have caused terror and fear throughout the city. Going by the *Sandesh* report, it seems as though a city immersed in Ram was attacked. The events that unfolded in Machchipeeth actually followed a very different sequence.

On 15 March, VHP and Bajrang Dal had given an all India level call for prayer and Ram dhun and in view of the prevailing tension, the Commissioner of Police had imposed Section 144 in the city from the same day. In contravention of the above order, a 500-strong rally, composed totally of outsiders, reached Machchipeeth naka around 3.10 p.m. The rallyists wore saffron bands, and several carried saffron flags borne on sticks and rods. Video clippings show them making provocative gestures and running in an unruly manner, occupying the whole road. Some six or seven police personnel also accompanied the rally on foot with a police van bringing up the rear. The rally turned violent before reaching Machchipeeth: many Muslim owned shops (including Indian Boot House and Tower Shoes) and *laaris* en route were burnt and looted. On reaching Machchipeeth, some of the rallyists rushed into residential lanes with trishuls and swords. All were shouting provocative slogans ('*Bandiao* [circumcized] go away to Pakistan,' '*Babar ki aulado Hindustan chhod do*' and the like). Some even took off their pants and danced around in the lanes.

Such was the scene that confronted Muslims of the area coming out of the mosque after Friday *namaaz*. The situation worsened with stones and bottles being thrown by residents and the 'Ram bhakts'. While pelting of stones and soda-bottles was going on, police reinforcements (in about four jeeps) arrived shortly. They immediately began firing with service revolvers and sten-guns. The police firing, which lasted about twenty-five minutes, was, however, exclusively directed at the residents of Machchipeeth. Some tear-gas shells were also lobbed into Machchipeeth. Army personnel reached the spot after about fifteen minutes of police firing and the situation was brought under control. While the residents took shelter in houses, the rallyists also disappeared. Thereafter, till about 4.00 p.m., the police conducted 'combing operations' in Machchipeeth. Abusing the residents, they barged into various houses and indiscriminately arrested thirty-four Muslims.

There was relative calm in the area between 4.00 and 7.30 p.m. in the area. During the evening namaaz at the mosque, small crowds chanting VHP and Bajrang Dal slogans had gathered on the terraces in Mama-ni-Pole. About fifteen were on the RK Roadlines' terrace, about twenty were on the terrace of Kalyan building and about thirty on the Uday Apartments' terrace. Ajay Dave, the municipal councillor of Manjalpur, N.K. Rathod, PI of the Ecocell and Niraj Jain, president of the Vadodara chapter of the Vishwa Hindu Parishad, were present on the RK Roadlines' terrace. In fact, it is from the terrace that stones were pelted at Muzzafar Khana mosque at about 7.30 p.m. About twenty rounds were fired from the RK Roadlines' terrace at the above mosque and in the general direction of Machchipeeth. The team noted that bullet marks are still evident on the structure of the mosque, and not on any other structures in the vicinity. Thereafter, police again combed Machchipeeth area and rounded up twelve Muslims from Bagh-e-Habib Apartments in the area. It is pertinent to note that the magistrate did not sustain the police charge of Section 307 when the arrestees were produced at court and they were unconditionally released.

Apart from Machchipeeth, the incident of four Muslim youth being picked up for carrying arms in a Tata Sumo singularly misrepresents reality. Going by *Sandesh* reports, it appears as though the youths had a whole cache of arms in the vehicle. The truth is that they had only one firearm and that the owner had a license for it. Likewise, there were misleading reports about Tandalja, which has a large Muslim population. It also housed the largest relief camp, giving shelter to more than 5,000 people from the city and nearby areas. *Sandesh's* reports on Tandalja were instrumental in fuelling rumours and spreading false information. In fact, on 18 March *Sandesh* was forced to publish a refutation issued by Shanti Abhiyan members in response to an article that there was tension in Tandalja.

Sensationalism

The most horrific acts of violence were repeatedly sensationalized with the use of a few devices. For example, large bold letters were used as banner headlines particularly when referring to gruesome acts like the burning alive of people. Photographs of burnt, mangled bodies were a common feature on the front page or the last page that usually carries local news. In the first week of violence in the state, colour photographs of scenes of the carnage were superimposed with a large red star carrying the latest figure of casualties. Photographs of trishul-wielding kar sevaks were splashed across the front pages in the first week. Both kinds of photographs served to instil fear and terror and to provoke intense passions and mutual hostility between the two communities.

Throughout the violence, *Sandesh* cynically promoted the idea of Muslims being anti-national and pro-Pakistan. Areas in the city and state with a large population of Muslims were described as 'mini-Pakistans'. On 7 March, a report claimed to have discovered Godhra's 'Karachi connection', an entire area in Karachi named Godhra. Similarly, on 1 March, the headline of a news item claims that a 'mini-Pakistan' is in existence in the Navayard area of the city. The article went on to say that such 'pockets' were being created in the city and instructed the police to take note of the reportedly 'criminal' UP migrant labourers who live in this area. That residents of the *basti*, Roshannagar, were living in complete terror at the time, was a trivial detail the *Sandesh* report preferred to ignore.

Similarly, on 1 March, a report claimed that the whole Sabarmati Express train would have been put to flames had it been on time and not delayed. The headline claimed: 'A mob of 7-8 thousand was waiting for the Sabarmati Express to arrive at Godhra.' The mob was, according to *Sandesh*, made up of 'religious fanatics'.

Conclusions

Sandesh effectively circumvented the code of conduct that disallows naming of communities involved in the violent conflagrations. Scattered across the newspaper were numerous reports where 'mobs of religious fanatics' abducted tribal women and, therefore, had to face the wrath of the people, or when rumours that 'religious fanatics' were about to attack a temple caused tension in certain areas in Baroda city, which brought 'devotees' out on the street to protect their place of worship.

When Muslims were at fault, names were taken, and perpetrators were clearly identified. When they were the victims of murderers, arsonists, looters, etc., attackers remained unnamed. No sources were quoted for headlines, even when they were simply lifted from speeches by VHP leaders. Headlines were also misleading, and often followed up by reports that did not substantiate, and even negated the headlines completely. Photographs were used which sensationalized events, and could incite communal anger, fear and terror among people. The anti-minority stand was obvious in the slant in news reporting.

Editorials and news items were often written in a manner to justify implicitly and explicitly the carnage after the Godhra incident. Through the worst phase of violence in the city, *Sandesh* consciously sought to project a communalised version of events, desensitising its readers to the enormous human tragedy and inflicting serious long-term damage to a society already fragmented along communal lines. It has been our experience that its Baroda readers, particularly Hindus, frequently quoted *Sandesh* reports to refute any arguments in favour of moderation and restoration of communal harmony. We found that people's own experiences in their neighbourhoods as well as reports in the national media were often relied on less than *Sandesh*'s reports. This is indicative of the influence that *Sandesh* was able to wield in the most savage phase of the violence and thereafter.

'Thank you, *Sandesh*'

The following is the text of a letter sent by Gujarat Chief Minister Narendra Modi to the editor of Sandesh.

The Editor
Sandesh

Dear Sir,
The incident of torching the coaches of Sabarmati Express and burning innocent people were extremely unfortunate for the entire state and for humanity at large. Following this inhuman act, the peaceful atmosphere in the state was disturbed. The state government had immediately tried its level best to restore peace. The newspapers of the state played a decisive role as a link between the people and the government. You have served the humanity in a big way.

It is state government's primary duty to restore peace, security and communal harmony when violence takes place. In this case also the state government has taken prompt action to restore peace in the state. The timely measures taken by the government turned out to be effective and normalcy was returned within a short period. It is noteworthy that the newspapers of Gujarat gave their full support to the state government in undertaking this difficult task.

I am happy to note that your newspaper exercised restraint during the communal disturbances in the wake of Godhra incident. I am grateful to you.
Yours sincerely,

Sd.
Narendra Modi
Chief Minister

A similar letter was sent to the editors of *Gujarat Samachar*, and some other Gujarati newspapers.

Source: Annexure 4, *Rights and Wrongs: Ordeal by Fire in the Killing Fields of Gujarat*. Report of the Editors Guild Fact-Finding Mission, New Delhi, May 2002.

Gujarat Samachar (Vadodara edition)

Gujarat Samachar, the other leading Gujarati paper, also played a role in heightening tensions over the most intense phase of violence. However, unlike *Sandesh*, it did not devote all its space to hawkish and inflammatory reportage in the first few weeks, and did carry reports highlighting communal harmony.

Reportage on the Godhra incident, in particularly, was inflammatory and irresponsible.

The main front page report on 28 February 2002 stated: '3-4 young girls have been kidnapped.' The source of information was not mentioned. On page ten, there was a report of VHP leader Kaushik Patel saying that ten girls had been kidnapped. The reporter had not cross-checked information either with the IGP or Railway Police. The report did not give names of any of the girls or any other details. One more report on gave details of an eyewitness, Hetalben, when the train reached Baroda. She said, 'Young girls from Amraiwadi travelling with us are lost.'

On 6 March, the back page carried a report with the headline: 'The plan was to torch the whole train, not just one bogey'. In yet another box item on the same page, a report states that 'a mob was ready for the second attack.' The source of the information is not mentioned. It seems that the story was based on a conversation with some Railway Police Force jawans. The way these reports have been presented is instigative. The same day's top story on the last page was about how the situation was gradually returning to normal.

Reportage of the situation in Vadodara

The caption of a story on the last page, 7 March was, 'What was the purpose of the youths roaming in white Tata Sumo with 12-bore rifle in position?' The sub-heading cries: 'They carried news clippings of the Godhra incident being pre-planned.' On 8 March, page three, the report of the chief minister's visit to Vadodara carried the caption: 'Mysteries of the Godhra conspiracy are opening up slowly . . .' However, the story does not open up a single mystery. Its 16 March story, 'Indiscriminate firing from Fatehganj Mosque,' was a complete fabrication.[9] A report on 16 March described incidents in Machchipeeth as if only Muslims were culprits. The headline claimed 'private firing on Ram bhakts'. The report described the whole incident as a pre-planned attack. The role played by the mob in the procession is not at all mentioned.

Other reports

- 18 March, p 1: Photograph of bombs recovered by police during combing operations in Danilimda area of Ahemedabad. The caption says: 'People talking of secularism should be asked if protecting criminals is secularism.'

- 21 March, p 10: 'Mob of 1000 encircled LIC building from all sides with a plan that mirrors Godhra'. This is a 3 column, 50-word story, which repeats the phrase 'pre-planned like Godhra' five times. The story is highly exaggerated. Another story just below this has similar qualities. It reads: 'Plan to torch 2 autorickshaws carrying 30 school children studying in English Medium school in Modasa prevented by the police.'

- 24 March, p 1: 'Sat kaival temple receives threat: Sarsa temple and *pathshala* threatened to be blown using remote control.'

- 24 March, p 2: 'Possibility of weapon attack. Secret agencies receive information; Religious and Educational institutions shall be targeted. All DSPs alerted.'

'Positive' stories

- Muslims saved a Hindu shopkeeper's shop in Halol (2 March, p 5).
- Residents of Ram-Rahim tekra in Ahmedabad is an example of communal harmony (5 March, p 1).
- Hindus saved life of a Muslim woman in Halol (5 March, p 5).
- No one wants riots. Rare scenes of communal harmony in sensitive areas of city (6 March, last page).
- Elol village near Himmatnagar is an example of communal harmony (6 March, p 5).
- A Muslim woman offered shelter to a Hindu family (7 March, p 3).
- At Bhoj village in Padra taluka, Muslims were given shelter in a temple. (7 March, p 8).
- Oh! He is our Rahim *Chacha* . . . our *guruji* . . . and they saved him (10 March, p 11). Article by Bhaven Kachchhi in Sunday supplement.
- At Lilapir Dargah of Talaja, devotees include all - Hindus and Muslims (11 March, p 5).
- A Muslim old woman saved from mob by a Hindu youth (22 March, p 2).
- A pregnant lady sent to hospital by a Muslim youth risking his life (28 March).

Gujarat Today

Gujarat Today is an eleven-year old Gujarati daily with a circulation of 70,000. It is published by the Lokhit Prakashan Trust of Ahmedabad. The paper was started by Muslim liberals and is probably the only daily which has a large Muslim readership. The print quality of the paper is low. Photographs are not very clear and there are no colour photographs. The paper carries news from villages and district towns not generally covered by the mainstream media.

It is important to analyse the role played by *Gujarat Today* given that it caters to the very section of people in Gujarat most critically affected by the state-wide violence following the Godhra incident and undoubtedly plays an important role in giving information and building opinion among Muslims. In this report we have covered the period from 28 February 2002 to 16 March 2002. One limitation in our analysis was that we were unable to access the issues of 1-5 March, and also the first and last pages of 28 February. Nonetheless, we feel that a broad picture emerges from our analysis which is indicative of the editorial policy the paper has followed through the critical situation faced by the Muslim community in Gujarat since 28 February.

Report on the Godhra incident (28 February)

The paper reported that kar sevaks caught hold of some Muslim tea-vendors at Godhra station and forced them to say *'Jai Shri Ram'* which sparked off the incident. This is also highlighted in a box on another page. The paper, in contrast to the more temperate language of its later reports, says that when the Sabarmati Express arrived at Vadodara station, . . . 'the saffron mob of Bajrang Dal and VHP ran like dogs, attacking people with their swords . . . the kar sevaks got down from the train shouting slogans like 'Har Har Mahadev, Bharat Mata ki Jai' and filthy abuses . . . 'Kill Muslims, cut Muslims . . .' The paper also carried a report and photograph of the Hindu youth, Arun Paswan, who was also attacked at Vadodara railway station.

What surprised us was that the editorial of the 28th focused exclusively and in great detail on the railway budget announced the previous day. There was no reference to the Godhra incident. Since we did not have the entire paper of the 28th, we do not know whether the incident was condemned elsewhere in the issue of the 28th. However, we feel that an editorial comment on the incident was due, and the editorial provided the most appropriate space to project the paper's viewpoint on the incident.

Information

The paper provided important and useful information for its readers. Some of these were:

Details of phone and fax numbers of police control rooms in Gandhinagar, Ahmedabad, Vadodara and Godhra. These were issued on the 28th itself to enable victims and relatives of injured persons to contact the police for information; details of relief camps in Ahmedabad—their location, kinds of facilities available (as well as those necessary) in the camps, as also appeals for assistance; reports and updates of incidents in the state. These reports are detailed, and include the names of attacked shops and their owners.

Investigative reports

The paper carried detailed investigative reports of the violence. Some of these were: Details on conditions of people in the relief camps, including issues of legal assistance, marriages organized and deliveries of babies in the camps (6 March); investigation into the Naroda Patiya incident, with details relating to the procurement of petrol, diesel and gas cylinders used for burning; use of the inflammable chemical 'Lakgel' for burning (8 March). This has not been reported in any other paper.

Reports of communal harmony through the violence

Most of the space in the newspaper over the first two weeks was devoted to extensive reportage on the carnage. However, space was made available every day to profile incidents of communal harmony. Given the terror, insecurity and alienation that Muslims in Gujarat felt over those first few weeks of violence following Godhra, it is commendable that *Gujarat Today* consciously sought to project the more humane side of inter-community relationships to its Muslim readers through these reports. For example, there was a report on how the lives and properties of 175 Muslims of Naroda in Ahmedabad were protected by the local shepherds; how Hindu doctors of Bhavnagar saved properties from burning and made efforts to treat the injured; relief of foodgrain and clothes provided by Hindus to victims in Jhagadia; and a group marriage of Hindu and Muslim youth in Mangrol. Also reported was news of Prantij, where a woman sarpanch successfully stopped riots occurring in her village.

The 8 March edition gave news related to peace committees in Vagra, Palej, Dholka and Bharuch. On 10 March, the paper had a report on how Hindu families saved the lives of fifteen Muslims in Kavitha village near Borsad. While there are reports of Juhapura, where Muslims saved Hindus, there is also a report on how looting of both Hindus and Muslims took place. The 12 March issue carried news of a Hindu family of Dehgam who sheltered twenty Muslims in their house, and a boxed item on a relief camp in Bhalej village, Kheda district, run by Hindus and Muslims. The 15 March issue carried a report of how Muslim women saved the lives of Hindus. News of unity among Hindus and Muslims of Lambadia and Sami were reported in other issues of the paper.

Role of the police

The paper attempted to maintain a balanced perspective on the role of the police over the first two and a half weeks of communal violence. Maintenance of peace in Padra was attributed to the local police, while the arrest of twenty-eight Muslim youths in Vadodara is strongly criticised. There is a report on Varnama where the police refused to entertain complaints against specific individuals. However, the arrest of a VHP functionary in Kutch was lauded.

Analytical and editorial reports

Barring the absence of editorial comment in the 28 February issue on the previous day's incident at Godhra, we feel that *Gujarat Today* has maintained a good balance in its editorials and commentaries on the Gujarat violence. These include several editorials reflecting concern with the fall-out of the riots and how their effects might be mitigated. The editorials over the editions surveyed did not always address the communal riots/violence. Editorials on only five of the thirteen days were about the violence in the state. The paper carried commentaries by prominent liberal intellectuals and humanists of Gujarat, such as an article by Mahesh Dave which fearlessly reprimanded the government for its role in the riots (8 March), a translation of a Siddharth Vardarajan article which had appeared in the *Times of India* (9 March), accounts by Indu Kumar Jani (in his Sunday column) of the kinds of materials supplied to relief camps, and articles by Nagindas Sanghvi titled: "India will be destroyed not by the atom bomb but by superstition and communal fanaticism" (7 March) and 'Ram gave up Ayodhya and the throne, but his followers are prepared to shed blood' (16 March).

Conclusions

Based on a quick and by no means exhaustive analysis of coverage of the riots by *Gujarat Today* from 28 February to 16 March, we feel that the paper, on the whole, managed to maintain a good balance in its reporting, and was fair and even-handed in its commentaries. This is significant since *Gujarat Today* is a Muslim-owned paper which is primarily read by Muslims. The paper was restrained in its reporting and its choice of visuals, temperate in its language and eschewed shrill and potentially provocative matter. Where rumours were mentioned, they were presented as such and not captioned with misleading headlines, as was done by some other newspapers. It regularly carried items highlighting interdependence of communities and incidents of help and co-operation extending across community barriers. It investigated incidents and carried detailed information that did not appear in other newspapers, thereby providing a useful service to its readers. Overall, our analysis suggests that *Gujarat Today* played a responsible and positive role during the violence in the state, for which it deserves to be commended.

A Brief Note on the Electronic Media

Cable TV channels

Local political leaders used the local electronic media in the most despicable manner. The intentions of the following leaders belonging to the ruling party and their affiliates becomes very clear if one examines the speeches of these leaders on local TV channels (namely JTV, Deep and VNM). The speeches of the following leaders were particularly provocative and aimed to incite the crowd to violence: Ajay Dave, Nalin Bhatt, Deepak Kharchikar, Neeraj Jain, Bhartiben Vyas (Mayor of Baroda), Jitendra Sukhadia, and others. If these were the speeches on TV one can well imagine the role of these people during the violence at the grass-root level. (For example, on 18 March, Ms Bharti Vyas convened a 'Shanti Samiti' meeting that was attended by the police commissioner and the collector, as well as leading political figures of various parties. She made appropriate pacifist remarks in this meeting and then on the same day she made inflammatory remarks against the minority community in the VMC council.)

On 14 March, a group of PUCL representatives told the police commissioner that local TV channels needed to be warned. We tried to obtain copies of the offensive tapes to submit to the NHRC, but were not given these. The police commissioner gave notice to the local channels, whose telecasts were off the air for two days, after which they resumed their work with a vengeance. In the last week of March, owners of two TV channels, VNM and News Plus, were arrested, when in fact the other two channels, JTV and Deep were far more inflammatory. It is significant that when people were housebound in the first week of terror and violence, with curfew all over the city, local cable operators were airing aggressive nationalist films like *Border*, *16th December*, *Ghadar*, etc.

Some examples of misuse of cable TV channels

Date	Name of Channel	Content
27 February 2002	VNM Channel	Ajay Dave's (VHP) statement that we will retaliate with violence and create history (in relation to Godhra incident)
From 27 February, a week	JTV	Kept repeating for more than images of the Godhra incident many times a day, thereby attempting to create feelings of outrage among Hindus.
15 March 2002	Siti Cable	Common man on the street said how Hindus want Ram Mandir. We are beginning an *andolan* today which we will stop after we achieve our goals.
15 March 2002	Deep Channel	Showed rally after *shiladaan*. 3 local leaders Deepak Kharchikar (Shiv Sena), Niraj Jain (Bajrang Dal) and Ajay Dave (VHP) gave speeches and interviews at the Machchipeeth *naka*. These contained anti-Muslim sentiments. 'Muslims will have to live the way we want otherwise we will pull them out of their houses and kill them.'
16 March 2002	VNM or News Plus In Cable	Ajay Joshi : 'We will be training Hindu youth to be *ladayak* (warriors, aggressive?)'

29 March 2002	VNM or News Cable	Mayor Bharti Vyas said 'like Hirankashap destroyed evil, we will also destroy *deshdrohis* (traitors)'.

Samples of fan mail at *www.narendramodi.org*

The CM of Gujarat is proud of being email and Internet savvy and he has often let it be known that he has a website. Given below are some samples from his website aimed at cynical self-promotion. If there is any need for 'proof' of his anti-Muslim, and, therefore, unconstitutional attitudes, they are here at this site.

- Dear modi ji, you are like a god to us. thank you for saving Hindus. but you are not doing enough. we will not be satisfied until you send your sena out to Muslim countries like Pakistan, Afghanistan to rape Muslim women kill and burn Muslims. thank you rakesh kumar trivedi raktri74@hotmail.com
- SIR, I FAIL TO FIND WORDS TO EXPRESS GRATITUDE TO YOU FOR THE WAY HINDUS HAVE BEEN PROTECTED IN THIS STATE DESPITE ALL THE CRITICISMS ALL OVER THE COUNTRY. YOU HAVE ENDEARED YOURSELF TO ALL THE GUJARATIS. THE WHOLE STATE IS SOLIDLY BEHIND YOU. HATS OFF TO "ASLI MARD" !!! p.j.desai ricky071@rediffmail.com
- Dearest Modi sir, Lots of thanks for all that u have done to us. We (Hindus) were a victim of Islamic violence since long. I remember killing of Hindu pilgrims in Vaishno Devi, Amarnath and in almost all over India innocent Hindus were killed by Muslims only on the name of religion and jihad. The entire underworld is run by Muslims. It is very sad that in spite of all these years of Muslim terrorism, some of our leaders still support the Muslims only to get their votes (Congress for e.g.) . . . In such a situation you have taken all the courage to stand against the Muslims and give justice to the majority, you

really deserve to be thanked. Come to our city and u'll realize that people are virtually worshiping you. I understand that the stand you are taking is a difficult one, and i also know that there will be even some Hindus too who will dislike you are stand, but a vast majority is with you and love you. Pls continue and don't bother about those critics, we will make sure that you remain the CM forever. Thanks a lot once again. I wish there were few more Narendra Modis in this country. . .
—Yours Truely Rupal (rupal_333@yahoo.com)

Rumours

The long history of communal violence in India is replete with instances where rumours have formed part of a modus operandi of a very special kind. By instilling fear and suspicion they prepare the ground for mischief by interested elements and simultaneously ensure the agreement of large sections of the public in what appear to be acts of self-defence.

Essentially fictitious, rumours tend to capitalise effectively upon people's latent fears, phobias, and vulnerabilities, and are effective vehicles for misinformation. Combined with propaganda in the form of malicious pamphlets and inflammatory 'news reports' they help in sustaining and prolonging structures of oppression. Together they generate an atmosphere of fear and mistrust in which peace initiatives are hampered. Rumours were in constant circulation in Vadodara city and around throughout the weeks of communal tension and violence. They palpably increased and reinforced prevailing levels of tension, fear, and insecurity. By combining fear and mistrust they lent immediacy and a concrete edge to popular hostilities towards the 'Other'.

Rumours had their basis in mutual threat perceptions of each other which was partly based on the perception of state authorities not being able to maintain law and order. They also were an outlet for the neurotic energies accumulated, which in better times could have been channelized constructively towards formation of *mohalla* (neighbourhood) committees and the like.

Documented below are the different types of rumours that circulated in and around Vadodara city.

Decapitated bodies in a temple

In early March 2002, soon after the first intense phase of violence, a rumour about four decapitated bodies that had been thrown into a temple, adjoining the Muslim-dominated suburb of Tandalja, spread rapidly. It did not last long, but its implications were clear. Tandalja is one of the few suburbs to have come up somewhat recently with a predominant Muslim population, outside the walled city. It has a sprinkling of reasonably well-to-do Muslims living alongside common citizens. Owing to its primarily Muslim identification, the locality is often referred to as the 'border' or as 'mini-Pakistan' and figures in the so-called 'threat-perception' of a sizeable section of middle-class Hindus. However, in sharp contrast to such stereotypes, Tandalja stood as an example of peace through the long period of disturbances in the city—and despite several attempts by outside groups to incite violence. There were also constant rumours about an imminent Muslim backlash emanating from the locality. Certain neighbouring colonies, under the inspiration of the ruling BJP leaders, even initiated a move to have Tandalja declared a 'disturbed area'.

Raja Masani murder

There was a category of rumours which dealt with actual events but altered important details such as to produce contrary effects. On 22 March 2002, a Muslim teacher, who ran coaching classes in the Dandia Bazar area and was married to a Hindu woman, was lynched to death in his office by a group of masked men.[10] In Sayajigunj, this news was constructed as the death of a Hindu who ran cooking classes. *Sandesh* reported that the victim was a debauch who ran coaching classes as a pretext to seduce young woman. On those very premises, the paper reported, the teacher had a bedroom where he used to sleep with women.

Avdhutnagar, Makarpura

In Avdhutnagar, Makarpura, during one of those moments when violence had abated somewhat, a group of Muslims were returning home to collect their belongings under police escort. An organized mob, a few hundred strong, brutally attacked them while the police stood by passively watching the crime unfold. Two people died on the spot and many were seriously injured and were hospitalized. The incident became the subject of a rumour but with essential facts altered. It reported that Hindus were assaulted heinously; as a result 22 of them were killed and many hospitalized.

An impending Muslim attack

A widespread rumour, which also lasted the longest, talked about an impending retaliatory attack from Muslims. The expected timing of the attack was constantly deferred from Id to Holi and then to Shivratri, without the rumour losing credibility. This was despite the fact that it was Muslim lives, houses and business establishments which had been the relentless target of coordinated mob fury and destruction for weeks together. Or, perhaps, it was precisely because this was common knowledge that the rumour gained credence.

Two versions of the rumour circulated. The first spoke about a few truckloads of heavily armed Muslims seen on the move somewhere in the city's vicinity, looking for an opportunity to launch an attack. The second version, which came into circulation later, referred to Muslims moving in a Tata-Sumo armed with AK47 assault rifles—a weapon that by now is synonymous in public imagination with 'Islamic terrorism'. In character with rumours, it was not long before the single Tata-Sumo metamorphosed into four. It is always difficult if not impossible to trace the exact or original source of a rumour. However, reports suggest that the Tata-Sumo rumour originated in Sama, spread by the BJP corporator of the area, Pradip Joshi. Reports from residents of colonies around the Abhilasha Char Rasta in Sama indicate that the police were instrumental in spreading this rumour. A police van went round informing people about the expected attack and instructing them to remain alert against it. This imparted greater authenticity to the rumour.

Rumours and night vigils

Rumours originating in such contexts had become the staple of almost every middle-class residential colony, holding them in a vice-like grip. The stark evidence of a pulverized population huddled away in miserable 'relief camps' or in apprehensive, confused Muslim ghettos notwithstanding, Hindu neighbourhoods energetically turned to the task of organizing the defence of their own residential quarters. Committees came up quickly, enlisting defence squads consisting specially of able-bodied men of the colony. Armed with *dandas*, iron rods, hockey sticks, or any other household implement for that matter, the men kept night-long vigils for weeks together. Gates were secured, at times even barricaded; in some places the boundary walls were raised higher.

The vigils were punctuated with breaks for tea and snacks supplied by the women of the colony. Late night dinners for all members of a colony were not uncommon. Cards and carom boards helped to while away the long hours during which the men stood guard against the coming attack. It may not be out of place here to note that between riots and rumours, a new public space came to be etched, howsoever provisionally, where men and women (the latter largely segregated within the family in normal times) could socialize. Between them they also supplied the ballast for shoring up—or even redefining—community bonds and boundaries against an imaginary foe.

Hindi TV and the Gujarat Violence*
Anil Chamaria

You may have had access to several television channels but do you know the truth about Godhra and what happened in Gujarat later? What has been projected on these channels about

Godhra? That there was a conspiracy behind the attack on the Sabarmati Express and the burning of passengers. Official sources have even claimed that the ISI could be responsible, though it has yet to come up with evidence. Our channels were silent on this, as if they were following the government.

Since the Sangh Parivar and Narendra Modi kept asserting through the channels that the widespread violence in Gujarat was an outcome of Godhra, how come no channel independently tried to find out what Godhra itself was the outcome of? How come these channels that invite psychologists to comment on the most minor of incidents did not care to find out that in villages surrounding railway stations and bus stations, it is not unusual for a crowd of thousands to collect even for the smallest incident?

No channel felt the need to find out whether prior to the burning of the train in Godhra any other violent incident took place. We now have reliable information to the effect that the RSS workers and sympathisers going to Ayodhya behaved on the train and the stations at various places on the way in the same manner as they do when, at Ram Nauvmi, a procession goes past a mosque and sparks off riots. The accounts of what happened at Bhalesar in Faizabad on 24 February would make anyone shiver.[18] But this news was not carried by the channels, perhaps because none of them wanted to hamper the passage of the kar sevaks. *Jan Morcha*, a Faizabad newspaper, carried this news. It said that Muslims were identified when made to divulge their names and then beaten up badly. Despite this, local Muslims leaders and intellectuals made an appeal to maintain peace. No Hindutva leader or group felt the need to respond to this. No channel saw fit to carry what happened in Bhalesar as part of its reports on such events. Godhra might have been avoided if such reports had come in. There would have been no excuse for Gujarat.

Such reports not coming through cannot be dismissed as an

---

*   Hindi TV aur Gujarat,' *Kathadesh*, April 2002, translated from the Hindi by Kamini Mahadevan oversight. Forming the base of the incidents that followed, they are proof of a deliberate attempt by the authorities to close their eyes to what was happening. When preparations were on for the VHP's march to Ayodhya, the channels were beaming the BJP's official claims that the party and government had nothing to do with the mobilization. But the channels failed to find out how members of this sectarian party were helping the VHP activists prepare for this march. Reporters of *Jansatta* and the *Indian Express* filed a report just before Godhra that the BJP and the governmental machinery were working together in preparing for the Ayodhya march. Rail and other facilities were being arranged for those heading to Ayodhya. How did channels that claim to be on top of the latest news miss out on this item?

When Godhra happened, many channels, especially the Hindi ones which supported Hindutva, got ready to mount their attack. On the one hand they acted as if they were non-sectarian and responsible, on the other hand they repeatedly flashed headlines about the burning of the bogies carrying the kar sevaks. A clip of a police official was carried by Zee TV that clearly accused 'Muslims' for the attack on the bogies at Godhra. Once this logic in response to Godhra was established and gained acceptance, then channels like Aaj Tak and Zee TV donned the cloak of non-sectarianism. Aaj Tak repeatedly advised its reporters not to mention any religion specifically, that they should avoid using terms like minority and majority. When what is happening is not just a riot but people of a certain religion being subject to attacks worse than those of 1984 in the shadow of the government, what does not identifying the victim mean? The victims of Godhra were called 'Ram Sevaks' but when Muslims were attacked, news reports on these channels became 'secular' and tended to avoid identifying them as Muslims. But when a potential narrative of 'Muslim attackers' was available to be conjured up, reporters did not flinch from naming names. On Aaj Tak, one reporter in his 'piece-to-camera' mentioned, naming a Muslim, how shots were being fired from the building across the street. He wanted to show how 'violent' the Muslims were and, by implication, that what was happening to them was justified. That they could only be attackers; they could not be defending themselves.

Aaj Tak and Zee TV were carrying reports as if they were desperate for a certificate from the government. Finally, Aaj Tak got a pat on the back from the chief minister. Modi said he had received full support from this channel. Zee TV was not to be left behind. Instead of interviewing Arun Jaitley and grilling him on the failure of the government, they invited him to make a statement in their studio, affirming that like the government, they too considered Godhra to be an international conspiracy.

On one hand was this stance of the Hindi channels and on the other, when Star News started giving reports of open attacks on the Muslims, there was a debate that this would provoke further riots. The Star News (NDTV) team was attacked from every side. Star was banned from many parts of Gujarat. But satellite channels do not function like newspapers, by which news can be successfully restricted to an area. BBC and CNN were openly telling viewers how mosques were being razed and converted into temples. How some groups from outside could come and attack the minority neighbourhoods in villages. The violence which persisted for months, and that was being justified by Godhra, was finally exposed by NDTV. Rajdeep Sardesai went to Godhra and stated that the investigators believed the attack was not a conspiracy and that the kar sevaks on the train had created havoc along the way. In their chargesheet, too, the police appear to have been unable to make out a case of conspiracy.

It is unfortunate that many reporters of Hindi television channels came across as 'Hindus'; when they began taking steps to prove they were 'secular', telephone calls from members of the Hindutva organizations started pouring in. And that pressure proved too hard to bear.

Notes

1 'Media not playing a constructive role: PM,' *Times of India*, 5 March 2002.

2   'BJP builds Bush shield for Modi,' *The Telegraph*, 7 April 2002.

3   'Language papers say it in black and white,' *Times of India*, 5 May 2002.

4   Editors Guild Fact-Finding Mission Report, New Delhi, May 2002 p 28.

5   'Rioters on loose, government gags media,' *Indian Express*, 2 March 2002.

6   See Bhavdeep Kang, 'Read the fine print,' *Outlook*, 8 July 2002.

7   Siddharth Varadarajan, 'The Ink Link: Media, Communalism and the Evasion of Politics'. In K.N. Panikkar, *The Concerned Indian's Guide to Communalism*, New Delhi, Viking, 1999, pp 160-229.

8   'Angry Muslims fire on and attack Ramshobha Yatra: What happened in Machchipeeth that caused the city to burn?' *Sandesh*, 16 March 2002. The violence in Machchipeeth is now being used to justify the orgy of violence that followed much like the way in which Godhra has been consistently used to justify the genocide.

9   See area reports in *Violence in Vadodara: A Report*. People's Union for Civil Liberties (PUCL)—Vadodara and Vadodara Shanti Abhiyan, June 26, 2002.

10 The case of Raja Masani, a Muslim teacher married to a Hindu woman, has been described above in Chapter 4.

The Aftermath

9

Little Relief, No Rehabilitation*

The People's Union for Democratic Rights (PUDR) sent a fact-finding team in early April 2002 to investigate the violence in Gujarat and its implications for the rights of citizens. Apart from speaking to a cross-section of victims in twenty-one relief camps in six districts, the team interviewed many officials, including the revenue secretary (in-charge of relief and rehabilitation), Government of Gujarat, and the collectors of Panchmahals, Anand and Sabarkantha districts, about what was being done to rehabilitate the survivors of the violence.

People are often found in camps far away from their homes; villages, urban mohallas and even families have been scattered between camps. The number of people living in the camps fluctuates as people move from the houses of their relatives to the relief camps and back. Some people's attempt to return to their houses also adds to the instability in numbers—few of them are successful and most come back. In some instances, their Hindu neighbours inform the victims that the atmosphere is not conducive to return, in others there is active opposition to their return, accompanied by threats and even more violence. The number of people found in the camps also depends on the

*   Extract from Chapter V of People's Union for Democratic Rights (PUDR) report, '*Maaro! Kaapo! Baalo!*': *State, Society and Communalism in Gujarat*, New Delhi, May 2002. (The extracts have been supplemented by other reports—*Editor*).

time of day, with some residents trying to find work in safe areas close to the relief camps.

'A company of broken people'

The Shah-e-Alam Camp is located in the Shah Alam Dargah. It is approached through an ancient gate which opens into a large courtyard type clearing. Near the entrance there are twenty-two toilets for 2,200 families or 8,000-10,000 inmates. The thick stench is nauseating. As we enter and remove our sandals, the flagstones burn the soles of our feet. On the left there is a large room, which serves as an office-cum-meeting place. People are milling all around. Women, men, children of all ages are scattered across the floor of the dargah. The muezzin calls them to prayer. Not many respond. They are a company of broken people.

The Vadali Camp is no more than a large open *maidan* with a cloth *shamiana* strung overhead. It provides little protection from the heat. The sides are open. When we visited, several hundred women were sitting huddled together in small groups. The *maidan* is in front of a now defunct cinema hall—the Veena Cinema. At night, over 600 women and nearly 600 children crowd into the premises of the cinema to sleep. The men sleep outside. The toilets are inadequate and the entire compound is slowly becoming a large latrine. They have been living like this for over a month. The only politician to visit is a local Congress leader—he came once. We are the first women visitors.

Source: Women's Panel, *The Survivors Speak*, p 25

Nobody, it seems, had a complete list of the relief camps functioning in the state. District authorities lack a comprehensive list of camps located within a district, and only recognize some camps. A random sampling of camps by our team revealed a consistent pattern across districts—among other things, of the near absence of any government provision. It is clear from the official resolution and our conversations with officials that the state does not wish to undertake the responsibility and incur the cost of proper relief measures.

How many displaced?

Official figures: 1,11,414 persons or 1.1 lakh
Figures given by NGOs working in relief camps: 1.75 lakh in
relief camps, 30-40,000 with relatives, i.e. over 2 lakh displaced.
Anand district: Official figures: 1,254 persons in camps
Our figures from just one camp: Kohinoor Camp, Anand town:
1,155 persons
There are 17 camps in the district.

Source: PUDR

Setting up of Relief Camps

The Gujarat government did not set up a single relief camp. As
the attacks on Muslims continued and spanned virtually the
entire state, they fled from their houses in search of refuge. It
took the victims in the rural areas a long time to find safe and
secure shelters, in some cases over a week. Many of them hid as
best as they could in the fields, hills and forests for days together
and then travelled long distances in different directions in an
atmosphere full of terror and risk. Some found temporary refuge
in neighbouring villages, while others tried to return, hoping
that the attacks would have ceased. Some were killed along the
way. Those who managed to reach safety informed the police
about others still hiding in the fields. In some cases, the police
rescued the Muslims and brought them to the camps or other
safe places such as residences of relatives, or mosques and
madrasas in villages and towns with substantial Muslim
populations. Sometimes even presumed safe locations turned
unsafe, as happened in Nadiad town, which housed many
displaced people from villages near and far.

The state administration failed totally in providing safe
locations of its own and relied wholly on the existence of certain
villages or towns where attacks were less probable. The
displaced, too, did not expect the State to provide shelter,

especially after its role in the violence. The only refuges available were those set up by Muslim-dominated panchayats and/or Muslim religious trusts, which took upon themselves the task of providing protection, feeding and housing the victims. Dead bodies, as and when they were discovered, were also brought by the police to these locations or collected by the camp organizers. For a whole week after the violence started, provision of relief was neither conducted nor contemplated by the administration.

On 6 March, the state government came out with its policy resolution regarding the provisions for relief (Resolution No. RHL 232 002/ 513/(3) S-4). The resolution glosses over the government's bounden responsibility to provide safe and sanitized shelters for victims. District collectors (e.g in Anand, Panchmahals) interpreted the lack of orders to organize relief camps as specific orders not to to do so. The revenue secretary at the state capital confirmed to us that this is indeed what had been intended.

The revenue secretary's explanation is revealing: 'In the scenario of ongoing communal attacks, victims would feel secure only with their own communities.' This is a telling comment (albeit unintended) on the administration's own performance. Victims did approach the police and district administration on innumerable occasions for help and safety. In many cases, help was not forthcoming, in others, police connived with the mobs or at best watched the killings, in still others the Muslims were saved and left at the charity of Muslim residents in other villages.

When questioned why operation of the camps was not later taken over, the reasoning was equally facile: that the State could not provide security; that it could not set up separate Hindu and Muslim camps; that there was nothing wrong with registered NGOs coming to the aid of the administration. If the State, with its monopoly over arms, cannot provide security, how does it expect NGOs or camp organizers to do so? What the government is unwilling to admit is that these NGOs are really religious organizations or trusts. The government failure to provide relief, thereby pushing people into the fold of various religious trusts, will only have the effect it officially deplores—of further communalizing society, and forcing different religious groups to arm themselves for self-defence.

The Gujarat government resolution stated that the district administration would provide assistance up to 31 May only to those camps that satisfy a number of conditions. These stipulate that the organizers should be a registered society or trust except those already running camps, in which case they need special permission. The camp should have at least 100 inmates. The camp should be located in a clean area, have toilet facilities, medical care, drinking water, and a clean and healthy kitchen. In addition, the camp organizers are to maintain a register recording details of all inmates, the losses and injuries suffered, their time of arrival, departure and place of departure. Violation of any of these conditions can lead to closure of the camp.

Yet there is no clause specifying what happens to the inmates in the case of closure, or in cases where the administration refuses to provide registration to the camp. Where medical, sanitation, water and toilet facilities are lacking, the administration does not take the responsibility of providing this. The role of the administration is restricted to providing a liaison officer and a medical officer to inspect the camp.

The outcome of such a policy is not difficult to imagine. A substantial number of camps in every district have not been recognized by the administration, such as the camps at Kadi (Mehsana district), Mehemdabad, Kesra and Mehlaj (all in Kheda district). Not surprisingly, therefore, while the number of camps in the official list was ninety-five as on 13 April, unofficial sources at the time put it at 146 camps in the entire state. While the revenue secretary claimed that there were six camps in the whole of Anand district, we found seven camps in Anand town itself and in all, seventeen camps in the district. In village Mehlaj, about 500 people from twenty-two villages have taken shelter, but when the village panchayat asked for government aid, the response it received was that because no one in the village had been affected by the riots, no aid could be given. At this camp, grain is being sent by an organization, Jan

Kalyan. Similarly, when the panchayat at Matar in Kheda district applied for registration of the camp in the village at the beginning of April, they were told that it was time to wind up the camps and hence new camps could not be registered at this stage.

Some camps that were initially recognized have been subsequently derecognized since they did not meet the stipulated requirements. The relief camp at Jinjer in Kheda district is a glaring example. Two- to two hundred and fifty residents continued to stay in the camp (as of end April) even as the government refused to make any provisions for them.

Given the scale of displacement, it is impractical to expect any private organization to deliver everything. For the state to then penalize them by withholding recognition without making any alternative provision is criminal. Evidently, the state neither wants to help victims itself nor enable others to do so.

Running of the Camps

The camps recognized by the government are not in much better shape either. The only help accorded to the inmates of these camps is a food ration amounting to 500 grams of cereal and 50 grams each of pulses, edible oil, sugar and milk, and a dole of Rs 5 per person per day. The supplies are supposed to be made on a weekly basis.

At some of the recognized camps that the team visited, supply of rations was irregular and far short of the slated amount. The Kohinoor Rahat Camp in Anand town, for example, started functioning from 3 March when displaced people started arriving. With 700 people, the camp got a week's ration on 6 March. The next week's ration did not arrive. Over the fortnight the number of inmates had grown to 1,155 people from 378 families belonging to 95 villages. The next ration on 2 April was sanctioned for 247 people and the amount supplied was even less than that sanctioned. Pleas for more supplies fell on deaf ears. The collector of the district had little to say except that the camp organizers were required to supply accurate figures. What the liaison officer was doing or meant to do is thus unclear. With the exception of the camps at Ahmedabad city, the team could not find a liaison or medical officer in any of the camps.

One explanation given by a local official was that the control room for relief and rehabilitation is located at Gandhinagar, which has to keep track of migration to and from the camps everyday. There is a lot of migration both ways: in Mehmedabad the inmates numbered 1984 on 3 March and had come down to 732 by 11 April. Of these, 534 had left for their village while 718 had gone to stay with relatives. In the Shah Alam camp at Ahmedabad, the inmates numbered 10,537 on 3 March and grew to 13,500 by 16 April. For some inexplicable reason the authorities have only kept track of the number of people going out of the camp and not those coming in. The figures of inmates available with the government are bound to be serious underestimates. The collector at Anand informed the team that there is no mechanism to sort this out. The decision of the government is final. In effect, then, a system is in place aimed to deny relief: through non-registration of the camps, through faulty recording of the number of inmates and through the lack of a system of redress.

Basic amenities such as clean drinking water, shelter from the elements, medical and sanitation facilities are completely absent in virtually all the camps, especially in the rural areas and taluka towns. Santrampur and Kalol relief camps are glaring examples of the total lack of drainage and sanitation, and are sitting ducks for the outbreak of epidemics. The collector of Panchmahals, where these camps are located, washed her hands of the problem by saying that the policy had no provisions for tents and toilets. Reports suggest incidence of measles, typhoid, gastroenteritis in the camps. In Godhra alone, sixty cases of measles were reported by doctors doing voluntary work in the camps. On 18 April, Union health minister C.P. Thakur admitted that cases of measles had been detected yet restricted the figure to eight in five camps! The summer heat and monsoons will only make things worse.

Given the absence of rehabilitation and the continuing rioting and tension, relief camps will need to continue for a long time. Government initiatives need to improve substantially in both quantity and quality.

Rains, epidemics threaten relief camps
Ruchir Chandorkar

Ahmedabad: The riots may have subsided but life continues to be a struggle for hundreds of families still living in relief camps in the city, who are defying the government's squeeze on supplies. The rains have only compounded the problems for these families who either don't have any home to go back to or don't feel it is still safe enough to return home.

The Shah-e-Alam camp has around 4,000 people, most of them without shelter from rains. Suhana Pathan, a volunteer at the camp, says: 'The people are living out in the open and when it rains, they occupy any dry place they are able to find. Even the places that are covered with plastic are giving way. Even the food becomes watery as it is cooked in the open.'

With the rains, the threat of outbreak of epidemics has increased as the camp is ill-equipped in even providing basic medicines. 'The medicine stocks are low and we are not being provided with even basic medicines like Paracetamol and Avil. The threat of diseases like cholera, jaundice and malaria is looming large and with no medicines, I don't know what am I supposed to do?' says Mehmood Malik, camp's dispensary in-charge.

The Aman Chowk camp in Bapunagar follows the same tale of neglect. The camp has been closed, according to the government, but the people won't leave. 'We were forced to close the camp because of pressure but we still have some eighty families staying here. We are doing what we can and providing shelter and food on our own.'

The camp is surrounded by gutter water. When asked about what the municipal corporation was doing about it, Sajjad Ahmed says: 'We have complained to the authorities but no action has been taken as yet. Forget medicines, we haven't had drinking water supply for the last two days.'

Refugees at Dariyakhan Ghummat are being provided with some assistance. The clerk at the camp says: 'The two days when there was quite a lot of rain, we faced a major question of how to accommodate 2,400 people. The government now seems to have taken some initiative and started building tin-roof shelters for the camp people.' At Juhapura, the Sonal Theatre camp also has started putting up such tin-roof shelters to protect the people from the rains.

Amarjeet Singh, health commissioner, on the other hand, denied the fact that the camps were lacking in hygiene and medicines. 'The camps are being looked after properly by our medical teams and we carrying out our daily checks. If there is a shortage of medicines at any place, we will cover that. That will not be a problem.'

Source: *Times of India* (Ahmedabad), 2 July 2002.

Schooling has practically come to a standstill, apart from religious classes in some of the camps. The government has made no provision for this. There is a need to initiate some income-generating schemes for the camp inmates. Many inmates of camps presently lack every sort of personal belonging that is considered necessary for day-to-day life. Many do not have a single change of clothes or money.

Inadequate Rehabilitation

Proper rehabilitation of victims involves a number of things. First and foremost is an environment free from fear, which at the very least demands that the identified attackers should be absent from the victims' surroundings. Secondly, it requires that victims have homes to live in with the belongings necessary to run a household. Third, they should have means to earn a livelihood: be it employment, or the tools and means to carry on a trade or profession. Where earning members are killed or disabled, sufficient ex-gratia assistance is required to enable families to support themselves.

Ex-gratia payments for loss of life and injury

The governmental response to loss of lives and injury is available from three resolutions issued by the revenue department. The first dated 28 February (No. RHL/232002/513/S-4) provides for an ex-gratia payment of Rs 2 lakh for those killed and injured (mostly Hindu) in the train burning at Godhra. A resolution of 2 March fixed the ex-gratia payment for lives lost in the post-Godhra carnage (mostly Muslim) at Rs 1 lakh. Following press reports and a public outcry at the discrimination even in death, the government, by a resolution of 9 March, chose to bring down the compensation for the Godhra victims to Rs 1 lakh. This is evidence not just of how cussed the government is against Muslims, but how little it cares even for Hindus. The sensible thing to do would have been to have uniformly increased it to at least Rs 2 lakhs for everyone. By the second week of April, compensation had been paid for about 450 deaths. Only recognized deaths (i.e. those on the official list) are being compensated—the death toll, in fact, is much higher.

This assistance amount in case of death is among the lowest paid to the victims of any communal killings in the recent past. In the Bhopal riots of December 1992, the ex-gratia amount was Rs 2.2 lakh. Since prices have approximately doubled since then, the equivalent amount today is around Rs 4.4 lakh. In Bhagalpur in October-November 1989, the amount paid was Rs 1 lakh, its present day equivalent is Rs 2.8 lakh. In the Congress-organized carnage of Sikhs in Delhi in 1984, which is being compared to the present carnage, both in the public sphere as well as by the government in Parliament, the amount paid was Rs 2 lakh. Initially, the government ordered Rs 10,000 as compensation, which was increased to Rs 20,000 by the R.N. Mishra Commission of enquiry. In 1997, the High Court awarded a total of Rs 2 lakh as compensation with additional interest payable from October 1984 till the date of payment. The amount worked out to Rs 6.9 lakhs in 1997. Its present-day equivalent is over Rs 9 lakhs. It should also be noted that the state of Gujarat has amongst the highest per capita GDP and, therefore, has a responsibility to provide better ex-gratia assistance, taking into account both the level and cost of living of the people and the ability of the state government to pay.

Even in terms of injuries sustained, the government has been both miserly and blatantly discriminatory between the Godhra victims and others. The 28 February resolution fixed an ex-gratia payment of Rs 5,000-50,000 for permanent disability and Rs 1,000-5,000 for temporary disabilities. For the predominantly Muslim victims of the subsequent genocide, a 2 March resolution (RHL/232002/513/(2)/S-4) provides no payment for temporary disabilities at all. Even for permanent disabilities, the amount has been substantially scaled down: Rs 2,000 for disability up to 10 per cent, Rs 3,000 for disability between 10 and 30 per cent, Rs 5,000 between 30 and 40 per cent and Rs 50,000 for above 40 per cent disability. These figures were based on a 1992 valuation and not upgraded. In this petty valuation, whether the government assesses an injury as 10 or 40 per cent becomes finally immaterial. For some like Mohammad Javed from Kadi village, whose hand was blown off by a bomb, the loss of a hand also means the loss of livelihood. He can no longer perform the work of cleaning that he used to do.

The procedure for obtaining assistance for medical expenditures of those who were treated privately is designed to deprive them of even this help. First, the onus is on the victims to obtain a disability certificate from the doctor, obtain a counter-signature from the civil surgeon and produce all this before the collector. Victims who suffer injuries that do not cause permanent disability are denied even this paltry medical assistance.

'Hum paanch, hamare pachcees'

After refusing to run any relief camps for the victims of the communal violence and then cutting off government rations in order to shut down privately-run camps, Gujarat chief minister Narendra Modi went one step further. In a controversial speech delivered during his 'Gaurav Yatra' at Becharji on 9 September, Modi accused the hapless riot victims of contributing to a 'population explosion'. He was playing on the popular RSS grievance that Muslim men are allowed to have four wives. The speech was taped by the state intelligence department and when a copy subsequently made its way on television, the intelligence chiefs were sacked. This is what he said:

Excerpt from Modi's speech as played on www.ndtv.com:

'I told them that I got water from the Narmada in the month of Shravan, if they had it their way, they would have got it in Ramzan. What should we do? Run relief camps for them? Do we want to open baby producing centres? *(Hum paanch, hamare pachees)* We are five and we will produce 25 children. Where does religion come in the way of family planning? Gujarat has not been able to control its growing population and poor people have not been able to get money.

'They make a long queue of children who fix tyre punctures. In order to progress, every child in Gujarat needs education, good manners and employment. That is the economy we need. For this, we have to teach a lesson to those who are increasing the population at an alarming rate.'

According to NDTV, the State Intelligence Department has sent a report in its letter J/2/BJP/YATRA/525/02 dated September 12 to the Additional Chief Secretary, Home on the allegedly inflammatory content of the chief minister's speech. In paragraphs 10 and 11 of the report, the text of the objectionable utterances has been quoted, while paragraph 13 makes the observation that religious feelings of minorities may be hurt due to this and may lead to increase in communal tension in the state.

On 18 September, days after the tape went on the air, Modi transferred additional director general R.B. Sreekumar to the police reforms department. He had joined the state intelligence bureau just four months earlier. Two other officers were also shunted out.

Unfazed by the controversy, the VHP announced it would make thousands of copies of Modi's anti-Muslim remarks and distribute them in Gujarat.

Assistance for damage to property

The single most striking feature of the attacks was destruction and looting of houses and property. It was far more generalized than killing. In village after village, houses, shops and kiosks were torched or demolished. In Kheda district alone, over 3,000 residential houses have been completely destroyed, according to official figures. This looting, arson and destruction has affected people cutting across classes, from landless casual labourers and middle-class people to rich traders and landowners. The losses suffered by the rich are enormous and decades will be required to make up for what has been lost. For instance, Bohra trader Kasimbhai lost a rice mill in Mehmedabad which is estimated at Rs 30 lakhs. The losses of the poor may be small in absolute terms but represent everything they have. Making up the loss is harder and they are likely to be pushed further to destitution. People have lost everything from utensils, beds and bedding, clothes, cash and valuables to houses, tools, implements, means of livelihood and grain stocks.

The assistance for damage to houses, property and household belongings is dealt with through four resolutions. The first dated 5 March provides for cash doles and assistance for household kits. The cash dole is fixed at Rs 15 per person per day, for a family of a maximum of five persons, for a maximum period of fifteen days. Though basically a relief measure for those displaced, this has been linked to a more than 50 per cent damage to the dwelling place. Thus, people whose dwellings are not substantially damaged and have been forced out because of threats to life are not eligible. It is also not payable to those residing in relief camps. The period of payment of the dole has not been extended even though return is not possibile, over two months since the displacement. The assistance for household kits is a one-time payment of Rs 1,250 per family for those whose household goods have suffered damage of more than this amount. Both these payments are dependent on a survey by the administration. As far as the team could ascertain, the administration did not inform or otherwise enable the victims to be present during this survey to explain their loss.

Assistance for movable and earning assets has been fixed at the actual loss with an upper limit of Rs 10,000 through another resolution dated 11 March 2002. This resolution is based on earlier such resolutions framed in 1986 and 1989. While the 1986 resolution fixed the government assistance limit at Rs 5,000, the 1989 resolution had raised it to Rs 10,000. However, while framing the current resolution it did not occur to the government that thirteen years had elapsed and there was a need to change the ceiling limit to at least compensate for higher prices. The eligibility criterion for availing of this assistance requires that the affected person should not have participated in the communal disturbance and should not be named in any criminal complaint. However, a number of FIRs concerning attacks by Hindu mobs have falsely named Muslims as accused. This criterion would further victimize those falsely implicated.

A resolution dated 20 March 2002 has fixed the compensation amount for houses lost between Rs 5,000 and Rs 50,000—the same as that fixed in 1992. The process of assessing house damages was begun when the displaced people were too scared to venture out of the relief camps. Thus the assessment of damage to the house—whether damaged, burnt or demolished—was done without an idea of the original structure. In Kanij village of Khera district, where victims have gone back to their houses, compensation received for burnt and destroyed houses ranges from Rs 1,000 to Rs 25,000. It is not surprising, therefore, that people continue to stay in canvas shelters outside their burnt houses—the assistance paid to them is insufficient even to repair some of the houses which are partially damaged. About fifty victims of Kadi in Mehsana district have got cash varying from Rs 200 to Rs 10,000 for burnt houses or shops. In Mehmedabad camp, we heard that a large number of villagers and jhuggi dwellers of the town have been given Rs 1,700, probably for damaged houses.

The final resolution dated 16 March 2002 fixes the assistance for industries, shops and self-employed people. Here the government provides a 4 per cent interest subsidy for three years on loans of up to Rs 1 lakh sanctioned by banks and financial institutions. Apart from this, payments of sales tax can be deferred for five years and of electricity duty for one year. This again is an exact replica of the policy framed in 1992.

The entire rehabilitation package is seriously flawed. It refuses to recognize the norms set throughout the country for compensation of damages. It relies on policies drafted a decade or more ago without even taking the bother of inflating the amounts specified by the price index. It is insensitive to the problems of the poor. There is no compensation, for example, for the loss of belongings, loss of days of work, loss of crops, cattle and grain stocks. The meagre compensation being doled out by the government may help some victims tide over their immediate consumption needs. To call it rehabilitation, however, is a fraud.

A pittance as payoff
Manas Dasgupta

Ahmedabad: The Gujarat government claims to have already disbursed more than Rs 56 crores as direct cash benefits under various heads to the riot victims. However, representatives of the victims dispute the government statistics and say that more than 90 per cent of those affected are yet to get anything. Ten per cent had received some 'meagre amount' . . .

Gaffarbhai Memon, who claimed a loss of Rs 50,000, has been paid nothing, Sayed Ahmed Shaikh, who estimated a loss of Rs 80,000 has been paid a paltry Rs 1,000 and Kurshidbanu Shaikh, who owned two houses and estimated her loss at Rs 1.60 lakhs, has been paid Rs 3,250. Even assuming that they had been exaggerating their claims, how can a family start life afresh with only Rs 1,000? Even the paltry compensation smacked of discrimination. A Hindu household which did not suffer any losses and is still living in the same house has been treated as a riot-victim just because it is a mixed locality and paid a compensation of Rs 5,000. But a Muslim, next-door, whose house has been totally destroyed has received a mere Rs 250. 'Are we also not citizens of this country? Why this discrimination,' asks Yasin Shaikh.

Shaukatkhan Tyrewala, general secretary of the Qaumi Relief Committee set up to carry out negotiations with the Government on behalf of the minority victims, said some of them had been paid as little as Rs 15 or Rs 50 for repairing their damaged houses. 'Why this crude joke in the name of compensation,' ask the victims. The committee said that while the victims of the earthquake in urban centres last year were paid a compensation of Rs 1.50 lakhs with soft-term loan facilities for another Rs 3 lakhs, the Government was not prepared to pay even Rs 50,000 for the houses damaged in the riots. Nothing remains in the house of Ruksahnabanu Mohammad Hussain in Amdupura locality. 'The hooligans did not even spare the floor tiles which were dug out before the house was looted and set afire,' Mr Shaikh pointed out. But what she got from the Government as the 'full and final settlement' was only Rs 2,000. 'Can anyone rebuild a house in a city with Rs 2,000?'

The situation is no different for the Muslim industrialists who have suffered heavy losses. Sheetal Submersible Pump company owned by Akhtar Mansuri was in ruins. Mr Mansuri submitted all relevant papers, including the insurance cover, to the District Industries Centre estimating his loss at Rs 45 lakhs. The reply from the DIC was a second shock to him after the riots. It did not dispute his claim but sanctioned only a 'loan' of Rs 1 lakh.

The compensation policy for the riot-hit industries, including small shops, has a major loophole. They can either avail a soft-term loan or a 10 per cent subsidy, not both. Accepting the Government subsidy means they will have to borrow the rest of the money from the market. With even small shop owners hard-pressed, the fate of the owners of the chain of hotels where everything was destroyed and the utensils looted is worse.

Source: The *Hindu*, 23 June 2002

———————————

The prime minister visited Gujarat on 4 April, over a month after the trouble began. He announced an additional compensation of Rs 1 lakh for those killed, rehabilitation of widows and orphaned children, textbooks and school uniforms for children, improvements in the living conditions of relief camps, 35 kg of food grains to victims below the poverty line, and Rs 50,000 for destroyed houses and Rs 15,000 for those partially damaged. None of this has been disbursed and, given the complete silence on this count since that date, in all likelihood it will never be. When the government was in a fix in Parliament over the question of dismissing the Narendra Modi government, the prime minister declared the release of Rs 150 crores from the Centre on 1 May. The amounts quoted and the schemes declared are meagre in the face of the destruction and killing. But that is the smaller worry. The real issue is whether compensation, relief and rehabilitation are rights of the citizens and their provision is a duty and responsibility of the state. Or will populist slogans and political expediency determine peoples' lives and livelihood?

Alternative livelihoods?

The effect of the genocide on livelihoods will be a long-term one. Several have been rendered jobless or destitute. Ghaffarbhai of Limkheda, a bidi maker has not been able to return to his village for two months, or get work; several young men of Sawala have been unable to drive their autorickshaws and earn a rupee in two months, because it is not safe to pass through Hindu areas. The government's meagre and partisan policy of rehabilitation does not even begin to address the magnitude of the issue.

Several of those now living in camps used to work as agricultural labour in fields belonging to Hindus (e.g. in the fields of the Patels of Sardarpura) or as workers in Hindu owned workshops, brick kilns or factories. They will obviously be unable to find employment there again. In some cases, the VHP and Bajrang Dal has threatened the owners with dire consequences if they continue to employ Muslims while in other instances the Hindu owner of an establishment has deliberately retrenched the Muslim workers. This was the consequence of a systematic campaign of economic boycott of Muslims undertaken by the VHP and Bajrang Dal through leaflets and meetings from 1 March. Casual workers in big and small cities continue to be particularly targetted by the campaign. The looting and/or burning of Muslim hotels, restaurants, trucks and factories also mean loss of employment—not just for the owners and managers but also for the employees of these establishments, both Hindu and Muslim.

Given that till mid-May the state had failed to provide even basic security for Muslims to reach their places of work—two

Muslim workers in Ahmedabad were killed en route to work in early May—or create any alternative sources of livelihood, economic rehabilitation of the victims is obviously last on the government's agenda.

The Return to 'Normalcy': Closure of Relief Camps

The government did not set up relief camps. When organizations did, in a number of cases the government refused to recognize these. In those that did receive the state government's tardy, grudging 'recognition', the food supply, and resources disbursed were meagre to begin with and did not increase commensurate with the increase in refugees. Security of the victims in camps was left almost entirely in the hands of the 'community'. And when the pressure started building on the state government to restore 'normalcy', in the Gujarat government's dictionary, it was defined by 'the winding up of relief camps'. A curious conundrum emerges—the camps are to be closed down because normalcy has to be established. And, of course, for the rest of the country, normalcy has been established because the camps have been closed down.

The government resolution (RHL 232 002/ 513/(3) C.4) had granted permission for running relief camps up to 31 May. This resolution was passed on 6 March 2002 long before the fact of continued communal violence in the area became apparent. For many living in relief camps across the state this deadline is far too soon.

By end April, some district collectors had started forcibly closign camps. Through a GO dated 26 April, the Dahod collector, posted to the district just a few days previously, abruptly closed down four camps in Dahod district with immediate effect.

Nowhere to go and no one cares
Manas Dasgupta

Ahmedabad: The BJP government in Gujarat has still not tired of harassing the minorities. They have now been ordered to leave the protection of the relief camps and walk into an uncertain future. Narendra Modi's officials are on the prowl. Eight camps were ordered shut earlier this week in Ahmedabad catching the organizers unaware. The district officials apparently wanted to prove the union home minister, L. K. Advani, right. When Mr Advani was briefing the media that only 12 camps were operating in the city providing shelter to some 15,300 people, actually 22 camps were sheltering some 49,000 riot victims.

The authorities instantly stopped supply of essential commodities and drinking water to the camps though not one of the inmates had moved out or was provided alternative shelter. The camp organizers are in a quandary. They can neither force the inmates to go back to their shattered houses nor can they afford to run the camps indefinitely without governmental assistance.

In those camps still in operation, pressure is on the organizers to send back home as many people as possible. Khalid Shaikh, who runs camp number 15, was told to send home at least 175 of the 800-odd inmates. It is another thing that those forced to return to their homes in some of the worst riot-hit areas of Idgah, Amdupura and Chamanpura are yet to get any compensation from the government, their damaged houses are yet to be repaired and a sense of fear and insecurity still prevails among them.

'We are being hounded out like criminals,' regretted Mr Shaikh, 'for committing the crime of running a shelter camp for the riot-hit'. Teams of officials from the district collectorate had visited his camp, his office and even his home to 'persuade' him to close down the camp and send the inmates home.

A government official is deputed to each camp to take a head-count and coordinate relief, yet teams of officials from the district collectorate descend on the camps now and then to crosscheck. 'Sometimes the teams come thrice a day to take a head-count as if the inmates are prisoners and cannot stir out of the camp even for a minute,' says Farid Shaikh, who runs camp number 45. Government assistance depends on the head-count taken by the teams and not on the number of inmates registered in the camps . . .

It is true that from about 1.50 lakh inmates in 121 camps at the height of the communal riots, the number has come down to about 60,000 in 19 camps in different parts of the State.

But except in the rural areas, not many have returned to their homes willingly.

The pressure to close down the camps had been mounting on the organizers for the last six weeks or so and many who could not withstand it either requested the inmates to return or handed over the camps to the district authorities to be closed down promptly forcing the inmates either to return to their un-repaired homes or take shelter with friends and relatives wherever feasible in some unaffected minority-dominated areas.

In the camps of people such as Khalid Shaikh who refused to give in to pressure, the Government dangled a carrot before the inmates. If they agreed to return to their homes voluntarily, they would be given priority in clearing their dues, a clear hint that those remaining in the camps would get nothing.

But for the Modi administration, promises are made only to be broken. 'They had made similar promises some three months back also, but nothing came of it,' pointed out Mr Shaikh. The inmates he sent packing home got nothing for a week though the promise was to pay them the compensation within two days. And those who were paid the 'compensation' feel ashamed to even talk about it . . .

The reason given for closing down the camps is the coming monsoon and the need to coordinate the relief work, but the motives are different. Besides the fact that they are a grim reminder of 'state-sponsored terrorism', many of the camps in the urban centres are located in the municipal schools which have to be reopened. And the Government is not willing to provide alternative sites for the camps as any such idea will be resisted in the Hindu-dominated areas and it does not want to follow a 'ghettoization' policy.

But the main reason for the early closure seems to be the political compulsion to clear the way for the Assembly elections. Elections cannot be held till the inmates are resettled and the relief camps closed down. The BJP and Mr Modi are keen on an early election to encash the communal sentiments generated by the riots . . .

Source: The *Hindu*, 23 June 2002

Continuing Insecurity

A number of Muslims do want to go back to their villages. Those with fields need to prepare for the next planting season and avoid their land being encroached upon by others. But a fundamental requirement for going back is a basic sense of security. This comes with food, with shelter, with means of livelihood, and with the knowledge that those guilty of perpetrating the attacks against them are being prosecuted. In Gujarat today, the state is unable to guarantee even one of these to Muslim victims. In Sanjeli, where villagers were sent back after their camp at Dahod was closed, the government has provided an escort of twenty-four BSF men. Yet, villagers continue to feel insecure—at the height of the attack which left almost 600 houses burnt and sixteen people killed, a mob of 30,000 had surrounded the village. Even if the BSF were to save them from further attack, there is little to subsist on. Their houses have not been rebuilt. Their tools and implements, kiosks and shops have been totally destroyed. Only a few have received the limited compensation. Back in their village the victims huddle in the burnt-out shells of some houses, in the midst of row upon row of desolate charred structures. The guilty roam free. This is what normalcy looks like this Gujarat summer.

There are many who do not want to return like the villagers of Anjanwa and Pandarwada who suffered grievous loss of life and betrayal by neighbours. Others will be unable to return, since the family breadwinners have been killed or seriously injured. Where can they go—the two orphaned children who survived Sardarpura; Sultani from Eral, who was raped and widowed with two small children to raise; old and disabled Benaben of Katwara who lost all her savings for her daughter's wedding; Mohammad Javed of Kadi who lost his hand?

In any case, Sanjeli is a rare case, where BSF men were sent as security. In most cases, the state has not made simple arrangements for the protection of Muslims who go back to see their houses, survey the damage, or explore the possibility of returning. In camp after camp, there are accounts of Muslims

328 Gujarat: The Making of a Tragedy

who went back, overcoming their very legitimate fear, being beaten up. If their houses and shops were as yet unharmed or simply looted, they were now torched to give them the message that they should not come back. The police who accompanied villagers back to their villages to see the damage and gauge the possibility of going back, repeatedly failed to protect them.

Kulsum Ghani Champaneria of village Sathamba of Bayad taluka, Sabarkantha district, went back to her village on 10 April. The tea-shop she used to run, intact till then, was burnt down and she was told to go back to the camp. Muslim villagers of Vadagam and Bhiloda of Sabarkantha district also had similar experiences. In early May, 150 families of Sayala village in Panchmahals left the security of the Godhra relief camp and tried to return to their homes. Threatened with dire consequences, they were forced to return to the camp.[2] The police took Pathan Jafar Khan back to his home in Baranpura, Vadodara, to assess the damage. A mob attacked from all sides. The policemen ran and those in the Special Reserve Police tent stationed there refused to come out and help.[3]

It is unlikely that the state governments and district administrations are unaware of the price paid by Muslims for returning to their villages, where they have done so. In camps in Mehmedabad, Matar, Anand we were told that the district administration and the police are asking the people to return-even conditionally. In some villages, the conditions include dropping FIRs or the names of the accused. In other places, they have been told to stop wearing all signs of religious identity or offering namaaz, if they are to be 'allowed' to come back. Almost everywhere that Muslims have gone back to their villages, it is on the basis of similarly tainted compromises. In some instances, as in Randhikpur, the villagers are battling on trying to get some justice, and refusing this conditional return.[4] Such resistance is possible only if they have the option to stay on in the camps.

The state forcing closure of camps without even the semblance of rehabilitation or simple protection to victims, well before its own earlier deadline is thus not an innocent desire to establish normalcy. It is a calculated move to ensure that the Muslim victims go back to villages to live on terms set by the attackers, quietly and without a fuss, subsuming their identity. This then is the bloody politics of 'peace': Golwalkar's vision of a second-class status for minorities come true.

Notes

1. *Indian Express*, 26 April 2002.
2. *Times of India*, 1 May 2002.
3. *Frontline*, 10 May 2002.
4. Raja Bose, 'Muslims held to ransom over FIRs,' *Times of India*, 7 May 2002.

Why free and fair elections are not possible in Gujarat today
Extracts from the Election Commission of India's order on
Gujarat
No. ECI/PN/35/2002/MCPS, 16 August 2002.

Extent of Affected Areas: The state government, in its presentation to the Commission, emphasized that the riots were confined to pockets in a few districts of the State, with 13 districts remaining unaffected . . . Significantly, additional director general of police R.B. Sreekumar stated before the Commission that 151 towns and 993 villages covering 154 out of 182 assembly constituencies in the State, and 284 police stations out of 464 police stations were affected by the riots. This evidently falsifies the claims of the other authorities that the riots were localised only in certain pockets of the state.

Voters displaced: (O)n-the-spot inspections have revealed that a substantial majority of electors who had to perforce leave their houses and in many case, flee from their villages to save themselves from the arson and carnage . . . have not yet returned to their houses or villages. In most of the cases, their houses stand totally demolished or burnt, and in many others, their houses have been so badly damaged that the same have been rendered totally unfit to live in. Their return to their houses is prevented primarily on two counts. First, slow progress of reconstruction/repair of their demolished/burnt/damaged houses because of inadequate/no compensation paid to them by the state government, and, second, a fear psychosis still pervading the minds of the displaced persons, particularly those belonging to the minority community . . .

Law and Order: Though the situation on the surface seems to be normal . . . there is, however, an undercurrent of fear and tension prevailing in the state particularly amongst the minority community . . .

Everywhere there were complaints of culprits of the violence still moving around scot-free, including some prominent political persons and those on bail. These persons threaten the affected persons to withdraw cases against them, failing which they would not be allowed to return to their homes. In Dakor (Kheda district), the team was told by a delegation, in the presence of senior police officers, that the culprits had been identified before the police but no arrests had taken place and the main culprits continued to threaten the villagers to withdraw their FIRs . . .

The progress of cases filed as indicated by the state government does not indicate the number of people named in FIRs but not yet arrested for their crime. In fact, in several instances prominent persons named have not been booked at all . . .

The Commission is thus of the considered view that the law and order situation is still far from normal . . . The slow progress in relief and rehabilitation work, on the one hand, and non-arrest and non-punishment of the guilty, on the other, have hampered the process of normalcy returning to the state, the victims carrying the fear and anxiety of another backlash. Similar feelings are shared by persons from the majority community as well living in minority-dominated areas. The people have lost confidence in the local police force, the civil administration and political executive. Someone who met the Commission, in fact, said how could the situation mend when there was not even regret for what had happened.

In this environment, election campaigns evoking passions will threaten a violent backlash. So confidence-building measures have to be taken up in earnestness and with urgency. Foremost among these would be to arrest and punish the guilty for their crimes, irrespective of their status and rank . . .

10

Apart, Yet a Part
Ghettoization, Trauma—and Some Rays of Hope

Editor's Note: After such large-scale, politically orchestrated violence—the purpose of which was to polarize society on communal lines—it is perhaps inevitable that the process of involuntary ghettoization in Gujarat will gather pace. Targetted for living amongst Hindus, abandoned by the police in their hour of need and now subject to the Sangh Parivar's call for an economic boycott, Muslims in the state are likely to seek security in numbers. The first part of this chapter looks at some examples of this trend. At the same time, the trauma of what the victims have been through will remain with them long after the physical, bodily scars of the violence have faded. Mental health issues, especially those relating to women and children, have already emerged as a key concern for the medical community. The second part of this chapter, thus, deals with the demons and fears that have started plaguing the minds of the victims, especially children.

When Prime Minister Vajpayee visited Ahmedabad in early April, an emotional Elaben Bhatt—founder of the Self Employed Women's Association (SEWA)—told him: 'We are ashamed that the Prime Minister of our country has to visit Gujarat at this time. What has happened in Gujarat is terrible. The country was divided in 1947. Today it is as if all our hearts are divided. If the people of Gujarat get the government's support for security, then is normalcy far off? When will this happen? There can never be peace by making Muslims insecure. This is not nationalism. Why don't our political parties understand this?'[1] Since then, the violence has stopped but the State is doing nothing to end the sense of insecurity ordinary Muslims feel. In such a situation, a major part of the burden of rehabilitating Gujarat's beleaguered Muslim citizens must necessarily rest upon the shoulders of civil society, upon the state's Hindus.

Rehabilitation is not just about providing houses and jobs but also about belonging and inclusion, empathy and solidarity. It is about standing up for justice and decency. There may have been very little decency on display in Gujarat since the burning of the Sabarmati Express but despite the best efforts of its political leadership, the state is far from being a moral black hole. The last section of this chapter recalls those small candles of light which the ordinary citizens of Gujarat held up amidst the darkness that was imposed on them from above.

Fear and Ghettoization

How do we give our children an education?
Afrozben[2]
Afrozben is a senior volunteer in-charge of Rang Avadoot, one of the seven camps in the Juhapura area, and which sheltered approximately 400 victims, including sixty-two children, from Naroda Road, Ahmedabad, as well as some from areas as far off as Vadodara. All the children were from middle-class families and had been attending private schools. Her own son studies in class II in Paldi, Ahmedabad.

'Where is there safety for our children, I ask you? The Bajrang Dal attacked the schools, broke down sections, beat up the watchman and demanded that the principal hand over lists of minority children in the school. Similar events took place in Little Flower, Don Bosco, Trinity, GLS, all English-medium schools.[3] Two of them have already sent notices to parents asking them to take Transfer Certificates for their children as they could no longer guarantee their safety.' With tears silently streaming down her cheeks, Afroz continued, 'After the riots started, my son's results dropped drastically, we ourselves are so frustrated, how are we to see to our children? When he went to sit for his exams, we'd be pacing up and down outside . . . his mother, father, grandfather . . . all afraid that something may happen . . . how will I educate my son like this? . . . I'm thinking of leaving Gujarat, *inshallah*, I cannot bear this any more. He is my only child, what if something happens to him?'

Her voice wavered, 'And my son loves India, he loves the Indian flag, he keeps seeing the film *Gadar* . . . He has such a strong Indian identity, we could not bear to tell him that Indians were behind the riots, that the Bajrang Dal Hindus were behind it. He thought that Pakistan was behind the riots and we let him believe that . . . and he was so angry when he found out we had been lying to him.

'In these camps we have been so busy just keeping people alive that we have had no time to address questions of education. Admissions have to be completed this week—it is very necessary. But who will take these children into schools is the question?

'Fellowship programmes for children in boarding schools in other states? How can a mother let her child go away from her after what has happened, who will guarantee her child's safety? Will those who put them in such schools give it to us in writing that our children will be safe, will the schools give it to us in writing? How can we trust that our children will be safe in boarding schools, even in other states?'

Afroz finally broke down, sobbing uncontrollably: 'I have never talked about myself like this before . . . I've always been told not to get emotional, to keep my control . . . I'm opening up to you for the first time today because I can't bear it any more, I'm so scared for my son . . . .'

When she recovered she asked in a grim voice, 'The questions I have for the authorities in this state are: Which are the schools for our kids? Is there safety on the roads? Is there safety in the schools? Will we find our children when we go back to get them at the end of the day? Will the teachers not be callous even if our children can go back to their schools? Will my son's teacher not say "Why are you back? Smile Iqbal!"

'The basic question is: How do we give our children an education?'

Even in rural areas, an economic boycott of Muslims
People's Union of Democratic Rights

After half a year, for the Muslims, who survived the attacks in March, resuming their work and earning a livelihood is proving to be a problem. In many villages, Muslims are being told that even if they do return—after meeting all conditions, including retracting the names of accused Hindus—they will not be allowed to carry on any economic activity.

For the Muslims who own lands, returning to the villages to take charge of their lands and beginning cultivation is an important means to rehabilitate themselves economically. In Ghodasar, for example, the Muslims collectively own about 150 bighas of land. The few Muslims who have returned to the village, after writing compromise affidavits, plan to sell off their lands and leave. Those staying in nearby villages such as at Jinjar categorically state that they too would like to sell off their lands and settle elsewhere in places with a greater concentration of Muslims. At present their fields are lying fallow, and Hindu farmers are taking their cattle to graze there.

At Delol village, Muslims have been issued dire threats and prevented from returning. In June and early July, some of the Muslims had managed to work on their fields and crops had come up in some of their fields. But following a bomb blast in July, Muslims are not being allowed to return. In their absence, the Hindus of the village have started grazing their cattle on these fields, ruining the standing crop. In Palana village of Kheda district, where only a few Muslims own land and are willing to return, the Hindus have found a different way of squeezing the landowning Muslims: the threat here is that they would be denied access to water from the borewell for irrigating their fields.

Given this scenario, leasing their land on sharecropping

arrangements is being viewed as an interim solution by the displaced Muslims till they return to take charge of cultivation themselves. With no Muslim presently residing in such villages, the lands have perforce to be leased out to Hindus. In Anjanwa, for example, Hindus and adivasis are share-cropping Muslim-owned fields. The Muslims eventually plan to sell off their land and have some kind of a 'settlement', and move out of the village altogether. Abdul Rahim Ahmed, who lost his grandchildren in the killings, has had to give out his seven acres of land to the deputy-sarpanch of the village on a sharecropping basis. In Kanjari village of the same district only some of the Muslims have been successful in leasing out their lands on sharecropping. However in better-off areas like in the districts of Kheda and Anand, Muslims are unable to even find Hindus to sharecrop their fields.

Inability to return to their villages also cripples those not owning land. But for the landless, the situation remains grim even where they have undertaken the risk of going back. Agricultural labourers in Palana village (Kheda) have been told that no one would employ them henceforth. Similarly, a number of Muslim workers of Ghodasar previously engaged in agricultural and other occupations are not being hired for casual work in the village.

Small traders and independently-owned businesses have also been seriously affected. Some of them are simply being prevented from carrying on their work. An instance is the case of Muslims of Laval village engaged in some petty trades such as tailoring, selling groceries, etc. They have been told that they would not be allowed to resume their trades and could come back only to work as labourers in agriculture or in other places.

Source: PUDR, *Gujarat Genocide, Part Two* (September 2002).

Winds of hatred wrench best friends apart
Why Sajid and Mehul do not have a chance.
Basant Rawat
The following is an excerpt from a leaflet being distributed by the VHP in the streets of Ahmedabad.

Let us resolve:

- *From now on I will not buy anything from a Muslim shopkeeper.*
- *I will not sell anything from my shop to such elements.*
- *Neither shall I use the hotels of these anti-nationals, nor their garages.*
- *I shall give my vehicles only to Hindu garages. From a needle to gold, I shall not buy anything made by Muslims, neither shall we sell them things made by us.*
- *Boycott whole-heartedly films in which Muslim hero-heroines act. Throw out films produced by these anti-nationals.*
- *Never work in offices of Muslims. Do not hire them.*
- *Do not let them buy offices in our business premises, nor sell or hire out houses to them in our housing societies, colonies or communities.*
- *I shall certainly vote, but only for him who will protect the Hindu nation.*
- *I shall be alert to ensure that our sisters-daughters do not fall into the love-traps of Muslim boys at school, college, workplace.*
- *I shall not receive any education or training from a Muslim teacher.*

They grew up together in Naroda. Best friends, they went to the same college to graduate in commerce. Last year, they became partners in a gas agency. Sajid Quereshi and Mehul Patel shared a dream and nurtured an ambition: to expand their business and become the top suppliers of cooking gas to city hotels. But the dream is in tatters now, torn to shreds by the winds of hatred generated by the Godhra massacre. Sajid has decided to pull out of the partnership. 'It is a very sad situation, but then one has to accept reality. The reality is that a Hindu and a Muslim cannot remain business partners in this state,' said the twenty-one-year-old.

He bears no ill-feeling towards Mehul. The signs are clear: it is time to end the partnership, which is no longer practical even if both want to work together. 'There are people who would not hesitate to browbeat my friend. So why endanger his life unnecessarily,' said Sajid.

Sajid's decision reflects the deep scars the riots have left on his young mind. 'We have to read the signals. The signals are that any Hindu having a business partnership with a Muslim will not be tolerated. This is what the miscreants wanted to convey when they ransacked and looted one of the city's biggest stores, Pantaloons. It was targetted just because it has a Muslim partner,' he pointed out. His parents are also pressuring him to pull out of the association with his Hindu friend so that both of them are safe.

Mehul, too, hasn't missed the signs. 'I will do whatever Sajid wants. If he feels that we should break our business partnership, we will do that. We will not force him to continue to be our partner,' he said. It was Mehul who had offered his friend the partnership a year after they passed out of college. Sajid had accepted promptly, investing Rs 2 lakh. Another Rs 2 lakh had to be put in later.

But 27 February changed everything. Sajid and his family landed at the Shah-e-Alam relief camp after a mob razed his house to the ground with a bulldozer the day after when the retaliation for Godhra erupted. Their office was spared as not many knew that Mehul had a business partner, but the second office in Sajid's house was destroyed.

Sajid's friends had rushed to his aid and tried to move his family to a safer location. 'But we were surrounded by the mob. When one of my friends, Umang Patel, pleaded with the mob to spare us, he was beaten. The mob spared him only after they were told that Umang is the nephew of state VHP joint general secretary Jaideep Patel,' he recalled.

Source: The *Telegraph*, 30 March 2002

Trauma

The unbearable burden of bearing witness
Kavita Panjabi, Krishna Bandhopadhyay and Bolan Gangopadhyay

In Gujarat hundreds of children now look at you with blank eyes and 'delightful' smiles frozen on their faces. The only time they express themselves is in the dread of night when they wake up screaming in terror. The violence they have experienced is unspeakable, ruthless the cruelty. What meaning will they find in the savage present that we have bequeathed to them—if they regain the capacity to do so—and how will they in turn shape it?

In every minority camp the organizers and parents told us that when the children first arrived, they were severely traumatized; they could not sleep—and if they did, then they woke up howling with fear in the middle of the night. Many had gone completely silent, others would cry quietly through the day, while some would play, re-enacting amongst themselves the attacks and murders, the violence and arson, that they had survived. While some children interacted with us normally, most in each camp still showed signs of acute depression and trauma.

In Shahpur, the majority community camp, the children were initially a bit wary, then they relaxed in warm and friendly conversation, especially after the organizers left us alone with them. One striking factor about the majority camps is that, unlike the minority camps, these are populated only by the poorest sections of the community.[4] Most of the people in these camps left their homes in a fear exodus, either as the fires in the neighbouring minority areas which had been set ablaze threatened to destroy their homes, or in anticipation of retaliatory attacks. As a result, some of the children in the Shahpur camp had actually seen their homes burnt, or even looted 'by sword-wielding men', but were confused about the identity of these men. Some said they were the same who attacked their neighbours of the other community, others said they were *miyas*. None of the children had witnessed a single murder, rape or burning of any human being. This team did not see any such evidence of trauma in these children: however, their narratives, like those of minority children, were rife with confusion about the role played by neighbours of the other community, and questions of trust and hostility.

Saddam Hussain
Eight years, from Randhikpur village, Panchmahals district.

As we talked to various other people, Saddam sat with us, a cheerful grin on his face. It took us time to realize that this grin never left his face—it was the wall he had set up between himself and the world. The patches of eczema on his arms betrayed the traumatized state of his mind. Latifabehn, one of the camp organizers, told us: 'He just sits there silently; he talks if you feed him.' His brothers, Mohsin (12) and Yakub (10), flanking him protectively, one on either side, maintained a stoical silence right through. Latifabehn gave Saddam a thick nutrition tablet to chew on, and he started to talk:

'I used to live with my mother Amina Bibi and these two brothers. When the tola arrived in our village, my brothers were not there. My mother had sixty rupees with her. When the tola of thirty to forty men attacked us, she stuffed the sixty rupees into my hand and pushed me into a run. I ran. But then I saw the men get hold of the women and I could not make myself run any more . . . I hid myself . . . (his eyes started to wander into space) . . . then . . . then they stripped my mother naked . . .' As he uttered *'usko nanga kar diya'*, his grin broadened, then he clamped his eyes shut and buried his face in his arm. It was painful to see this child lift his head again, very soon, and try to continue. We could not bear to hear him narrate the rest himself and stopped him.

Latifabehn later told us what she had heard from him. 'He saw the brutal rape of his mother. His neighbour B—[5] and her sister were also there with Amina. They managed to run away, only to be gang-raped three days later by another tola. He saw his mother raped successively by three to four men, then he saw them chop off her head and hack her body with sickle and talwars (swords) . . . After the tola left Saddam found only dead bodies around him. He started to run in a frenzy. When he got tired, he would stop, buy himself some food from the sixty rupees his mother had given him, then start walking again. Ultimately he reached a police station. The police located his mama (maternal uncle) in Baria and handed Saddam over to him. His mama brought him to the camp where he met up with his two brothers. Now all three say they do not want to go anywhere else. Not 'home' to Randhikpur—where the sixty to seventy Muslim houses have all been burnt—and not to Baria with their mama either.'

Regarding the boys future, Latifa said firmly, 'We will not force them to go where they do not want to go. They are too scared. They will stay right here with us. They can then go to the madrasa, they will be educated there and can live in the *yateemkhana* (orphanage) of the madrasa.'

'Saddam regularly weeps in his sleep. "I will kill them if I see them . . . I was scared then, but I recognized them, they are from the nearby villages . . . I remember their faces." he says' ended Latifa.[6]

Juned Salim Sheikh
Seven years, from Anjanwa village, Panchmahals district.

We first met Juned, another orphan, with Saddam in the Iqbal High School camp. He sat with us with a vacant wide-eyed look, neck bent at an angle, head falling into chest, like he had lost all interest in holding it up. Nothing interested him—food, crayons and drawing sheets, conversation—he remained unresponsive with just this numbness in his eyes. The only time they flickered was when we asked him if he had anybody of his own in this camp, and he whispered, 'Dadaji' (grandfather).

We met Abdul Rahim Ahmed, his dadaji, very briefly that day. Dadaji just said *'Uska dimag ab theek nahin hai*—Something is wrong with his mind now . . . 3-4 whole days he stayed hungry, kept fleeing from one place to another . . . the horrors he witnessed, houses looted and burnt, 13 people killed, much more . . . all this has affected his mind. Now the child asks after the cows and buffaloes, and says, "Is this our home"?'

Juned's eyes haunted us through the night. Instead of setting straight out for Kalol in the morning we decided to go back to his dadaji first. At Iqbal High School we were told that the group from Anjanwa had left—they had been shifted to Satpul where the camp was relocating . . . There, we found Juned and dadaji, Juned's dadi (grandmother) Amina, their daughter Rabia, and daughter's young son-in-law Faroukh. Juned sat curled listlessly in dadaji's lap as the latter spoke:

'Juned's father Salim and mother Afsana had died of TB and sickness. Juned lived with us. One of his uncles, my son, was killed in the attacks. His wife and children are here. They also slashed Juned's kaki (paternal aunt), Maqsooda's neck with a sword, stoned her, and killed her four-year- and two-year-old children. Then they threw them all into the well. We all used to live together . . . our houses and everything we had was burnt.' At this point Juned stirred. Dadaji lifted him onto the ground and asked him to go away to the other children.

He continued, 'Three days later Maqsooda was recovered from the well . . . we found her still alive . . . her children were dead. Juned witnessed all this with us, with his dadi and me . . . his mind did not function like this earlier . . . now he asks, "Is this our home?" His mind is boggled now, earlier he used to be fine. Now he wakes up in his sleep and starts running away, he shouts, "Run! Run!"'

Then Juned's grandmother spoke up, 'My daughter Rabia's daughter-in-law, Zubeida, was also killed and thrown into the well. Zubeida's two-year old son Adnan was killed too.' . . . At this point, Rabia, who had been listening quietly, burst out, 'When the tolas came, we started running for our lives. I got separated from my son Farooq and his family. Then I ran into an adivasi who asked me to remove my clothes, 'to become one with him,' to take on his religion . . . I pretended to agree to his demand, but asked him to give me water and clothes first . . . then I managed to run away into the jungle. The next day I went to the police, took them to the well, and got the bodies pulled out of the well, got their names written. Two-year-old Adnan's body was recovered with its legs cut off. When I went to lift it, the police beat me with a stick, asking me to stay away from it. [At this point Rabia voice breaks, she buries her face in her hands, then pulls herself together and continued.] When my daughter-in-law Zubeida's body was recovered, it was hacked into two from the abdomen down . . . others had arms cut off . . . the police did not let me see the other bodies after that . . . little Adnan's legs had been cut off . . .' She broke down sobbing hysterically.

While dadaji and Rabia were talking to one of us, another member of our team noticed a youth of around twenty-two years sitting close by with a numb look on his face. He did not answer when asked his name. Upon a repeated query; his lips moved a little but he failed to speak. Then a voice answered, 'I am Mohammed, he is my son Farooq. Farooq is also Juned's aunt's son.'

Mohammed continued: 'A few days back we had celebrated Id with full vigour. Some relatives were also staying at our place. It was around 2.30 in the afternoon when Farooq saw a huge mob coming to attack us with sharp weapons in hand. We all started to run. Unluckily, my family was gheraoed by the attackers. They started forcing us to utter "Jai Sia Ram". And then they plunged swords into the bodies of five members of our family. Their dead bodies were mauled and thrown into the nearby well. They killed Juned's aunt and her two children with swords and threw their bodies into the well. Farooq was escaping along with his wife Zubeda and son Adnan. At first they hit Farooq and snatched Adnan from his lap . . .'

Farooq finally opened his mouth: 'They snatched Adnan from me and even pulled Zubeida away. I hid myself behind the bush. From there I saw Zubeida being stripped and raped by the Bajrang Dal people. After that they killed her, cut her into two halves and threw the pieces into the well.' Tears streamed down his face momentarily. 'They even killed my one-and-a-half year old Adnan and threw him into the well. Then they burnt our house.'

As we left, all were crying bitterly to themselves except Farooq. One of us held his hands firmly and could feel that they were trembling. A sudden grim look in his eyes said these were the hands which had failed to save his wife, to protect little Adnan.

Dadaji said quietly, 'Juned had seen all this happen . . . he saw what they did to Zubeida and Adnan too . . . after they had thrown everybody into the well and left, Juned and I went and just sat looking into the well for hours . . . we could not move . . .'

Juned's blank eyes had led us to these layers within layers of terror, grief and suppressed fury.[8]

Source: *Extracted from* The Next Generation: In the Wake of Genocide, *A Report on the Impact of the Gujarat Pogrom on Children and the Young by an independent team of citizens, July 2002. Supported by Citizens' Initiative, Ahmedabad.*

No respite from stress and trauma
Medico Friends Circle

Doctors from Medico Friends Circle visited nine relief camps and three hospitals in Ahmedabad, Vadodara and the Panchmahals in April 2002.

Post-traumatic stress disorder (PTSD) is a well-known sequelae of any disaster, and is accepted as a public health issue to be tackled by the health services in such situations. However, the only emotional support to victims of violence is being provided by camp volunteers, who have no training for this kind of work.

Because the team visited the camps nearly two months after the beginning of the violence, it could observe that a certain routine had been established. Survivors of the violence have made efforts to restore some normalcy in their lives. Still, the team also found pervasive psychological stress and trauma. Those who had witnessed killings and/or lost members of their own families were the most severely affected. Many broke down while recounting their experiences. Many suffered from the more visible symptoms of psychological distress: bouts of crying and complete withdrawal. They also reported insomnia and nightmares.

In general, stress and trauma among survivors manifested in both physical and psychological symptoms. People expressed feelings of frustration, helplessness and fatalism, agitation, anger and depression. Certain attacks, like those in Naroda Patiya and Chamanpura, were so brutal that that they have become part of collective memory. Even those who have not witnessed those episodes refer to them again and again. Survivors are always conscious that they could be once again subject to violence of that scale and brutality. Many live in constant fear of what can happen to them as insecurity and earlier memories haunt them.

Paralysed by fear

At Kalol, the team met M, a seven-year-old boy, on the insistence of one of the volunteers. She said M required immediate medical attention. The boy lost both his parents and most family members in the violence.

The team visited M at his grandmother's house, where he now stayed. He was sitting with a maternal uncle (Mammu) on the parapet outside the house. The moment he saw the team approach him, and before anyone touched him or spoke to him, he burst into tears.

The doctor in the team sat at a distance, and, softly, asked M to walk towards him. Clearly, M did not want to walk. He got up with tears rolling down his face, insisting that he could not walk. However, the doctor's soft encouragement finally convinced the boy to walk for the first time in two months, first holding his uncle's hands, then holding the doctor's hands, and finally on his own. As he walked, he dragged his right leg, which he insisted was injured.. However, when the doctor examined the leg to locate the source of pain, and the extent of damage, M did not complain of any pain.

The team's doctor diagnosed M's case as a probable 'conversion reaction'. The child's inability to walk was not due to any physical injury but due to extreme psychological trauma. The doctor prescribed some exercises for the child and reassured him and his relatives. The team was told that M had witnessed his parents being burnt alive. His grandmother, who was looking after him, was also detected to be suffering from severe depression.

———————————————

Another manifestation of stress was in an increased level of reporting of non-specific symptoms. This may be compounded by the fact that, in most camps, people are living out in the open, exposed to the heat. They complained of headache, body ache, palpitation, stomachache and disturbed sleep. Among women, in many camps, team members found instances of disturbances of the menstrual cycle, such as polymenorrhoea (frequent menstrual bleeding) and dysmenorrhoea (painful menstruation), which were concurrent with the outbreak of violence. There is a strong possibility that these problems are stress-related. Women were very concerned by these changes. They were also distressed by the difficulties of managing menstruation without adequate water and bathing facilities.

It was equally disturbing to see children with various stress-related problems. Women reported that their children would wake up at night crying, and get agitated on hearing loud noises. Children were afraid of anybody in police uniforms; they expressed fears that they would be killed or burnt; they did not want to leave the camp. Some were deeply disturbed and clearly needed professional help for their psychological problems.

———————————————

Games revolve around death for these children
Leena Misra

Ahmedabad: Last Friday in a relief camp at Modasa, eight-year old Sabina and her friends were spotted digging holes in the ground, filling them up with mud, pouring water and then embedding a piece of marble on it. The exercise went on till someone asked them what they were up to. Pat came the reply: *Kabar-kabar khel rahe hain* (We are playing a game of graves!). And what was the piece of marble for?, the visitor asked. 'It is the epitaph for those buried inside,' retorted Sabina. This is the Garib Nawaz relief camp of Modasa in Sabarkantha district, four months after the riots. What she saw shocked Paulomee Mistry of an Ahmedabad-based voluntary organization, Disha, who had gone there to distribute livelihood kits as a part of their intervention programme. 'It was gut-wrenching,' she exclaimed after the experience. But there was more. A little ahead, at the Makdoom relief camp hosting 120 families, she met five-year old Ruksana with her friends Altaf, and Kabir who were also playing with mud and water, digging similar pits. Another set of make-believe graves, but these were bordered with green grass and stones after being filled.

For the children living in relief camps, life has begun to revolve around death. Having witnessed the lives of their dear ones end in the most gory manner, they talk about mobs, fire, blood and death as if they were talking of cakes, pastries, chocolates or toys.

During intervention programme at two relief camps of Himmatnagar, organizers roped in a group from Mumbai to conduct a puppetry workshop for children. One girl of around ten created a girl puppet out of paper, and when asked to build a story around it she said, 'This is Aapa (elder sister). She is very sad because people came to her house and stole and destroyed everything,' recounts Paulomee.

City-based psychiatrist Dr Hansal Bhachech who has been working with riot-hit children recounts cases where he caught children playing 'riot-riot'.

When working at the Shah-e-Alam camp, Bhachech heard the oft-repeated account of Kausar Bano, the pregnant rape victim from Naroda-Patiya, from a child. He was aghast. 'They must have overheard it from elders, and their imagination ran wild.'

Says Paulomee: 'On account of the polarization the drop-out rate in the schools is also high, which means most of these kids will go without a decent education. And this is the biggest fear.'

Source: *Times of India* (Ahmedabad), 10 July 2002

UNICEF had conducted a training programme for medical officers (MOs) deputed to provide medical care at the camps. Using a structured protocol, they screened 723 children for signs of mental trauma and found that 239 children required counselling (according to the protocol). This need was rephrased as 'parental support' in the interim report data. In addition, 12 children required referral to a psychiatric specialist.

These findings seem to underestimate the extent of trauma. There was no information about whether the symptoms recorded in the protocol were probed or only recorded if reported spontaneously. Also there were no details about which children were screened.

No assessment has been made of the mental state of adults. However, the experiences of heinous attacks, and a prolonged period of unabated violence, have taken a heavy toll. The extremely hostile and insecure atmosphere prevents people from moving out to look for work. This has led to feelings of depression and anger. Uncertainty about the future, and a loss of faith in civil society and the State, has led to a feeling of desperation.

Medical professionals and camp volunteers had strikingly different attitudes to people's mental health needs. The MOs providing medical care at camps consistently undermined the importance of dealing with psychological trauma. Any sign that people were returning to a routine was taken as proof that they were not traumatized. This was illustrated when the team attended a vigilance meeting of medical officers deputed to the relief camps. When a team member mentioned that disturbed appetite could be a sign of PTSD, an officer immediately retorted, 'Oh, they eat very well . . .' Even more disturbing was authorities' general disdain for the suffering of those whom they treat. A senior government health administrator opined, 'The camp inmates do not have brains to understand that they are suffering from stress and mental trauma.'

On the other hand, camp volunteers are extremely concerned about the mental state of survivors. They spend several hours talking to people and listening to them. In several places, they have organized makeshift schools for the children, and also games. Their role in providing emotional support to survivors is very important.

Source: Extracted from Carnage in Gujarat: A Public Health Crisis, *Report of the investigation by Medico Friends Circle, New Delhi, May 2002.*

Reprisal fear triggers exodus again

Ahmedabad/Vadodara: Two days after the terrorist attack on the Swaminarayan temple in Gandhinagar and on the eve of another VHP-sponsored bandh, it is back to relief camps for many. People from areas like Naroda-Patiya, which witnessed a massacre during the last VHP-backed bandh on 28 February have started moving back to camps fearing another round of reprisals.

Some are of course staying put but they are wearing their nationalism on their sleeve. A huge poster on the Shah-e-Alam Darwaja proclaims, '*Mazhab nahin sikhata, aapas meing bair rakhna, Hindi hai hum, Watan hai Hindustan hamara*'(Religion does not preach enmity, we are all Indians).

The Akshardham strike has triggered another round of panic, especially in the sensitive Panchmahals and Dahod districts, with hundreds leaving their villages for the "relative safety" of towns. In the Panchmahals, villages close to Halol, Kalol, Lunawada and the district headquarters Godhra have seen people trooping to these towns fearing possible retaliatory attack. In Dahod too, villagers from areas like Piplod, Randhikpur and Limkheda have come over to the relative safety of Dahod town . . .

'What if there is another backlash like 28 February?', asks Ershad Sayyed. Sayyed, who has taken shelter at the dargah along with 100 others, left his rented premises in Naroda-Patiya on Wednesday afternoon. Maqsud Qureshi, who lives in the Muslim mohalla of Naroda Gam said, 'I am carrying whatever little cash I had and some clothes. I hope nothing happens.' The number of people at the Qureshi hall riot-relief camp in Mirzapur has jumped from 1,300 to 2,300 overnight with frightened residents pouring in from Shahpur and Naroda-Patiya . . . Mustafa Ahmedbhai Sheikh, resident of Shahpur, lamented: 'My house and my paan shop were looted and burnt on 28 February. Just when the situation was getting back to normal, this terrorist attack has made us refugees again'. Samsad Bano, a resident of Khemchand ni Chali in Naroda-Patiya, said, 'Last night the local police said that whosoever wants to move to safer places may do so. What else could one do in such a situation?"

Source: *Times of India*, Ahmedabad, 26 September 2002.

Hope

An oasis of peace in communally-ravaged Gujarat
Sanjay Pandey

Ahmedabad: They have done it again. For the fourth time in a row, Ram-Rahim Nagar slum residents in Behrampura have not allowed their respective faiths to create a vertical rift among them or to be engulfed by the communal violence which surrounded them.

After easily sailing through turbulent times in 1969, 1985 and 1992, the locality once again did not witness any violence or disturbance. When everything burnt in communal frenzy, harmony reigned supreme in these slums despite having a mixed population of Hindus and Muslims.

Mutual trust helps 20,000 people living in this slum to overcome any communal hailstorm. 'Humanity is our religion here,' says Pyar Ali B. Kapadia, president, Ram-Rahimnagar Jhupdawasi (slums) Mandal adding that nobody is concerned about each other's faith.

This secular colony instead has become a refuge for some 300 riot-affected people housed in a nearby mosque.

Poverty being their common enemy, co-existence of Hindu and Muslims is at its best. People here are least concerned about the mandir-masjid issue. 'Everytime the mandir-masjid issue is raked up, tension crops up and innocent people die,' says A.H. Badami, a retired clerk from the central excise and customs department, adding that the issue should be buried forever.

Source: *Times of India*, 4 March 2002

Some Hindus still live in the heart of Juhapura
Robin David

Ahmedabad: A Hindu living in Juhapura is incongruous for those who have witnessed the recent riots in the city. Juhapura after all is the largest Muslim ghetto in the state and the general belief is that a Hindu choosing to live here is unimaginable in these communally-charged times.

The fact, however, remains that a handful of Hindus continued to live there in relative peace even during the worst of the riots. Some of them live shoulder-to-shoulder with riot victims who have fled there to find safety in the relief camps, and yet they have not been attacked or threatened to leave. The feeling may not be shared by those in the neighbourhood of Juhapura who feel threatened by the miscreants. Only last week, about forty-eight families of Kaumudi Society adjoining Juhapura had fled from their homes.

But Madhuben Navnitlal, who runs a small 'chana' shop, has lived in Ward E, the heart of Juhapura, for the last thirty years. She and her two grown-up sons say they have left their fate to both Mataji and Allah and will continue to stay in the only home they know.

'In the past thirty years of our stay here, I have seen nine riots. We continued to live here even after my husband died fifteen years ago. And now, there is no point in shifting somewhere else every time violence breaks out. Moreover, I would have to shell out about Rs 3 lakh to buy a house in a Hindu-dominated area, something I can't afford,' she says.

Says her son Ashok, 'Our neighbours are like parents to us. Not only do they protect us, they also bring food and rations during curfew. We feel safe here.' Ironically enough, the family had run away only during the post-Babri Masjid demolition riots. Their neighbours like Khatijaben Khalifa and Anwarbibi have marked the house with some symbols of Islam so that no one targets it. The same neighbours form a protective cover around them.

Source: *Times of India*, Ahmedabad, 17 June 2002

For Bhagwandas, this Vadodara mosque is life
Sajid Shaikh

Vadodara: His name is Bhagwan and he is the officiating priest of a dargah. Bhagwandas Haribhai Patel (77) is a chaste Hindu devoted to a Muslim saint, Kasim Dulha. For thirty-eight years, Patel has been functioning as *mujavar* (priest-cum-caretaker) at Kasim Dulha's 250-year-old *mazaar* near the Laxmi Vilas palace gate and has protected it by putting his own life at risk.

'I came to the dargah as boy of fifteen in 1941. I was afflicted with an illness that no medicine could cure. I prayed here and got well. I began spending my evenings at this dargah and in 1964 became the *mujavar* here,'Patel says.

He has no formal training in Islam, has not learnt Urdu or Arabic but knows the essence of the religion. Despite his lack of training in Urdu, he rattles off Urdu couplets and preaching of Sufi saints like an expert. '*Maut se koi basar nahi, saman sau baras ka pal ki khabar nahi* (One can't escape death, one can collect belongings for 100 years but don't know what will happen in the next moment),' he says.

Patel is not the exception at Kasim Dulha's dargah but rather the rule. For 250 years, this dargah has always had a Hindu *mujavar*. Before Patel, Madhavrao Anandrao Satham, a Maharashtrian Hindu, officiated as the *mujavar*. Even today, 95 per cent of the devotees at the dargah are Hindus. 'All *mujavars* till date have been Hindus. A majority of devotees are Hindus.

Patel's dedication to Kasim Dulha initially made him a social outcast. 'I had to walk out of my home, face taunts and word was spread that nobody should speak to me or have any relation with me. But none of these stood the test of time because my conscience was clear. Today, I am not only accepted but respected in society,' Patel says. He has passed his values and beliefs to his two sons, Deepak and Roshan, who help their father at the dargah. Many Hindus living nearby help maintain the dargah and deter mobs from desecrating it during riots.

Patel is not the exception at Kasim Dulha's dargah but rather the rule. For 250 years, this dargah has always had a Hindu *mujavar*. Before Patel, Madhavrao Anandrao Satham, a Maharashtrian Hindu, officiated as the mujavar. Even today, 95 per cent of the devotees at the dargah are Hindus. All mujavars till date have been Hindus. A majority of devotees are Hindus.

Source: *Times of India*, 21 March 2002

Why not a few 'Lajja Yatras'?
Chitra Padmanabhan

Streets always have stories to tell, be it the patter of playful feet, the soft hush of a baby's pram, the camaraderie of friendship or secluded corners of sweet nothings—even the sharp jabs of conflict. But a balance of life is maintained in the public space, for streets have a compulsion to connect.

Sometimes, all streets become dead ends. The public space becomes a site of corrupted meanings; witness Gujarat in the last six months. What is celebrated as Narendra Modi's 'Gaurav' Yatra—launched finally in September—is in reality a bullish flag-march through streets turned communal battlefields. It is meant to stake out territory, keeping all recent wounds alive. There will be very few who do not realise that its purpose is to tease and provoke the simmering embers of hatred and rekindle the bonfires.

Not to be outdone, the opposition parties too, have decided to employ similar tactics of 'yatra' and 'procession'. Politics in Gujarat is obviously moving from the processual to the processional.

It does seem that citizens' groups too should take an active polemical lead from all this. Why can't concerned citizens' groups organise and embark on a qualitatively different kind of procession? Why only a Gaurav Yatra' that seeks to manufacture the sectarian illusion of some exclusive 'Gujarati-ness'? Why not a few Lajja—or Shame—Yatras to actually exhibit for public viewing, from up close, the scale of brutality of a partisan state. A yatra that creates a powerful and universal humanist aesthetic to cleanse the public space.

One such political and activist alternative has already been movingly demonstrated, when over 3,000 A'mdavadis, dispossessed of homes and families, livelihood and security, denigrated and terrorised, shed their numbness to curate Independent India's most ambitious, moving multimedia installation of life as art.

Despite a pall of fear, a huge turnout of victims of the two-month long carnage finally spoke out at the 'Sah Nirman Rally', walking a five kilometre stretch they had not dared step upon these last few months.

Organised by the Society for the Promotion of Rational Thinking (SPRAT) with groups, including Citizens' Initiative, Swaraj, Darshan, Prawah, Democratic Youth Federation of India, ActionAid, Abhikram, Mazdoor Kisan Shakti Sangathan (MKSS), Janpath and the Gujarat Sarvajanik Relief Committee, and supported by 120 organisations across Gujarat, the rally was like an underground stream that gushes to the surface with an awesome purity of purpose.

The Sah Nirman Rally was dedicated to the memory of Deepak Kosti, a tailor in his early 30s, who was killed on February 28 when he tried to save the dargah of Hazrat Syed Shahid, at Bapu Nagar. The dargah was a part of his life, he prayed there every day. The caretaker of the dargah was a friend of the family. Standing alone before a baying mob as if to physically stop it, Deepak was killed by a revolver fired at close range. The dargah has been vandalised; only the graves remain.

It was at that spot that the 3,000 men, women and child victims—accompanied by artists, writers and citizens' groups— came together to display the extraordinary range of material that had been worked upon by toiling rioters: the wood of doors, the metal of vehicles, the alloy of time in clocks, the steel and rubber of sewing machines, fans and cycles - all torched by gas or chemical fires. And, yes, the memories of charred flesh branded in the eyes of the living.

It was the kind of procession that would make blood turn to ice. The shell of a Maruti van atop a camel cart carried the legend: *'Toward the 21st century India! Maruti Van on 27th February Rs 1 lakh. Now fit for the junkyard'*. A motorless sewing machine on a push cart read, *'Once it clothed, now itself naked! Value before, Rs 1600, now Rs 200'*. Cindered doors and windows torn out of their jambs, a few remaining pots and pans hanging from a slender thread spoke of a 'House Hanged'. An enlarged copy of a cheque for Rs.180 as compensation for a house destroyed, told its own story: 'The worth of my house on 27th February–Rs 50,000. Now, Rs 180.'

And what of the human chain of women who had seen their husbands and children perish in the inferno that raged ceaselessly for several days? Or the orphaned children who held aloft placards asking, 'Where are our parents?' In their eyes reflected the flicker of a home that once was, a loved one who was; in one eye was embedded the image of a tree also consigned to the flames, along with humans. It had a nest in it. As if to prove that the image was no metaphor, the gutted tree with the nest was displayed on a camel cart. The opaqueness of death was palpable.

And like all civilizational journeys of the dispossessed, which transform the landscape of the oppressor in subtle ways, by creating long-lasting expressions born of lived experience, this one was no different. There is always a sense of heroism involved in turning around a context that is like a tightening noose and coaxing meanings never intended by the perpetrator. It is these meanings, often categorised as art, that ambush the authoritarian mind and rejuvenate the human spirit.

But, like many epochal moments of our time, this event too went unnoticed by the media. The Chief Election Commissioner was in town that day and was the cynosure of all electronic eyes and ears. The media provided little evidence of this stunning display of reclamation of space and voice by a group of victims. Which is why it is all the more important to record and salute this incident.

What is interesting is the means they adopted to do so, even if it was for a day. To speak out against the injustice of a partisan state was the basic idea. But by using elements of their lives as artefacts, by conceptualising the rally as a moving multimedia installation, the organisers grasped one important fact: Such conscious acts have the potential to become active counters against an aesthetics of violence that parasites on the religious faith of people.

That is why the Sah Nirman Rally is important. It created a scaffolding of self-expression to counter brutality by bestowing individuality to every loss, and making every 'thing' seem human through the associations they evoked. The rallyists restored to the materials the memories of their real selves.

There cannot be a better beginning to a long fight against injustice than a Lajja Yatra transforming into a Gaurav Yatra honouring the humanist spirit of individuals like Deepak Kosti.

Source: The original version of this article appeared in *Hindustan Times*, 13 September 2002.

Notes

1 Self-Employed Women's Association (SEWA), *Shantipath: Our Road to Restoring Peace*, Ahmedabad, p 27.

2 As told to an independent team of citizens in *The Next Generation: In the Wake of Genocide*. A Report on the Impact of the Gujarat Pogrom on Children and the Young, Ahmedabad, June 2002, section 4.

3 'Muslim schoolkids targetted,' *Hindustan Times*, 6 April 2002

4 In some of the better off sections neighbouring the minority community areas, the former were warned to evacuate before the latter were set on fire.

5 Latifa said B— managed to survive only because she passed out and was mistaken to be dead. When she regained consciousness, she found herself surrounded by the dead and mangled bodies of her three-year-old daughter, her sister, and her sister's two-day-old child who had been delivered while they were on the run. The bodies were also weighed down with heavy stones. B— too had found her way to this camp. She was in the next room as we talked to Saddam. Her testimony has been recorded in *The Survivors Speak*.

6 Saddam Hussein and organizer Latifabehn, interviewed in the Iqbal Primary School camp, Godhra city, 6 May 2002.

7 Juned's grandfather, Abdul Rahim Ahmed, grandmother Amina, their daughter Rabia Bano, Rabia's husband Mohammed, and their twenty-two-year-old son Farooq interviewed in the Satpul camp, Godhra city, on 6 and 7 May 2002.

11

The Elusive Quest for Justice
Delhi, 1984 to Gujarat, 2002

Vrinda Grover

In the last weekend of March, almost a month after the violence against the Muslims of Gujarat began, I visited Ahmedabad to attend a meeting on legal strategies to respond to the unending crisis. There were many questions on everyone's mind. When the State is an accomplice—an abettor of the crime—and the police are in empathetic collusion with the 'mob', can the perpetrators be made accountable? Who will investigate? Who will lodge First Information Reports (FIRs) promptly for every murder, every incident of mutilation, rape, burning and loot? Who will collect evidence diligently? Who will faithfully record the testimonies of the victims? Who will arrest the accused? Who will prepare a case that will withstand judicial scrutiny and prove the guilt of the accused beyond reasonable doubt?

As the erstwhile Ahmedabad police commissioner, P.C. Pande, himself admits to the anti-Muslim bias of the state police force and the chief minister transfers the few officers who worked impartially to maintain the rule of law, the chorus for an independent investigation grows louder. But where is such an independent investigating agency to be found? The National Human Rights Commission (NHRC) has asked for the Central Bureau of Investigation (CBI) to step in but the sheer scale and magnitude of the carnage is way beyond the capacity of this premier investigating agency. In any case, the state government has refused to requisition the services of the CBI.

Gujarat unquestionably ranks as India's worst State-sponsored pogrom since Partition. As the macabre dance of death and destruction unleashed on the Muslim community for almost three months in Gujarat slowly abates, the concern is shifting to ensuring that the guilty are prosecuted and punished. However, a glance at the history of communal violence in India reveals that few if any have ever been punished for taking part in or masterminding a communal holocaust.

Thanks to the public outcry, the police in Gujarat have been forced to go through the motions of filing chargesheets in certain high-profile cases. However, the legal outcome is largely a foregone conclusion. A useful reference point here could be the anti-Sikh pogrom engineered and executed by the Congress (I) in Delhi in November 1984. Like Gujarat, here too the agencies of the State, particularly the police, subverted the law of the land in complicity with the ruling party. Later, many prosecutions were initiated and some prominent leaders of the Congress (I) too were tried. The conduct of these trials and the decisions in these cases provide many insights to discern what lies ahead in Gujarat.[1] Indeed, so far, the Gujarat government and police seem to be diligently replicating the 1984 pattern of investigative sabotage which their counterparts in Delhi perfected in order to ensure the dismissal of riot-related cases at the trial stage.

Subverting the First Information Report

The process of investigation into any offence is set into motion by the recording of a First Information Report (FIR) under Section 154(1) of the Code of Criminal Procedure, 1973 (CrPC). The First Information Report is that information relating to the commission of a crime, which is given to the police first in point of time, on the basis of which the investigation commences.[2] Discussing the importance of the FIR, the Supreme Court has observed that this information, 'when recorded, is the basis of the case set up by the informant. It is an extremely vital and valuable piece of evidence for the purpose of corroborating the oral evidence adduced at the trial and can hardly be overestimated from the standpoint of the accused.'[3] In any criminal trial, the FIR unquestionably plays a pivotal role. Lacunae, discrepancies and contradictions in this document would impinge upon the investigation as well as gravely impact on the trial and its final outcome.

For the registration of FIRs, victims of the Gujarat genocide had to turn towards the same police force which had, at best, been indifferent bystanders and at worst actively colluded in, connived at and instigated the killing and looting of the Muslim community. Now it is this very police force which is expected impartially, diligently and accurately to record the complaints of the victims. The long-standing recommendation of the National Police Commission of 1997 that the functions of maintaining law and order and investigation of crimes must be delinked and should be performed by two distinct and independent wings of the police force, assumes significance in this context. All hopes are now pinned on a police force which has been systematically communalized over the past four to five years and which is under the direct control and command of the state executive.

In the initial phase in Gujarat, few, if any FIRs were lodged by the victims. The reasons for this are obvious. Those who had survived the murderous attacks were in hiding or in refugee camps. The FIRs were required to be lodged at the police stations within whose jurisdiction the incidents had occurred and where the victims used to reside. The victims were reluctant to step out as the trip to the police station was not free from risks and hazards. The police seized this opportunity to record FIRs without consulting the victims. Most of these record general facts and accuse no one in particular. These distorted documents serve no real purpose except to prevent the victim from lodging a true narration of facts.

Also, as reported by PUCL, Vadodra, in its submission to the NHRC, in many instances the police point-blank refused to register the FIR. In Bhutadi Zampa and Old Padra Road, the police refused to lodge FIRs of affected Muslims. In Ahmedabad,

Mohan Bundela, convenor of an NGO, Jansangharsh Manch, saw a police officer help burn down a large number of Muslim hutments on 1 March by supplying the mob petrol from his official jeep. It was only after he moved the High Court that an FIR was registered on 10 April.[4] In Sabarkantha district, 137 riot victims moved the High Court claiming the police had not recorded their FIRs.[5] Baba Harsulia of Raj Motors managed to note the car number and identify three persons who were part of a mob who burned his large tractor showroom in Himmatnagar. The *Times of India* reported: 'Baba mentioned the details in his complaint. But it didn't help. 'First, the police tried to convince us that it would be in our best interests if the complaint was withdrawn.' When they insisted, the police cited technical problems. But the arguments 'were simply meant to block the complaint, where we identified some in the mob,' says Harsulia.[6] In response to the Sabarkantha petitition, the additional advocate general agreed to record the statements of the victims.

The People's Union for Democratic Rights documents that similar petitions have been filed before the Gujarat High Court from Kalol in Mehsana district seeking the registration of FIRs and recovery of looted goods and from Radhanpur village in Patan District where a BJP MLA has been identified as one of the attackers. The report comments that the Gujarat High Court, despite receiving such petitions, did not seize the opportunity to frame guidelines and monitor the implementation of procedures prescribed by law.[7]

On 24 April 2002, the NHRC's special representative deputed to track the ground situation in Gujarat reported back to the Commission that the situation in regard to FIRs was grim. Pointing out that in most FIRs, the accused persons are shown as unknown, the NHRC noted that, 'Even when complaints of the aggrieved parties have been recorded, it has been alleged that the names of the offenders are not included. In almost all the cases, copies of the FIRs which the complainant is entitled to, has not been given . . . Further, for far too long, politically-connected persons, named by the victims of the crimes committed, remained at large, many defying arrest. These are grave matters indeed that must not be allowed to be forgiven or forgotten.[8]' It was only after the NHRC insisted that an FIR be filed in the case of the rape and murder of a sixteen-year-old girl from Eral village that the police finally acted, arresting the BJP's Kalol unit president, Chandrasinh Parmar.[9]

As reports of the reluctance of the police to record proper FIRs mounted, the Gujarat government reluctantly issued instructions (on 29 April) that all those who wanted to lodge or FIRs give statements but had been unable to do so earlier should now have their statements recorded. Instructions were also given to the police to record FIRs or statements at relief camps itself.[10]

Despite statements issued by the central and state governments, the situation on the ground remained unchanged and a majority of the victims were unable to lodge FIRs with the police. For example, many victims and volunteers who went to police stations to try and file FIRs reported being harassed and intimidated by the police. One student volunteer of Citizens'Initiative complained, 'A friend of ours was harassed by policemen when he accompanied Waheeda, a victim, to help her file an FIR.' He further recounted that his friend was taken to a room where he was cross-examined like a criminal. Another volunteer, Ankit, said that he was once asked if he was 'a Hindu or a Muslim' at a police station where he was helping a victim.[11]

Even if victims and volunteers who went to great lengths to file an FIR are successful in getting the police to take cognizance, there is no guarantee that the complaint will actually be acted upon. The case filed by Mohan Bundela provides a typical—and chilling—example of what can happen if a complainant is too persistent. After the High Court directed that an FIR be registered in the case involving a police officer, sub-inspector Modi, providing fuel to a mob from his official jeep, the officer concerned sought to bring pressure to bear. Bundela was forced to move the High Court again. The police 'has not examined any of the witnesses named by the petitioner in his FIR nor has taken any action to apprehend the culprits. The registration of the FIR was a mere formality because of the kind intervention of the Court', his petition stated. The police, he said, had no intention to carry out any sincere investigation.

> In fact, the petitioner has come under dire threats for having registered the FIR and on 21 April, the makeshift office of the petitioner at the same place where the 240 hutments were earlier burnt, was attacked around 4.30 p.m. by a mob and several persons travelling in a Tata Sumo Jeep. The culprits placed an explosive material and tried to blow up the door of the office and succeeded in breaking the lower part of the door. As per the information of the petitioner, the attack was carried out by the same persons who had earlier burnt down the hutments. It is also learnt that the PSI is himself instigating the culprits to terrorize the petitioner so that the petitioner does not pursue his earlier complaint.[12]

Upon the failure of the police to record FIRs, some victims and survivors have also filed private complaints before the court of the Chief Judicial Magistrate under Section 202 of the CrPC. Private complaints, as is well known, require the complainant to first lead evidence and satisfy the court that there exists sufficient ground to proceed against the accused and only then would a trial commence. It is quite unlikely that the victims who are already overwhelmed by the task of piecing together their lives would be able to sustain this onerous and time-consuming task.

A Familiar Pattern

The actors have changed but the script remains more or less the same. Almost two decades ago, the Ranganath Mishra Commission enquiring into the anti-Sikh violence of 1984 noted similar lapses and dereliction of duty on the part of the police. The Mishra Commission had warned that shoddy police investigation might prejudice the trials before many of them began. The Commission noted that,

> When oral reports were recorded they were not taken down verbatim and brief statements dropping out the allegations

362 Gujarat: The Making of a Tragedy

against the police or other officials and men in position were written. Several instances have come to the notice of the Commission where a combined FIR has been recorded in regard to several separate incidents . . . Tagging of so many different incidents into one FIR was bound to prejudice the trial, if any, as also the accused persons, if called upon to defend themselves in due course . . . The Commission was also shocked to find that there were incidents where the police wanted clear and definite allegations against the anti-social elements in different localities to be dropped out while recording the FIR.[13]

In Gujarat, even where FIRs have been recorded, they are rendered totally useless as the police has quite deliberately omitted the names of accused persons. 'Only cases referring to mob attack are being registered. Police turn a deaf ear to cases where perpetrators have been identified.'[14] In the Best Bakery case, Zahira Sheikh filed a complaint naming all the accused. She was, however, not given a copy of the FIR by the police, in violation of Section 154(2) CrPC. On 2 March, she went to the police station and found that the FIR registered by the police was false as it stated that the victims were burnt in their sleep.

The police have skillfully manipulated many FIRs so that the accused is only a nameless and faceless mob. An illustration of this is FIR No. 75/2002 dated 1/3/2002 recorded at Vatva police station against an unidentified mob of about 5,000 to 6,000 persons for indulging in arson and rioting at Vatva Gam Waghriwas and nine other places. The mob also attacked the police and burnt a person who has still not been identified.[15] Such FIRs, that hold the key to bringing the culprits to book, neither name any persons as accused nor narrate the specifics of any particular incident. They may, in all probability, prove to be a useless piece of paper unable to initiate any investigation or trial. In many instances, the FIR was registered only after the victims agreed to drop the name of the accused especially if they belong to the BJP or Bajrang Dal.[16]

It must be pointed out here that in many cases relating to the 1984 massacres, the accused were acquitted by the trial courts due to the non-mentioning of names of the accused in the FIR.

Another apprehension voiced is that the police are manipulating statements to scale down cases of cold-blooded murder under Section 302 of the Indian Penal Code (IPC) to dacoity and 'murder in dacoity' under Sections 396, 397 and 398 of the IPC. This would tone down the offence and give leeway to the offenders as the latter penal provisions entail a less stringent punishment.

But by far the most serious and far-reaching dereliction by the police has been the recording of omnibus/running FIRs. Section 154 CrPC mandates that every piece of information relating to the commission of a cognizable offence, whether in writing or orally, shall be reduced to writing and shall be signed by the person who renders it.

As in Delhi, 1984, the police adopted an innovative and illegal method of registering FIRs. Instead of registering a separate and distinct FIR with regard to each and every cognizable offence, a single omnibus FIR is recorded. The contents are general, vague and bereft of details. The incidents reported therein relate to different places, time and accused persons. Some FIRs have been registered where the accused are both Hindus and Muslims and have been booked as part of the same mob.[17] In one FIR, totally unconnected events are clubbed together. The events are spread over several places and at times even several days. An illustration of this is the omnibus First Information Report No. 36/2002 of PS Kalol, Panchmahals.[18] This FIR records different incidents spanning from 28 February to 1 March as well as several areas:

- One incident of 'five to six thousand Hindu men' confronting '2,000 men of Muslim community' at 4 p.m. on 28 February at Rabbani Masjid.
- An incident on 1 March in a hospital compound in which one Muslim was killed by a different mob.
- The killing of 10 Muslims fleeing from Delol by an 'uncontrollable Hindu crowd' at Ambika society on 1 March.

- Arson and attack in Boru village on 1 March by 'about 2,000 Hindu men of surrounding villages' who were 'uncontrollable.'[19]

Such FIRs are also being used by the Gujarat police to preclude the registration of accurate, detailed and specific FIRs by the survivors whose statements are merely annexed to such an omnibus FIR. Such FIRs will ensure that the investigations and prosecution of criminal offences would be no more than an exercise in futility.

It may perhaps be useful to recall that in November 1984, a similar omnibus FIR was recorded for the colony of Trilokpuri in Delhi where over 200 Sikhs had been slaughtered and burnt within forty-eight hours. The investigating officer, while deposing before the trial court, admitted 'that there were oral instructions of his senior officers that all incidents of riots are to be clubbed together and to be dealt under FIR No. 426 of 1984 and no separate case was being registered.'[20]

Recording FIRs in this manner will inevitably entail serious and grim consequences. In *State v. Kishori and Ors*, ASJ O.P. Dwivedi observed:

After the assassination of late Prime Minister Mrs Indira Gandhi on 31.10.84, anti-Sikh riots broke out in different areas of the capital killing thousands of Sikhs. Law and order machinery was completely paralysed because of inaction/connivance of the police. This is apparent from the fact that for hundreds of murders that took place in the area of P.S. Kalyan Puri only one single FIR, i.e. FIR No. 426/84 was registered and that too did not contain any specific details regarding the names of the persons killed or the names of the rioters who took part in the killings. In the name of investigation a farce was carried out. Even the formality of preparing a site plan of the places where various incidents occurred was not completed in most of the cases. Ultimately, to show the compliance of law, an omnibus challan in respect of FIR No. 426/84 was submitted to the court and along with it the statements of some of the victims were also attached. It was left for the courts to sort out specific cases which could be proceeded in accordance with law. It seems the prosecution expected that the trial will be equally a farce and cases would be summarily disposed of thereby drawing a curtain on the legal drama.[21]

Confronted with such omnibus FIRs on the basis of which it was impossible for any trials to proceed, the trial courts had to instruct the police to split the FIR and file separate challans for separate incidents and places. Clearly, not only was valuable information lost in the process but trials were hampered and justice for the victims further delayed.

Yet another feature found common in many of the FIRs lodged by the police in Gujarat is that they are prefaced by a detailed account of the burning of the Sabarmati Express at Godhra on 28 February 2002. This point is well illustrated by FIR Nos. 98/2002 and 100/2002 at P.S. Naroda Patiya, both of which carry identical paragraphs describing the murderous attack by a mob of Muslims on VHP activists and supporters and train passengers. If the idea is to trace the history of the carnage in Gujarat, it would then be relevant to describe the provocative and unruly conduct of the VHP passengers, of which there is not a whisper. Is the reference to Godhra to supply the defence of grave and sudden provocation to the accused?

Both these FIRs pertain to Naroda Patiya, one of the worst affected areas in Ahmedabad, where the mayhem left at least 91 dead. In them, a few prominent VHP, BJP and Bajrang Dal functionaries are named as leaders of the mob. But both FIRs suffer from the infirmities mentioned above, inasmuch as they are vague and general and do not assign specific acts to anyone. It is imperative for a successful prosecution that these shortcomings are overcome by recording detailed and accurate statements of survivors under section 161 CrPC.

The mischief does not end here. A bare perusal of FIR Nos. 98/2002 and 100/2002 shows that the police continue to collude with the Sangh Parivar attackers. Both name the same five accused i.e. Kishan Korani (a BJP leader), P.J. Rajput, Harish Rohera, Babu Bajrangi and Raju Chobe (Bajrang Dal and VHP). The FIRs are dated 28 February 2002 but the place of the offence is different. Thus the police themselves provide a fool-proof alibi to these high-profile accused persons by charging them with separate incidents that occurred in different places on the same day. It is apprehended that eventually both the FIRs will nullify each other and the accused persons will go scot free.

First Information Reports registered in the manner described above will certainly undermine the very foundations of the prosecution case. In cases relating to the 1984 carnage, the recording of vague and delayed FIRs by the police allowed the majority of the accused to evade justice on such technical escape routes provided by the police immediately after the violence. Trial courts expressed their helplessness in giving the accused the benefit of the doubt where the very foundation and basis of the cases, the FIR, was meaningless. History must not be allowed to repeat itself but already it may be too late. In early July, a Godhra court acquitted nine persons, accused in a case of burning and destruction of shops in Lunawada town in Panchmahal district, for lack of evidence.[22] This incident was one of the first cases of violence after the Godhra train attack. The defence counsel was local BJP MP Bhupendrasinh Solanki and the trial lasted barely over a day.

With VHP prosecutors, riot accused need no defence . . .

In the Lunawada case, the accused were acquitted in record time because of faulty investigation by the police. But what happens when the public prosecutor helps sabotage the case? This is a question many are asking since the Modi government has appointed many lawyers affiliated to the Vishwa Hindu Parsihad as prosecutors in riot cases.

Amit Mukherjee writes: 'Dilipbhai Trivedi, state general-secretary of the VHP, is also a public prosecutor in Mehsana, pleading in courts on behalf of Muslim riot victims. Several other public prosecutors owing allegiance to the BJP and the VHP will be entrusted with the responsibility of representing riot victims in court . . . In Ahmedabad, it is reported that at least nine of the sixteen public prosecutors are active workers of Sangh Parivar groups. Among the prosecutor panel in

Ahmedabad are two VHP members who also fought cases of the riot-accused free.'

Since many of the accused are VHP activists, justice could prove elusive. Yusuf Charkha, a Godhra lawyer, told Mukherjee: 'You should see some of these government pleaders in action. Instead of pinning down the accused, they seem to be pleading their cases.' Trivedi, however, defended his position. 'An individual performs different roles in life. In court I am an advocate, but when I am with the VHP I perform as is expected of me'.

Mukherjee continues: 'There are allegations that the selection of public prosecutors for the riot cases has been done by the BJP government in such a way that "ideology, rather than competence, has taken precedence". "I do not expect justice to be done in such circumstances. Their political ideologies will come in the way," says senior advocate Girish Patel.'

Source: Amit Mukherjee, 'VHP lawyers to fight for riot-hit victims', *Times of India*, Ahmedabad, 23 August 2002.)

The Need for Independent Investigation

In view of widespread allegations that FIRs have been poorly or wrongly recorded and that extraneous considerations or players have influenced investigations, the NHRC has recommended that certain critical cases be entrusted to the CBI. These are the Godhra incident, which is at present being investigated by the Godhra police, the Chamanpura (Gulberg Society) and Naroda Patiya massacres in Ahmedabad, the Best Bakery case in Vadodra and the Sardarpura case in Mehsana district. The NHRC further observes that it is a central principle in the administration of criminal justice that those against whom allegations are made should not themselves be entrusted with investigations of those allegations.

In addition to the NHRC, the National Commission of Minorities, various civil liberties and citizens' groups and writ petitions filed in the Supreme Court have asked for investigation by the CBI. The Modi government, however, categorically refuses a CBI probe. The feeble and unconvincing response of the central government has been to cite existing rules, which permit investigation of cases by the CBI only if the state government makes a request for the same. The system of checks and balances, division of powers and functions envisaged by the framers of the Indian constitution had perhaps not conceived of a situation where the central and state governments would both collude to deprive certain sections of the Indian citizenry of their fundamental rights. To reiterate what the NHRC has stated, 'It would thus be a travesty of the principles of criminal justice if such cases were not transferred to the CBI. Worse still, the inability to do so could severely compromise the fundamental rights to life, liberty, equality and dignity guaranteed by the constitution to all the people of India on a non-discriminatory basis.'[23]

Predictably in a state led by a RSS *pracharak*, the investigation of even the most gruesome and horrific incidents does not inspire any confidence. In both the Naroda Patiya and the Gulberg Society incidents, 'inconvenient' police officers have been transferred. Barely a week after the two incidents, for example, assistant commissioner of police P.N. Barot was given charge of the investigation. The first thing he did was to question how his police colleagues—who had already filed FIRs naming Bajrang Dal and VHP leaders for their role in the attacks—'could have identified 5-6 people in a mob of thousand'.[24] The resulting chargesheets project these massacres as the product of not just anger over Godhra but also of provocation by the Muslim victims. In the Gulberg Society case, where at least thirty-nine people were massacred on 28 February, the chargesheet filed virtually justifies the mob killings and blames former MP Ehsan Jafri for the incident. It states, 'It was after firing by Jafri that the mob got violent and attacked the locality.'[25] While at least one news report appearing after the chargesheet asserts that Jafri never fired a shot,[26] the police seem to have forgotten that the right to self-defence in the face of a murderous mob is available in law to the victim. It is also a well-known fact that before allegedly firing from his licensed revolver, Jafri for hours tried to implore politicians and the police to rescue the residents of Gulberg Society. The police, however, did nothing. In fact, the police should be prosecuted for criminal negligence among other offences.

Along similar lines runs the chargesheet filed in the Naroda Patiya incident, where more than ninety Muslims were murdered on the day of the Gujarat bandh, 28 February.[27] It states that the two communities clashed with each other. But the Hindu mob turned violent after a Muslim driver of a mini-truck ran over a Hindu youth, killing him. Also the recovery of a mutilated body of a Hindu person sent the mob on a rampage. While in both the Gulberg Society and Naroda Patiya chargesheets, locals as well as some lower-rung functionaries of the Bajrang Dal and BJP have been arrested, significant by their omission are the names of the BJP city unit president and Naroda MLA, Maya Kodnani, VHP state president Jaideep Patel and police inspector K.K. Maisurwala of the Naroda police station. Several eyewitnesses had provided the police signed statements blaming these three for the violence; however, though the Naroda Patiya chargesheet appends numerous statements by victims and eyewitnesses, none blaming these senior politicians has been included.[28]

Criticizing the Ahmedabad police's chargesheets in the Naroda Patiya and Gulberg Society cases, K.P.S. Gill, who was security adviser to the Gujarat government at the time, said, 'Nobody, least of all the courts, would believe what these preliminary chargesheets have to say.'[29] He also said that 'if any court of law believes this story then it would be the biggest travesty of justice. These police statements and stories will not stand in court, and can be proved wrong through evidence'.[30] The NHRC, too, has taken strong exception to the biased chargesheets. In as much as they are reported to depict the victims of violence as the provocateurs'.[31]

When cases of much less significance and consequence have been frequently handed over to the CBI for investigation, the persistent refusal of the central and state government to permit the CBI to investigate heinous crimes like Naroda Patiya and Gulberg Society can only lead to one conclusion—that they are not interested in the truth being discovered and justice being done.

How the Police Sabotage Investigations

A successful prosecution depends on effective, professional and honest investigation by the police. To prove the charges of murder, rioting, looting etc., the prosecution will have to marshal evidence before the court that proves all the ingredients of the offence as well as the guilt of the accused beyond reasonable doubt. The prosecution will be able to accomplish this task and meet the strict standards of proof laid down by criminal jurisprudence only if the police, i.e. the investigating agency, collects the essential oral, ocular, documentary, material and scientific evidence.

Identifying the accused

Since in many incidents the attacks were by large mobs and the victims can recognize many of the members of these illegal assemblies, it is essential that without any delay the police conducts Test Identification Parades to enable the complainant and witnesses to identify the accused persons. Test Identification Parades are supposed to be conducted as a matter of prudence by the police, particularly in cases where prior to the incident, the complainant does not know the accused. It is the job of the investigating officer to arrange for the Test Identification Parade to be conducted in the presence of the Magistrate. The complainants or witnesses cannot be expected to conduct these parades themselves or even demand them. In the present circumstances of Gujarat, where the entire investigation process is overshadowed by police inaction and complicity at several levels, there is serious doubt whether the police will fulfill this requirement. The failure of the police to do so will adversely affect the prosecution of these cases. As evidenced in the trial of cases relating to the 1984 anti-Sikh massacre, in the absence of a Test Identification Parade, the identification of the accused for the first time in Court has no evidentiary value.

In *State v. Ashok*, ASJ S.N.Dhingra noted that,

> From the testimony of above two witnesses it is apparent that
> the husband and *devar* of Harbhajan Kaur were killed during
> the riots. At that time when the riots had taken place she was
> able to identify two of the persons but due to lapse of time
> now she was not able to identify those persons. Had the
> investigation been done properly and had the accused persons
> subjected to TIP soon after the incident, the witness would
> have been able to point as to who were the persons who had
> killed her husband and *devar* and if the trial had been
> expeditious and the time of eleven years had not been wasted
> by the Administration deliberately, the neighbours who had
> mercilessly killed innocent persons would have been brought
> to book and punished according to law.[32]

Again, in *State v. Om Prakash & Ors.*, ASJ S. S. Bal held
that: 'Merely pointing out towards the accused persons that
they were the members of the mob for the first time in the dock
does not fix the identity of the accused persons in the absence
of TIP.'[33]

Widespread incidents of looting of shops, homes and
commercial establishments have been reported from Gujarat.
To bring the rioters to book it is necessary that the looted
property is recovered in accordance with the law. The police
should also intelligently use as evidence the recordings by
internal circuit cameras fitted in showrooms and major stores,
and employ them to identify both the accused and the stolen
property. However, reports in this regard are not very promising.
In Ahmedabad, the police did not deploy the still and video
cameras they had during the violence. In Vadodara, where the
police did film the violence in the initial phase, it has not 'had
time to view these films'. The *Times of India* reported: 'From
day one of the riots at Vadodara, almost all officers of the rank
of police inspectors and above could be seen moving in the field
with a video cameraman. But nobody knows what these cassettes
contain.'[34]

In the carnage of 1984, the police adopted an illegal method to recover looted property. They announced that looted property should be deposited on the road or at police stations and that no action would be taken against looters. This enabled the rioters to escape prosecution altogether. This is borne out by the statement of the accused himself in *State v. Ved Prakash etc.* where ASJ S.N. Dhingra noted that,

> In his statement u/s 313 Cr.P.C. accused Kishori had stated that police made pronouncements in the area that those who have looted the houses of Sikhs, they should put out looted articles on the road. These statements were made by Inspector Rathi who was from Special Staff. These announcements were made after police had come to block number 32 . . . Thus, from this statement of accused u/s 313 CrPC it is clear that police was in league with the accused persons and riot was a consequence of this league.[35]

Witness statements

For the successful prosecution of the cases being lodged in Gujarat, the police must cite as witness more persons than just the complainant. As most of these crimes have been committed in broad daylight and in full view of the public, neighbours and family members must be joined as witnesses. This would enable corroboration of the complainant's testimony during trial.

In the perfunctory investigation that followed the 1984 massacre, the police deliberately did not join more than one witness to corroborate the statement of the complainant. At trial, the court was often reluctant to convict only on the basis of the sole testimony of the complainant. In other cases, the statements were deliberately recorded inaccurately by the police, which resulted in discrepancies and inconsistencies in the statements under Section 161, CrPC and the depositions of the witnesses before the court. All these lacunae only ensured that a majority of the trials resulted in acquittals.

In *State v. Ram Pal Saroj etc.*, ASJ S.N. Dhingra noted that,

> Police had not made any other person as witness in this case. In fact, there is no investigation done by the police except

recording the statements. Statements recorded by the police are also very sketchy and some times the statements are actually not made by the victims but they have been recorded by the police officials sitting in the police station and it is alleged that these statements were made by victims. In most of the cases it is found that in order to help the accused persons police has given wrong facts in the statements. The victims of the riot cases when appeared in the court had given altogether a different story . . .[36]

Faced with the refusal of the Gujarat government to permit the CBI to investigate the crimes, there is a real apprehension that in the name of investigation a charade may be carried out. It is imperative that the statements recorded under section 161 CrPC are accurate, relevant and detailed. Later at the stage of trial such biased and shoddy investigation will enable the accused to escape the clutches of law.

While a majority of the 1984 trials resulted in acquittal, in a few cases the judge did not allow the machinations of the police to succeed. In *State v. Ved Prakash etc.*, ASJ S.N. Dhingra observed that,

There is no doubt that there are contradictions in the statements recorded u/s 161 and the statement made in the court but these contradictions are due to the unfortunate attitude of the police and the Administration . . . Under these circumstances, when the police and the accused joined hands against the victims, there is no wonder that there are contradictions but I consider that truth and justice cannot be made casualty because of the vicious nexus between the police and the accused persons. I, therefore, consider that witnesses cannot be discredited because of the non-recording of accurate statements by the police. [37]

Corroborative evidence

To meet the strict standards of proof, the police during investigation are required to not only record statements of witnesses but also collect corroborative evidence. This can be in the form of a site plan, post-mortem report to ascertain the cause of death, voter's card, electoral lists to establishing the identity and residence of the deceased, scientific and forensic evidence as most of the victims were burnt. In the case of Best Bakery, an expert panel from Baroda Medical College has confirmed that the bones recovered are those of humans. Scientific evidence has confirmed the gory killing of two residents who were reported missing. DNA tests will further confirm the identity of the deceased.[38] In other cases also, the police must seek the assistance of experts to collect evidence. As charge-sheets are being prepared and filed in Gujarat, it is important that civil society initiatives are vigilant and compel the police to investigate rigorously. The rioters have already wiped much of the evidence of the heinous crimes out; the police must not be allowed to destroy the rest. Judicious use must be made of photographs. The police can also summon video footage, in the custody of different news channels, to corroborate witness testimonies.

In the past, the police have weakened the prosecution case by conducting shoddy and casual investigations. As noted in the judgement relating to the 1984 massacre in *State v. Mangal*, ASJ O.P. Dwivedi noted that, 'Neither any inquest proceedings were conducted nor even dead body of Mohan Singh or of any other riot victim was got identified nor the post-mortem examination reports were filed on record. Even a rough site plan of the scene of crime was not prepared. Investigation was conducted in a most perfunctory and casual manner.'[39] In *State v. Shayam Vir* ASJ S.N. Dhingra noted that,

> It is not only that police did not do its duty of investigating the crime properly but it is that police deliberately did not collect the evidence against the accused persons who were involved in this fiendish act of murder of more than 200 persons. The record filed with the court shows that the police was a party in protecting the accused persons and in wiping out the evidence against the accused persons . . . Any court to draw an adverse inference against police and the investigating agency being hand in glove with the rioters and acting under the directions of those unseen powerful persons who were behind all this.[40]

Sexual Violence

Reports such as *The Survivors Speak* have documented incidents of extreme forms of sexual violence against Muslim women both in urban and rural Gujarat.[41] Muslim women and girls of all ages were routinely gang-raped by the mobs. Unlike earlier incidents of communal and caste massacres, where patriarchal notions of family and honour served to invisibilise the sexual violence inflicted upon women of the targetted community, this time the affected women and their families have openly named the alleged rapists and also tried to get the police to register criminal cases. There are complaints that the police have grossly under-reported sexual crimes against women. The above-mentioned report notes, 'For instance, in Panchmahals district only one rape FIR has been filed, though we heard of many other cases'.[42] Even in the case of Kausar Bano, it took a letter from the leader of the Opposition to the Prime Minister for the FIR to be registered.[43]

It must be mentioned here that even in so-called 'peace time', rape continues to remain a difficult crime to prove and the rate of conviction in rape cases is generally very low. Most of the cases of rape that have been reported from Gujarat are either instances of gang-rape[44] or rape of minors[45] or rape of pregnant women.[46] Accordingly, they would all fall within the purview of Section 376 (2) of the IPC, or what is commonly called 'custodial' or 'statutory' rape. Section 114 A of the Indian Evidence Act would be attracted in such a case. Thus if the woman states in her deposition before the Court that she did not consent, the Court shall presume the absence of consent and the accused shall have to rebutt the same. However, the prosecutrix will be required by law to establish sexual intercourse by the accused persons. In the circumstances that prevailed in Gujarat, obviously no medical examinations of the victim or accused was possible. It has been recommended by the Women's Panel report referred to above that in view of the extraordinary conditions that prevailed in Gujarat, the legal requirement of medical examination should not be insisted upon.

In many of these cases, corroborative evidence in the form of witnesses to the rape are available to test the veracity of the complainant. If the court fails to take cognizance of these exceptional circumstances, then exacting requirements and legal procedure and evidence will succeed in throttling the truth.

In the 1984 massacre too, women were subjected to rape and other brutal sexual assaults but there is till date no official legal record, redressal or acknowledgement of these crimes. A glimpse of the sexual crimes committed against these women can be found in their testimonies before the trial court, when they came to depose in cases pertaining to the murder of their family members. Women have described in their evidence before the court how the attackers tried to strip them and they offered valuables to save their honour, and then the statement abruptly ends.

Recent statements of the joint commissioner (crime) P. Pandey are not very encouraging. He has stated that it would be difficult to punish the guilty, at least in the rape cases, as in most cases the victims were killed and their bodies burnt, thereby destroying all evidence. The fact, however, remains that the police is making no attempt to gather scientific and forensic evidence which in corroboration with statements of eyewitnesses may make out a strong case in court. Fearing that justice may never be dispensed to the women who have courageously spoken out and named the rapists, some NGOs and women's groups have demanded that a special tribunal be constituted for adjudication of rape cases. The Gujarat government has yet not responded to this demand and in the meanwhile, whatever evidence was available is fast disappearing.

Ignoring the Conspiracy Angle

It would be no exaggeration to say that the violence that has engulfed Gujarat since 27 February 2002, was not a spontaneous reaction but a well-organized and planned attack on the Muslim community. The sheer scale, duration and pattern that the attacks followed would belie any argument of spontaneous outrage. The truth is known to the victims and survivors. If the legal machinery, including the police and the courts, is to retain any legitimacy and validity in the eyes of the people, the conspiracy to decimate and destroy the Muslim community in Gujarat must be investigated, proved and the guilty brought to book. The police must invoke the law of conspiracy to arraign for trial, politicians and others who master-minded this orgy of violence. There are many leads that point towards such a conspiracy. Apart from the alleged meeting of ministers and others on the eve of the Gujarat bandh on 27 February, the killing, arson and loot followed a chillingly similar pattern. The availability of kerosene and gas cylinders in such large quantities for purposes of rioting again points towards the organized distribution of inflammable materials. An investigation into the source and distribution of weapons used during the violence would also help in discerning the contours of the conspiracy. Mobile phone records could be another source of information that must be explored by the police to determine who were involved in planning, instigating and directing this carnage. The attacks on industries, and large commercial establishments on the Ahmedabad Highway clearly showed that the rioters had definite and full knowledge of the religious identity of the owners. This information was not common knowledge and had obviously been supplied from an authoritative source.

Though much police effort has gone into trying to establish a conspiracy in the Godhra case, the massacres which followed are not being probed for this angle. The chargesheet filed for the Godhra train killings is perhaps the only one which invokes the law of conspiracy. According to the chargesheet, the accused attacked the Sabarmati Express with prior knowledge and planning with intention to kill. According to an investigating officer, the use of over 100 litres of inflammable liquid early in the morning points to a conspiracy. The same yardstick, however, is not applied when investigating attacks on Muslims in the rest of Gujarat.

It would be pertinent to mention here that although some senior Congress (I) politicians were prosecuted for their alleged role in the 1984 massacre in Delhi, the prosecution failed to prove the charges against any one of them. Acquitting one such politician, the Court observed that, 'The riots in Delhi had followed a definite pattern which indicated that there was some planning, prior conspiracy but the conspiracy angle was totally overlooked during investigation. Thus, the "eye of the storm" remained elusive. Even after the riots were over, no serious effort was made to book the guilty with an honest intention of getting them punished through a court verdict.'[47]

In *State v. Kanak Singh*, the court expressed dissatisfaction at the manner in which the police had conducted their investigation.[48] Ordering the acquittal of the accused, he stated,

> It is apparent that Kanak Singh and Ram Pal Saroj were the local Congress(I) leaders, they seem to have silently encouraged the riots and perhaps they were also part [of] the conspiracy of allowing the rioters to have free hand into the area but police had not gone into the aspect of conspiracy. . . Accused, therefore gets benefit of police and state apathy towards 1984 riot and in showing no interest by the State in investigating the conspiracy part of riots.

Need for Effective Prosecution

The recommendations made by the NHRC with respect to the prosecution of crimes are significant and the Gujarat government must be compelled to implement these. The NHRC has recommended the constitution of Special Courts which should try these cases on a day to day basis. An expeditious trial is necessary, as the experience of 1984 cases shows that delays usually take a heavy toll. With the lapse of time, the memory of witnesses about time, date, exact spot of occurrence and other details predictably gets blurred, leading to discrepancies and inconsistencies in their testimonies Protracted trials may translate the saying that 'justice delayed is justice denied', from a cliché to reality.

The trials of those accused for the massacre of Sikhs in Delhi in 1984 dragged on for over a decade and some trials are pending even now. In several of the cases, witnesses had either moved or died, evidence in some cases had even been auctioned by the police and those witnesses who still struggled for justice were defeated by the passage of time and the natural erosion of their memories of incidents that occurred ten to seventeen years before their day in court.

The next recommendation of the NHRC, that special public prosecutors should be appointed, is equally significant as a professional, competent, independent and impartial Public prosecutor alone can represent the case of the victims of this carnage. Victims of the 1984 carnage have spoken of intimidation by defence lawyers even as their government assigned lawyers stood quietly aside.

Under the Indian criminal justice system, crimes are deemed to be committed not against an individual but against the State. It is therefore the job of the State to prosecute those who commit offences. The difficulty, however, arises when the State acquires a communal visage and, through acts of omission and commission stands indicted as an accomplice. It must be remembered that under Section 301 of the Code of Criminal Procedure, the public prosecutor alone is authorized to prosecute an accused and the role of a private counsel in a criminal trial is limited to assisting the prosecution. Strenuous efforts must, therefore, be made to seek the appointment of honest and upright special public prosecutors for the trial of cases of the Gujarat carnage. The fact that the Godhra prosecutor is to be paid Rs 7,000 a hearing while the public prosecutors trying the riot cases will get Rs 400 a day irrespective of the number of cases they hear does not augur well.[49]

No Equality Before the Law

In pursuit of its Hindutva ideology, the Modi government in Gujarat has blatantly followed discriminatory practices and policies. Chapter III of the Indian Constitution guarantees to every citizen certain fundamental rights. Article 14 provides that the State shall not deny to any person equality before the law or the equal protection of the laws within India; Article 15 expressly prohibits discrimination against any citizen *inter alia* on the grounds of religion; and Article 21 enshrines the principle that no one should be deprived of life or liberty except according to procedure established by law. From 28 February 2002 onwards, the Gujarat government suspended the operation of these Fundamental Rights for a section of Indian citizens viz. the Muslim community. Arbitrarily and illegally, the State infringed the fundamental rights of Muslim citizens.

This discriminatory approach is also found in the legal response of the State. The Gujarat government initially announced Rs 2 lakh compensation for the victims of Godhra and Rs 1 lakh for the others who were murdered in Gujarat. Again, initially an enquiry was ordered into the train attack at Godhra alone and not the mass murder which followed throughout the state. Similarly, while the pogroms against Muslims were not considered terrorism, the initial response of the Gujarat government was to arrest those accused of involvement in the Godhra train attack under the Prevention of Terrorism Act (POTA).[50] It was only after a public outcry that the Modi government backtracked on all these decisions, reducing the compensation of the Godhra victims to Rs 1 lakh (rather than increasing compensation for the Muslims to Rs 2 lakh), broadening the scope of the Justice Shah Commission (now headed by Justice Nanavatty), and dropping POTA charges against the Godhra accused.

However, the discriminatory approach persists in more ways than one. The overzealousness of the investigating agency in the Godhra case has even led them to administer 'truth serum' to seven of the prime accused. This practice is highly objectionable and was described as torture by the UN in 1999. Under Indian law, evidence procured in this manner is inadmissible in court. What is, however, most disturbing is that in glaring contrast, a rather uninspiring, unconvincing and dispirited investigation is being conducted into all other crimes that have rocked the state for over three months. As for 'truth serum', the police are wary of repeating the Godhra experiment on those accused in the major mass murder cases against Muslims. 'Big names that the police have failed to list as accused for riot-related killing and looting might tumble out. This possibility could prove to be a deterrent for use of truth serum to question Ahmedabad's riot accused,' a senior police official was quoted as saying.[51]

Another aspect of the state government's discriminatory attitude is the manner in which it has registered cases against Muslims who tried to defend themselves when they were under attack during the mob violence. According to one estimate, no less than 19 Muslims are currently in jail in Gujarat for using force to defend themselves from the murderous mobs.[52] Perhaps the most celebrated case is that of Dr Yunus Bhavnagri, a dentist and former national rifle shooting champion. On 28 February, he opened fire on a violent mob outside his flat at Delight Apartments in Ahmedabad, killing two persons and injuring one. According to some accounts, he opened fire only after someone in the crowd shot into the house first. After registering a case of murder against Dr Bhavnagri, his brother Aamer Yunus Bhavnagari and one Aslam Harun Golibar, the police subsequently realized no case could be made out and thus opted not to file a chargesheet within the stipulated ninety day period. Curiously, the Gujarat High Court pulled up the police for this and for not preparing a case against the three, and recommended that two police officers—including additional police commissioner Satish Sharma—be suspended.[53] On appeal, the Supreme Court stayed this order.[54]

Law on Genocide

Since 28 February, for almost three months, genocide has been orchestrated in the state of Gujarat. Article 1 of the Convention for the Prevention and the Punishment of the Crime of Genocide, 1948, states that genocide is a crime under international law, and defines it as acts committed with intent to destroy, in whole or in part, a national, ethnical, racial or religious group. In Article II, genocide includes any of the following acts: (a) Killing members of the group; (b) Causing serious bodily or mental harm to members of the group; (c) Deliberately inflicting on the group conditions of life calculated to bring about its physical destruction in whole or in part; (d) Imposing measures intended to prevent births within the group; (e) Forcibly transferring children of the group to another group.[55]

By the definitions of the Genocide Convention, there is no question that the carnage unleashed in Gujarat was an act of genocide, culpability for which must necessarily extend all the way up to the top. However, the offences enumerated in the Indian Penal Code fall short of comprehending, defining, describing and punishing the crime of genocide. This statutory limitation, compounded by the partisan conduct of the State, has seriously crippled the criminal justice system. The criminal justice system is not equipped to deal with any sort of group crimes where political forces are at play. Genocide represents the most brutal side of such crimes. The cases of 1984 show clearly how in a situation of mob crimes, where over 3,000 people lost their lives in a span of three days, where bodies and evidence were burnt or destroyed to thwart the legal system, agents of that system—whether it was the police or the investigators or the courts—were unable to grapple with the complexities of such a mass-scale crime. The genocide in Gujarat once again puts a system that is already under severe strain to the test.

Matters of 'Faith' Put Above the Law

The scant respect that the BJP and the Sangh Privar have for the law and the judiciary is well known from their public pronouncements in the context of the Ayodhya dispute. They demonstrated their contempt for the rule of law on 6 December 1992 and on many subsequent occasions, including the recent withdrawal by the VHP, on 23 June 2002, of written assurance that they will abide by the verdict of the Supreme Court in the Ayodhya matter. The Gujarat killings too are being projected as acts in defence of Hindutva and the accused as martyrs.

Whenever it suits the BJP it arrogates to itself the right to settle disputes, using brute force and veiled threats. In Sabarkantha, Panchmahals and Vadodara rural districts, in response to the arrest of BJP workers named in complaints and FIRs by the police, the BJP threatened to launch a 'jail *bharo*' campaign,[56] while the VHP declared a bandh on the arrest of its cadre.[57] The VHP has also engaged a team of 50 advocates to defend those facing prosecution, who according to VHP have fought a 'religious battle'.[58] In order to help the police show that they are taking action against the attackers (and in the process help themselves too, VHP leaders are paying poor Hindu boys to volunteer as the rioters, knowing they will get bail and there will be few convictions.[59]

Along similar lines run the *mafipatrak*—letters of apology— which the Muslim victims are being coerced to sign in Gujarat if they wish to return to their homes and land.[60] The letter, on the one hand, exonerates and pardons those who attacked them and burnt and looted their homes, and on the other holds the provocative conduct of the Muslims responsible for the murderous attacks that they suffered. It also stipulates a code of conduct that the Muslims are required to observe and which accords to them the status of second-class citizens. After allowing the carnage to take place, senior officials of the Modi government are now trying to propound the theory of 'forgive and forget'.[61] How ironical that a party that came to power on the strength of raking up an alleged dispute that dates back to the sixteenth century should now talk of reconciliation. Confronted with a criminal justice system that has an unenviable track record in failing to punish those guilty of communal holocausts, and a government that instigated and directed a genocide against them, some Muslims feel that the *mafipatrak* may provide them safety of life and property, a task abandoned by the elected government of Gujarat and even of India.

Conclusion

The analysis presented above indicates that the present system of criminal justice is woefully inadequate to deal with State-sponsored genocide. The criminal justice system assumes the existence of an independent investigating and prosecuting agency, insulated from political interference, which is not the case in Gujarat. Experience shows that when situations of mass violence, where the executive and the investigating agency are both implicated, are sought to be addressed within the rubric of the Indian Penal Code, the Criminal Procedure Code and the Evidence Act, the legal system is unable to grapple with the situation. A case for the total breakdown of the constitutional machinery needs to be made out.

While the 1984 massacre and its aftermath remain useful points of reference, it must be mentioned here that the scale of destruction of life and property witnessed in Gujarat remains unparalleled. Also, the Gujarat carnage was the consequence of systematic infiltration and communalization of all agencies of the State by the Hindutva forces ruling the State. The apathy and inaction of the police cannot be explained by simple arguments of the police force being outnumbered by 'uncontrollable mobs' or that they had been given instructions to not take any action. The police force in Gujarat has been deliberately and systematically communalized, the outcome of which is that they no longer owe allegiance to the rule of law.

It is with much scepticism and anxiety that people today approach the justice delivery system. Scepticism, because the record of the justice system in punishing those guilty of communal violence and killings is abysmal. And anxiety that if even now, the gravest hate crimes go unpunished, the Sangh Parivar will with impunity soon hunt down all those they classify as their 'enemy', an ever-growing category. In such a scenario, it is hardly surprising that increasingly citizens are looking towards international fora for redressal of their grievances.[62]

Fatalistic pronouncements on the fate of our criminal justice system apart, there is a strong democratic urge in people—victimized even as they have been by the State—to continue to fight for justice where they are. This is expressed in their unceasing attempts to file FIRs, speak of their experiences and seek out every possible avenue for justice. This spirit perhaps may find some counter to our flagging system. Some urgent steps must be taken to give some strength, some props for the system to tackle the scale and magnitude of these crimes. Some ideas and suggestions are given below. These include:

- CBI investigation of the most gruesome incidents enumerated by the NHRC and Citizens' Initiative.
- Constitution of a Special Cell housed by police officers deputed from cadres outside Gujarat to monitor the investigation of all cases.
- Appointment of Special Public Prosecutors with proven record of professional and impartial conduct.
- Special Courts to conduct day-to-day trials.
- Judicial notice and cognizance to be taken of the exceptional circumstances in which investigation has been conducted and evidence collected.

That the criminal justice system is in crisis is grudgingly admitted by most. But if the perpetraters of the Gujarat genocide go unpunished, then democracy itself will be in peril.

Notes

1 Vrinda Grover, *Quest for Justice: 1984 Massacre of Sikh Citizens in Delhi*, mimeo, 2002. This report documents and examines the responses of the legal system to the 1984 massacre. All judgements relating to the 1984 carnage cited in this article are from this report.

2 AIR 1975 SC 1453

3 AIR 1973 SC 501

4 'SI charged with aiding mob transferred,' *Times of India*, Ahmedabad, 10 June 2002.

5 Amit Mukherjee and Radha Sharma, 'Police not naming names in FIRs,' *Times of India*, 26 March 2002.

6 *Ibid.*

7 People's Union For Democratic Rights, *'Maaro! Kaapo! Baalo!'*:

State, Society, And Communalism in Gujarat*, Delhi, May 2002 (henceforth *PUDR*).

8   Final Report of National Human Rights Commission on Gujarat, 31 May 2002 (henceforth *NHRC*), p 13.

9   Milind Ghatwai, 'BJP leader held for "rape" as mother refuses to give in,' *Indian Express*, Ahmedabad, 14 May 2002.

10   *Mid-Day*, 30 April 2002.

11   'Legal redressal eludes victims,' *Times of India*, 10 June 2002.

12   Petitition filed in the High Court of Gujarat at Ahmedabad by Mohanbhai B. Bundela, Convenor, Jansangharsh Manch, 6 May 2002.

13   Report of the Justice Ranganath Misra Commission of Inquiry, Volume I, August 1986, p. 63

14   'Police not naming names in FIRs,' *Times of India*, 26 March 2002.

15   *Indian Express*, (Ahmedabad), 6 June 2002.

16   *NHRC*, p 13.

17   'Advocates expect delay in riot cases,' *Times of India*, 16 June 2002.

18   *PUDR*, pp 61-62.

19   The FIR mentions the fact that the mobs were 'uncontrollable' several times.

20   *State v. Kishori*, Karkardooma, Delhi, S.C. No. 42/95, FIR No. 426/84, ASJ S.N. Dhingra quoting the deposition of Inspector Badan Singh (pp 6-7).

21   *State v. Kishori and others*, Karkardooma, Delhi, S.C. No. 53/95, FIR No. 426/84, p 1.

22   'Godhra court acquits 9-riot accused,' *Times of India*, Ahmedabad, 6 July 2002.

23   *NHRC*, p 19.

24   Joydeep Ray, 'The spirit of inquiry: khaki sympathy for saffron accused, Ahmedabad cop casts doubts on FIRs,' *Indian Express*, 11 March 2002.

25   'Jafri 'blamed' for his murder,' *Indian Express*, 4 June 2002.

26   Kingshuk Nag, 'Jafri may not have fired at all,' *Times of India*, Ahmedabad, 9 June 2002. This report has not been contradicted by the police.

27 'Once again, police blame victims,' *Indian Express*, 5 June 2002.

28 *Ibid.*

29 'Naroda, Gulberg chargeheets blame Muslims, upset Gill,' *Times of India*, 11 June 2002.

30 *Hindustan Times*, 11 June 2002.

31 'NHRC upset over "bias" in Gujarat FIRs,' *Times of India*, 10 June 2002.

32 Karkardooma, Delhi, S.C. No. 12/96, FIR No. 426/84, pp 5-6.

33 Karkardooma Courts, Delhi, S.C. No. 46/94.

34 Sourav Mukherjee and Sachin Sharma, 'Where are the police videos on the riots?,' *Times of India*, Ahmedabad, 10 July 2002.

35 Karkardooma, Delhi, S.C. No. 70/95, FIR No. 426/84, pp 12-13.

36 Karkardooma, Delhi, S.C. No. 57/95, FIR No. 426/84, p 3.

37 Karkardooma, Delhi, S.C. No. 70/95, FIR No. 426/84, pp 11-12.

38 *Indian Express*, 25 May 2002.

39 Karkardooma, Delhi, S.C. No. 51/95, FIR No. 426/84.

40 Karkardooma, Delhi, S.C. No. 34/95, FIR No. 426/84.

41 See Chapter 6 above.

42 *Ibid.*

43 Eleven weeks after the incident, the police arrested the prime accused, Ratilal Rathod alias Bhavani Singh, for the crime. 'Kausar Bano case sees some action,' *Times of India*, Ahmedabad, 16 May 2002.

44 IPC Sec 376 (2)(g)read with Explanation I.

45 IPC Sec 376 (2)(f).

46 IPC Sec 376 (2)(e).

47 *State v. Mangal*, Karkardooma, Delhi, S.C. No. 51/95 FIR No. 426/84.

48 Sessions Case No. 18/95 in the Court of S.N. Dhingra, ASJ, Karkardooma Courts, Delhi (Judgment 30.11.96).

49 Amit Mukherjee, 'Rs 7,000 for Godhra prosecutor,' *Times of India*, (Ahmedabad), 21 June 2002.

50 Joydeep Ray, 'POTO in Gujarat means Prevention of Terrorism for Ourselves, not Muslims,' *Indian Express*, 19 March 2002.

51 Sourav Mukherjee and Raja Bose, 'Police divided over using truth

serum on rioteers,' *Times of India* (Ahmedabad), 21 July 2002.

52 M. Jowher, Society for the Promotion of Rational Thinking, Ahmedabad, personal communication to Siddharth Varadarajan.

53 'HC recommends suspension of two cops,' *Times of India* (Ahmedabad), 9 July 2002.

54 *Times of India*, 30 July 2002.

55 Convention on the Prevention and Punishment of the Crime of Genocide. Reproduced as Appendix 1 in Leo Kuper, *The Prevention of Genocide*, Yale University Press, 1985.

56 'BJP's *jail bharo* campaign gives cops jitters,' *Times of India* (Ahmedabad), 13 May 2002.

57 Leena Misra, 'Police fighting shy of netting big fish,' *Times of India* (Ahmedabad), 15 May 2002.

58 Joydeep Ray, 'Riots: Parivar picks team for legal battle,' *Indian Express*.

59 Vinay Menon, 'VHP playing innocent Hindus to admit rioting,' *Hindustan Times*, 4 May 2002.

60 Milind Ghatwai, 'A stamp paper of hate: Muslims asked to sign on the twisted line,' *Indian Express*, 11 May 2002.

61 Vipul Mudgal, 'Forgive and forget deal in Gujarat,' *Hindustan Times*, 14 April 2002.

62 Proposals have been made for genocide trials abroad. See for example Balakrishnan Rajagopal, 'Gujarat: A Plea and a Proposal,' *Hindu*, 27 March 2002.

12

India's Reaction to the International Concern over Gujarat

A.G. Noorani

After experiencing considerable embarrassment over a series of adverse references to the Gujarat violence by Western and particularly European governments, Nirupama Rao, the spokesperson of the Ministry of External Affairs (MEA), was instructed on 22 April to register the Vajpayee government's protest. 'We would like to make it clear,' she said, 'that India does not appreciate interference in its internal affairs.' Referring to Finnish Foreign Minister Erkki Tuomiojia's interview to the *Indian Express* as an example of the 'utilization of the Indian media by foreign leaders', Ms Rao said that India did not like 'visiting dignitaries making public statements in order to pander to their domestic lobbies.'[1]

Since Finland is not known as a country with a large Indian or South Asian diaspora, the MEA's remarks were obviously aimed at the British. Barely a week earlier, details of a British High Commission cable to London on Gujarat were leaked to the *Hindustan Times,* much to the embarrassment of the Vajpayee government. The cable, which was based on a tour of the state by a High Commission team, apparently held that the attacks on Muslims in Gujarat had been planned well before the Godhra carnage and that in some places, the police had been instructed not to act.[2] Broadly similar conclusions appear to have been reached by the German and Dutch missions in New Delhi, as well as by the European Union.[3]

The official spokesperson of the MEA may be pardoned for speaking sharply on foreign comments on the Gujarat pogrom of Muslims. Ms Nirupama Rao was doing her duty and speaking as instructed by her government. The government deserved censure for what she said. The same cannot be said of Justice (Retd.) J.S. Verma, Chairman of the National Human Rights Commission (NHRC) who is responsible for his own words.

Justice Verma's remarks at Chennai on 21 May are not in consonance with the tenets of international law. 'We have a well-built internal mechanism for taking corrective actions. We have (the) NHRC, (the) Supreme Court and a vigilant and vibrant democracy to take care of things. There is no need for any foreign intervention on this.'[4] The assertions of fact in the first part of the remarks are palpably untrue. The assertion of claim to an exclusive domestic jurisdiction on human rights is outdated. Especially since, just a week earlier, at a seminar in Jaipur, Verma J. was quoted as saying the violation of human rights as witnessed in Gujarat could not be passed off as an internal matter. 'Human rights are everyone's concern and any such violation could be challenged by anyone from anywhere in the world.'[5] At the same seminar, Attorney General Soli J. Sorabjee was also quoted as saying India cannot brush aside concern voiced by some foreign countries on the Gujarat situation. 'Old dogmas of state sovereignty have changed and the international community can now express legitimate concern,' he said.[6]

Verma J. would, apparently, permit 'outside intervention' if there was 'a deficiency in the national mechanism'.[7] European Countries did not establish the European Court of Human Rights because their 'national mechanism' was weak, but because they recognized that concern for human rights transcends national frontiers. Verma J. is as exercised as any *babu* in North Block or South Block. 'We have to be careful that the human rights programme is not hijacked by vested interests.'[8] The reference to 'vested interests' was a familiar one. After attending a session of the UN Human Rights Commision in Geneva, the Congress (I) spokesman, Mr V.N. Gadgil, noted on 24 April 1992 that the question of human rights had climbed to the top of the international agenda. So the best way to face the reality was to establish an HRC at home. It could play a useful role in this respect: 'Its findings will act as correctives to the biased and one-sided reports of some of the NGOs (non-governmental organizations). It will also be an effective answer to the politically motivated international criticism.'

Mr Gadgil's candid exposition was foreshadowed by a PTI report under a New Delhi, 16 February 1992 dateline quoting 'official sources'. India was 'considering a proposal' to set up an HRC. 'This is being done to obviate the risk of Amnesty International and other such bodies being "hijacked" by forces "inimical" to the unity and integrity of the country . . .' The sources also denounced the civil liberties bodies in the country.

The correct position was well stated by President Jimmy Carter in one of his earliest pronouncements as President, in a speech at the United Nations on 17 March 1977. He declared emphatically that 'no member of the United Nations can claim that mistreatment of its citizens is solely its own business. Equally, no member can avoid its responsibilities to review and to speak when torture or unwarranted deprivation of freedom occurs in any part of the world.'

It is necessary, therefore, to recall today the rejoinder which India's Permanent Mission at the United Nations submitted to that body in reply to the charges levelled by the International League for Human Rights against the then Government of India for violation of the UN Charter. The rejoinder, published on 7 June 1976, flatly declared that 'the protection of the fundamental human rights is the concern of each sovereign state and is a matter which is essentially within the domestic jurisdiction of member states of the United Nations.'

The document went on to complain bitterly that 'this sort of gratuitous interference in India's internal affairs is certainly not calculated to serve the best interests of the people of India, but rather to encourage the subversive elements to try once again to destroy the framework of constitutional democracy that the Government of India has been sustaining in a country with a formidable diversity of problems of scaring magnitude.'

A quarter century later, the mindset remains frozen with chauvinistic fears laced with hypocrisy. The Annual Reports of the MEA are State Papers admissible as evidence of State Practice in a court of law. The last decade's Reports, to go no further, record India's persistent 'intervention' on human rights in distant Fiji. It went so far as to pronounce its rejection of Fiji's new Constitution as being racially discriminatory. India was, of course, within its rights in expressing its censure on that score.

What is significant is that neither the march of legislation, domestic and international, nor case law, nor world currents affect the mindset of our government. The UN General Assembly unanimously adopted the Universal Declaration of Human Rights in 1949 with India's support. Article 51 (c) in the Constitution of India enjoins the Indian State to 'foster respect for international law and treaty obligations in the dealings of organized peoples with one another.' One such treaty which India ratified on 27 March 1979 is the International Covenant on Civil and Political Rights and the Covenant on Economic Social and Cultural Rights. If Verma J. will read the Protection of Human Rights Act, 1993 carefully, he will find that the definition of 'human rights' in S. 2 (1) (d) covers those 'guaranteed by the Constitution *or embodied in the International Covenants* and enforceable by courts in India.'

In a recent decision, the Supreme Court of India referred to the Convention on the Elimination of All Forms of Discrimination Against Women (CEDAW) and observed: 'The International Covenant on Economic, Social, and Cultural Rights contains several provisions particularly important for women. Article 7 recognizes her right to fair conditions of work and reflects that women shall not be subjected to sexual harassment at the place of work which may vitiate the working environment. *These international instruments cast an obligation on the Indian State to gender-sensitize its laws and the courts are under an obligation to see that the message of the international instruments is not allowed to be drowned.* This Court has in numerous cases emphasized that while discussing constitutional requirements, court and counsel must never forget the core principle embodied in the international conventions and instruments and as far as possible, give effect to the principles contained in those international instruments. The courts are under an obligation to give due regard to international conventions and norms for construing domestic laws, more so, when there is no inconsistency between them and there is a void in domestic law . . . In cases involving violation of human rights, the courts must forever remain alive to the international instruments and conventions and apply the same to a given case when there is no inconsistency between the international norms and the domestic law occupying the field.' It cited four previous rulings in support of its ruling. This was a case of sexual harassment.[9]

Article 40 of the Covenant on Civil and Political Rights contains a commitment to submit Reports on compliance into the Covenant. These reports are examined by the Human Rights Committee set up under Art. 28 of this Covenant. India submitted its first Report on 4 July 1983, four years after ratification.[10] It was examined by the Human Rights Committee in New York on 28 and 30 March 1984 in three meetings.[11] India's Attorney General, K. Parasaran, was closely questioned. The Second Report was due on 9 July 1985. It was submitted on 12 July 1989. It was examined by the HRC on 26 and 27 March 1991 in four meetings.[12] The Third Report was submitted in late 1995 or early 1996. It was due on 9 July 1990. It was examined by the Committee on 24-25 July 1997.

Members of the Committee seemed extremely well informed and closely questioned India's representative. On all three occasions, India's response was formal rather than substantial. It relied on the texts of the constitution and the laws. They wanted details on *performance* and criticized laws such as the Armed Forces (Special Powers) Act, TADA and the National Security Act as being incompatible with the Covenant. They were concerned at instances of torture and death in police custody and failure to bring offenders to justice. What is important is that a pattern of international accountability has been firmly established. Questioning on the second and third occasions was sharper than on the first. NGOs brief members of the HRC thoroughly. Three attorneys general were grilled by the committee.

What else is this if not acceptance of the duty to account to an international body for India's observance of human rights? The legal effect of India's adherence to the UN Charter as well as the two Covenants is implicit acceptance of the proposition that human rights fall outside the exclusive domestic jurisdiction provision of the Charter (Art. 2 (7)). As far back as in 1923, the Permanent Court of International Justice at The Hague construed the expression 'solely within the domestic jurisdiction' of States in the case of *Tunis-Morocco Nationality Decrees*. It held that once a matter is covered by an international treaty, it ceases to be solely a domestic affair.

International law and institutions have progressed by leaps and bounds since the Second World War and especially in the last two decades.

There exists the office of a UN High Commissioner on Human Rights established with Indian support. India actively supported the Declaration on the Rights of Persons Belonging to National or Ethnic, Religious and Linguistic Minorities which the UN General Assembly adopted in December 1992. In December 1996, the Special Rapporteur appointed by the UN Human Rights Commission, Abdel Fattah Amer, visited India and reported on 'the situation of' Muslims, Christians and Sikhs. An authoritative text book on International Law holds that 'States may no longer plead this rule (domestic jurisdiction) as a bar to international concern and consideration of internal human rights situations'.[13]

Three years ago, on 22 January 1999, then minister for external affairs Jaswant Singh became 'furious' when German ambassador Heinrich-Dietrich Dieckman conveyed his concern about the attacks on Christians. On 12 January, the ambassador had characterized the attacks mildly as 'an internal affair with international implications'. His government had instructed him to raise the matter. His meeting with Singh was held soon after the launch of the minister's book *Defending India,* in which he wrote: 'While Mrs Gandhi's support for Sri Lankan Tamil aspirations was correct and justified, her policy of materially supporting Tamil militant separation was wrong'—a sound distinction.

Section 405 of the US International Religious Freedom Article 1998 lists fifteen forms of protest against such wrongs, ranging from 'a private demarche', 'an official public demarche' and 'a public condemnation' to sanctions. The first Annual Report under the Act revealed that on five occasions (from 22 October 1998 to 22 February 1999) US officials had discussed with Indian leaders attacks on Christians in India. US ambassador Richard Celeste met Union home minister L.K. Advani (October 22) and even the chiefs of the Bharatiya Janata Party (November 6) and the Vishwa Hindu Parishad (January 12). Indian expressions of concern on the lot of the minorities in Bangladesh, Pakistan and Sri Lanka are well known. In the mid-1980s, a demarche was made to Malaysia on Hindu temples there. Wrath on foreign comments on the human rights situation in India is utterly inconsistent with this record.

It is now universally accepted in international law that violation of human rights is a matter of international concern. The MEA's Canutian warnings will not stem the tide of protests which the Gujarat carnage has provoked.

The technique is a familiar one and it has worked on occasions—impute motives to critics; complain of hostility and violation of India's sovereignty, work up synthetic anger and smile in secret as 'regrets' follow. On 24 January 1999, President K.R. Narayanan said that the Staines murders 'belonged to the world's inventory of black deeds.' Far worse happened in Gujarat. Can the world be asked to ignore that? Atal Bihari Vajpayee had no qualms about peddling the Modi line on the Gujarat carnage in Singapore on 9 April: 'The riots have been brought under control. If at the Godhra station the passengers of the Sabarmati Express had not been burnt alive, then perhaps the Gujarat tragedy could have been averted. It is clear there was some conspiracy behind this incident.'

The BJP's spokesman, V.K. Malhotra, criticized the use of the word 'genocide' to describe the Gujarat carnage.[14] Article

II of the Genocide Convention (1948) says: 'Genocide means any of the following acts committed with intent to destroy, in whole or in part, a national, ethnical, racial or religious groups, as such: (a) Killing members of the group; (b) Causing serious bodily or mental harm to members of the groups; (c) Deliberately inflicting on the group conditions of life calculated to bring about its physical destruction in whole or in part . . .' India is a party to this convention.

We live in times when international humanitarian law has developed. Like Topsy, it simply grew. This is the age of international criminal law, and international criminal tribunals. Prime Minister Vajpayee is willing to lend an Indian Judge to Cambodia to try Khmer Rouge leaders. There is also such a thing as 'universal jurisdiction' in respect of 'crimes against humanity', as Augusto Pinochet discovered. Even heads of state are not immune from accountability to foreign courts. Narendra Modi will be ill-advised to travel to Europe. Like Charles II, he should vow never to go abroad. L.K. Advani will be of little help. He himself is accountable to the law.

Notes

1   'Gujarat Remarks: India lodges a strong protest with Finland,' *Indian Express*, 23 April 2002. Tuomioja had said: 'What happened in Gujarat is of great concern for us. It was mentioned at the Luxembourg meeting of the EU. The pictures of the carnage are very disturbing.'

2   Saurabh Shukla, 'Riots were planned: UK Mission,' *Hindustan Times*, 14 April 2002.

3   Batuk Gathani, 'E.U. diplomats call it planned violence,' *Hindu*, April 2002; Saurabh Shukla, 'Muslims specific target of riots, says Germany,' *Hindustan Times*, 23 April 2002; 'EU draws parallel with Apartheid, Nazis,' *Indian Express*, 22 April 2002.

4   *Telegraph*, 22 May 2002.

5   'Gujarat violations not just an internal matter: NHRC Chief,' *Hindu*, 14 May 2002.

6   'Can't shut world out says Sorabjee,' *Times of India*, 14 May

2002.

7   'Outside intervention in Gujarat not needed: NHRC chief,' *Hindu*, 22 May 2002.

8   *Ibid.*

9   Apparel Export Promotion Council vs. A.K. Chopra (1999) Supreme Court Cases 759 at p. 776.

10 CCPR/C/10/Add. 8; 13 July 1983.

11 CCPR/C/SR 493, and 498.

12 CCPR/C/SR 1039 to 1042.

13 Malcolm N. Shaw, *International Law*, Cambridge University Press, fourth edition, 1997 p 202.

14 'Not "genocide": BJP,' *Hindu*, 27 April 2002.

Essays and Analyses

The Dialogue of Vali Gujarati and Hanumanji

Ranjana Argade

'Says Wali, my heart has been stolen by Dilli/ Will someone go and tell Mohammed Shah this.' When Wali lost his heart to Delhi, he is said to have sent an appeal to Mohammed Shah. Today, when rioteers have destroyed the tomb enshrining the grave of that very Wali Gujarati (or Wali Dakhini) in the most heart-rending communal violence Gujarat has ever seen, whom should we turn to? Would his spirit enshrined there not be crying, 'Rioteers have knocked down my tomb/Oh, my Shahji, to whom should I complain!' But the Shahji in politics has turned deaf. There is no redemption for Wali's spirit. It haunts the restless hearts of the troubled since 28 February, when the tomb above the grave was broken and an idol of Hanumanji placed inside.

Wali was a renowned poet of Urdu, a sister language of Hindi; Urdu also forged the link between Deccan and Gujarat. It is a pointless debate whether Dakhini or Aurangabadi or Wali Gujarati is the same, for even after his end, Wali's spirit is not at peace. It must be muttering, 'Where in the firmament can one hide / when one did not find a resting place in one's own alley.' Don't these ignorant people realize that the grace and power emanating from the resting places of poets like Wali turn them into shrines even though they are simple graves? We do

*   Ranjana Argade, '*Mere sukhan suun jalwagar*,' *Jansatta*, 8 March 2002. Translated from the Hindi by Kamini Mahadevan.

not build a temple where we cremate our dead. Just think of it, will we find it appropriate for Hanumanji to be sitting above Wali's grave? Why has Hanumanji fallen into the hands of such unrighteous people? The Hanumanji who had the strength to set aflame Ravana's Lanka was also a saint. He must be deeply troubled there at Wali's tomb now perhaps. Together, they must be thinking of some message for us.

One is reminded of the lines of the Hindi poet, Shamsher Singh, in which he considers writers as the ones willing to sacrifice everything for peace on earth. He asks quite correctly, are our leaders watching everything? Where and who are these leaders? But forget our leaders, what are we observing as writers? Are we not noticing the spreading virus of sectarianism in literature? To place a denominational flag on the graves of poets like Wali is an acceptance of sectarianism in our language and literature. We organize seminars on Kabir, produce articles and books on him, and loudly affirm that his was the lone voice against sectarianism in medieval times—but, today, we remain mute witnesses to the shameful happenings in our times. Can we relegate our responsibility to others? A poet belongs to that society, that soil which gave birth to him, not to any language or akademi.

And Wali was our poet. Of our town, of our language. This is also true for writers who are not 'activists' but confine themselves to the beauty and nuances of the word and meaning.

According to the fortieth *shloka* of the second chapter of the Vayu Purana, Hanuman was the son of the Wind God and was a master of the treatises on words. At other places it is said that Hanuman was a master of treatises on grammar. In the twenty-ninth *shloka* of the Kishkinda Canto, Ram says to Lakshman, 'He must have surely learnt grammar several times over, because in all his speech not once has he made a mistake.' This Hanumanji must be conversing with the spirit of Sufi Wali much like Shamsherji's poem in which Homer beckons the Indian poet, Sardar Jafri, and Shakespeare's genius spills over into Ujjain's valleys. For him, Tagore, Hafiz, Tulsi and Ghalib— all illuminate his heart and mind. Wali's spirirt and Hanuman must together be laughing that, unwitttingly, the rioters have brought together those that politics had rent apart. The power of Hanuman's tail, the power of knowledge, and Wali's power of dialogue, send us the message that whatever the designs of politicians, politics and rioters, we people should remain united.

Yet, after all this musing, how can the truth be refuted that the Wali who wrote of Hindu-Muslim unity in these words— '*Hey, suleh kul ke johraan mere sukhan suun jalwagar/aj bas ke basat musharbi su dil mera dariya*' (My verses are imbued with the goodness, the qualities needed for the happiness of all/ The path of my faith is wide, open like a river)—his grave has been flattened into dust by the violence this time. Has this grave and shrine been destroyed forever? What do you say, my friend?

14

Genocide of the Idea of Gujarat*

Shail Mayaram

Mohandas Karamchand Gandhi was born in 1869 in Porbandar on the Gujarat coast, in a family of vaishyas, a merchant caste. His mother was a Parnami (a cult with a strong Islamic derivation) and he himself espoused Vaishnava dharma, a moral and religious philosophy with a highly incorporative vision. This economic and cultural context created an extremely fortuitous conjuncture that produced one of the greatest men ever. Gandhi could, arguably, only have been born in Gujarat.

Gujarat, of all the regions in the Indian subcontinent, is culturally and demographically one of the most complex. Its arid, coastal and forested areas provided ecological niches for several groups, their diverse livelihoods, cultures and institutional arrangements. Gujarat's ports find mention in the Mahabharata as the sites of a polity ruled by a clan called the Yaduvansh kshatriyas. The ports were not just junctures for trade and commerce. These ancient and medieval markets were the doors and windows of the subcontinent where India reached out to the world and obtained a thousand-fold in return. The exchange of goods and commodities was only one aspect of the transaction. There was also a simultaneous exchange of languages, of ideas, of literary genres and metaphors, of sciences and other aspects of cultural and intellectual life. Not surprisingly, Gujarat's kings financed and patronised shrines of different religions that had to do with the worship of the

* The *Hindu*, 16 May 2002.

Sun, of the goddess, the Jain tirthankaras, Muslim saints.

The medieval-modern identity of the Gujaratis is derived from a vibrant relationship with their neighbours—Persians, Arabs, Baluchis, Sindhis and others. Gujarati traders and merchants were an eclectic community exposed to transcontinental trade and global cultures. Many converted to Jainism, the *sramana* tradition that involved a radical critique of caste hierarchy and the ritual dominance of the Brahmin. And then there were the large number of Shi'ite communities also with commercial interests—the Bohras, the Aga Khani Khojas, the Isna-Asharis, the Memons and others. These groups contributed to the State's prosperity. The cultural encounter brought into being a region with an extremely complex linguistic, literary, sectarian, legal and politico-institutional diversity. In the realm of language and literature, for instance, Gujarat was one of the first areas of the subcontinent to develop a *desh bhasha* or popular language. The more popular Rajasthani and Gujarati replaced Dingal or the old bardic language sometime around the thirteenth century. These were the first languages of northern India to possess a rich literature in both prose and verse, which ranged across genres such as *lok gathas*, *khyats* (chronicles), *vanshavalis* and *pirhiavalis* comprising genealogies, clan, lineage and biographical histories. Many of these have been referred to as indigenous forms of recording history and are written rather than oral.

Gujarat is today one of the Indian states with the largest number of Muslim communities, including groups that combined the idea of the worship of the ten *avatars* with Quranic cosmology. As Hindu and Muslim ideologies launched their competition over numbers early in the 20th century they sought to 'convert' a large number of these 'deviant' Hindu and Muslim sects. A century later, the language of these fundamentalist groups has changed. Gujarat's various Islamic ideologies stand totalised into caricatured versions of the Taliban. All Muslims stand collectively blamed for what happened at Godhra.

Gandhi died many times before Nathuram Godse actually killed him: once in Noakhali in 1946 and several times over during the Partition. He continues to suffer a cycle of ceaseless deaths in contemporary Gujarat as he is butchered time and again by Godse's successors, who call themselves Hindu. The tragedy of Gujarat, to my mind, is not only in terms of countless lives and the charred social fabric that our minds have hardly even begun to comprehend. The tragedy is that what happened involved the genocide not only of households, neighbourhoods and communities, but also of the idea of Gujarat. It is pointless quibbling about whether this conforms to the criteria of genocide in international law, which itself provides a highly limited definition and needs to be interrogated. After this genocide, Gandhi can never again be born in Gujarat.

The philosopher, Ramchandra Gandhi, sees in the Gujarat violence a recurrence of the Mahabharata, when the entire Yadava clan suffered the curse of Gandhari. Holding Krishna responsible for the wiping out of the Kuru clan, Gandhari pronounced: 'So also will your people kill themselves in fratricidal frenzy!' Drunken Yadavas indulging in revelry further tested the patience of the irritable Guru Durvasa. The Guru cursed the man pretending to be a pregnant woman by clothing a mace over his stomach. In parodying reproductivity, life itself had been mocked. The Guru condemned the mace to a prolific reproductivity, making possible the weapons of total destruction. The two curses devastated the Yadavas and their leader, Krishna.

Ramachandra Gandhi's reading of the replay of the Mahabharata in Gujarat can be further deepened. In the death of Krishna, from a hunter's arrow, died the androgynous self that has been so significant in the religious life of the subcontinent. Krishna had embodied two principles that bridged the limits of a simple, gendered self, conceived of as exclusively either male or female. Krishna with Radha is *ardhanarishvar*, together with Arjuna he is *nar-narayan*. The divine envisaged in an intimate relationship with the human: the god as both lover and beloved and the god as friend and confidante. The death of Krishna also meant the end of the *ganarajya*, Dwarka. It brought to a close the limited history of the republican principle that had competed with the monarchical in the political organisation of the subcontinent.

In Gandhi was reborn the subterranean principle of androgyny, for he celebrated the woman in himself. His elaboration of Vaishnava dharma made possible the presence of both Rama and Krishna. In his Ram dhun were also the strains of the distant devotional music of the Baul singers of Bengal. After all, medieval-modern Vaishnavism had travelled from Bengal to Braj and spread to the larger Brajbhasha-speaking area. In Gandhi's deeply Vaishnava and Hindu identity was also a celebration of the love and compassion articulated in Islam, Christianity and Buddhism.

Gandhi's strength came from the cultural resources of the region he was born into. Contemporary Gujarat has ensured that Gandhi will never again be born there. Lord Ram, the *maryada purshottam*, would never have allowed the *praja* of Ayodhya to desecrate a place of worship whether a mosque, church or ancestral shrine; Krishna would never have sided with the play of *adharma* in Gujarat. The Hindus affiliated to the Sangh Parivar have today ensured that Ram can never again be born at the Janamsthan in Ayodhya and Krishna can never return to rule from Dwarka.

15

The Pathology of Gujarat*

Achyut Yagnik

In the collective memory of Gujarat, the opening years of the twentieth century are synonymous with the Great Famine followed by widespread plague. Similarly, the opening years of this century will become synonymous with the Great Earthquake followed by communal carnage. While the early years of the last century witnessed large-scale out-migration of rural Gujaratis opening up new directions, the present crisis will lead to intra-state migration and out-migration of urban and rural Gujarati Muslims resulting in further ghettoization. Simultaneously, the worldview of the vast majority of the Hindutva-oriented Gujarati middle class will most likely shrink, further reducing the space for any kind of dialogue.

The Great Famine of 1900, known in popular parlance as *chhappaniyo*, (referring to Vikram Era 1956) set in motion the migration of not only peasant communities but dalits as well. Realizing the limit of land-based activity, the peasant communities began diversifying into modern sectors— commerce, industry and technical education. Even the Brahmins and Banias from Hindu upper castes and Muslims with a trading background—Bohra, Khoja and Memon—were part of this trend. A few took the route to Africa and Fiji. The combined impact of such migration resulted in greater urbanization within Gujarat and the expansion of a prosperous Gujarati diaspora.

The second wave of migration from rural Gujarat started in

*   *Seminar*, May 2002.

the mid-twentieth century after land reform measures were initiated by the Congress government in Bombay and Saurashtra states. In 1911, less than 20 per cent of the population of Gujarat was concentrated in urban areas and of that only 18 per cent resided in two cities with more than 100,000 population. By 1951, 27 per cent of the population was urbanized and of that, 36 per cent was concentrated in six cities with more than 100,000 population.

Though industrialization started in the mid-nineteenth century, the modern production processes were largely controlled by the mercantile elite that had dominated trade and commerce for centuries. Within the 'great tradition' of mercantilism in Gujarat, there existed a powerful stream that propelled every new generation to cross boundaries and establish new frontiers. The beginning of the first textile mill against many odds exemplified this spirit of entrepreneurship. But the value system that governed entrepreneurship remained the age-old code of competition with compromise.

After the first quarter of the twentieth century, the trend towards greater entrepreneurship in industry and agriculture became marked. Modem and technical education contributed to the rise of new professions—medicine, engineering, agricultural science, pharmacy and banking. The land-owning communities diversified from agriculture into these new avenues but continued their linkages with agriculture and the two worlds reinforced each other.

Between the first and second waves of urbanization, just when mercantile dominance was giving way to the entrepreneur, Gandhi entered the public sphere. Having grown up in a mercantile-turned-administrator family, conversant with the feudal dimensions of Saurashtra society and Mahajan culture, he sensed the looming crises. Mercantile society, dominated by Jain and Vaishnava Banias, thrived on competition and generally resolved conflicts of interest through compromise. While the structure of society was feudal, public life and business dealings were governed by the *kajiyanu mon kaalu* norm, that is, 'conflict is always inauspicious'.

However, with the rise of a new entrepreneurial class, the rules governing social and business life were slowly rewritten by the new entrants so as to emphasize ruthless advancement. Gandhi grasped this transition and tension which is why he strongly advocated inter-community harmony, peaceful co-existence and, above all, the primacy of means over ends.

For the first couple of decades after Gandhi's death, the march of this new dominant class towards urbanization intertwined with industrialization and capitalist development of agriculture, manifested in the green and white revolutions. During this period age-old socio-economic practices—the *haalipratha* or bonded labour system in South Gujarat and *vethpratha* or forced labour system in the erstwhile princely states—started disappearing because of state intervention, even as the *grahakvati* or *jajmani* system was on the decline due to market forces. A new structure of domination emerged, characterized by ruthless exploitation of agricultural and migrant labour by denying them minimum wages as well as the displacement of large numbers of tribal and other backward communities through projects for irrigation, electricity and water.

The social sphere revealed another dimension of the changing scenario. The sex ratio in urban areas steadily decreased from 965 at the turn of the century to 896 in 1961 and 893 in 1971. In Class I cities, the figure fell from 909 to 851 and 861 for the same years. This suggests both greater in-migration on the one hand and increasing violence in the private sphere on the other.

Parallel to these developments was the last contribution of Mahajan culture in the form of the establishment of new national level institutions, such as the first Indian Institute of Management, the National Institute of Design and the School of Architecture in Ahmedabad. At the same time, the entrepreneur class in smaller towns established new colleges, in which exploitation of teachers and students reflected another expression of their dominance. This trend is exemplified by the fact that by 1970, Chimanbhai Patel, the rising star of the Congress, controlled more than seventy colleges and successfully subverted the university system. This period also witnessed the hijacking of the cooperative sector—banks, milk dairies and agricultural produce market yards—by the entrepreneur class.

By the late 1960s, the social composition of Ahmedabad had radically changed. More and more people from other parts of Gujarat as well as other states such as UP, MP and Rajasthan, started flocking to the city in search of economic opportunities. The contradictions of rapid urbanization first became visible in Ahmedabad with the outbreak of Hindu-Muslim conflicts from the early sixties, culminating in the eruption of one of the worst post-independence communal riots in 1969. These riots marked the demise of the Mahajan culture as the old city elite among both the Muslims and Hindus were unable to contain the violence. Another feature of these riots was the beginning of the partisan role of the state and the emerging nexus between the political leaders and criminals.

The 1970s witnessed the Navnirman student's movement, essentially an urban upsurge against those who were repeating *ad nauseum* the slogans of green and white revolutions. By 1980, however, the power elite had put these developments behind them and moved on to hardcore industrial projects, developing the 'golden corridor' from South to North, projecting in sharp focus the image of a mini Japan for Gujarat. Even the political leadership of the intermediate and lower communities were incorporated into this culture. The entrepreneurial class marched on and their ethos became the *mantra* of an ever expanding middle class. The rising middle class of Gujarat, unlike in the 1950s, was no longer dominated by the upper castes. A number of communities from the intermediate castes and socially and educationally backward castes, as well as Scheduled Castes and Scheduled Tribes, had moved upwards and become part of the middle class, sharing its aspirations and world view.

To recover from the setback caused by the Nav Nirman movement, the Congress formulated an election strategy around a combination of caste and community known as KHAM (Kshatriya-Harijan-Adivasi-Muslim combine). After the great success of this formula in the Assembly elections of 1980, the upper castes for the first time sensed a political and economic threat to their domination. To them it appeared that their political power was slipping away and being transferred to the 'backward castes and communities'. The educated middle class, mainly the Brahmins, Banias and Patidars, reacted sharply by starting an agitation against the reservation system in 1981.

Probably for the first time in independent India, a modem industrial metropolis experienced such extreme forms of caste violence. The clashes between the *savarnas* and the dalits in the industrial periphery of Ahmedabad gradually evolved into a caste war that spread to the towns in eighteen out of the then nineteen districts. In many villages dominated by land owning Patidars in North and Central Gujarat, dalit *bastis* were burnt. Caste tension resurfaced in 1985 in the second anti-reservation agitation. The issue this time was the increase in job quotas of the non-dalit socially and educationally backward castes; yet the victims were all dalits. As a result of these two agitations, the Brahmin-Bania-Patidar combine acquired a savarna unity.

The BJP leadership, drawn mainly from the upper castes, indirectly participated in both anti-reservation agitations. But they realized that in order to expand their social base and dislodge the Congress, they would have to co-opt 'backward communities' including SC and ST groups. From 1985 onwards, the Sangh Parivar tried to consolidate its social base through a series of symbolic *yatras* and by 1990, was able to win over a large section of urban dalits and OBCs. The riots of 1990, after Advani's arrest during his rath yatra from Somnath to Ayodhya, saw dalits and Muslims in pitched battle in industrial Ahmedabad.

In the 1990s, the Sangh Parivar tried to win over tribals who constitute 15 per cent of Gujarat's population. They did this by systematically creating a rift between the so-called 'Hindu tribal' and the 'Christian tribal', mainly in the areas south of the Narmada. dalits, tribals and socially and educationally backward castes were drawn towards Hindutva, seeing in the ideology an opportunity to achieve social acceptance from the savarna society.

At the same time the Hindu Gujarati diaspora was adrift in the western world, in search of an anchor, which they found in the ideology of Hindutva. Since they maintained close linkages with their family and community, Hindutva was nurtured both at home and abroad and in turn gave many Hindus a new meaning and direction to their lives.

In the first half of the twentieth century, the rising Gujarati entrepreneurial class along with the middle class expanded and consolidated their economic and social control, deriving meaning and direction from two ideals—independence and nation building. After Independence, the pace of their expansion became more marked as they grew both in number and in their control over the modern economic, educational and political apparatus. With the weakening of the mercantile and Gandhian ethos, degeneration within the Congress and the diminishing of the focus provided by the nation-building project, this class became devoid of moorings in any value system.

Despite outward modernization and institution building, modern values of equality, fraternity, justice and secularism remained weak. In the ensuing vacuum, Hindutva provided both an identity beyond caste and community as well as sanction to pursue their own agenda of greater political, economic and social control. Also, Hindutva as ideology scarcely raises any ethical questions for its supporters. In the case of Gujarat, this aspect made it more attractive for the entrepreneurial middle class that wants to perpetuate its hegemony.

Even prior to the events of February-March-April this year, the aftermath of the earthquake provided a glimpse of the future that lies ahead for Gujarat. In the immediate relief phase, we saw discrimination against Muslim communities by both the state machinery and volunteers of the Sangh Parivar. Indeed, the demarcation between the two was hardly visible. In the rehabilitation phase, discrimination was extended to dalits, Kolis (OBC community) and pastoralists whose damaged property was neither surveyed nor were their compensation amounts fixed in a just and proper manner. Though many of them continue to struggle on these issues, the middle class has hardly raised any

414 *Gujarat: The Making of a Tragedy*

voice of protest.

When villages had to be shifted to new sites, the dominant communities of Patidars and Darbars ensured that dalits, other 'backward communities' and Muslims were allotted separate venues away from their village. In many cases, two villages were formed, thereby revealing the upper caste sense of exclusiveness, as also their shrinking horizons.

If the 'violence' around the post-earthquake relief and rehabilitation was 'invisible', the violence in ongoing communal conflagration is there for everyone to see. The Sangh Parivar and the state apparatus have once again coalesced, this time to loot, burn and murder, and then shield each other. Citing the Godhra carnage, the entrepreneur class and burgeoning Hindu middle class found no difficulty in justifying open violence, including the lawlessness of the state. It is significant that in the private sphere, the same class has perpetrated violence within their own family in the form of foeticide and infanticide. The 2001 Census reveals that the latest sex ratio in urban Gujarat is 879 females per 1,000 males, the lowest figure in the last hundred years.

It goes on to add: 'The overall sex ratio is affected by migration from rural to urban areas in search of employment, education, etc. The sex ratio in the population category of 0-6 years is, however, relatively immune to such bias/aberrations and can be said to be a relatively stable indicator. On this count also, the state of Gujarat has fared badly as the 0-6 year sex ratio has decreased from 928 in 1991 to only 878 in 2001.' The five worst blocks in this category are Unjha, Mansa, Visnagar, Mehsana and Prantij where the number of females ranges from 781 to 734. The same blocks witnessed communal violence in varying degrees.

At this juncture, one may ask whether the visible and invisible violence is turning Gujarat into a dark zone. If we examine the geography of the present communal violence closely, we find that Saurashtra and Kutch remained relatively calm. Except Rajkot and Bhavnagar, which were disturbed for the first two days, all the other towns and most villages remained quiet. South

Gujarat too remained peaceful, with the exception of Surat city that saw some unrest in the early days. It is also significant that the tribals of South Gujarat did not participate in the violence unlike the tribals of the northeastern Bhil belt. Even in rural North and Central Gujarat which have been at the centrestage of violence, a number of Hindu communities—dalits, Thakor, Rajput and pastoralists—protected and sheltered Muslims.

The next assembly elections, whether held now or later, will be decisive in more than one way. Even if the Congress were to win, it would be unable to stop the onward march of the entrepreneur class and the middle class, and the accompanying invisible violence. What might perhaps change is the blatant state support to visible violence. The dominant classes would be forced to introspect and reconsider their worldview only if the deprived and oppressed strata throw up radical challenges through people's movements.

16

Caste, Hindutva and the Making of Mob Culture*

Ghanshyam Shah

Dalits and shudras, particularly other backward castes (OBCs) constitute the overwhelming majority of the population in Gujarat. Nearly 70 per cent of the workforce of these social groups are casual labourers and 'self-employed'; and 20 per cent are white collar employees in cities. This essay attempts to probe and contextualize their role in the present communal carnage and is a response to press coverage and the observations of some scholar activists regarding 'large scale' participation of dalits and OBCs in rioting, looting and killing.

Soon after the ghastly communal carnage in Surat in 1992, a proportion of the Hindus expressed intense 'communal consciousness'. They took positions of 'we' verssus 'they' and considered their community to be superior to others. But the majority of them were not active participants in the riots.[1]

Inter-caste and community stereotypes are widely prevalent in all societies. Gujarat is no exception. The process of hardening of stereotypes began with discourse on religion-centred nationalism. What we are witnessing now is its ugly face. This has been intelligently built up and in Gujarat, since the 1965 Indo-Pak war on the Kutch border. It was coupled with the *gau-raksha*, i.e., anti-cow slaughter campaign. The first major planned large-scale communal riots followed. Since then, the fear psychosis and sense of injustice among the majority

*   *Economic and Political Weekly*, 13 April 2002.

community has been constantly whipped up. The myth that Muslims were favoured by the State has been systematically articulated and spread. Time and again, Muslims have been branded as anti-national, fundamentalist, conservative and backward, and so on. The Hindus are reminded that they are apostles (*'upasak'*) of *'shakti'*—the worshippers of Maha-Shakti with trishul in the hands of Shiva, *sudarshan* in the hands of Krishna, bow and arrow in the hands of Ram. Hindus are cajoled to take arms against the enemies.[2] They are reminded that weakness, timidity, unmanliness are great sins and bravery and masculinity are great *punya*, i.e., virtues. Such interpretations of Hinduism have been systematically spread through informal conversation, rumours, public lectures, children's comic books, printed and audio-visual media by all units of the parivar. Newspapers and journals, 'kathas' of the religious saints, booklets and other forms of popular literature orchestrated the same message.

Violence in the present riots has been publicly applauded by VHP leaders.[3] The testing of nuclear bombs by India and Pakistan, the Kargil war, the 11 September holocaust in the US, and the December attack on Indian Parliament, frequent terrorist acts in Kashmir and the constant live bomb of Ram Janmabhoomi add fuel to fire. A carnage like Godhra inflames passions. During the last seven years, the state has patronized and institutionalized anti-minority activities by the Sangh Parivar.

On the other hand, overall traditional ethical values of honesty, harmony, tolerance and mutual dialogue in the public domain are getting eroded with rising corruption in all fields of life and criminalisation of politics. The proponents of Hindutva were jubilant in the 1969 riots that it was their 'victory over Muslims'. They felt that the riots offered them an opportunity to teach Muslims a lesson and avenge the historical defeat of Prithviraj at the hands of Mohammad Ghauri.[4] The past—real or imaginary—is constantly kept ignited. Statues of Shivaji and Rana Pratap have been installed in all cities during the last three decades inculcating poison of Hindutva against 'others'.[5]

Rioting is an act of a mob, pogrom and genocide are not. But they cannot be carried out without mob support. The strength of the mob varies from hundred to five thousand and, in a few cases, the number is larger. All participants in the mobs do not indulge in looting, destroying and burning property and killing. On the basis of my observations of 1969, 1973 and 1992 in Gujarat, I submit that mobs in such situations consist of four types of actors. The organizers, who meticulously prepare plans and evolve strategies. Many of them are not on the site. They also chart out the route for the attacks in different localities. VHP leaders had admitted that the list identifying Muslims was prepared on the 28th morning. The organizers are primarily the top rank leaders. The majority of them happen to be brahmins. And more important, they subscribe to the brahminical ideology of the varna system.

The second set of actors are the skilled and experienced personnel constituting the core. They have mastered the craft of breaking shutters and doors, pulling down ceilings and walls, using electrical devices for setting fire and burning people, using swords and other weapons. In the present riots, gas cylinders and other chemicals were used to destroy property. They function in a group of ten to twenty with all the necessary equipment. The leaders of the group (more than one) are committed 'Hindutvavadis', believing that they are performing their dharma, and are trained like all terrorists, be they Muslim or Christian fundamentalists. For them, their caste or other identity is not important, though it would seem that the majority of them belong to upper and middle castes. The rest are professional goons routinely involved in criminal activities. They are called and mobilized by the organizers who provide patronage and political protection. H, who actively participated in the 1969 and 1973 riots in Ahmedabad, told us, 'By now I have done all sorts of business. There is no red-light area between Bombay and Ahmedabad which I have not visited . . . I use to gamble and live on it . . . I believe there is nothing wrong in killing people.' At that time he was twenty-five years old and had passed his MA with psychology. He was Bania by caste

and the son of stockbroker. He was close to the Jan Sangh.[6]
The number of such hooligans has increased manifold in Gujarat
with the rise of unemployment, casualization of labour and
criminalization of politics. They are from all social groups: upper
and middle castes, dalits and OBCs including Gujaratis and
non-Gujaratis.

The third component comprises agent provocateurs engaged
in spreading rumours, shouting slogans, instigating and directing
mobs. They are activists of the various Sangh Parivar outfits.
They are not more than five in a crowd of fifty. Their number
multiplies with the size of the mob. In many places, they are
accompanied with professionals like doctors and advocates,
social activists, active members of the Parivar. The fourth
segment consists of 'other' participants who, in the charged
atmosphere, lose their individual identity and submerge into
the mob. Their number increases and their fear disappears when
they find that they are not prevented by the law and order
machinery. During the present riots, the police at several places
encouraged them to loot. They belong to all castes depending
upon locality. In posh and middle class neighbourhoods, they
are from upper and middle castes, local as well as outsiders.
The composition is different in working class localities. Persons
belonging to OBCs, dalits and non-Gujarati immigrants are
found in large number. Some also participate in looting,
throwing stones, burning property and, sometimes, assisting in
physical assaults. Their involvement in hideous acts, however,
is rare.

All the participants are not necessarily anti-Muslim. For
instance, Sanjay, thirty-eight years old, is an OBC who joined
the mob in Naroda Patiya, Ahmedabad on 28 February. He
went there to see what was happening. People were throwing
stones on the mosque and Muslim bastis and shouting anti-
Muslim slogans. He too was angry about the Godhara incident
that 'our people were brutally burnt'. Out of anger, he also
joined the mob throwing stones on the mosque. The same person
after three hours rescued fifteen Muslims and sheltered them
for three days at great risk. His neighbours helped him. Take

another example. Ramesh, eighteen years old, from an upper-caste family in Baroda, saw a crowd on the street. He went there out of curiosity. His friends were throwing petrol bombs. His neighbour gave him a bomb and asked him to throw it. He did. He was upset when he came to know that they were trying to kill Muslims of the adjoining locality. During the curfew, he and his younger brother went to the targetted Muslim locality to see Karim Chacha of whom they were very fond. A number of persons told us that their Muslim friends were nice and kind 'but Muslims are bad and cannot be trusted'. Against the onslaught of propaganda, they are unable to differentiate their personal experiences with the rumours.

Dalits, OBCs and Hinduism

The major challenge for the proponents of Hindutva is to build unity among all Hindus without disturbing the dominance of the upper castes and classes. The Bharat Sevashram and Hindu Milan Mandir, outfits of the Hindu Mahasabha launched in the 1920s, have been more active in Gujarat since the 1970s. Besides undertaking activities to unite various sects and organizing religious festivals, they carry out welfare and relief measures for the poor. The main thrust of these organizations is to build unity and harmony among the upper and lower castes. They reject the notion that Sudras occupy an inferior and degraded position, though they do not reject the caste system. Cooperation and unity of upper and lower castes for the protection of the Hindu dharma and Hindu *samaj* is called for. Hindutva consciousness and Hindu inspiration are the starting point for the realization of power necessary for the self-protection of Hindus. According to these organizations, low caste Hindus are the most hardworking, strong and able to bear much suffering. 'Because of their numerical strength, they are truly the spinal code of the Hindu "*jati*" (race). Lakhs and crores of these people are getting disassociated from Hindu samaj because they are humiliated and looked down upon. As a result, the Hindu jati is becoming weak and powerless.'[7] They are the real kshatriyas who protected the Hindu samaj in the ancient period against all calamities, aggressions and shocks. The Hindu jati can become strong only by uplifting them in moral, good behaviour, education and other fields. It is the responsibility of the upper caste members to 'reform' them for their own protection and protection of the Hindu samaj. The Vishwa Hindu Parishad (VHP) also subscribes to the above theory. *Vishwa Hindu Samachar*, the organ of VHP edited by K.K. Shastry, former president of Gujarati Sahitya Sabha, often exhorts its readers: 'All Hindus should unite against "vidharmis" (people of other religions) . . . "Savarna" (upper caste) Hindus should now become alert and not widen the gap between the castes. They must compromise with the dalits . . .'

The Rashtriya Swayamsevak Sangh, (RSS) emphasizes unity and harmony among all Hindus irrespective of castes. Accordingly to them, the caste system is based on 'scientific' principles. The prevailing discrimination is a distortion. Deendayal Upadhya argued in his widely read book among the Sangh volunteers, *Integral Humanism,* 'In our concept of four castes (Varna), they are thought of as analogous to the different limbs of Virat-Purush [the primeval man] [. . .]. These limbs are not only complementary to one another, but even further, there is individuality, unity. There is complete identity of interests, identity of belonging [. . .]'.[8]

The RSS has floated an organization, 'Samajik Samrasata Manch' (SSM), i.e., Social Assimilation Platform, to attract Ambedkarists and other dalits for the purpose of developing Hindu unity. Hedgewar, the SSM says, did not support caste and class divisions. The prevailing divisions should be ignored. 'We are one'. He emphasized: 'We are all Hindus, Where is untouchability? Today we have only one varna and jati that is Hindu.' According to the proponents of the SSM, the central thrust of Ambedkar's ideology is dharma. He was a strong critic of the Brahmin caste which exploited society in the name of religion. But that was, according to a RSS leader, the fault of Brahmins and not of religion. Ambedkar's views on Pakistan are twisted to show that he was against Muslims. It has been argued that he adopted Buddhism and not Islam or Christianity because he feared those religions would make people anti-national.[9] The RSS has recently published a book by a dalit swayamsevak who asserts that he had not experienced any discrimination in the organization. The foreword of the book is written by another dalit who is the editor of *Sadhana,* organ of the Gujarat RSS. He observes, by citing his experiences, that Gandhians and Congress leaders practice discrimination but he had no such experience within RSS in the last twenty years.[10]

After the 1969 riots, RSS 'shakhas' (units) increased from less than 30 to 45 in 1973. Now they have reached over 1,500 and the RSS is aiming at a target of 2,000 in the next three years. Besides shakhas, the RSS organizes health relief and income generation welfare programmes on a regular basis in more than 200 locations in the state. It has adopted a few villages for 'total development'. Though the RSS claims that it does not encourage rituals, various activities carried out by 'the organization are not free from them. VHP and other outfits also undertake several welfare programmes involving upper caste professionals like doctors and teachers for philanthropic work for the poor. They also often coordinate their functions with other sects like Swaminarayan, Swadhayay, Gayatri Pariwar, Pustimargis and also occasionally caste organizations. Despite all efforts, in normal times Hindu identity has not superseded caste identity.'[11]

The BJP, like the Congress, distributes election tickets on caste lines and reinforces caste-based divisions in the election campaign. The Sangh Parivar hardly raises a voice against discrimination and atrocities against OBCs and dalits in Gujarat. Their journals do not report such incidents. The RSS believes the true swayamsevak refrains from finding fault with the samaj. He has to remember constantly that 'We Hindus are one.'[12]

There are a number of sects or individual saints who try to build unity among castes within Hinduism. They came into existence at different points of time. They are critical of superstitions and 'irrational' rituals practised by other sects. Though some of them favour the caste system, they are critical of untouchability. Sachchidanand, one of the radical Hindu saints, works for the eradication of the degraded status of backward and dalit castes. Being a strong critic of caste, the varna system and untouchability, he asks 'How can Varna-based Sanskriti, i.e., culture and heritage, be beneficial to all sudras, ati-sudras, untouchables and women?'.[13] He has been acclaimed as Narmad, the father of the Gujarati 'renaissance', for his social reform and literary work. The swadhyay movement opposes the caste system. But at the same time, it supports the 'chaturvarna' system. According to Athavale, the founder of the sect, the 'chaturvarna' system created by Shri Krishna has no hierarchical differences of low and high. It is a materialist arrangement for distribution of occupations so that people need not have to worry about their bread and shelter. He repeatedly emphasizes that 'no man born on this earth is lowly and degraded'. The sect highlights self-dignity, dignity of labour, individual identity, culture and devotion. It has motivated persons from upper castes to work for the lower castes. The swadhayay has a large following among OBCs such as Machchis, Kharvas, Kolis, Vagharis, dalits and adivasis. Though in their routine discourse, these sects do not discuss Hindutva ideology and Sangh Parivar programmes, their reconstruction of history is not substantially different than the later.[14]

The Swaminarayan sect, which started in the early nineteenth century, does not talk about nationalism and rashtra. All the above-mentioned sects keep a distance from electoral politics, neither supporting nor opposing the BJP or Congress. They did not support the Ram Janmabhoomi campaign. However, during the past ten years they have begun to praise and support the activities of the RSS for raising Hindu consciousness (various issues of *Sadhna*). None of them expressed even grief for the large-scale killing in the present riots.

Gujarat does not have a significant number of radical groups—Hindu Left, Gandhians, liberals, socialists, etc. It has not witnessed an anti-brahmin or backward caste movement. Some religious sects mobilized backward castes with a view to Sanskritize social customs. Since the early twentieth century, several OBCs have followed the path of Sanskritization for their upward mobility. A section of the Kolis of central and north Gujarat claim kshatriya status. In course of time, they began to don the sacred thread at the Vedic rite of Upanayana. Mythologies for honour and insult are created and religious rituals of the Rajputs are imitated.[15] In the 1950s and 1960s, the Gujarat Kshatriya Sabha reinforced and legitimized their sentiments of being kshatriya. Caste as well as Hindu consciousness was invoked. Symbols like the sword, trishul, and swastika are deployed to rally members not only around caste but simultaneously around Hinduism. They perceive these as emblematic of their identity.

Some sections of dalits also followed the Sanskritization path. Under the influence of Gandhi, they kept their distance from Ambedkar's struggles. However, with the growth of the urban middle class and rising atrocities against dalits, the influence of Ambedkar's ideology began to attract the younger generation of dalits in the seventies. The movement of Dalit Panthers grew. Though conversion to Buddhism has not spread, assertion for rights and dignity increased. Occasionally, they joined hands with other oppressed groups. But during the last ten years, the movement is at a low ebb. Middle-class dalits do assert their individual rights but collective actions are absent. They do not link their problems with those of the rural dalits who are often victims of atrocities and blatant discrimination. Several dalit leaders have tried to intervene in the present riots and provided protection to some Muslims. But this has remained on a small scale with localized impact in a few localities. Valjibhai Patel, the leader of the Dalit Panthers who led several dalit struggles in the mid-1960s, feels lonely and deserted. He laments that, 'With this new generation it seems everything has changed. They have forgotten resistance against injustice and atrocities . . . In order to increase the capacity for assertion Babasaheb taught us to get educated. But now its outcome is opposite. Education has come and it has created huge battalions of arm-chair intellectuals. Their capacity for retaliation and assertion has declined. Sensitivity is replaced by thick skin. Careerist approach, selfishness and mindset for compromise and adjustment have destroyed the dalit movement. So-called dalit leaders and organizations have almost become captive of political leaders . . .'[16] Many secular minded individuals share this agony.

Notes

1 Shah, Ghanshyam (1994a), 'Identify, Communal Consciousness and Polities', *Economic and Political Weekly*, 29 (19), May 7.

2 Atmanand, Swami (1982), Hindu Samaj Samanvaya, *Bharat Seaashram Sangh, Ahmedabad.*

3 Bhatt, Sheela (2002), 'VHP Leader's Startling Revelation,' *Mainstream*, 60 (13) March 16.

4 Shah, Ghanshyam (1970), 'Communal Riots in Gujarat,' *Economic and Political Weekly*, 5 (3-5) Annual Number, January.

5 Togadia, Pravin (2000), *Sadhana*, July 8.

6 Shah, Ghanshyam (1974), 'Anatomy of Urban Riots: Ahmedabad 1973,' *Economic and Political Weekly*, 9 (6-8) Annual Number.

7 Atmanand, *op cit.*

8 Jaffrelot, Christopher (1998), '*The Sangh Parivar Between Sanskritistion and Social Engineering*' in Hansen and Jaffrelot *(eds).* The BJP and the Compulsions of Politics in India, *Oxford University Press, Delhi.*

9 Dhengadi, Dattopant (1993), Samajik Samrasta, *Samjik Samrast Manch, Karnavati.*

10 Patange, Ramesh (undated), *Hau, Manu Ane Sangh*, Sadhana Pustak Prakashan, Karnavati.

11 Shah (1974) *op cit.*

12 *ibid.*

13 Sachchidanand, Swami (1988), *Adhogatinu Mul Varna Vyavastha*, Samanvay Prakashan, Ahmedabad.

14 Shah, Ghanshyam (1994b), 'The BJP and Backward Castes in Gujarat,' *South Asian Bulletin*, 14 (1).

15 Ghanshyam Shah, *Caste Association and Political Process in Gujarat.* Popular Prakashan, Bombay.

16 Patel, Valjibhai (1999), *Karmashil ni Kalame*, Valjibhai Patel Sanman Samiti, Vallabha Vidhyanagar.

17

The VHP Needs to Hear the Condemnation of the Hindu Middle Ground*

Ramachandra Guha

All decent and peace-loving Indians shall be depressed by the recent events in Gujarat, but a historian of Indian nationalism has a right to be more depressed than most. This particular historian had spent the first half of February studying the letters and papers of Chakravarti Rajagopalachari, 'Rajaji', a man who at various times served as chief minister of Madras, home minister of the government of India, and governor general—a philosopher, statesman and writer once described by Mahatma Gandhi as 'the keeper of my conscience'.

Amidst a mountain of correspondence between Rajaji and the likes of Gandhi, Patel, Nehru and Ambedkar, I came across a curious exchange of letters with a lesser known patriot named Valji Govind Desai, who was a long-time follower of the Mahatma and the translator of some of his works. In the festive season of 1947-48, Rajaji, as governor of West Bengal, had given away the prizes at the horse-races on the Calcutta Maidan. Valji Desai wrote to Gandhi in protest, and after Gandhi was shot dead on January 30, passed on the complaint to the offender himself. 'Don't you think', asked Desai, 'you are making our independence ugly by lending your prestige to an institution which was condemned by Bapu without any reservation?'

* The *Telegraph*, 9 March 2002

Rajaji's first instinct was self-defence. He too condemned gambling, he said, but considered that the presentation of a cup to the winner of a horse-race was no worse than, or no different from, the presentation of a medal to a student who comes first in an examination. Rajaji then had second thoughts about the exchange, whose pettiness he transcended by saying: 'But let us drop the matter in the universal grief. I may be even wrong with regard to horses. Let us unite on the Hindu-Muslim issue.'

Rajaji was, among other things, a learned and devout Hindu, and the author of celebrated translations of the Ramayana and the Mahabharata. He believed that a unique feature of his religion was 'its specific and positive doctrine of catholicity'. 'The Hindu tradition', he once wrote, 'prescribes that it is not open to any Hindu, whatever the name and mental image of the Supreme being he may use for his devotional exercises, to deny the Gods that others worship. He . . . cannot deny the divinity or the truth of the God of other denominations.' It was, indeed, as a positively catholic Hindu that Rajaji worked for inter-religious harmony. Thus his plea to his fellow Gandhians in February 1948; a plea that rings compellingly true in February and March of 2002. For the brutalities in Gujarat have recalled the brutalities and bloodshed of the Partition riots of 1947-48. The same tales of burning and loot, the same animal frenzy, and—despite it and defying it all—the same singular tales of refuge given by exceptional members of one religious community to terrified members of another.

'Let us unite on the Hindu-Muslim issue.' That, at a particularly trying time in our history was the call of a wise man like Rajaji, and that, now, is the message conveyed in statements recently issued by two of our most respected writers. In a moving letter to the President of India, Mahasweta Devi has appealed to him 'to immediately intervene as the constitutional head of the country to protect the lives of innocent citizens and prevent the carnage from spreading any further.' Speaking with characteristic forthrightness of this 'hour of national shame', Mahasweta called upon the President, and the rest of us, to help 'put an immediate halt to this needless waste of human life and help restore sanity.' She asked for the banning of extremist religious organizations—whether Hindu or Muslim—and for exemplary legal action to be taken both against those who burnt the train at Godhra and those who instigated the riots in retribution.

No living writer has a record of public service as distinguished as Mahasweta's. She has undertaken a lifelong struggle on behalf of vulnerable and victimized Indians: be they forest tribes, landless peasants, battered women, tortured prisoners or persecuted minorities. At times, the happenings in Gujarat have depressed even this indomitable woman. 'There was once', she told me over the phone, 'a solitary man in a loin-cloth who walked to restore peace between Hindus and Muslims. But were he to walk now in his native Gujarat they would kill him too.' Then, quickly, the will and the character reasserted itself. *'Hum maidan nahin chhodenge',* insisted the seventy-eight-year old, *'hum maidan* nahin *chhodenge.'* We will not leave the field. We will stay, and fight on against the reactionaries and the fundamentalists.

From Bangalore, Mahasweta's call has been seconded by a letter to the President by her fellow Jnanpith awardee, U.R. Anantha Murthy He too calls it a 'period of national shame'. Anantha Murthy writes that 'a growing number of Hindus, including myself, feel that no temple that has caused so much blood to be spilt can ever represent the sentiments or the spiritual yearnings of Hindus.' The Ayodhya campaign, he continues, 'has only consolidated fundamentalist feelings amongst both Hindus and Muslims and sown deep distrust amongst neighbours and friends. Some politicians seeking to build a Muslim or Hindu vote bank may see in the controversy an opportunity, but for most citizens, the issue of whether a new temple is built or the mosque rebuilt is largely irrelevant to their daily lives. It only impinges on them in adverse ways, as when innocent Indians of all faiths become victims of violence.'

Anantha Murthy has followed up his letter to the President with an appeal to the swami of the Pejawar *mutt* in North Karnataka, a highly respected religious leader who, for reasons not easy to fathom, has supported the Vishwa Hindu Parishad's malevolent activities in Ayodhya. Anantha Murthy has asked the Pejawar swami to reconsider his support. As he points out, 'unlike Islam and Christianity, Hinduism is not a historical religion. It does not need to know where or when Rama was born. The Rama for whom thousands of men, women and children have been killed is not the Rama our saints and poets have praised or the Rama whom Gandhiji called out to when he died. I request you not to support this murderous campaign in any way.'

I used the term, 'malevolent', but Anantha Murthy's appellation, 'murderous', is more accurate and wholly just. For close to twenty years now, the Ayodhya campaign has led to episodic bursts of violence. In 1989, the *Ramshila puja* or brick-worship ceremony, led to a riot in Bhagalpur in which more than 2,000 people lost their lives. The next year, L.K. Advani's Toyota *yatra* from Somnath onto Uttar Pradesh left a trail of dead bodies and burnt houses in its wake. Then, in 1992-93, the demolition of the Babri Masjid sparked off a wave of violence and counter-violence in Mumbai and other places. And now we have these horrific incidents in Gujarat. The temple, were it ever to be built, will not be a celebration of divinity but, rather, a chilling testimony to manufactured violence and consciously willed murder. The marble pillars that are currently being made for its construction are each inscribed with the blood of a hundred innocent victims.

The activities of the Hindu fanatics are condemned by the secular democrat, speaking on behalf of the Constitution of India. They are condemned by the non-denominational patriot who fears that communal violence will besmirch our name in the international community, which will come to regard us as an unstable fundamentalist state: as, indeed, a Hindu Pakistan. They are condemned by the pragmatic economist and businessman who worry that riots will lead to a dramatic dip in India's investment ratings. (Each day of violence in Gujarat led to an estimated loss of Rs 500 crore.)

These worries are entirely legitimate. But the VHP and its

cohorts need also to be condemned by the Hindu middle ground, the millions of thus far silent Indians who have seen their ancestral religion taken over and grossly distorted by a bunch of power-hungry individuals. It is these voices that one now needs to hear, and hear more often. Once, men such as C. Rajagopalachari and Mahatma Gandhi were the political voice of Hindus. They stood for catholicity and tolerance and for progress and social reform, building friendships with Muslims and Christians and Sikhs, working to remove the disabilities faced by women and low castes, thus to more effectively and painlessly bring this old faith into the modern world. Their work won wide acceptance and support amongst Indians, but perhaps especially amongst their fellow Hindus. Can it really be that these Hindus are now content with having Ashok Singhal and Giriraj Kishore stand in for Rajaji and Gandhi?

18

Where Will It End?*

Mahasweta Devi

Gujarat's actions and behaviour are aberrant and, I think, unlike any other place in the world. Perhaps the events of Sunday 5 May 2002 in Ahmedabad—murder, violence and pillage—took place to teach K.P.S. Gill a lesson. They seemed to mock him and say, 'Did you really think we would be subdued so easily? We shall continue to do exactly what we have done in the past.'

And they do, time and again. I had personally visited the villages near Baroda in Gujarat and seen and heard things first-hand. There is the immediate threat of further communal violence on asylum-seekers and they are told to leave the relief camps. Where they will go, where they will get shelter, what will happen to the babies and the young boys and girls?—the refugees are burdened with all these questions by a callous state that seems to feel no sense of responsibility towards its citizens.

Chhota Udepur is a taluka town. Its one-time *raja* was an adivasi, and the region has a strong adivasi concentration. This strength is numerical only—in social terms they are backward and downtrodden. The relief camp in Chhota Udepur is providing shelter to Muslims chiefly from villages like Panvad and Tejgadh. The Saba Charitable Trust is running the camp there and distributing rice, wheat and flour provided by the government. Now the biggest concern is rehabilitation. Why only Chhota Udepur? This is an extremely pressing problem

---

* Mahasweta Devi, '*Kothai Shesh?*', *Aajkal*, 8 May 2002. Translated from the Bengali by Ankita Mukherji.

even in the surrounding villages. Those who have come from the cities and villages of the Tanjalda region are in a similar situation. And yet the state roars—'Dismantle the relief camps, go back to where you came from'. Where they have come from, the majority community has saffron blood in its veins. The stench of divisiveness and hatred is in the air. If only returning was that easy. With some help from the adivasis each of these villages has been looted and houses and property set on fire. However '*Insaf*' reports that there have been no incidents of rape or of people being burnt alive.

In the meantime, of all the news that I have been getting from diverse sources, there is one bit of information that is truly explosive. Some forty Muslim families from the Tezgarh panchayat have returned to their villages. Thirty-nine houses were burnt down. One had not been attacked—a place with big rooms probably used to store grain.

The most positive incident in the entire Gujarat affair went without comment. Some seventy families have gone back from the Chhota Udepur camp to Tejgadh.

For the government, these relief camps are like raw and bleeding wounds and it wants them to close. 'Wind down!' Their marching orders are issued constantly. And if you leave aside the cities, in rural Gujarat, the block officers reign supreme. And they are all acutely anti-Muslim. 'Remove the refugees' was the order they were being given day after day. And then, after much needless delay and hair-splitting, these same people distributed the promised relief package. These seventy families I know about have no idea how much compensation they are entitled to, but they have all received between fifteen and forty or forty-five thousand rupees. However to try and rebuild their houses, buy basic household necessities and clothes as well as revive their ruined businesses with the amount paid to them is absolutely impossible. In many of Gujarat's villages I have seen that adivasis have mud huts or huts made of a combination of bricks and mud. But non-adivasi homes are *pukka* buildings, villages have paved roads, there are STD booths and even mobile phones. After all, Gujarat is considered one of the wealthier states. Those who have returned to Tejgadh are in need of financial help. I say this to my readers—I make no special mention of any of the organizations working here. Those who receive death threats every day on the telephone and yet continue to work, I will speak only of them. Three or four times a week they travel to places up to a hundred kilometres away. I ask you to stand by these afflicted people. While on the subject, I would like to talk about two more things:

1. In rural Gujarat, the rehabilitation of refugees to their rightful homes might actually take place if there is enough determined effort. Descriptions of camps in rural Gujarat have been provided by a number of NGOs. The government may not torch their homes at this very moment but it *will* eventually uproot them and cast them away from all the towns including Ahmedabad and seize their land. It *will* do this. In such a situation rehabilitation will be extremely difficult. It is hard to take on the might of the state.

2. People are trying to go back to the ideals of Gujarat, India and that greatest of men, Mahatma Gandhi. I am thinking of Amlan Dutta's hunger strike. I have also heard that students of Shibpur's B.E. College and Jadavpur University have gone on hunger strike for a day or two. After the police went into the bylanes of Baroda and killed some refugees—people associated with PUCL, some fifty of them, Hindus and Muslims—went to the district police headquarters with their faces covered in black cloth, as though issuing a challenge: 'Why should the police get tired hunting us down? Here we are, shoot us!'

The police place them in custody in the mornings and set them free in the evenings. Today, in the twilight of my life, I believe that fasting and picketing are perhaps the greatest forms of resistance. My diabetes prevents me -- had I been able to, I would have taken to the streets of Ahmedabad and undertaken a fast unto death.

19

NM and Kalinga? Impossible, Thrice Impossible, Brother Gill!*

Prakash N. Shah

As I pick up my pen I realize it is exactly three months since Godhra. Our natural expectations of clean governance have been thwarted by the administration of NM.[1] Setting aside the exception of the anti-Sikh riots of 1984, the bloody shame of a pogrom has been thrust upon Gujarat for the first time since India became a Republic. But we reserve our comments on that for now. We also put aside the question of NM's action-reaction theory in the context of the behaviour of the kar sevaks on the way to and from Ayodhya by rail. We certainly reiterate our feelings and our demand that every timely step, ranging from critique to punishment, be taken along specific guidelines as regards the inhumanity of the Godhra episode. But at this moment, at the very start of this comment, we wish to remind you of the pain we had expressed in the very first week of March; namely, that whatever was done by the Sangh-recognized government and the Sangh family outside the government was such that Musharraf, of all people, could sit in judgment against you and me. A question of propriety does arise when the military dictator of a fundamentalist state starts advising a secular democratic nation about the standards it ought to maintain.

*   Prakash N. Shah, 'Namo ane kaling? Asambhav, trivaar Asambhav, Bhai Gill'. Nirikshak 16 (360): 2-3, 1 June 2002. Translated from the Gujarati by Francis Parmar S.J.

But why we have come to such a pass that he can take such a liberty is also a question that arises.

Early in the morning we were reminded of Musharraf. The immediate cause, a couple of statements from K.P.S. Gill. I must confess I've always had nagging doubts about the authority of military and police chiefs to advise us on matters pertaining to democratic processes and civil society. My simple understanding is that minimizing the need for the military and the police defines a mature society. We did not find it a happy state of affairs when in 1985, during the rule of Madhavsinh Solanki, at the time of the anti-reservation riots and the communal twist given to the riots, we, as a non-party civic group, under the leadership of Umashankar Joshi, approached our governor B.K. Nehru with a request to hand over the city to the Army. But what other option is there when the government itself is a wicked partner in inciting anti-peace actions that lead to violence and anarchy? We remember Umashankar recalling the famous lines of Ramanbhai Neelkanth[2]: 'He who awakens the evil inclinations of others / Sets in motion a dangerous game / Having broken the embankment of a full lake / Who has ever succeeded in controlling the torrent?' So, in these circumstances, it is not unnatural for Gujarat to accept, with some reservation, the arrival of the military and the appointment of Gill as security advisor to CM Narendra Modi—be it against his wish or according to Article 355.

Be that as it may, only last week, barely forty-eight hours after the departure of the army, disturbances in Godhra and Gomtipur-Rakhial (Ahmedabad) erupted; and reports of bomb blasts in Vadodara and elsewhere keep coming in. Given this situation, Gill's voice sounds a note of sanity and security. He has said, "I can curb violence, but true peace is in the hands of the elected government and its administration as well as in the hands of the people." But along with this, a significant thing that he mentions is the Kalinga episode. Gill reminds us that seeing the enormous cost—in bloodshed and destruction—of the victory of Kalinga, Emperor Ashoka undertook introspection and underwent transformation. A similar process of introspection on what happened or what has been done, Gill adds, usually takes place among people and the administration about ten days after any outbreak of violence. This has been his experience while combating violence. But here in Gujarat month after month, the time goes on and yet the Kalinga-touch of Ashoka still eludes us.

I find Gill extremely naïve indeed! Who will remind you, my dear chap, that once there was a sage among us by the name of Kripalani. It was a time when Indira Gandhi had fielded her own candidate, V.V. Giri, against the official candidate of the Congress, N. Sanjeeva Reddy. She appealed to the very Congress MPs to vote according to their conscience (and not according to the whip). The great Kripalani retorted immediately, saying, 'My dear lady, try to understand this much. Even if you're a thief, you have to have the stature of a Valia (a great bandit) for your conscience to be stirred. For petty thieves, where is the question of conscience?' Not that we have the authority of giants like Kripalani, but we can definitely say this much to Gill: for the Kalinga-touch, one needs the measure and stature of Ashoka.

Who is the person in this case? In a special issue of *Seminar* (May 2002) on Gujarat, Ashis Nandy has recalled his first impression of Narendra Modi whom he met more than a decade ago when he (Modi) was a little known Sangh pracharak or BJP official: "It was a long, rambling interview, but it left me in no doubt that here was a classic, clinical case of a fascist . . . Modi, it gives me no pleasure to tell the readers, met virtually all the criteria that psychiatrists, psychoanalysts and psychologists had set up after years of empirical work on the authoritarian personality . . . I still remember the cool, measured tone in which he elaborated a theory of cosmic conspiracy against India that painted every Muslim as a suspected traitor and a potential terrorist. I came out of the interview shaken and told (Achyut) Yagnik that, for the first time, I had met a textbook case of a fascist and a prospective killer, perhaps even a future mass murderer' (p 18). If Ashis Nandy, sitting so far away, takes no delight in recalling this, you and I, as concerned citizens of Gujarat and as soldiers of social transformation do not like it either. But in the people's struggle to get out of the bloody encounters and the chain of dissension, we cannot afford to ignore the evidence of our eyes and ears and memory.

However, I intend to discuss, by way of example, the appointment of the Justice KG Shah Commission and the addition of Justice G.T. Nanavati as head, for the judicial enquiry into the carnage at Godhra and the subsequent events. I am doing this in the hope some touch of the Kalinga episode may be felt if not by the so-called leader, at least by some of his followers and especially by the common people, willy-nilly regaining their senses after the initial madness. The appointment of Justice K.G. Shah (and him alone) was controversial from the beginning. You could even say that the question of the Commission's credibility was raised, either formally or informally, in different ways, by both, the National Human Rights Commission and the National Minorities' Commission; the demand for the appointment of a sitting supreme court judge did not come only from our civic voices or from the leader of the opposition, Sonia Gandhi, but also from the Minorities' Commission itself, appointed by the present NDA Government. Here too, those in the know of things had recalled the Supreme Court's observation while overturning the ruling of this retired judge of Gujarat, which said, 'this judgment is not based on the understanding of any evidence but on imagination.'

Since Nanavati, a retired judge of the Supreme Court is sitting on this Commission, as the natural head, there is now some easing of tension. Nanavati is conducting a judicial enquiry into the anti-Sikh riots of 1984. The Gujarat BJP and its supporters keep raising the bogey of 1984 to escape the responsibility of the present. But if the NDA government, under the leadership of the BJP, feels the need of a new Commission for a truthful and full investigation of 1984, it must accept the concept of honest investigation into the events of 2002. In a conversation with Manoj Mittal of the *Indian Express* Justice Nanavati has said, 'Accusations of well-planned violence, of the connivance and inaction of the government and the fact that most of the casualties were from the minority community are the similarities between these two carnages.' Some people defend 2002 by citing the example of 1984; they angrily demand a fresh examination to replace the 'farce' which was the old enquiry. But why do the same people soft pedal the application of the same demand to the events of 2002? The answer to this question is, in a way, clear—and that is, the finger points towards them.

But we want to draw the attention of the wider civil society of Gujarat to the official release of the government regarding the appointment of Justice Nanavati:

'The government had appointed a judicial Commission for an investigation into the Godhra Railway massacre and the subsequent violent events. But unfortunately, some vested interests tried to drag this noble, trustworthy and popularly acceptable institution of a judicial enquiry Commission with a retired judge, into controversy. They have taken advantage of the disturbed atmosphere to keep the enquiry Commission in a state of controversy. Now that peace has been restored, the government has taken an important decision to reconstitute the present judicial Commission. This has been done for the sake of maintaining the dignity of an institution like that of a judicial Commission, for the bright future of the state and in the public interest, as well as with the noble aim of avoiding any doubts about the good intentions of the government.'

Widespread public opinion and pressure from the Centre have forced the Gujarat government to seek the services of Justice Nanavati. But instead of accepting them with grace, it gives in with contempt. You can see that the government had raised a contentious point by appointing the useless Justice K.G. Shah Commission. In fact, such a Commission should have been of high calibre, trustworthy and acceptable in the popular mind. When the government finally realized this, instead of accepting it with an open heart, it resorted to making half true statements about the reasons that led it to reconsider its decision; thus, while repairing the damage, it kept snapping and pampering its own ego. And to crown it all, it did not feel the need to announce that from now on, this Commission would work under the leadership of Justice Nanavati. The government's attitude was not that of correcting a mistake, but that of being forced to recant and eat its own words.

There is quite a lot of anticipatory joy in certain circles of the Gujarat BJP with regard to the holding of elections before March 2003. Following on the heels of the Central observer for the state, Ramdas Agrawal, the national president Jana Krishnamurti is about to visit us to make a rough estimate. It remains to be seen to what extent the popular vote in Gujarat is ready to come forward with mature reflection to renew the license of a leadership that has not shown the least sign of the Kalinga touch. Putting ideologies aside, even on moral grounds, I have no doubt that NM's license must be revoked. But that does not mean that the civil society of Gujarat has to place its confidence in those who are opposing NM within the BJP. The frightening capacities of NM which were perceived by Ashis Nandy may be the individual achievements of this leadership, but they must have been fed by a specific ideology also. Besides, we must ask where were all those people now banding together against NM, during the recent carnage? What were they doing and do they have an iota of regret or remorse? Not only this. The civil society of Gujarat is not likely to let them off without asking them what their ideological stand is, whether they have had the sense to see the dangers of fragmenting the nation on communal lines.

The main point is that without a strong fabric of civil society, popular struggle against internal and external terrorism will not be of much use. No doubt, military intervention and deployment are needed, but only occasionally. There is a definite role to be played by the government, the ruling party, the opposition; but its test, aim and ballast are one and the same—civil society.

Notes

1   Narendra Modi, the Chief Minister of Gujarat (translator).
2   A reputed Gujarati author (translator).

20

Just Another Day in Ahmedabad

Gurpal Singh

Mail Number Eight
5 July 2002

Shocked by everything I had heard about the violence in Gujarat and the pathetic state of the survivors staying in relief camps, I arrived in Ahmedabad on 16 May.

I spent most of my time playing with the children in some of the camps for over a month. I also kept e-mailing my family and friends about the situation here. Reading my last few e-mails, some friends probably felt I was becoming too emotional, zealous, obsessed and raving mad about the situation here and they gave some good-natured advice that I should take a break from it all and move away from Ahmedabad to gain some perspective. I did not agree fully with them but, anyway, partly following this advice I went off for a few days when I found some work and returned to this strange city on 3 July. Here are some impressions, thoughts, experiences upon my return.

I took an auto from the station and immediately set about finding out if the driver was Muslim or Hindu. This is something I don't have to do (as yet) in any other city, but is important here because some Hindu drivers would be uncomfortable going to certain areas that I visit. Everywhere in this city there is a heightened sense of awareness of your religion. It was not difficult to surmise that this driver was a Muslim—most Hindu drivers advertise their religion by putting stickers of gods and temples in front of the steering, and often trishuls on the top, and most of the Muslim autos have absolutely no marking on them . . . and in a few you can find traces of recently removed stickers that may have had a picture of some mosque or some inscription in Urdu, hastily covered with black paint.

I asked to be taken to the Shah-e-Alam camp and the driver smiled . . . This driver, Javed , told me that the survey for his burnt house had not been done even now and he had no idea when he would get his compensation. There are just too many like him who will have to wait for god knows how long to get back what was snatched away from them due to a breakdown of the law and order machinery. He has to manage a family of four and he said that even now he was living on borrowed money as he was not earning enough every day to pay back what he had to borrow. He was staying with his brother in his one-room tenement and there were a total of eleven people staying in that room. With a wry smile he also told me that he has been eating things he has never eaten before. Well, at least he was in a cheery mood, unlike my friend Usman Bhai at the camp.

When I had last seen him, he was hopeful of getting his compensation cheque soon. Now he seemed devastated. He had been given a cheque three days ago, the amount was Rs 3,000. According to him, it was a little less than one-hundredth of the value of what he had lost. In desperation, he asked me if I could do anything to fix a meeting for him with the 'higher-ups'. I did not have the heart to tell him that for one, I too was powerless, and besides, he was not the only one with whom this was happening and there were lakhs of others whose amounts were even more incredible. He probably knew all this and I doubt if he really expected me to offer anything more than moral support. All I could do was hold his hand and all he could do was cry silently.

Usman Bhai is about fifty-five, from Naroda Gaon, one of the worst affected areas during this genocide and he along with his family and others from there sleep on the floor on the right side of the dargah. I took him to the left side to meet another family from the Anupam cinema area. They have been together in the same camp for four months now but it is impossible to know everyone. At its peak, there were 12,000 people in the camp. Even now there are nearly 5,000. Riaz Bhai lived near Anupam cinema, and he had received a compensation cheque of Rs 12,500 for the three-room house that was completely burnt. One wall of his Hindu neighbour's house was slightly blackened from the fire, and that neighbour has got a cheque of Rs 22,500. Riaz Bhai cannot go back yet because his neighbours have threatened him not to return. He is quite a fearless man but he feels it is pointless to register a complaint, as the cops who will take the complaint were themselves involved in this pogrom. I wanted him to meet Usman Bhai as I had found in Riaz Bhai a strange kind of resilience and a will to fight and I thought it would wear off on Usman, who seemed quite broken and physically much weaker than when I last saw him. Sadly, this backfired, because I found a change in Riaz Bhai too since I last met him. He too seemed broken and defeated and his story only made things worse. I ended up adding to the depression when I mentioned that things were much worse in rural areas.

I decided to cheer things up by playing with the kids. I found that many of the children I played with had left but there were many more who wanted to make friends and play. The children decided that they wanted to sing and tell stories. While we were doing that, one of the kids near me, a six-year-old, was keenly observing the ants and insects around. I smiled and picked up one ant and put it back. The boy immediately stamped on it and said softly that it was a Hindu ant. When I asked him to repeat what he had said, he smiled sheepishly and ran away. This for me was a new experience and I had no idea how to deal with it. If there were more Hindus coming forward to show them the 'other' face, it may have been easier. Later, one of the kids who knew me from before took me aside and begged me for a rupee. This too is a disturbing new development. For over a month since I have known them, these kids had never begged. I went back to Usman Bhai. It was my turn to cry on his shoulder.

Usman Bhai's immediate neighbours (that is, the family sleeping three feet away) offered me some water and told me how they appreciated my playing with their kids. An old lady kept blessing me and would not stop. I had never seen her like this before. And I wished there were others with me to share the burden of her blessings. When I told her about what the little boy did with the ant she set out to look for him in order to admonish him . . .

While I was in the office, there were many women standing in line waiting for their turn to choose clothes from a consignment of old clothes that had come from Delhi. Some were in the process of choosing them and others had already done so. Many were complaining about the fact that of there were so many strange skirts and tops which our girls will never wear. One man in the office said *jo milta hai khushi khushi le lo*—a better way of saying that beggars can't be choosers. I guess that was true, but they must have wondered why they had been reduced to this . . .

Later, we went to the Behrampura camp at the municipal school that has been officially closed but there are forty-six families living there. Shareefaben, a volunteer, was arguing with the principal of the school, pleading with him to let the people stay on as they were huddled in two rooms which were not being used by the school. In any case, they could not go home as their houses were burnt, the compensation was not paid and besides, the landlord of the chawl where they stayed had blocked the entrance to the chawl. He had built a shop and a wall and the matter was being negotiated. She told him that she had spoken to K.P.S. Gill too, and was hopeful of a quick solution. Soon the principal relented and Shareefaben saw me and came to appraise me of the situation. She also told me that the government had not bothered about where to send the people, but had stopped giving grain. It was now coming from an NGO but she did not know for how long they would be able to sustain it. As we were talking we noticed that an old lady was having an argument with the driver of the municipal truck that was parked outside. It turned out that he had told her that she was going to be loaded on to the truck with all the others and dumped outside Gujarat, and when she told him triumphantly that the principal had agreed to let them stay, he had said that he will now take her in the other truck pointing to the garbage truck parked a distance away. Shareefa, always the fighter, confronted him but he brusquely denied this.

The old lady, Batul bibi, in the meantime came to me and asked me about the promise I had once made to take her to the eye doctor. Several days ago when my mother was here too, helping out at this camp, she had learnt that this lady was suffering as her spectacles had been left behind in her house as she ran for safety to this camp on 3 March. She had gone back much later to find her house burnt down and she could not find her glasses or even the paper which had her power number. Her eyes had been burning all these days and no one from the relief committees took this seriously enough. Mom had asked me to do the needful as she was leaving that day and I had promised to do so, but like the others, had not taken the problem seriously enough. It was time to redeem myself. She wanted to be taken to a particular doctor who had been kind to her and had operated her free of cost. As we were leaving the camp, another old lady, Amina bibi, said that she too had the same problem, so the three of us went off to find the benevolent doctor. As we reached his gate we saw a large, freshly painted sign that said *OM* on the outside wall. Amina bibi was scared on seeing this and was of the opinion that we should go back, but Batul bibi insisted that the doctor was a wonderful man and would treat them well. I too added my two bits by saying that *OM* was something to be revered and chanted and nothing to be scared of. Dr Vipul and his wife, Dr Sandhya, were indeed wonderful people and treated these ladies free of cost. The few people in the waiting room who seemed uncomfortable about Amina bibi's dirty burqah and Batul bibi's shabby salwar kameez, were duly ignored and we went back happy, singing the praises of the wonderful couple. Amina bibi is to be operated for cataract in three months time.

When I had asked the doctor if he was scared of the VHP or the Bajrang Dal landing up at his door because he was defying their call for a social boycott of Muslims, he had replied that he was indeed, but he was more scared of God, so he did what he had to do. I have, in any case, changed their names in this e-mail to protect their identities. My family perhaps wishes that I could change my name in these e-mails too. They are concerned and keep telling me to keep a low profile, which I must admit, I am doing, because all said and done, I am no superhuman. I too, am scared of being marked and victimized. But perhaps I am playing into their hands too. The politics of fear and hatred thrives on people like me. Hatred can only be conquered by love and fear by courage, so I keep telling myself to try and be braver. Anyway, I still do wish that there were more people speaking out and standing up to be counted. There is safety in numbers! They cannot victimize everyone! Even if some are victimized, I think it can only do them good. Look at three illustrious people who were badly victimized during the Emergency . . . One rose to be the prime minister, another his deputy, and the third is the defence minister! It is a pity that they choose to look the other way when others are victimized here in Gujarat.

Through this long and tedious e-mail, I can only give you a tiny part of the whole picture, but whatever I see is unacceptable to me as a human being, as an Indian, and as a Sikh . . . I still don't know if my absence from Ahmedabad helped me gain any perspective. I already did realize, even while I was here, that there were larger socio-economic and political factors at work. What is reinforced in my mind is the fact that the situation is extraordinary and nothing will solve itself without participation from people like you and me.

21

I Salute You, Geetaben, From the Bottom of My Heart*

Siddharth Varadarajan

Two weeks ago, the resident editor of the *Times of India* in Ahmedabad sent our office in Delhi a photograph so shocking it made my stomach churn. Shocking not just for what it depicted but because, to paraphrase Roland Barthes, 'one was looking at it from inside our freedom.' This was my India. This is my India.

On a hot and dusty patch of asphalt lies the naked body of a woman, Geetaben, her clothes stripped off and thrown carelessly near her. One piece of her underclothing lies a foot away from her body, the other is clutched desperately in her left hand. Her left arm is bloodied, as is her torso, which appears to have deep gashes. Her left thigh is covered in blood and she is wearing a small anklet. Her plastic chappals sit sadly alongside her lifeless body and in the middle of the photo frame is a gnarled, red, hate-filled remnant of a brick, perhaps the one her assailants used to deliver their final blow.

Geetaben was killed in Ahmedabad on 25 March, in broad daylight, near a bus stop close to her home. She was a Hindu who in the eyes of the Hindu separatists currently ruling Gujarat had committed the cardinal sin of falling in love with a Muslim man. When the Sangh Parivar mobs[1] came for him, she stood her ground long enough for him to flee. But the killers seemed

* *Times of India*, 19 April 2002.

more interested in her. She was dragged out, stripped naked and killed. No lethal dose of Zyklon-B delivered surreptitiously in a darkened, secluded chamber. Geetaben's murder was never meant to be a furtive, secret affair. The holocaust that Chief Minister Narendra Modi's administration presided over was engineered in the knowledge that the Indian State never punishes murderers with political connections. Delhi 1984, Bombay 1993, Gujarat 2002. Neither Congress, Third Front or BJP believes in Nurembergs.

In these troubled times, when heroes are scarce and villains abound, Geetaben deserves to be worshipped. She is Gujarat's *Jhansi ki Rani*, its La Passionaria. I salute you, Geetaben, from the bottom of my heart for your one brief moment of defiance. For, even in death, with your helpless, innocent body bloodied and your clothes ripped apart, you showed more courage, humanity and dignity—and more fidelity to your Hindu religion —than Prime Minister Atal Bihari Vajpayee has done in the past month. When the day of reckoning comes, no one will dare ask you where you were when Gujarat was burning. But when Yama waves a dossier at Mr Vajpayee and asks him how many lives he saved, what will he answer, I wonder. Will he hang his head in shame as he did at the Shah-e-Alam camp in Ahmedabad? Or will he lecture the Hindu God of Death about Godhra and jihadi Muslims, and claim, as he did on 16 April, that if only Parliament had condemned the Sabarmati Express carnage, the genocide which followed would never have happened.

When I heard what Mr Vajpayee said at the BJP rally in Goa in April, I experienced the same contaminating, nauseous sensation of being present at a crime scene that I felt when I saw the photograph of Geetaben. Though the prime minister now claims he was misquoted, whichever way his words are parsed, what he told his party faithful at Goa was bone-chilling. 'Wherever Muslims are,' he said, painting a broad brush to describe not just the followers of Islam around the world but the one-fifth of India's citizens who happen to be Muslim, 'they don't like to live in co-existence with others, they don't like to mingle with others'.

At the best of times, such a statement would be unforgivable. But when you consider that he was talking about the killing of as many as 2,000 Muslims in Gujarat—and to an audience which believed this genocide was justified—one can only react in horror. Already, the Sangh is enforcing an economic boycott of Muslims. There is hardly a single Muslim business left in Gujarat. Photocopying stalls near Gujarati courts turn Muslim lawyers away. Men with beards are not served in restaurants and shops in the state. Muslim mothers pray their children won't call them *ammi* on the street. Instead of speaking out against this, Mr Vajpayee actually had the gall to say Muslims do not wish to live in peace.

For tens of millions of Indians, including those who might have flirted with the BJP, Mr Vajpayee's remarks have served as a wake-up call. At the Shah-e-Alam camp, he said the riots had shamed India. But what he said at Goa has shamed India even more.

For all his fulminations against *jihad*, Mr Vajpayee's ideology is equally *jihadi*. His party does not believe in people living in peace, in ensuring that the citizens of India—whether Hindu, Muslim or other—have the wherewithal to live as human beings. The BJP does not respect the rights of citizens or of the nation as a whole. Instead, a bogus, hollow ideology of 'Hindutva' has been erected to cover up their utter contempt for the rights of the people of India.

If historians use the phrase 'Muslim separatism' to define the struggle to carve out a Muslim nation from India in the last century, the project of the RSS-BJP could well be called 'Hindu' separatism. Separatism or secessionism is not just about the desire to create physical distance; it is as much about striving to distance oneself from the political, cultural and philosophical mores of the country. The BJP's separatist project poses as 'Hindu,' but it aims to secede from the philosophical and cultural foundations of India, including Hinduism, and from the political principles that Indians have evolved over the past 200 years of struggle for their rights.

The aim of this project is to establish a state where all Indians, including Hindus, will be devoid of rights except those which will be bestowed upon them as a privilege. Today, Mr Vajpayee tells Muslim, Christian and Sikh Indians at Goa that 'we (i.e., the BJP) have allowed you freedom of worship.' Tomorrow, Hindu Indians will be told what they are 'allowed' to do. Those that transgress—like Geetaben, or Medha Patkar, journalists and others—will be dealt with. Gujarat has thrown a challenge to the country. The writing is on the wall. Either we stand up to defend the rights of all citizens; or we will all go down eventually.

Note

1   'Two BJP leaders held for Geetaben's murder,' New Indian Express, 27 March 2002.

Appendix 1

Reprinted here is the English text of the speech delivered in Hindi, by Prime Minister Atal Bihari Vajpayee at a public meeting in Goa in 12 April 2002.

I was in Cambodia just recently. It is the Kamboj state of the past, where magnificent temples that kissed the sky were built in the tenth and the eleventh centuries. It had Hindu states ruled by Hindu kings. There were others too among the citizens, but there was justice towards all. Sometimes the kings also used to fight among themselves. The wheel of victory and defeat rolled on. But during their centuries' long history there isn't a single instance of a Hindu king destroying temples or breaking idols when he attacked another Hindu king. The kings who were victorious used to build a new temple. If Vishnu was being worshipped there earlier, later Shiva began to be worshipped. If Shiva was being worshipped at one time, then other deities began to be worshipped later. Nevertheless, no king destroyed a temple or damaged the deities' idols at the time of attacking another king. This is our culture. This is our outlook, which treats all faiths equally.

Yet, accusations are being hurled today that secularism is under threat. Who are these people accusing us? What is the meaning of secularism for these people? India was secular when Muslims hadn't come here and Christians hadn't set foot on this soil. It is not as if India became secular after they came. They came with their own modes of worship and they too were given a place of honour and respect. They had the freedom to worship God as per their wish and inclination. No one thought of converting them with force, because this is not practiced in our religion; and in our culture, there is no use for it.

Today the 100 crore people of India are engaged in creating their future on the basis of their own culture. Sometimes, minor incidents do take place here and there sometimes they take the form of major incidents. But if you go to the root of these incidents, you will find intolerance, you'll find them to be a manifestation of growing intolerance. What happened in Gujarat? If a conspiracy had not been hatched to burn alive the innocent passengers of the Sabarmati Express, then the subsequent tragedy in Gujarat could have been averted. But this did not happen. People were torched alive. Who were those culprits? The government is investigating into this. Intelligence agencies are collecting all the information. But we should not forget how the tragedy of Gujarat started. The subsequent developments were no doubt condemnable, but who lit the fire? How did the fire spread? Ours is a multi-religious country, a multi-lingual country, we have many different modes of worship. We believed in peaceful and harmonious co-existence. We believe in equal respect for all faiths. Let no one challenge India's secularism. I have read somewhere in newspapers that the Congress Party has decided not to try to topple my Government. Shall I thank them for this? Or shall I say that the 'Grapes are sour'? How will the Government fall? Once they did topple it, but they couldn't form one themselves. Then a fresh mandate from the people was called for, and the people once again gave us an opportunity to serve them.

For us the soil of India from Goa to Guwahati is the same, all the people living on this land are the same. We do not believe in religious extremism. Today the threat to our nation comes from terrorism. Wherever I went around the world, the heads of state or of elected governments complained to me that the militant Islam is sowing thorns along their paths. Islam has two facets. One is that which tolerate others, which teaches its adherents to follow the path of truth, which preaches compassion and sensitivity. But these days, militancy in the name of Islam leaves no room for tolerance. It has raised the slogan of Jehad. It is dreaming of recasting the entire world in its mould.

You will be surprised to hear this—indeed, I too was surprised—that some terrorists belonging to Al-Qaeda were arrested in Singapore. The rulers of Singapore couldn't even have imagined that Al-Qaeda would be active in their country, too; that Al-Qaeda would hatch a conspiracy in Singapore too. Some fifteen or sixteen persons were arrested, an investigation is underway, which will reveal the truth. The same is happening in Indonesia. The same is happening in Malaysia.

Wherever Muslims live, they don't like to live in co-existence with others, they don't like to mingle with others; and instead of propagating their ideas in a peaceful manner, they want to spread their faith by resorting to terror and threats. The world has become alert to this danger.

As far as we are concerned, we have been fighting against terrorism for the past 20 years. Terrorists have tried to grab Jammu and Kashmir through violence, but we have countered them. Jammu and Kashmir is an integral part of India, and will forever remain so. No other country's dream will ever, come true. Now other nations in the world have started to realize what a great mistake they did by neglecting terrorism. Now they are waking up, and are organizing themselves. They are putting together an international consensus against terrorism.

We tell them through our own example that a large number of non-Hindus live in our country, but there has never ever been religious persecution here. We have never discriminated between 'our people' and 'aliens'. The modes of worship may differ, but God is one. Only the paths to reach Him and realize Him can be different. It is for this reason that India's prestige is growing, India's reputation is rising. I have also had an occasion to visit many other countries. Everywhere Muslims live in large numbers. And the rulers in those countries are worried lest those Muslims embrace extremism, We told them that they should educate people on the true tenets of Islam, that they should also teach other subjects in madrasas. Islam too should be taught, but emphasize that people should live together and that it is necessary to accept that faith cannot be propagated on the strength of the sword.

Real audio downloaded from the official website of the BJP in Goa, www.goabjp.com, and then checked against the translation put out by the Prime Minister's Office.

Appendix 2
Five Months in the Life (and Death) of a State

Darshan Desai

January-February: VHP mobilizes supporters for Ayodhya campaign.

24 February: Western Railways gives kar sevaks half the train free; compartments reserved under BJP MP/MLA quotas. VHP activists on Sabarmati Express to Ayodhya attack Muslim passengers, bystanders at UP stations.

27 February: 59 persons killed aboard Sabarmati Express at Godhra. Stray stabbings at Ahmedabad, Anand. PM asks VHP to abandon Ayodhya agitation, VHP says no, calls Gujarat bandh.

28 February: Hundreds killed in anti-Muslim violence organized across Gujarat. *Sandesh* reports Hindu women abducted, raped, mutilated by Godhra mob. Paramilitaries sent to Gujarat, army on standby.

1-2 March: Rape, killing, destruction of Muslim property continues. 16 districts affected. Army arrives 24 hours late. Official death toll 252, unofficially several hundred.

2 March: PM finally addresses nation on TV, says violence a 'blot'.

3 March: Violence continues, despite army presence. Official death toll 427. Advani blames ISI for Godhra. Ahmedabad students forced to abandon peace protest by goons.

4 March: Violence spreads to Surat, Bhavnagar, Rajkot. Modi offers riot victims half the compensation of Godhra victims. George Fernandes blames 'external hand' and ISI for Godhra.

5 March: Shankaracharya, as 'mediator', asks Muslim Law Board to agree to handover of 'undisputed' land at Ayodhya. National Human Rights Commission asks Modi to explain compensation bias.

6 March: Centre asks courts to 'fast-track' Ayodhya. Justice K.G. Shah asked to probe Godhra, subsequent riots. Violence in Ahmedabad and elsewhere. Over one lakh people in relief camps.

7 March: Gujarat University postpones exams. Police admits no Hindu women abducted in Godhra train attack.

8 March: Official death toll 636. All-party delegation of MPs visits Ahmedabad. US, UK etc. express concern.

10 March: Muslim Law Board rejects Shankaracharya's 'compromise' formula, wants court verdict. Violence against Muslims breaks out in Chotta Udepur.

11 March: PM says government will not allow puja at disputed site till Supreme Court (SC) verdict. Advani defends Modi in Parliament.

13 March: In SC hearing, Attorney General Sorabjee says nothing wrong in 'symbolic puja' at disputed Ayodhya site. Court rejects plea, forbids any 'religious activity'. VHP threatens to go ahead regardless.

14 March: PM says government will implement SC order in 'letter and spirit'. Ahmedabad police claim city will be curfew-free from 19 March.

15 March: In 'compromise', VHP allowed to take out *shila* procession in Ayodhya and offer prayers before Rama idol at old Babri Masjid site. PMO representative receives carved plinth from VHP leaders outside disputed land. VHP's Pravin Togadia proclaims 'victory'. Violence erupts after this shiladan and maha artis in Ahmedabad and Vadodara.

16 March: VHP, Bajrang Dal activists storm Orissa assembly. Three killed as parts of Ahmedabad, Vadodara, Bharuch remain under indefinite curfew.

17 March: In Bangalore, RSS says safety of Muslims depends on goodwill of Hindus. Ahmedabad not calm, arson, rioting and loot reported. Four killed in Vadodara. School exams in Ahmedabad and Vadodara postponed indefinitely.

18 March: Four killed in police firing in Bharuch and Sabarkantha. Prevention of Terrorism Bill passed in Lok Sabha.

19-21 March: More violence against Muslims in Ahmedabad, Bharuch (four killed), Himmatnagar. Gujarat minister Bharat Barot wants camps for Muslims closed, says they are 'security risk'. POTO defeated in Rajya Sabha (later passed in joint sitting).

22 March: Modi withdraws POTO cases from Godhra accused after reports on selective use against Muslims. Four killed and others injured in Ahmedabad, Vadodara. NHRC rejects Gujarat government report on violence as 'perfunctory'.

24 March-16 April: Violence, mainly directed against Muslims but also some group clashes, continues in different parts of state. Muslims cancel Muharram procession. Police combing of Muslim areas and shooting continue. Large parts of Ahmedabad still under curfew.

25-27 March: **Major reshuffle in police. Gujarat submits 400-page report to NHRC.**

31 March: Seven killed in fresh violence.

1 April: NHRC indicts Modi government for failing to protect life, liberty, equality and dignity of people, wants CBI to probe most heinous cases of violence including Godhra, Naroda Patiya.

2 April: Violence spreads to Kutch, Anjar.

3 April: Five members of Muslim family burnt at Abasana village. In Ahmedabad, Muslim man killed for being married to Hindu. Police attack Suleiman Roza camp, fire at inmates. Camp forcibly shut down. Muslim advocate shot inside home by police.

4 April: PM visits Gujarat, asks Modi to observe 'rajadharma', announces relief package. Violence despite PM presence.

5 April: Convoy of victims under police escort en route to Vadaodara attacked.

6 April: Four killed in Ahmedabad, National Commission on Minorities blasts Modi government.

7 April: Medha Patkar and journalists attacked at Gandhi Ashram during peace meeting.

8-29 April: Opposition and NDA allies call for Modi's removal, BJP refuses, issue stalls Parliament.

12 April: Vajpayee attacks Muslims in Goa speech. BJP rejects Modi's resignation.

18 April: Muslim schoolchildren stay away from exams out of fear.

22 April: External Affairs ministry attacks foreign governments for Gujarat criticism, even as toll from renewed bout of week-long violence hits 29.

30 April: NDA allies support BJP on Gujarat in Lok Sabha censure motion, PM promises Rs 150 crore for riot relief.

2 May: K.P.S. Gill appointed Modi's security advisor.

6-7 May: Rajya Sabha passes Opposition motion on Gujarat government. Army called out in Ahmedabad.

21 May: Army withdrawn from riot duty.

23 May: Official death toll: 950. Godhra chargesheet filed, no mention of wider 'conspiracy'.

25–30 May: Two killed in Kadi, Maulvi stabbed in Vadodara, bomb blast in Muslim areas in Vadodara and Godhra lead to tension, Muslims injured, killed in police firing, shops burnt in Bharuch, serial blast in Ahmedabad buses.

4 June: Chargesheet filed in Naroda-Patiya case against Sangh Parivar leaders.

9–11 June: Violence in Ahmedabad. Modi reneges on promise to rebuild shrines or allot land for refugees.

24-25 June: Chargesheet filed in Best Bakery case, three arrested for Gulberg murders. Violence in Vadodara.

30 June: Rural camps shut down. Government stops rations.

4 July: Forensic report on Godhra says fire set from inside coach S-6.

8-12 July: Muslims flee anticipating violence during Ahmedabad rath yatra. BJP refuses to change route. Yatra peaceful, huge police bandobast. Modi claims normalcy returns.

13 July: Fresh riots in Kheda.

19 July: Modi resigns, dissolves assembly. BJP wants early polls. Violence in Viramgam.

30 July: Election Commission team visits Gujarat to test viability of elections.

Note: This chronology does not list all the incidents of violence

Copyright Acknowledgements

My publishers and I would like to acknowledge the following newspapers, magazines, and reports for permission to reprint copyright material:

The *Times of India* (Ahmedabad) for: 'Godhra bogie burnt from inside, says report' (3 July), 'Jafri may not have fired at all' (9 June), 'Women not spared by the police' (3 May), 'Rain, epidemic threaten relief camps' (2 July), 'Want riots dole? First go home and get your phone bill' (29 March), 'Games revolve around death for three children' (10 July), 'Some Hindus still live in the heart of Juhapura' (17 June), 'VHP lawyers to fight for riot victims', (23 April), 'High-society looters roam scot-free' (16 September), 'Reprisal fear triggers exodus again' (26 September); to the *Times of India* (national) for: 'Treasure of Sanskrit scholar goes up in flames'(11 May),'An oasis of peace in communally-ravaged Gujarat'(4 March),'For Bhagwandas, this Vadodara mosque is life' (21 March), 'Even judges had to run for cover'(5 March), 'I salute you Geetaben, from the bottom of my heart'(19 April); the *Hindustan Times* for: 'Meet Prasad, the Muslim in Gujarat' (4 March), 'Why not a few "Lajja Yatras"?' by Chitra Padmanabhan (original version published in *HT* dated 13 Setember); the *Telegraph* for:'Winds of hatred wrench best friends apart' (30 March), 'The VHP need to hear the condemnation of the Hindu middle ground' by Ramchandra Guha (9 March), 'Where had all the soldiers gone' (2 March); the *Hindu* for: 'A pittance as a payoff'(23 June), 'Nowhere to go and no one cares'(23 June), 'A candle in the darkness'(23 June), 'Genoicide of the idea of Gujarat' by Shail Mayaram (16 May); *Amar Ujala* for 'Gujarat ki Hinsa aur Dalit' by Mohandas Namishray (24 May); *Kathadesh* for 'Hindi TV aur Gujarat' by Anil Chamaria; *Jansatta* for 'Mere sukhan su jalwagar...' by Ranjana Argade (8 March); *Aajkal* for 'Kothai Shesh?' by Mahasweta Devi (8 May); *Nirikshak* for 'Namo aur Kaling?' by Prakash N. Shah(1 June); *Seminar* for: 'Tribal violence and voice' by Ganesh Devy, 'The Pathology of Gujarat' by Achyut

Yajnik (May 2002); *Economic and Political Weekly* for: 'Caste, Hindutva and the making of the mob culture' by Ghanshyam Shah; *Outlook* for: 'I feel my mind has been destroyed' (May 2002), 'The Rape of Reason' by Barkha Dutt (May 2002); Rajdeep Sardesai for 'The media did not ransack shops, take lives, Mr Modi', (first published in *Indian Express*, 7 March); *Communalism Combat* for *Jan Morcha* report, 'Bajrang Dal activists on Sabarmati Express beat up Muslims'; Editors Guild Fact Finding Mission for: 'Thank you, *Sandesh*' and other select excerpts (May 2002); the National Human Rights Commission for: 'Report on the ruckus at Godhra station', 'On the failure of intelligence at Godhra' (31 May); Citizens' Initiative, Ahmedabad, for testimonies from *The Survivors Speak* of : Kulsim Bibi, Azharuddin, Abdul Usman, S—, Medina Mustafa, Ismail Shaikh, Naimuddin, Ayub, Naseem, Mehmooda, Janmat Sheikh, Saira Bano, (April 2002), 'A company of broken people'; People's Union of Democratic Rights for excerpts from *Maaro! Kaapo! Baalo*!: *State, Society and Communalism in Gujarat*, New Delhi, May 2002, on Randhikpur (pp14-15), Sanjeli (pp15-16), Sardarpura (pp7-9), Anjwana (pp9-10), Delol (p 11), Kidiyad (pp16-181), and excerpts from Chapter V, 'How Many Displaced?'; People's Union for Civil Liberties, Vadodara, and Vadodara Shanti Abhiyan for excerpts from *Violence in Vadodara: A Report*, Vadodara, May 2002, Anand district (pp114-115), Best Bakery (pp59-62), Kisanwadi, Wadi-Taiwada, Wadi-Panigate (pp 32-37), Raja Rasul Masani(pp 52-53), 'Police role in Vadodara' (pp132-135), excerpts from survey of print and electronic media in Baroda (pp 47-48, 140-160), 'Even before Godhra, a warning' (pp104-5); *Forum Against Oppression of Women* and *Awaz-e-Niswaan*, Genocide in Gujarat (pp15-19), Kavita Punjabi, Bolan Gangapadhyaya and Krishna Bandhopadhyaya, 'The next generation: in the wake of genocide' for 'How do we give our children an education' and 'The unbearble burden of bearing witness.'

Postscript: Akshardham and After

Two armed terrorists attacked the Akshardham Swaminarayan temple in Gandhinagar on 24 September. Thirty-three people, including many children, were killed before the two—who claimed membership of an unknown group, Tehreek-e-Qisas—were shot dead. As after Godhra, the VHP called a bandh, but this time the BJP leadership decided against a replay of the anti-Muslim violence which convulsed Gujarat from 28 February onwards.

The latest chapter in the still unfolding tragedy of Gujarat is proof that genocidal violence can have consequences far beyond the control of its original authors. Whether or not the terrorists were from Gujarat, elsewhere in India, or Pakistan, it is unlikely that 33 innocent people would have died in Gandhinagar that day had the State not presided over the murder of some 2,000 innocent people earlier in the year. Today, the terrorism of armed mobs backed by the police and ruling party has given rise to the equally abominable terrorism of young men who resort—or are incited—to violence against other innocents. By allowing a terrible injustice against citizens and then compounding this sin by not doing anything—even six months later—to ensure the perpetrators are brought to book, the government of Prime Minister Vajpayee has created a festering wound on the body politic of India. Nothing but pain, frustration, anger, hatred and violence can come out of such a wound. Foreign governments and agencies with hostile intentions will find a ready situation to exploit.

In the wake of Akshardham, one has heard calls for tolerance from all quarters. While tolerance is important, what the country needs is justice. In Gujarat, Muslims are being forced to do a 'compro'—to withdraw their complaints—in order to return to their destroyed homes. Any society that compromises with terrorism against one section of citizens will always be vulnerable to terrorism against another. Unless the government takes firm steps to punish those involved in the planning and execution of the Gujarat massacres—regardless of their political affiliation or official rank—the tragedy that began in Godhra will claim many more innocent victims.

Siddharth Varadarajan
29 September 2002

Errata:
Delete from p. 117—*Indian Express* 13 May 2002
Delete from p. 143—'says' from 'The grandfather says Ghulam Hussain was burnt alive.'